A GLENN REPAIR AND TUNE-UP GUIDE

Books by HAROLD T. GLENN

Youth at the Wheel
Safe Living
Automechanics
Glenn's Auto Troubleshooting Guide
Exploring Power Mechanics
Automobile Engine Rebuilding and Maintenance
Automobile Power Accessories
Glenn's Auto Repair Manual
Automotive Smog Control Manual
Glenn's Emission-Control Systems
Glenn's Tune-Up and Repair Manual for American and Imported Car Emission-Control Systems
Glenn's Foreign Car Repair Manual
Glenn's Triumph Repair and Tune-Up Guide
Glenn's Alfa Romeo Repair and Tune-Up Guide
Glenn's Austin, Austin-Healey Repair and Tune-Up Guide
Glenn's Sunbeam-Hillman Repair and Tune-Up Guide
Glenn's MG, Morris and Magnette Repair and Tune-Up Guide
Glenn's Volkswagen Repair and Tune-Up Guide
Glenn's Volkswagen Repair and Tune-Up Guide (Spanish Edition)
Glenn's Mercedes-Benz Repair and Tune-Up Guide
Glenn's Foreign Carburetors and Electrical Systems Guide
Glenn's Renault Repair and Tune-Up Guide
Glenn's Jaguar Repair and Tune-Up Guide
Glenn's Volvo Repair and Tune-Up Guide
Glenn's Peugeot Repair and Tune-Up Guide
Glenn's Fiat Repair and Tune-Up Guide
Glenn's Toyota Tune-Up and Repair Guide
Glenn's Mazda Tune-Up and Repair Guide
Glenn's Chrysler Outboard Motor Repair and Tune-Up Guide for 1 & 2 Cylinder Engines
Glenn's Chrysler Outboard Motor Repair and Tune-Up Guide for 3 & 4 Cylinder Engines
Glenn's Evinrude Outboard Motor Repair and Tune-Up Guide for 1 & 2 Cylinder Engines
Glenn's Evinrude Outboard Motor Repair and Tune-Up Guide for 3 & 4 Cylinder Engines
Glenn's Johnson Outboard Motor Repair and Tune-Up Guide for 1 & 2 Cylinder Engines
Glenn's Johnson Outboard Motor Repair and Tune-Up Guide for 3 & 4 Cylinder Engines
Glenn's McCulloch Outboard Motor Repair and Tune-Up Guide
Glenn's Mercury Outboard Motor Repair and Tune-Up Guide
Glenn's Sears Outboard Motor Repair and Tune-Up Guide
Honda One-Cylinder Repair and Tune-Up Guide
Glenn's Honda Two-Cylinder Repair and Tune-Up Guide
Suzuki One-Cylinder Tune-Up and Repair Guide
Yamaha Enduro Tune-Up and Repair Guide
Triumph Two-Cylinder Motorcycle Tune-Up and Repair Guide
Glenn's Chevrolet Tune-Up and Repair Guide
Glenn Chevrolet Camaro Tune-Up and Repair Guide
Glenn's Ford/Lincoln/Mercury Tune-Up and Repair Guide
Glenn's Chrysler/Plymouth/Dodge Tune-Up and Repair Guide
Glenn's Pontiac Tune-Up and Repair Guide
Glenn's Pontiac Firebird Tune-Up and Repair Guide
Glenn's Oldsmobile Tune-Up and Repair Guide
Glenn's Buick Tune-Up and Repair Guide
Glenn's Complete Bicycle Manual

GLENN'S

JOHNSON

OUTBOARD MOTOR REPAIR AND TUNE-UP GUIDE FOR 1 & 2 CYLINDER ENGINES

by Harold T. Glenn

HENRY REGNERY COMPANY · CHICAGO

Cover Illustration by Wayne Kibar

Printed in the United States of America
Library of Congress Catalog Card Number: 74-6927
International Standard Book Number: 0-8092-8317-4

FOREWORD

This is a comprehensive repair and tune-up manual for outboard motors. It is designed to be used as a classroom text or mechanic's reference book, or it can be used by a boating enthusiast who is interested in keeping his engine in tip-top shape. A quick-starting and dependable engine can contribute to an enjoyable vacation; a balky engine can spoil the fun.

The manual is organized about the conventional units of the outboard motor: the engine and the lower unit. Chapters are devoted to servicing the fuel and electrical systems. A separate chapter on engine tuning will enable the enthusiast to get all of the power from the engine that it was designed to deliver. A chapter on maintenance provides vital nontechnical information for fuel mixing and lubricating the units properly, to keep the engine operating dependably.

The first chapter deals with troubleshooting. It enables a mechanic to isolate trouble before beginning to disassemble the mechanism. It helps to pinpoint the trouble so that a mechanic will know what to look for as the unit is being disassembled. This feature can save valuable time when making repairs.

This book contains comprehensive and accurate specification tables, wiring diagrams, and exploded view of all mechanical and electrical units.

A special feature of this book is the use of many step-by-step illustrated instructions for representative types of carburetors, engines, and lower units. The illustrations and text are so closely correlated that no legends are needed. The illustrations have been especially treated to drop out the backgrounds.

The author wishes to thank Messrs. P. G. Geller and Bill King of Perry's Sporting Goods and Mr. Jim McDonald of Lane's Marine Sales & Service for their kind assistance in helping to set up some of the pictures for this book. Also, appreciation is expressed to Messrs. Edwin W. Hanson, John Tuzee, John Dobbertin, and Norman Schultz of Outboard Marine Corporation for their kind assistance in helping to set up the pictures and for furnishing information that is used in this Guide.

Especial thanks are due to Howard Young of Harbor Boat House for his kind assistance in helping to revise the book, to my wife, ANNA GLENN, for her devoted assistance in helping to proofread the text, and to Mark Tsunawaki for his contribution to the art work.

HAROLD T. GLENN

CONTENTS

GLENN'S

JOHNSO

OUTBOARD M
REPAIR AND TUN
FOR 1 & 2 CYLINDE

CONTENTS

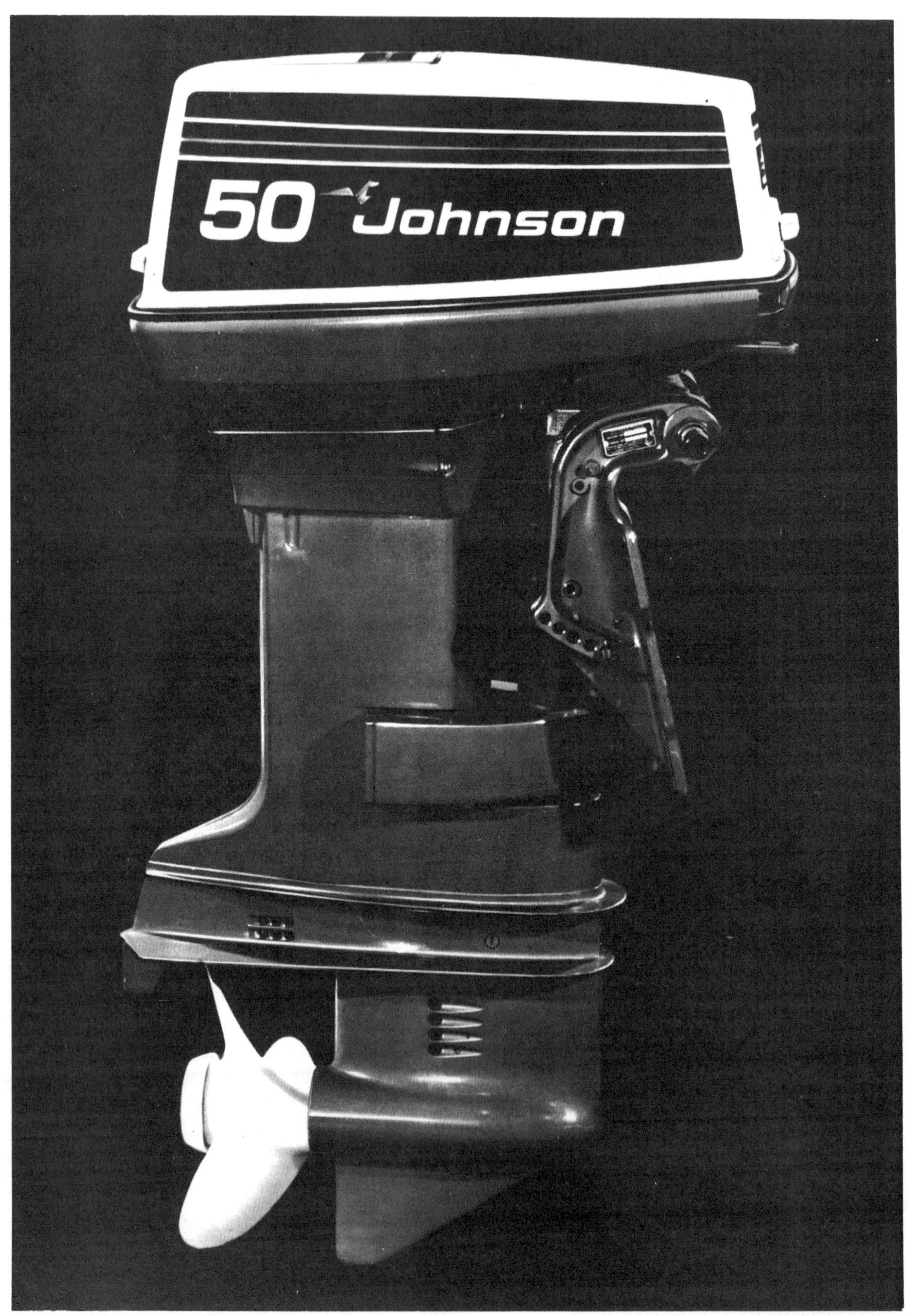

The modern outboard motor is a masterpiece of engineering design and efficiency.

1
TROUBLESHOOTING

When the engine won't start, it is very important to be able to run through an organized procedure in order to pinpoint the cause of the trouble. Basically, starting troubles can be localized to either the fuel system or the ignition system. After isolating the trouble to the defective system, go through the following suggested check list to determine the exact cause.

FUEL SYSTEM TROUBLESHOOTING

First make sure that there is gasoline in the tank. Sometimes the fuel supply burns up faster than you realize. On engines with a remote fuel tank, make sure that the air vent screw on the fuel tank cap is open, and then squeeze the priming bulb in the fuel line. When the carburetor float bowl is full of gasoline, pressure will be felt on the priming bulb. However, it is possible to force fuel past the needle and seat by additional pressure so that gasoline will flow out of the carburetor throat. **CAUTION: The fuel will leak onto parts of the engine and could cause a fire.** Make sure that all the gasoline is dried up before attempting to start the engine again.

If the carburetor float bowl is dry, check the line for an obstruction. Do this by disconnecting the fuel line from the engine quick-disconnect fitting, and then depressing the check valve in the fuel line connection. Squeeze the bulb and fuel should come out of the line, if it is not obstructed.

If the fuel line to the engine is clear, the trouble could be in the line to the fuel pump or to the carburetor, usually at the fuel line strainer. To check this out, disconnect the fuel line at thc carburetor and see if you can force fuel through it by squeezing the priming bulb. **CAUTION: When disconnecting a fuel line, use the proper wrenches, never a pair of pliers. CAUTION: When replacing a fuel line, don't tighten the nuts too much, especially on aluminum castings where the threads can be stripped rather easily.**

Remove a spark plug to check its condition. A wet spark plug means that the engine has been overchoked; a dry spark plug means that no fuel is reaching the combustion chamber. If the carburetor fuel bowl is full, but the spark plug is dry, the carburetor jets may be plugged.

If the spark plug is wet, go through the procedure for starting a flooded engine. Disconnect the fuel line or shut off the fuel supply completely, and then spin the flywheel several times to remove the excess fuel from the combustion chambers. Reconnect the fuel line, replace the spark plug, and then start the engine in the normal manner.

Check the fuel in the carburetor to see if water has gotten into it by catching a little of the gasoline in the palm of your hand. The water will appear as small beads or bubbles. If you blow on the mixture, the gasoline will evaporate, leaving the water behind.

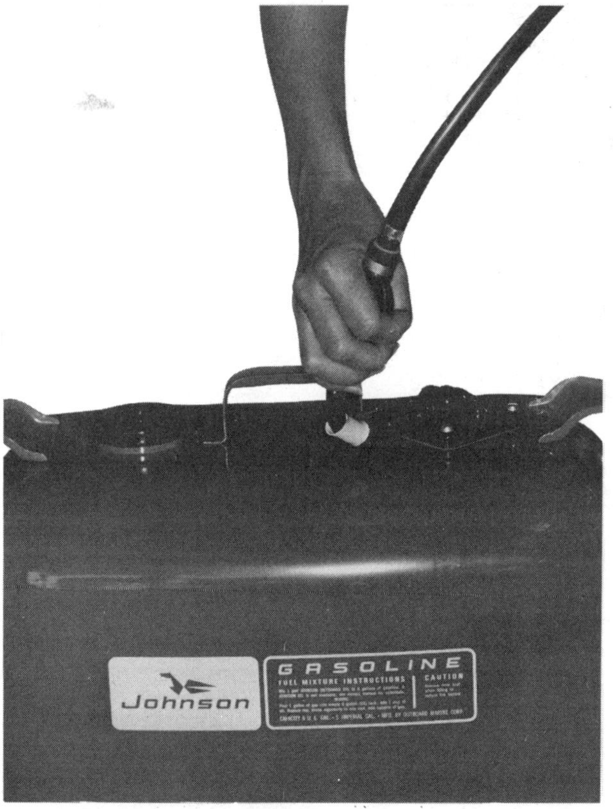

A primer bulb is used to lift fuel from a remote gas tank in order to prime the carburetor. If the carburetor runs out of fuel, the fuel pump may be defective, but the engine can be run by using the primer bulb as a fuel pump.

TROUBLESHOOTING CHART

POSSIBLE CAUSES	ENGINE DOES NOT START	ENGINE RUNS IRREGULARLY OR MISSES	ENGINE STARTS AND THEN CUTS OUT	ENGINE DOES NOT IDLE PROPERLY	ENGINE SPEED IS FASTER THAN NORMAL	ENGINE SPEED IS SLOWER THAN NORMAL	BOAT SPEED BELOW NORMAL	ENGINE OVERHEATS
FUEL TANK EMPTY	●		●					
FUEL FILTER NEEDS CLEANING	●	●	●				●	●
CARBURETOR LOW-SPEED MIXTURE OUT OF ADJUSTMENT		●		●				
CARBURETOR HIGH-SPEED MIXTURE OUT OF ADJUSTMENT		●				●	●	●
WRONG OIL IN FUEL MIXTURE						●	●	●
WRONG GASOLINE IN FUEL MIXTURE		●				●	●	●
NOT ENOUGH OIL IN FUEL MIXTURE						●	●	●
TOO MUCH OIL IN FUEL MIXTURE		●		●		●	●	●
MOTOR FLOODED	●							
SPARK PLUGS FOULED OR DEFECTIVE	●	●		●		●	●	
WRONG TYPE SPARK PLUGS		●		●		●	●	●
NO SPARK	●							
WEAK OR INTERMITTENT SPARK		●	●	●		●	●	
MAGNETO CONTACT POINTS NEED ATTENTION		●	●	●		●	●	●
SPARK PLUG LEADS INTERCHANGED	●							
WATER PUMP DEFECTIVE								●
COOLING SYSTEM IN NEED OF CLEANING						●	●	●
CAVITATION					●		●	
PROPELLER DAMAGED						●	●	
TILT ANGLE IMPROPERLY ADJUSTED							●	
TRANSOM TOO HIGH					●		●	
TRANSOM TOO LOW							●	
AIR VENT HOLE IN FUEL CAP CLOGGED		●	●				●	●

A troubleshooting chart is often helpful to determine the general area in which to look for possible causes of trouble.

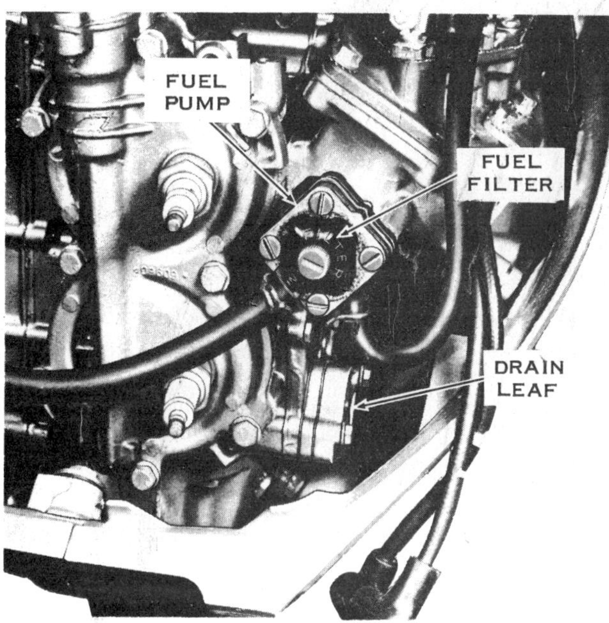

Most of the engines have a fuel pump, and the filter screen should be cleaned periodically. Always replace the gasket.

To see if the fuel pump is working, disconnect the fuel line and direct its flow into a container. You should be able to determine the condition of the pump before the carburetor fuel bowl runs out of fuel.

FUEL SYSTEM TROUBLESHOOTING CHART

1. **No fuel in carburetor**
   1a. Empty gas tank
   1b. Clogged fuel filter
   1c. Restricted vent in gas tank
   1d. Defective fuel pump
   1e. Main adjusting screw closed
   1f. Clogged carburetor screen
   1g. Clogged or broken fuel line
2. **Fuel in carburetor**
   2a. Flooding at carburetor
   2b. Choke not operating
   2c. Water in gasoline
   2d. Restricted carburetor jets
3. **Flooding**
   3a. Choke out of adjustment
   3b. High float level
   3c. Float stuck
   3d. Excessive fuel pump pressure
   3e. Float saturated and not buoyant

IGNITION TROUBLESHOOTING

To check the ignition system, disconnect one of the high-tension wires to a spark plug. Hold the end about 1/4″ from the cylinder head and spin the flywheel. There should be a good spark from the wire to the metal; or there is trouble in the ignition system. If there is a spark from the wire to the ground, but the engine does not start because of ignition system defects, then the trouble is generally with the spark plug. Also, if the ignition timing is out of adjustment, the engine will be hard to start. **CAUTION: There is always the danger of fire with gasoline around an outboard engine; therefore, make sure that the area the spark will jump to is dry and away from the carburetor or fuel lines.** If an approved tester is used, the danger of fire is minimized.

The firing end of this spark plug is black with carbon and wet, indicating that the fuel mixture contains too much oil, the fuel mixture is too rich, or the spark plug is not firing.

To check out a spark plug, remove it from the cylinder and connect the high-tension wire to it. **CAUTION: Don't remove more than the one spark plug so that engine cranking speed will be approximately normal.** Lay the spark plug on the base of the cylinder head, and then spin the flywheel. If there is no spark across the points of the plug, and there was a spark from the high-tension wire to the ground in the preceding test, then the spark plug is shorted. If the plug is good, check the gap and set it to 0.035″. **CAUTION: Make the adjustment by bending the outer electrode, never the center one.** *NOTE: If a gap gauge is not available, you can use two thicknesses of a business card in an emergency.*

IGNITION SYSTEM TROUBLESHOOTING CHART

1. **Spark plugs**
   1a. Fouled
   1b. Wrong type for engine
   1c. Residue on porcelain, especially in salt water areas
   1d. Cracked porcelain
   1e. Loose connections
2. **Ignition coil**
   2a. Weak
   2b. Shorted
   2c. Improperly mounted
   2d. Loose wires
3. **Condenser**
   3a. Weak
   3b. Shorted
   3c. Improperly mounted
   3d. Loose wires
4. **Breaker points**
   4a. Improperly adjusted
   4b. Pitted or corroded
   4c. Broken or weak spring
   4d. Breaker point loose in its mounting
   4e. Loose wires
   4f. Breaker point arm binding on pivot post,

To check the ignition system, hold the high-tension wire about 1/4″ away from a metallic surface. CAUTION: Make sure there are no gasoline fumes nearby to catch on fire. Spin the flywheel and a good spark should jump from the wire to the ground; if the ignition system is working properly. If the end of the high-tension wire is encased in a boot, as this one is, you can insert a screwdriver tip into the boot to make contact with the wire. Hold the screwdriver so that the shank is about 1/4″ away from a good ground to check the spark.

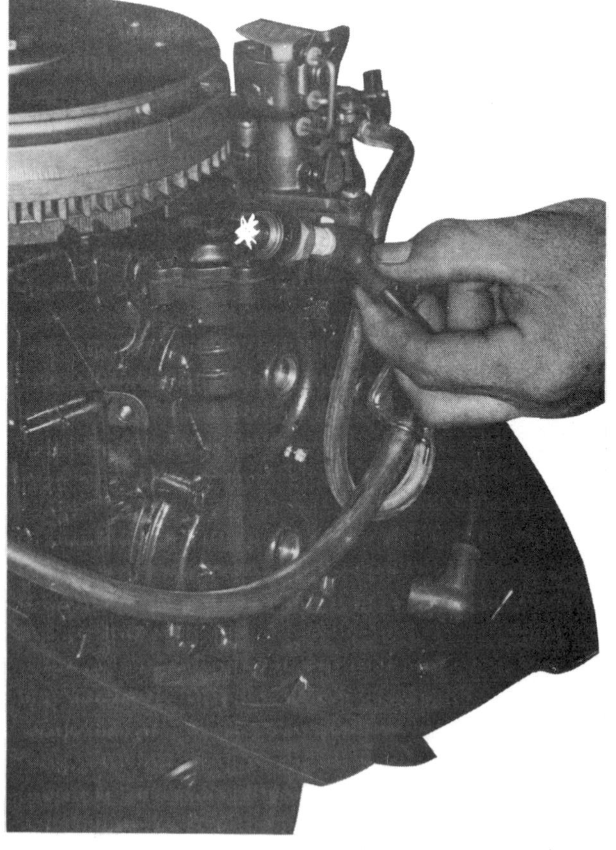

To check out a spark plug, connect the high-tension wire to it and lay the base of the plug on the cylinder head. Spin the flywheel and the spark should jump across the spark plug gap, if the spark plug is good.

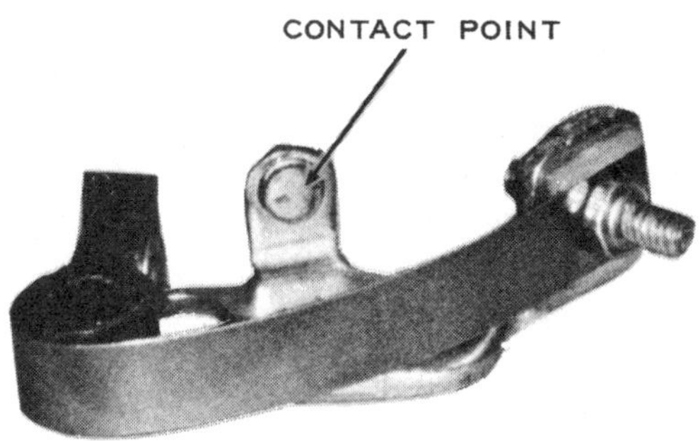

The frosted appearance of this breaker point is an indication that the ignition system was operating properly.

which can cause sluggish action, or the plunger rod can be binding in the bracket
   4g. Broken cam follower or plunger rod

5. **Wiring**
   5a. Loose, corroded, or poorly soldered connections
   5b. Broken wires (broken under the insulation)
   5c. Oil-soaked wires that cause leaks
   5d. Faulty ground or stop button connection
   5e. Faulty spark suppressors (where used)
6. **Flywheel**
   6a. Weak magnet
   6b. Cracked magnet
   6c. Improper clearance between magnet pole pieces and coil heels
   6d. Magnet pole pieces sticking or rubbing on coil heels

COMPRESSION

For an engine to start properly, the compression must be good. The amount of compression depends on the ability of the piston rings to keep the gases from escaping. The condition of the cylinder walls, piston ring grooves, and the rings is a factor. Turn the flywheel by hand with the spark plugs installed to check the compression. If compression is present, it can be felt when attempting to complete one revolution of the flywheel. An engine will run with low compression, but it will be difficult to start and certainly won't develop its normal power output. *NOTE: The compression should not vary more than 10 to 15 psi between cylinders.*

This black, pitted breaker point shows evidence of oil on the contact surface, which burned into an insulator. The oil can be placed on the contact point surface with your fingers or by using a dirty feeler gauge to measure the gap.

COMPRESSION TROUBLESHOOTING CHART

1. **Piston rings**
   1a. Top ring striking ridge in cylinder
   1b. Worn ring grooves
   1c. Rings sticking in ring groove
   1d. Insufficient ring tension
   1e. Insufficient gap clearance

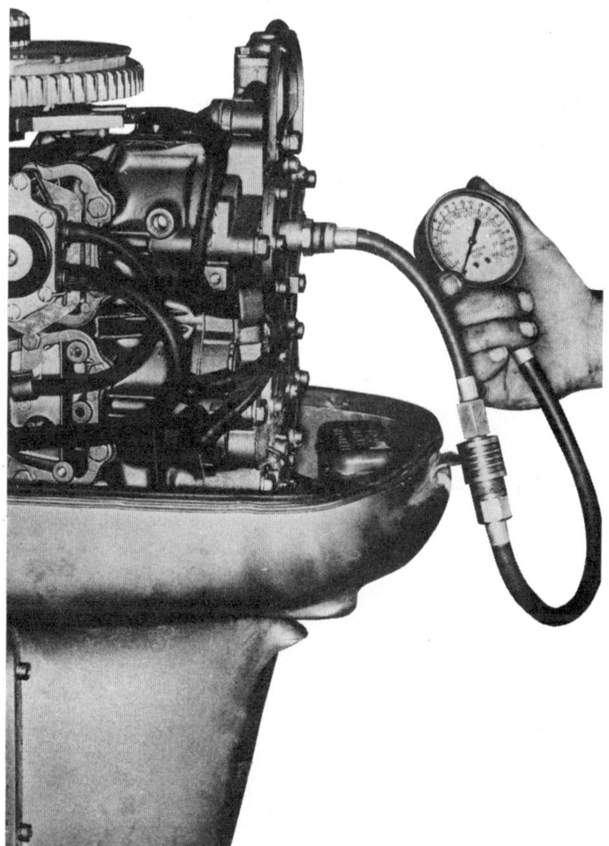

A compression gauge should be used to check the pressure inside of each combustion chamber. It is not possible to tune properly an engine in which the compression varies over 10 psi.

   1f. Excessive side clearance in ring groove
   1g. Undersize pistons
   1h. Scored or wavy cylinder walls

2. **Piston(s)**
   2a. Carbon accumulations in head
   2b. Broken piston, skirt, or ring land
   2c. Insufficient clearance at top of ring land
   2d. Out-of-round, tapered, or worn cylinders
   2e. Excessive piston-to-bore clearance
   2f. Inadequate lubrication
3. **Cylinder(s)**
   3a. Inadequate lubrication
   3b. Contaminated or poor oil
   3c. Exhaust ports clogged with carbon
   3d. Incomplete combustion
   3e. Incorrect type of rings
   3f. Improper cylinder wall finish
   3g. Hole in cylinder
   3h. Insufficient ring gap clearance
   3i. Distorted block or crankshaft

ROUGH OPERATION

An engine that is not operating smoothly can have trouble in the ignition or the fuel system. Closely allied with the fuel system is trouble with a reed valve which affects the fuel distribution to two cylinders of a multi-cylinder engine.

To check the ignition system, disconnect a spark plug wire, and then run the engine at its rough-operating point. Note the size of the spark that jumps from the wire to the terminal of the spark plug. Widen the gap to see if the spark becomes intermittent as the gap increases. This is a rather rough test, but it can be used to throw some light on the condition of the ignition system.

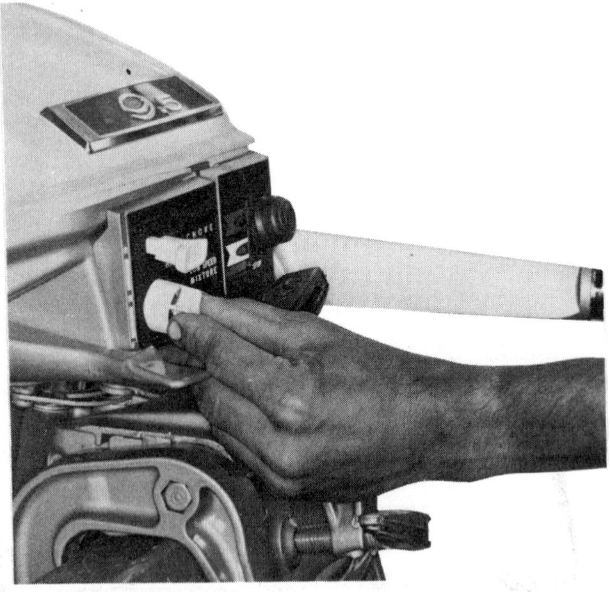

If the engine idles roughly, adjust the idle mixture adjusting screw to see if you can smooth out the idle. Turning the screw to the right (clockwise) leans the mixture. The high-speed adjusting screw at the base of the carburetor can be adjusted in a similar manner.

If the trouble is in the fuel system, it can be checked by changing the air-fuel ratio and noting its effect on the running of the engine. For example, with the engine running at its rough-operating point, close the choke valve slowly and note the effect that enriching the mixture has on the operation of the engine. If the engine smooths out with the choke valve partially closed, then the air-fuel mixture is too lean. The lean condition can be caused by a poor carburetor mixture adjustment or by dirt in one of the jets.

If the engine is running too rich, enriching the air-fuel mixture with the choke will cause the engine to slow down and run even rougher.

If the engine is running too rich, the trouble could be a leaking fuel pump diaphragm, which will allow raw fuel to enter the crankcase and mix with the carbureted fuel. This condition can be suspected if one carburetor of a multi-cylinder engine is running excessively rich. The trouble can be isolated further by removing the spark plugs to check their condition. A wet spark plug indicates an excessively rich mixture.

A defective reed valve will cause the engine to spit back through the carburetor air intake. In some cases, white smoke will come out of the carburetor throat. Hold your hand over the air intake and you may be able to feel raw gasoline being returned through the throat of the carburetor.

On a multi-cylinder engine, one reed valve block controls the air-fuel mixture of one carburetor, which may feed two cylinders. Remove the spark plugs of these two cylinders to determine which one is wet in order to pinpoint the defective reed valve.

ROUGH OPERATION TROUBLESHOOTING CHART

1. **Engine misfires because of ignition troubles**
   1a. Incorrect spark plug gap
   1b. Defective or loose spark plugs
   1c. Spark plugs of an incorrect heat range
   1d. Sticking breaker arm
   1e. Incorrect breaker point gap
   1f. Breaker points not synchronized
   1g. Loose wire in primary circuit
   1h. Defective distributor rotor
   1i. Corroded or pitted breaker points
   1j. Cracked distributor cap
   1k. Leaking or broken high-tension wires

1l. Weak armature magnet
1m. Worn cam lobes on the distributor or magneto shaft
1n. Worn distributor or magneto shaft bushings
1o. Defective coil or condenser
1p. Defective ignition switch
1q. Spark timing out of adjustment

2. Engine misfires because of fuel troubles
2a. Dirt or water in fuel
2b. Reed valve stuck open or broken
2c. Incorrect fuel level
2d. Carburetor loose at flange
2e. Throttle valve not closing completely
2f. Throttle valve turned to one side or incorrectly positioned

3. Engine misfires at high speeds
3a. Weak breaker arm spring
3b. Defective coil
3c. Coil shorts through insulation
3d. Breaker points improperly adjusted
3e. Poor breaker point contact
3f. Spark plug gap set too wide
3g. Too much spark advance
3h. Wrong type of spark plugs
3i. Excessive carbon in cylinders
3j. Poor compression
3k. Dirty carburetor
3l. Lean carburetor adjustment
3m. Crankcase magneto adaptor flange worn out-of-round

4. Engine backfires through the exhaust
4a. Cracked spark plug porcelain
4b. Carbon track in distributor cap
4c. Crossed spark plug wires
4d. Air leak at intake deflector
4e. Improper ignition timing

5. Engine backfires through the carburetor
5a. Poor quality fuel
5b. Air-fuel mixture too lean
5c. Excessively lean or too rich a fuel mixture
5d. Improper ignition timing
5e. Pre-ignition
5f. Improperly seated or a broken reed valve
5g. Improperly adjusted carburetor

6. Pre-ignition
6a. Spark advanced too far
6b. Incorrect type of spark plugs
6c. Burned spark plug electrodes
6d. Incorrect breaker point setting
6e. Excessive oil in fuel
6f. Poor grade of fuel
6g. Lean carburetor mixture
6h. Excessive engine temperature
6i. Carbon deposits in combustion chamber

HIGH FUEL CONSUMPTION

Excessively high fuel consumption is generally caused by carburetor defects. However, the efficient operation of the ignition system is essential for good utilization of the fuel that is drawn into the engine. To this extent, defects in the ignition system will cause the fuel consumption to increase.

HIGH FUEL CONSUMPTION TROUBLESHOOTING CHART

1. Carburetor troubles
1a. Cracked carburetor casting
1b. Leaking fuel line connection
1c. Defective carburetor bowl gasket
1d. Warped or bent bowl cover
1e. Plugged vent hole in cover
1f. High float level
1g. Loose float needle valve seat
1h. Defective needle valve seat gasket
1i. Worn needle valve and seat
1j. Ridge worn in lip of float
1k. Worn float pin or bracket
1l. Float binding in bowl
1m. Choke lever stuck

2. Fuel pump troubles
2a. Leaking around diaphragm cover
2b. Leaking fuel pump diaphragm
2c. Warped check valves
2d. Dirt or sediment in valves
2e. Corroded valve seats
2f. High fuel pump pressure
2g. Leakage at lines and connections
2h. Leaking gas tank
2i. Leakage at filler cap

3. Ignition conditions
3a. Retarded spark timing
3b. Leaking high-tension wires

The condition of the firing end of a spark plug can be used to determine the condition inside of the combustion chamber. This spark plug is running dry, meaning that the mixture is combustible and that the spark plug is doing its work well.

3c. Incorrect spark plug gap
3d. Fouled spark plugs
3e. Worn breaker points
3f. Faulty spark advance adjustment
3g. Defective condenser
3h. Weak ignition coil
3i. Pre-ignition

4. Compression troubles
4a. Worn or broken piston rings
4b. Worn pistons or cylinders

5. Miscellaneous troubles
5a. Loose carburetor flange
5b. Improperly adjusted or worn throttle linkage
5c. Restricted exhaust system
5d. Carbon in manifold
5e. Overheating engine
5f. Use of poor grade of gasoline
5g. Sticking reed valve
5h. Poorly seated reed valve

NOISES

Checking engine noises is one of the more difficult troubleshooting procedures because noises travel in the metal of the engine and sometimes appear to be coming from every part. However, it is possible to localize noises by using a stethoscope or a listening rod.

NOISE TROUBLESHOOTING CHART

1. Knocking in powerhead
1a. Loose flywheel
1b. Excessive bearing clearance
1c. Spark advanced too far
1d. Pre-ignition
1e. Excessive end play in crankshaft
1f. Out-of-round bearing journals
1g. Bent or twisted crankshaft
1h. Broken crankshaft

2. Knocking from the connecting rods
2a. Excessive bearing clearance
2b. Worn connecting rod
2c. Misaligned connecting rods and cap
2d. Bent or twisted connecting rod
2e. Worn crankshaft journal

3. Center main bearing noises
3a. Improperly installed main bearing
3b. Crankshaft striking the reed stops

4. Piston noises
4a. Excessive piston-to-cylinder bore clearance
4b. Out-of-round cylinder
4c. Loose piston pin
4d. Carbon in the top of the cylinder
4e. Piston pin bent
4f. Excessive clearance at the ring grooves
4g. Broken piston ring

5. Gear housing noises
5a. Propeller shaft worn or sprung
5b. Bearing worn
5c. Broken gears
5d. Propeller hub rubbing against the gear case cover
5e. Improperly fitted gears
5f. Worn gears
5g. Wrong conical angle
5h. Incorrect backlash
5i. Oil seal leakage
5j. Water in gear housing
5k. No grease in gear housing

MECHANICAL PROBLEMS

Generally, mechanical problems in an engine require it to be disassembled to correct the condition. The following Mechanical Troubleshooting Chart will assist in determining the possible causes of mechanical troubles.

MECHANICAL TROUBLESHOOTING CHART

1. Reed valve breakage
1a. Improper valve opening
1b. Corrosion of reed valve
1c. Poor valve seat

2. Excessive bearing wear caused by dirt
2a. Careless service methods
2b. Contaminated oil

3. Bearing wear caused by improper fitting
3a. Distorted connecting rods
3b. Mixed connecting rod caps
3c. Dirt between bearing and connecting rod bore
3d. Out-of-round, tapered, or worn journal
3e. Warped crankshaft or block
3f. Excessive crankshaft end play
3g. Scored bearing surface
3h. Improper clearance
3i. Use of wrong service tools

4. Bearing failure caused by corrosion
4a. Overheating
4b. Storage in damp place
4c. Water entering powerhead

5. Bearing failure caused by improper operation
5a. Overspeeding
5b. Spark detonation
5c. Improper engine break-in
5d. Racing a cold engine

5e. Using the wrong type or grade of oil
5f. Using an improper fuel
5g. Improper spark timing

6. Bearing wear caused by lubrication problems
6a. Excessive engine temperatures
6b. Insufficient engine warm-up time
6c. Insufficient quantity of oil

7. Engine speed faster than normal
7a. Cavitation
7b. Transom too high
7c. Propeller hub slipping
7d. Wrong propeller pitch

8. Engine speed slower than normal
8a. Carburetor out of adjustment
8b. Too much oil in fuel mixture
8c. Wrong oil in fuel
8d. Wrong type of gasoline
8e. Spark plugs fouled
8f. Wrong type of spark plugs
8g. Tilt angle not correctly adjusted
8h. Transom too high
8i. Transom too low
8j. Cavitation
8k. Weeds tangled on gear housing
8l. Propeller damaged
8m. Wrong propeller pitch

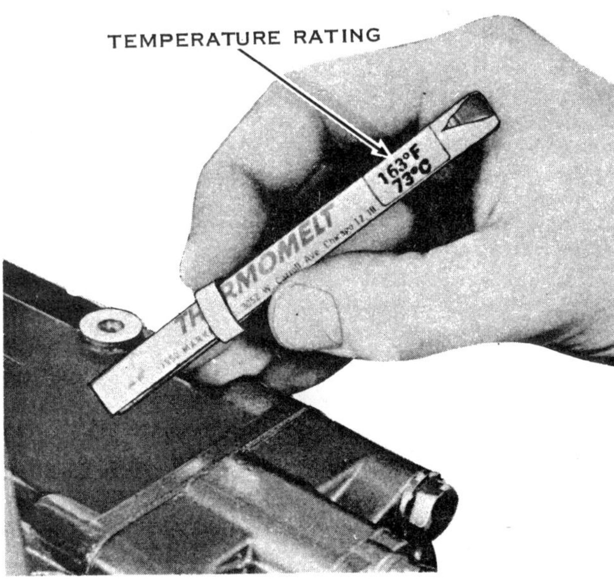

A Markal Thermomelt Stik can be used to determine engine temperature. The material is a heat-sensitive crayon, which melts on contact with a surface at a specific temperature. Use the stick to make a mark on the powerhead; it will appear dull and chalky until the surface temperature reaches the rating of the stick, and then the mark will melt, becoming liquid and glossy. On a painted surface, it may be necessary to hold the stick against the surface until it starts to melt. Two sticks are needed: a 125°F. Stik and a 163°F. Stik. With the motor at operating temperature, the 125°F. Stik should melt, but the 163°F. Stik must not melt, or you have trouble. If the 125°F. Stik does not melt, the thermostat is stuck open, and the motor is running too cold.

COOLING SYSTEM TROUBLESHOOTING CHART

1. Overheating with an external leak
1a. Loose cylinder block cover bolts
1b. Damaged cylinder block cover gasket
1c. Warped cylinder block cover or block
1d. Cracked cylinder wall
1e. Porosity of cylinder head

2. Overheating without a leak
2a. Incorrect ignition timing
2b. Improper fuel mixture
2c. Improperly adjusted spark advance linkage
2d. Defective spark advance linkage
2e. Pre-ignition

3. Overheating caused by restricted circulation
3a. Pump impeller loose on shaft
3b. Water inlet pipe seal ring not in place
3c. Pump blades broken or worn
3d. Water pump worn
3e. Clogged water jacket passages
3f. Water tube mislocated
3g. Water tube cracked or corroded
3h. Cover not securely tightened

ELECTRICAL SYSTEM TROUBLES

The battery supplies the current required to crank the engine. On engines with a distributor-type ignition system, the battery furnishes the current to energize this circuit. Some engines are equipped with an alternator to charge the battery. In the absence of an alternator, the battery must be charged by an outside source.

It takes specialized testing equipment and knowledge of its use to determine accurately the condition of an electrical unit. However, the following troubleshooting charts can be used for guidance in tracing out some types of electrical troubles.

BATTERY TROUBLESHOOTING CHART

1. If frequent charging is required
1a. Corroded battery terminals
1b. Alternator grounded or shorted
1c. Worn-out or inefficient battery
1d. Rectifier defective
1e. Short in charging circuit
1f. Excessive use of electrical units
1g. Short circuit in ignition switch

2. Battery does not take a charge
2a. Low water level
2b. Worn-out battery

- 2c. Cracked case
- 2d. Spilled electrolyte
- 2e. Internal short circuit
- 2f. Impure electrolyte

3. High water loss

- 3a. Too high a charging rate
- 3b. Old or inefficient battery
- 3c. Leaking battery cell
- 3d. Worn-out battery
- 3e. Cracked case
- 3f. Defective current regulation

IGNITION SYSTEM
TROUBLESHOOTING CHART

1. Oxidized breaker points

- 1a. High charging voltage
- 1b. Resistor of incorrect value
- 1c. High resistance in condenser circuit
- 1d. Incorrect type of ignition coil

2. Ignition coil failures

- 2a. Extremely high voltage
- 2b. Moisture formation
- 2c. Excessive heat from engine

3. Spark plug troubles

- 3a. Incorrect type of spark plug
- 3b. Too rich a fuel mixture
- 3c. Incorrect oil mixture
- 3d. Inferior grade of gasoline or oil used
- 3e. Overheated engine
- 3f. Too much carbon in combustion chamber
- 3g. Improper torque on spark plug

STARTING MOTOR
TROUBLESHOOTING CHART

1. Starter fails to crank engine

- 1a. Poor battery ground
- 1b. Jammed or broken drive
- 1c. Broken teeth on flywheel
- 1d. Grounded switch
- 1e. Solenoid shorted or open circuited
- 1f. Burned contact points in switch
- 1g. Improperly seated brushes
- 1h. High mica between commutator segments
- 1i. Shorted armature
- 1j. Shorted field or brushes

2. Excessive current draw

- 2a. Broken or jammed starter drive
- 2b. Dirty or gummed armature
- 2c. Shorted armature
- 2d. Grounded armature or field
- 2e. Misaligned starting motor
- 2f. Worn armature shaft bearings

CRANKING MOTOR TROUBLESHOOTING CHART

STEP NUMBER	METER READINGS (In Volts) As Hooked Up	With Starter Button Pushed	If It Reads	CAUSE
V-1	12	10–11	12 Below 10	Open Circuit Weak Battery
V-2	12	0–1	Over 1 Below 8	Loose Terminal Open Circuit High-Resistance
V-3	0	1/2–1	Below 1	Loose Terminal Broken Wire
V-4	0	1/2–1	Over 1	Loose Terminal
V-5	0	1/2–1	Over 1	Loose Connection Corroded Connection
V-6	12	1/2–1	Over 1	Defective Solenoid
V-7	12	1/2–1	Over 1	Loose Terminal
V-8	0	0	Over 0	Poor Ground
A-9 ①	0	125	Well Over 125	Defective Cranking Motor

① An ammeter of this capacity must use a shunt. **Caution: Do not connect a small ammeter in this circuit, or you will burn it out.**

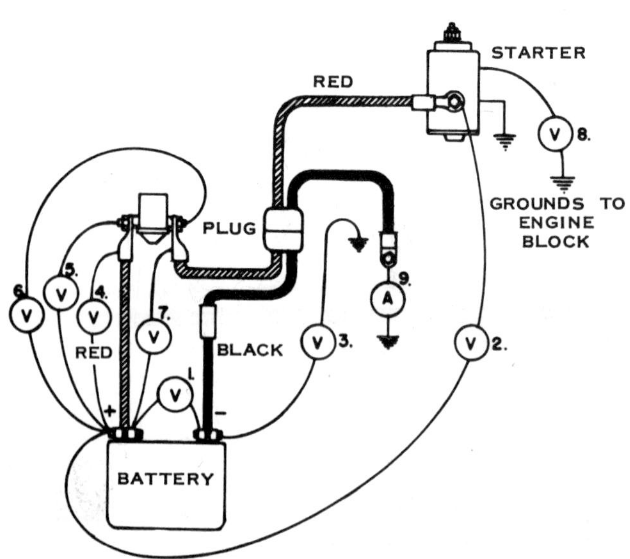

This diagram is to be used in conjunction with the Troubleshooting Chart to make accurate tests, which will determine the exact area of trouble.

2g. Misaligned armature shaft
2h. Loose field pole pieces
2i. Engine turns hard

3. Burned commutator bars

3a. Excessive arcing at brushes
3b. Excessive voltage
3c. Improperly seated brushes
3d. Open-circuited armature coils
3e. Open field circuit
3f. Weak brush spring tension

4. Excessive noise

4a. Defective starter drive
4b. Chipped or broken flywheel teeth
4c. Insufficient lubrication
4d. Worn armature shaft bearings
4e. Misaligned starting motor
4f. Loose starter mounting
4g. Sprung armature shaft

TROUBLESHOOTING THE CRANKING MOTOR

When a cranking motor does not turn, or doesn't crank the engine, the electrical system must be checked with an accurate voltmeter and ammeter to determine the sources of trouble. Use a 0-15 voltmeter and a 0-500 ammeter. The following chart is keyed to the illustration to give a useful step-by-step tracing procedure.

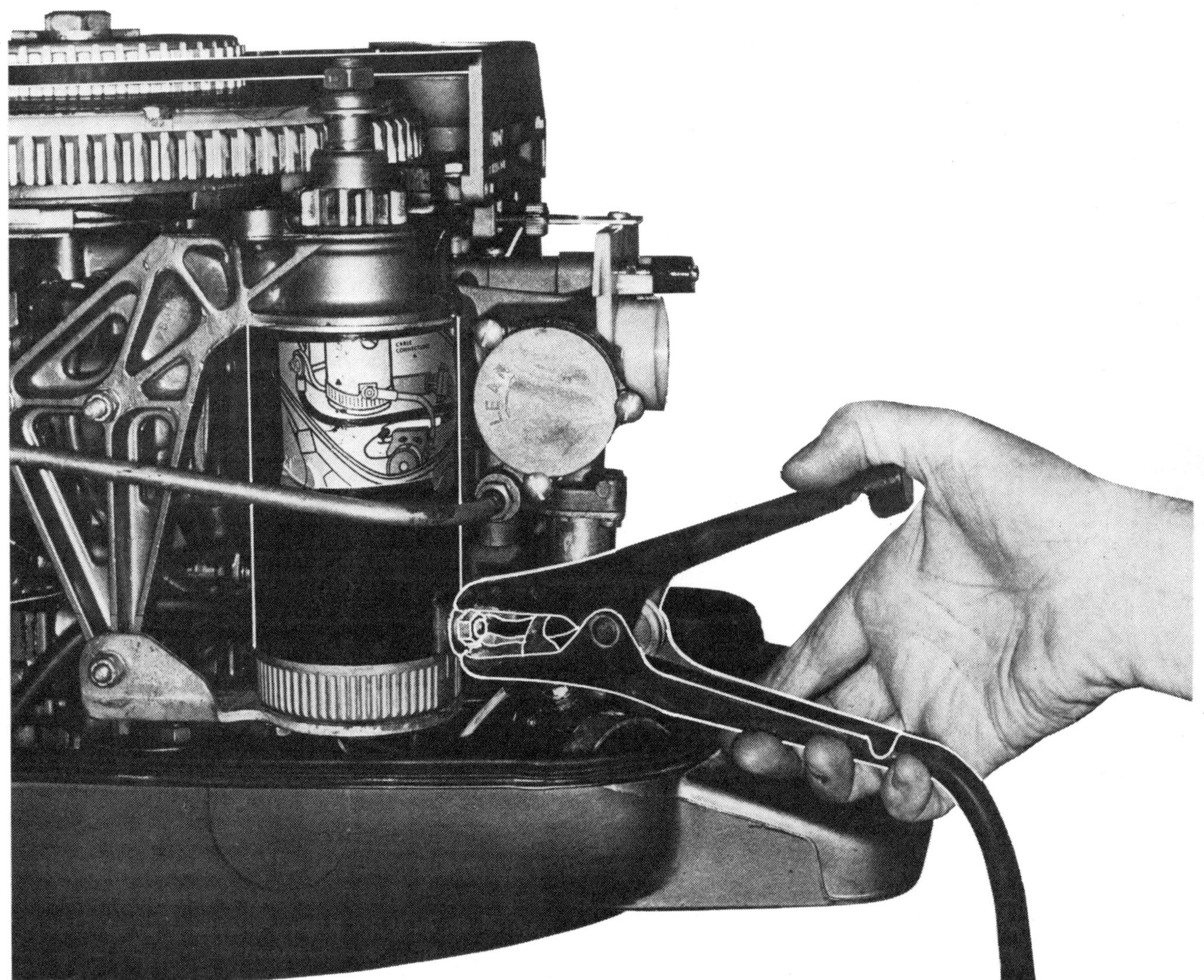

Cranking motor troubles can be caused by a defective relay. To check the relay, use a jumper cable to bypass the relay entirely, and the cranking motor should work unless it is defective. CAUTION: To avoid sparks near the carburetor, which could cause a fire, connect the jumper to the cranking motor terminal first, as shown, and then connect the other end of the cable to the booster battery.

2

MAINTENANCE

To install the engine on the transom, open the boat bracket clamp screws, and then install the unit, centering it with respect to the keel or centerline of the boat. Observe the position of the anti-cavitation plate with respect to the keel. The plate must be level with or slightly below the keel or bottom of the boat. If the anti-cavitation plate is more than one inch below the bottom of the boat, shim the engine, using 1/4″ strips of hard wood between the top of the transom and the boat brackets, as shown.

Installation of the engine on the transom should be given very careful attention. The clamp bracket not only must support the weight, but is subject to thrust, impact, inertia, and steering stresses. These forces are applied directly to the transom through the clamp bracket assembly. Therefore, to avoid damage to the transom and to prevent the engine from working loose during operation, it is important that the clamp screws are tightened securely and equally and that the larger

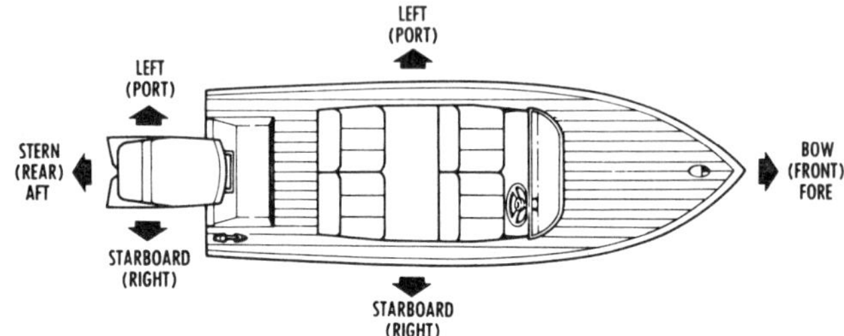

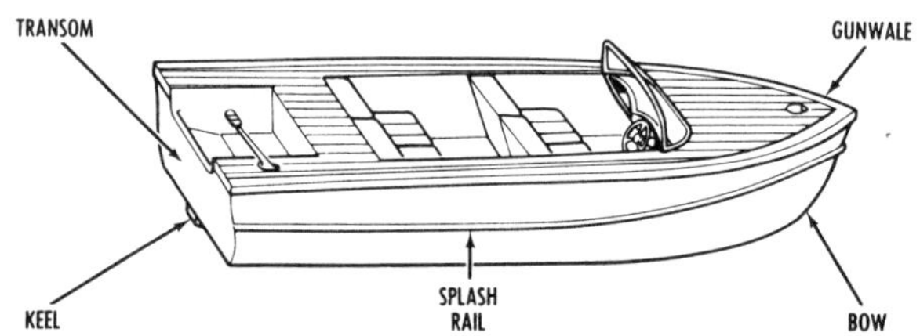

In this book, specific names are used to refer to the various sides of the boat and motor. These names are an accepted standard in the marine industry, and their usage remains the same regardless of the direction from which the boat is viewed.

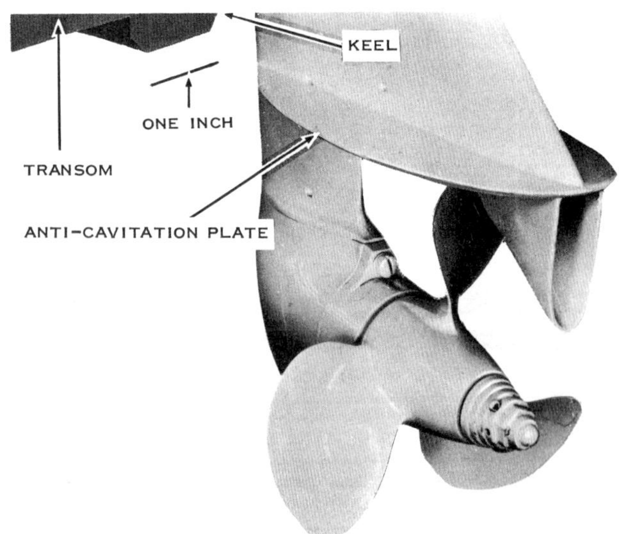

The anti-cavitation plate should be level with or slightly below the bottom of the boat when the engine is properly mounted.

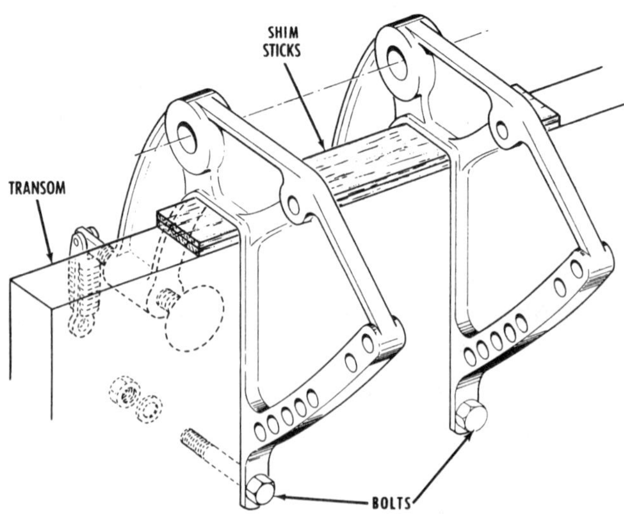

Shim sticks should be used under the motor mounting brackets if the anti-cavitation plate is more than 1″ below the bottom of the boat.

	NO. OF MOTORS	CUTOUT WIDTH A X HT.	Y HT.	Z HT.	TRANSOM HEIGHT B	SPACING C	CLEARANCE LENGTH D	THICKNESS E MIN.	MAX.	MOTOR CLEARANCE F	COVER HT. G	DRAIN WELL H
1-1/2 THRU 5 HP	1	22″	22″	22″	15 ± 1/2″ OR 20 ± 1/2″	–	15″	1-1/4″	1-3/4″	14″	18″	5-1/2″ MIN.
	2	43″	45″	49″		22″	15″	1-1/4″	1-3/4″	14″	18″	5-1/2″ MIN.
6 THRU 9-1/2 HP	1	21″	23″	27″	15 ± 1/2″ OR 20 ± 1/2″	–	21″	1-3/8″	1-3/4″	17″	22-1/2″	5-1/2″ MIN,
	2	43″	45″	49″		22″	21″	1-3/8″	1-3/4″	17″	22-1/2″	5-1/2″ MIN.
20 THRU 40 HP	1	28″	34″	34″	15 ± 1/2″ OR 20 ± 1/2″	–	21″	1-3/8″	2″	21″	29″	5-1/2″ MIN.
	2	50″	56″	58″		22″	21″	1-3/8″	2″	21″	29″	5-1/2″ MIN.
50 HP	1	33″	39″	40″	19.5–	22″	21.5″	1-3/8″	2″	21″	29″	5-1/2″ MIN.
	2	54″	60″	61″	20″	22″	21.5″	1-3/8″	2″	21″	29″	5-1/2″ MIN.

Operating clearances and mounting dimensions for the various models.

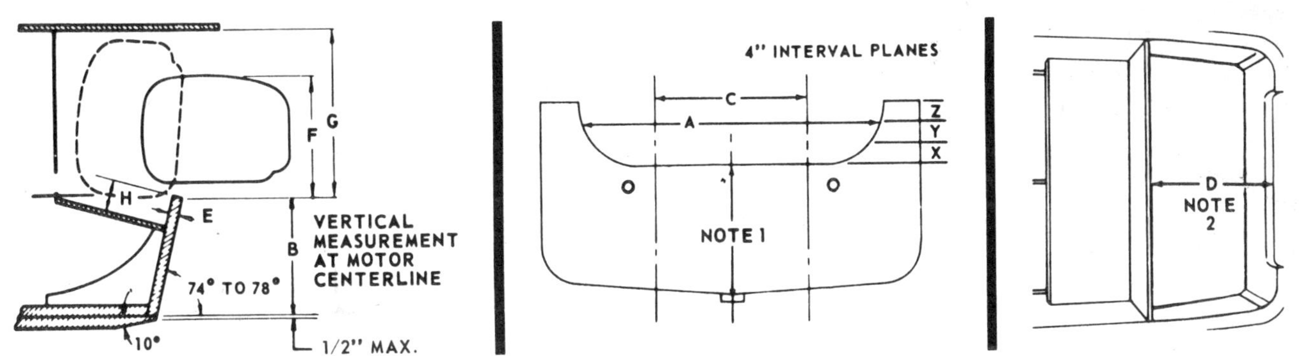

TRANSOM MOUNTING DIAGRAM

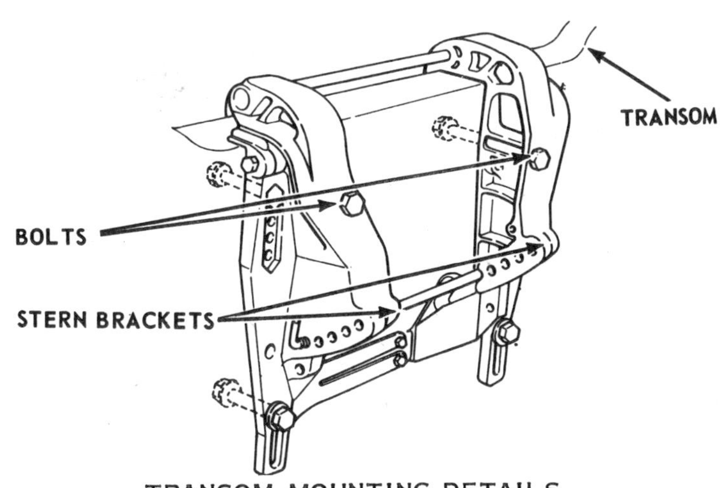

TRANSOM MOUNTING DETAILS

engines are secured to the transom with bolts through the brackets. **CAUTION: Failure to bolt the engine to the transom may result in damage to the boat and/or loss of the engine.** Apply a waterproof sealant to the bolts to prevent water from reaching the wood core of the transom. During operation, the clamp screws should be checked occasionally for tightness.

BOAT PERFORMANCE AND PROPELLER SELECTION

Many times the engine is blamed for inefficient operation when actually the fault lies with the boat or the installation of the engine on the boat.

Boat Speed

Consult the boat house bulletin charts for similar boat sizes and loading. These boats and engines are run with the best-suited propellers and with an optimum set-up (transom height and tilt angle, usually with an aft position of the center of gravity).

Center of Gravity

For maximum speed, move the weight aft until the boat porpoises or is about to porpoise. This reduces the wetted surface to a minimum. Only the rear half of the boat bottom should be wet.

Tilt Angle

The tilt angle should be set so that the anti-cavitation plate is about parallel to the bottom of the boat. The speed of boats that have the center of gravity located forward may be improved sometimes by tilting the lower unit out one pin hole. This will tend to raise the bow and reduce the wetted surface. If the lower unit is tilted in, the boat will ride with the bow down, wetting more of the bottom and thereby reducing speed.

Transom Height

A greater transom height will increase boat speed, but it makes cavitation more likely. The effect of transom height on speed is slight at speeds between 15-20 mph, but it becomes important at speeds of 30-35 mph and above.

Condition of Boat Bottom

For maximum speed, a boat bottom should be nearly a flat plane where it contacts the water. It should be especially straight and smooth in the fore-and-aft direction. The bottom is said to have a "hook" if it is concave in the fore-and-aft direction when viewed from below. When the boat is planing, this causes more lift on the bottom near the transom and allows

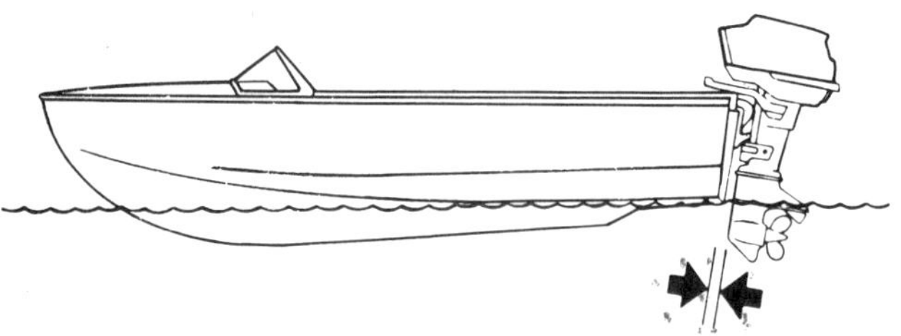

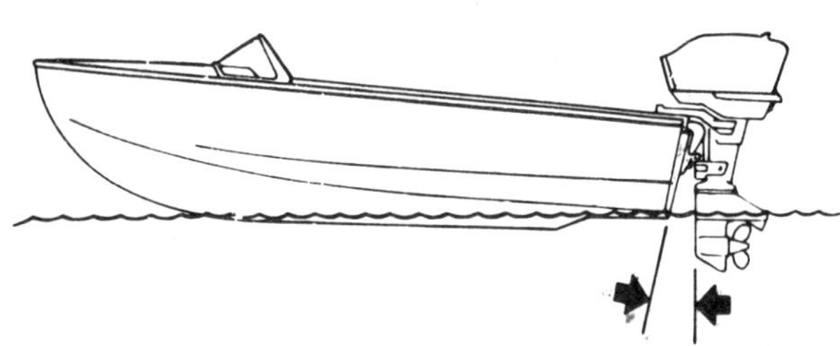

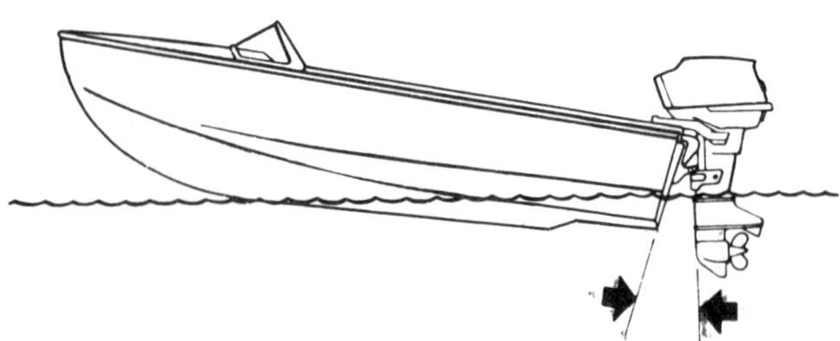

For best performance, the tilt angle should be adjusted so that the engine is vertical to the surface of the water. If the lower unit is tilted out too far, the bow of the boat will ride too high. If the lower unit is tilted too close to the ransom, the bow will plow, or dig into the water. NOTE: Changes in boat loading may require a change in the tilt angle.

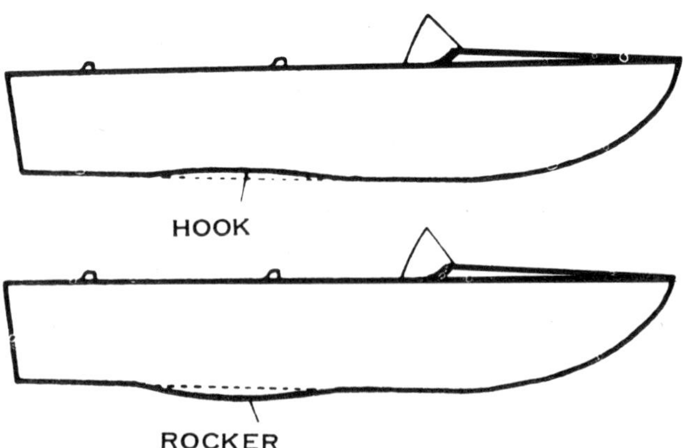

For maximum speed, the bottom of the boat should be a flat plane where it contacts the water. A boat bottom with either a hook or rocker can affect the speed and operation to a large degree.

the bow to drop, which greatly increases the wetted surface and reduces boat speed. A hook is frequently caused by supporting the boat too far forward to the transom while hauling it on a trailer or during storage. A "rocker" is the reverse of a "hook" and much less common. The boat has a rocker if the bottom is convex in the fore-and-aft direction when viewed from below. A boat with a rocker has a strong tendency to porpoise. Moss, barnacles, or other surface irregularities that increase skin friction of the boat bottom will cause a considerable loss of boat speed. Surface roughness of the gear case, caused by barnacles or corrosion, easily can result in a speed loss of 1 or 2 mph on boats in the 30 to 35 mph and higher class.

PROPELLER SELECTION

The speed at which a given boat will travel is governed mainly by the horsepower available. Use of the correct propeller will allow the engine to turn at the recommended rpm and develop full power. First, select a trial propeller, using the approximate boat length and load, if known. This usually will be the correct choice. Establish the exact transom height and tilt pin setting by test.

To check, make a trial run, using an accurate tachometer. It is important that the engine rpm remain within the recommended limits. The trial run should be made with a light load of one person. Under these conditions, it is desirable to have the engine rpm near the top of the recommended limit so that, under a heavy load, the speed will not fall below recommendations. If the engine rpm is too high, try a higher pitch or the same pitch cupped. Likewise, if the rpm is low, try a lower pitch propeller. There normally is a 300-500 rpm change between propeller pitches.

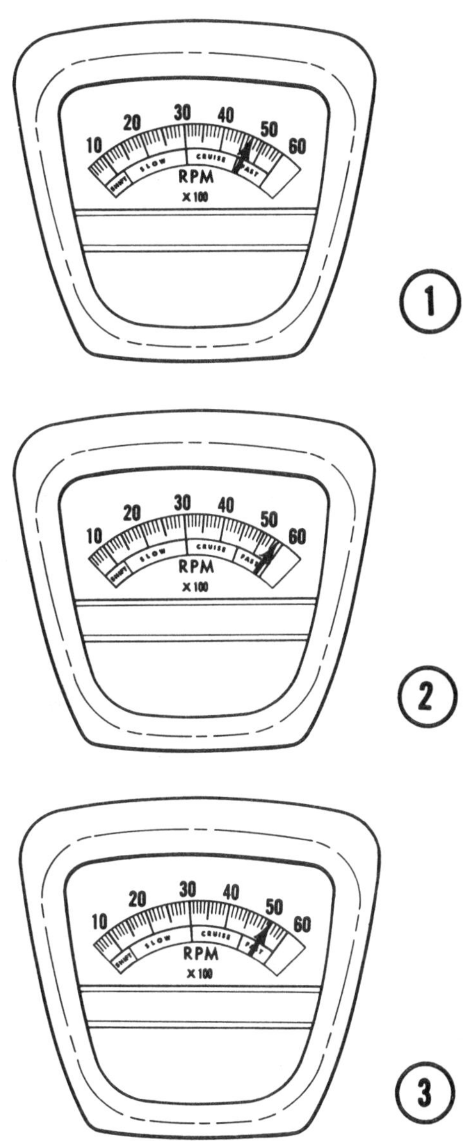

These three tachometer illustrations show the method of determining the correct propeller for a given engine-boat combination. (1) The first trial run, using an 11-1/2" diameter by 14" pitch propeller, showed a tachometer reading of 4,700 rpm. The manufacturer's specification for this engine is 4,800-5,400 rpm; therefore, this propeller is loading the engine too much and should be replaced with one having less pitch. (2) The second trial run, using a propeller 11-1/2" diameter by 10" pitch, shows a tachometer reading of 5,800 rpm, too fast for the load. To correct, increase the pitch. (3) The third trial run, using a propeller 11-1/2" by 12" pitch, shows a tachometer reading of 5,100 rpm, safely within the 4,800-5,400 specifications.

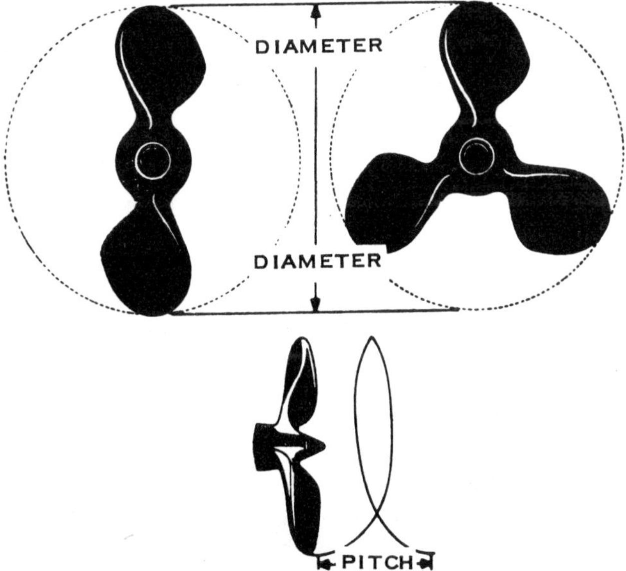

The two basic dimensions of a propeller are pitch and diameter. The pitch is the theoretical distance that a propeller advances if there is no slip. The diameter is the distance from the tip of one blade to the tip of the other.

For dual installation, the next higher pitch propeller may be best. For water skiing, it may be desirable to use the next lower pitch propeller; however, do not operate at full throttle when using a ski propeller and not pulling skiers. **CAUTION: If, in this connection, a propeller has too little pitch for the application, dangerous over-speed of the engine will result!** If a propeller has too much pitch for the application, acceleration will be slow.

Light, fast boats require higher pitch propellers, while heavier boats require lower pitch propellers. Use aluminum propellers in salt water areas to reduce the electrolytic action that can result in corrosion and pitting of metal surfaces.

FUEL CONSUMPTION

For a planing boat, the maximum miles per gallon is obtained with an engine that will just plane the boat (15-17 mph) at full throttle. Larger engines, or dual engines that will drive the boat faster, will give fewer miles per gallon. A given boat and engine usually will get the most miles per gallon at or near full throttle. An improper carburetor setting can reduce the miles per gallon by 10-15%.

INSTALLING THE PROPELLER

All models are equipped with a shear pin which is designed to break before the engine is damaged. The engine is equipped with a two-position lock which prevents the propeller from rising out of the water when the unit is run in reverse. The same lock can be used to tilt the powerplant all the way forward in order to change a propeller or to replace a sheared drive pin. To raise the engine, release the lock lever and then pull the engine as far forward as possible.

To replace a shear pin, pull the rubber propeller cap off the propeller shaft. Remove the sheared pin, align the shear pin hole in the propeller hub with the hole in the propeller shaft, insert a new shear pin, and then install the rubber propeller cap. It should be noted that a washer is used between the shear pin and propeller on all these engines, and this washer must not be left off as it performs the important function of protecting the softer propeller from being damaged by the shear pin if the propeller spins out. Also, if the washer is not in place, the embedded shear pin will be difficult to remove.

Extra drive pins and cotter pins should be carried for spares. If these parts are used, be sure to purchase new ones as soon as possible so that you always have a spare.

Most propellers incorporate a rubber shock absorber to prevent damage and to keep the drive pin from being sheared, unless the propeller hits a solid object. The shock absorber also prevents damage to the lower unit.

TILT PIN ADJUSTMENT

Holes are provided in the clamp bracket to permit changing the location of the tilt lock pin for proper adjustment of the title angle. The tilt angle of the engine should be set so that the anti-cavitation plate is about parallel with the bottom of the boat. The speed of boats which have the center of gravity located forward may be improved sometimes by tilting the lower unit out one tilt pin hole. This will tend to raise the bow and reduce the amount of wetted surface. If the

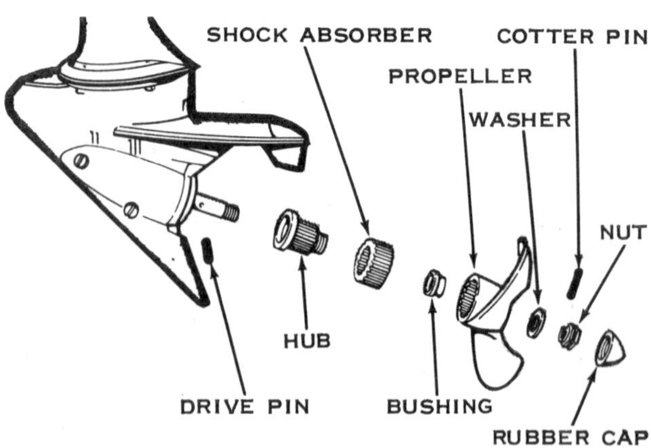

Some propellers are mounted with a shock absorber to minimize propeller damage and reduce the possibility of shearing the drive pin.

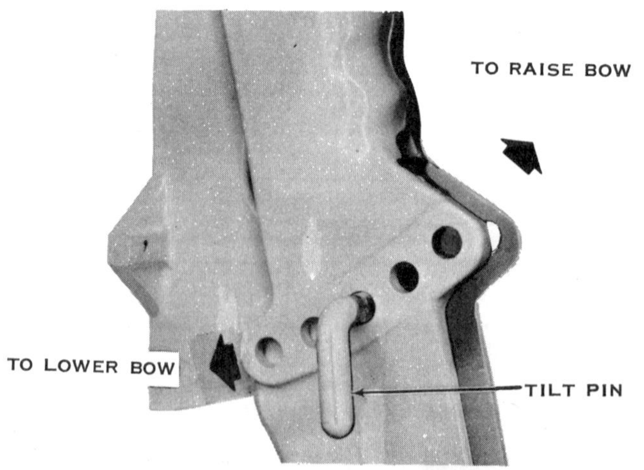

Holes are provided in the clamp bracket to allow you to change the location of the tilt lock pin in order to change the tilt angle of the engine.

lower unit is tilted in, the boat will ride with the bow down, wetting more of the bottom and reducing speed. Raising the bow generally will improve operation in rough water.

Under ideal conditions, efficiency will be best with the lower unit operating in a level position, because the entire thrust will then be applied parallel to the plane of motion. With some boats, under certain unfavorable conditions of loading, there will be a tendency to ride stern high or bow high. This condition can be corrected considerably by adjusting the tilt angle so that the boat rides level. Operation with excessive tilt will reduce performance noticeably and may induce cavitation. It is preferable, therefore, to level the boat by proper loading rather than by an extreme adjustment of the tilt angle. Except in very rough water, a properly designed boat will ride level and will plane without porpoising if the tilt angle is correctly adjusted and the boat is favorably loaded. **CAUTION: Do not operate the engine with the tilt lock pin removed.**

It should be noted that the tilt pin should be used to support the weight of the engine only when working on the propeller. Under no circumstances should the pin be used to support the weight while the engine is being towed on a trailer, because it was not designed for this type of strain. Generally the pin breaks, and the skeg drops to the pavement where it is damaged enough so that the entire lower unit must be replaced.

CAVITATION

Cavitation is indicated by intermittent or continued overspeed of the engine, accompanied by violent water agitation and a sharp reduction of boat speed. Cavitation occurs when the slip stream (flow of water past the propeller) changes from a smooth, consistent flow to a turbulent one. Under conditions of cavitation, the turbulent area or cavity around the propeller causes a very noticeable loss of forward thrust. Generally, cavitation is caused by one of the following: (1) The propeller's operating too close to the surface. This may be due to the transom's being too high, to an adjustment of the tilt angle that causes the lower unit to be too high, or to the boat's riding stern-high because of improper loading. (2) Turbulence in the slip stream, which can be caused by an obstruction, such as a wide or deep keel. This can be helped in most cases by tapering the keel in both width and depth from a point about 30″ forward of the trailing edge; however, for best results, the boat should have no keel in the last 4′ of stern. (3) Fouling of the propeller by weeds, rope, etc. (4) Damaged or broken propeller blades. A broken blade is indicated usually by excessive vibration.

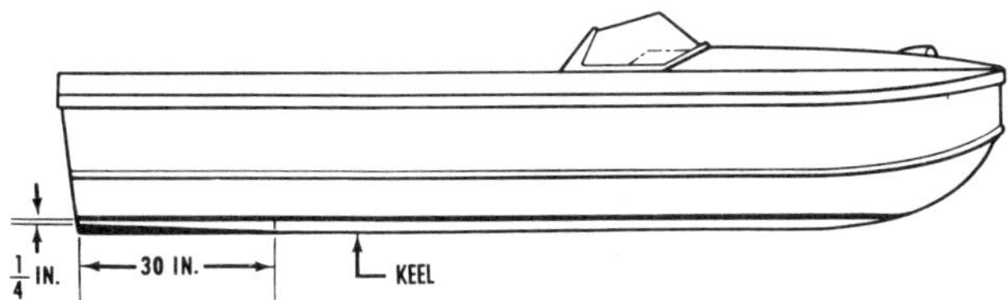

To avoid cavitation, the keel of the boat must be tapered, beginning about 30″ forward of the transom, so that it projects no more than 1/4″ below the hull at the transom end.

CAUTION FOR SHALLOW WATER OPERATION

When the shift lever is in REVERSE, the lower unit is locked in its normal operating position. The shock load of an impact could cause transom breakage, particularly when the boat is backing up. Proceed cautiously when in reverse motion and be careful of underwater obstructions. **CAUTION: Do not accelerate the engine to high speeds or the stern will dip and you may swamp the boat.**

PERFORMANCE FACTORS

Engineers have always known that weather exerts a

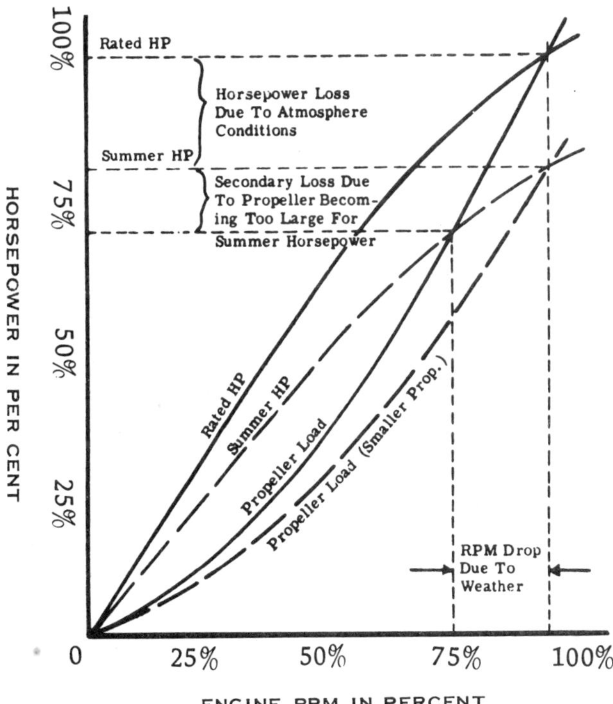

This graph shows how the changes in temperature affect the performance of an engine.

profound effect on the performance of internal combustion engines. Therefore, all horsepower ratings refer to the power that the engine can produce at its rated speed under a specified set of weather conditions.

Summer conditions of high temperature, low barometric pressure, and high humidity combine to reduce power. Reduced power, in turn, is reflected in decreases in boat speeds—decreases of as much as two or three mph, in some cases. Nothing can restore this loss of speed for the boatman except the coming of cool, dry weather.

To point out the practical consequences of weather: an engine running on a hot, humid summer day may encounter a loss of as much as 14% of the horsepower it can develop on a dry, brisk spring or fall day. The horsepower that an internal combustion engine can produce depends on the density of the air that it is consuming; this density, in turn, depends upon the temperature of the air, its barometric pressure, and its content of water vapor or humidity.

Accompanying this weather-inspired loss of power is a second, more subtle loss. At fitting-out time in early spring, the engine may have been equipped with a propeller which allowed it to turn at its rated speed at full throttle. With the coming of the summer weather and the consequent drop in available horsepower, this propeller will be too large. Hence, the engine will operate at less than its rated speed. Due to the horsepower-speed characteristics of an engine, this results in a further loss of horsepower and another decrease in boat speed. This secondary loss can be regained by switching to a smaller-pitch propeller which will allow the engine to run at its rated speed again.

FUEL MIXING PROCEDURE

An automotive low-lead gasoline is recommended for outboard motor use. An outboard motor is extremely sensitive to inconsistent fuel/oil mixing and to fuel mixtures resulting from different brands of gasolines and oils. Such changes often require frequent readjustments of the carburetor.

Mix the oil with the gasoline in the following ratios: Mix a 6 oz. can of 100:1 two-cycle motor oil with each 5 gallons of gasoline. Mix a 12 oz. can of 40/50:1 two-

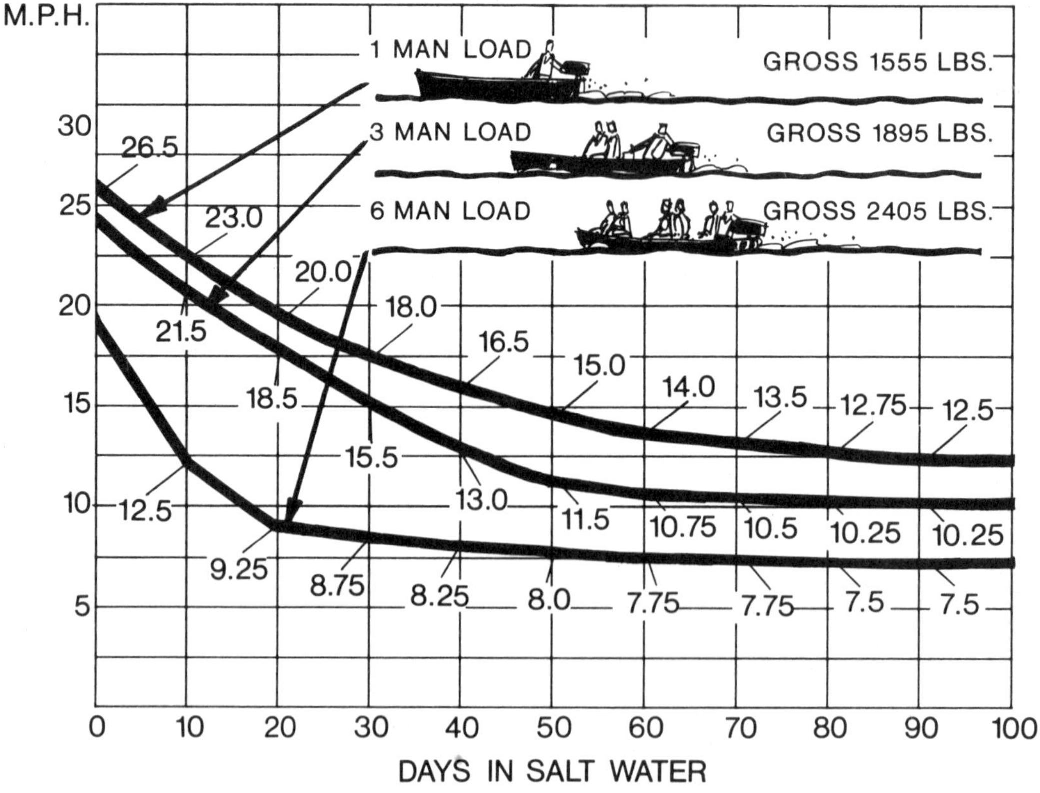

Bottom fouling is a major cause of poor performance. In salt water, barnacles and other marine life will grow on the hull while, in fresh water, the bottom picks up a light film of scum. In just a few days, these deposits can drastically reduce performance. In a fresh water test, boat speed dropped 6 mph with a two-man load in only 30 days. Cleaning the hull restored the original performance.

cycle motor oil with each 5 gallons of gasoline. An approved outboard motor oil of SAE 40 weight can be mixed in the ratio of 50:1 by adding 12 ozs. of the oil to 5 gallons of gasoline. **CAUTION: Don't use multi-grade oils or other automotive oils that have a large amount of detergents. Oils which contain metallic additives are exceedingly harmful to two-cycle engines. Their use can result in piston burning and scoring. CAUTION: Using less than the recommended amount of oil will result in very serious engine damage because of insufficient lubrication. Using more than the recommended amount of oil will cause spark plug fouling, erratic engine operation (poor carburetion), excessive carbon accumulation, and smoking.**

Always use fresh gasoline; never store gasoline in the fuel tank over an extended period. Cracked gasolines contain ingredients that change into gums when stored for any length of time. These gums and varnish products will cause carburetor troubles and spark plug burning. Always drain the fuel from the gas tank if the engine is to be stored for any length of time. An additive (Sta-Bil) is available and can be used to keep gasoline from forming gums over an extended storage period.

Sta-Bil is a fuel additive that can be used to keep gasoline from forming gum during storage. It should be used when the engine will be put back in service during the season and draining would be difficult.

OUTBOARD LUBRICANT AND GASOLINE CHART Model	Quantity of Oil per Gallon of Gasoline	Mixing Ratio Gas to Oil
†AD Series	1/3 Pint	24:1
†CD Series thru 1963	1/3 Pint	24:1
*CD Series 1964 thru 6R73	1/6 Pint	50:1
†FD, FDE Series thru 1963	1/3 Pint	24:1
*FD Series 1964 thru 20R73, 25R73 & 25E73	1/6 Pint	50:1
*JW, JH Series 1964 thru 4R73 & 4W73	1/6 Pint	50:1
†JW Series thru 1963	1/3 Pint	24:1
*LD Series	1/6 Pint	50:1
*MQ Series thru 9R73	1/6 Pint	50:1
†QD Series	1/3 Pint	24:1
†RD & RDE Series thru 1963	1/3 Pint	24:1
*RD Series 1964 thru 40R73	1/6 Pint	50:1
†RDS, RK, RX Series thru 1963	1/3 Pint	24:1
*RDS, RK Series 1964 thru 40E73 & 40ES70	1/6 Pint	50:1
†RJE Series	1/3 Pint	24:1
*RX Series 1964 thru 33R70 & 33E70	1/6 Pint	50:1
SC-10 thru 2R73	1/6 Pint	50:1
TN-25 thru 28	1/2 Pint	16:1
50R72 & 73, 50ES72 & 73	1/6 Pint	50:1
TR-10 thru 71, 72 & 73	1/6 Pint	50:1
†V4 Series thru 1963	1/3 Pint	24:1
*V4 Series 1964 thru 1973	1/6 Pint	50:1

Lubricant and gasoline recommendations for Johnson/Evinrude outboard motors. The gasoline must be a regular or premium leaded fuel. For new engine break-in, use 1/6 pint of oil per gallon of gasoline (50:1) only if Johnson/Evinrude lubricant is used. (†) Use 1/6 pint of oil per gallon (50:1) for these models listed with 24:1 fuel mixture only if Johnson/Evinrude lubricant is used. (*) See owner's manual for break-in instructions for models since 1964.

Mix the fuel in a well-ventilated location, preferably out of doors. **CAUTION: Don't smoke while handling gasoline.** Accurately measure the required amounts of oil and gasoline. Pour the oil into a remote fuel tank, and then add an equal amount of gasoline. Mix thoroughly by shaking vigorously, and then add the balance of gasoline and mix again. **CAUTION: Cleanliness is of prime importance in mixing fuel, as even a very small particle of dirt can cause carburetor trouble.**

Automotive oils are not suitable for outboard motor use, because many of them contain a dilution inhibitor which resists thorough mixing of the oil with gasoline. The resulting separation may put a layer of oil at the bottom of the tank, with gasoline at the top and with various proportions of the mixture between. Since the fuel pick-up tube is located at the bottom of the tank, the engine may receive an excessively high proportion of oil when the tank is full and almost straight gasoline when it is nearly empty. Therefore, at first, the engine may smoke excessively and foul the spark plugs. Later on, it may overheat and score the pistons because of insufficient lubrication.

Automotive oils with metallic detergents are very effective in reducing varnish formation and piston ring sticking in a four-cycle engine, where very little of the oil gets into the combustion chamber. But in a two-cycle engine, all of the oil must pass through the combustion area, where the metallic additives form deposits when they come into contact with the hot surfaces of the spark plugs, piston crowns, and combustion chamber. These deposits cause pre-ignition and detonation which result in piston crown burning, piston scuffing, and cylinder wall scoring. If the metallic particles bridge the spark plug gap, the plug will cease to fire.

Using the wrong oils or an incorrect mixture of oil and gasoline can result in piston scoring. Follow the manufacturer's instructions to protect your outboard motor.

WATER PUMP OPERATION

Normal operation of the water pump is indicated by a stream of water discharging from the idle relief outlet when the engine is idling. If at any time this stream is not evident, stop the engine immediately and check the hole with a piece of wire to be sure that it is not clogged. This stream indicates that the water pump is operating. **CAUTION: Avoid further operation until the water pump and cooling system have been checked.** Operation of the engine with an inoperative water pump or an obstruction in the cooling system will cause overheating and severe damage.

STOPPING

If the engine is to be ready for an immediate restart, stop by shifting into neutral and depressing the STOP button. If the engine is to remain idle for a period of time or if it is to be removed from the boat, stop it by disconnecting the fuel line and allowing the engine to run at idling speed until it stops of its own accord. If the engine is to be stored for a long period, it is necessary to drain all of the gasoline from the carburetor, and this can be done by packing some rags under it and removing the drain plug. An additive (Sta-Bil) is available for minimizing the decomposition of gasoline and it can be added to the last tankful.

REMOVING THE ENGINE FROM THE BOAT

Disconnect the remote controls and steering connections, if so equipped. Disconnect the fuel line. Loosen the clamp screws and detach the safety cable or chain, if so equipped. Keep the engine in an upright position, resting on its skeg, until all water is drained from the driveshaft housing. **CAUTION: If the engine is placed on its side while the water remains trapped in the driveshaft housing, some water may drain into the powerhead and enter the cylinders through the exhaust ports.** Be sure that all water drain holes in the gear housing are open so that the water can drain completely.

MAINTENANCE

Lubrication

The lubricant in the lower unit gear housing should be checked after the first ten hours of operation and every 50 hours of operation thereafter. Add OMC Type "C" Lubricant to bring the level to the vent plug, if necessary. Drain the gear case and refill every 100 hours of operation or once each season, whichever comes first. **CAUTION: While this is the factory recommendation, experience indicates that fish line could foul the prop shaft and cut the oil seal so that you could be out of lubricant at any time. Check the lower unit for such damage or an oil leak everytime you take the boat from the water.**

To replace the lubricant in the gear case, on all engines except the one-cylinder, remove the plugs and gasket assemblies marked OIL DRAIN and OIL LEVEL from the port side of the gear case. With the propeller shaft in a horizontal position, allow the oil to drain completely.

To refill the unit, insert the lubricant filler hose into the oil drain hole and inject lubricant until it runs out of the oil level hole. Install the oil level plug before removing the filler hose from the drain hole to create an air lock, and then withdraw the filler hose and install the drain hole plug. If a filler-type can is not available, install the drain plug and slowly fill the gear

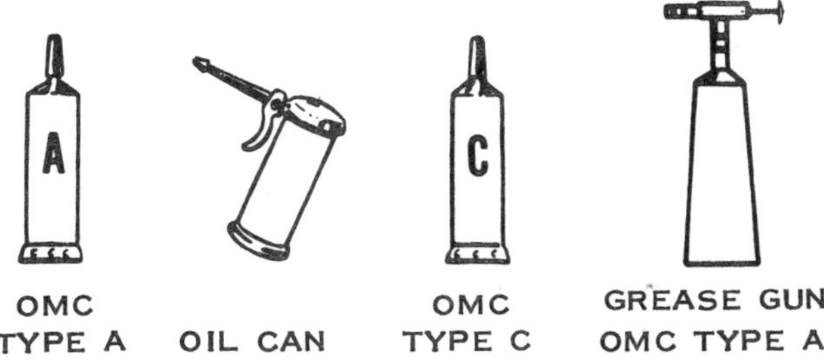

Types of OMC lubricants mentioned in the lubrication charts.

case through the oil level hose. Do this slowly enough to allow all of the trapped air to escape, and then install the oil level plug.

Fuel Filter

All engines have a fuel filter screen to prevent dirt particles from reaching the carburetor. The filter

LUBRICATION POINT	LUBRICANT	FREQUENCY (PERIOD OF OPERATION)	
		FRESH WATER	#SALT WATER
1. Gearcase	OMC Type "C"	Check level after first 10 hours of operation and every 50 hours of operation thereafter. Add lubricant if necessary.	Same as Fresh Water
		Drain and refill every 100 hours of operation or once each season, whichever occurs first.	Same as Fresh Water
2. Cam Follower, Carburetor and Choke Linkage	OMC Type "A"	60 days	30 days
3. Clamp Screws	OMC Type "A"	60 days	30 days
4. Throttle Shaft Bearings	SAE 90 Oil	60 days	30 days
5. Throttle Shaft Gears	OMC Type "A"	60 days	30 days
6. Gear Shift Lever and Shaft	OMC Type "A"	60 days	30 days
7. Locking Lever	OMC Type "A"	60 days	30 days
8. Swivel Bracket Fitting	OMC Type "A"	60 days	30 days
9. Tilt Lock Pin	OMC Type "A"	60 days	30 days
10. Starter Pinion Gear Shaft (Electric only)	SAE 10 Oil	60 days	30 days

#Some areas may require more frequent lubrication.

Lubrication chart

screen must be cleaned periodically. On the one-cylinder engine, the fuel filter is located inside of the fuel tank and is part of the fuel hose connector. A fuel shut-off valve is positioned in the fuel line directly below the filter. On the larger engines, the fuel filter is located on the fuel pump, and it can be removed by taking out the retaining screw. Always replace the gasket to prevent leaks.

OPERATING IN SALT WATER OR SILT

Operation in salt water or silt results in the accumulation of salt or mineral deposits in the cooling system water passages and around the cylinder water jackets. Unless removed regularly, these deposits will build up to the extent that circulation of the cooling water becomes restricted or cut off entirely. Also, the deposits act as an insulator, reducing the transfer of heat from the cylinders to the water. This loss of transfer will cause overheating, loss of performance, and serious damage.

Even though the interior surfaces of outboards are treated to resist corrosion, there remains a possibility of a mechanical build-up of salt and silt deposits that no form of protective coating can prevent; it can be minimized by occasional flushing with fresh water. While no complete protection for exterior surfaces is known, there are ways in which electrolysis and corrosion damage can be minimized. By following the simple steps below, you can increase materially the life of all exposed parts and decorative finishes.

An outboard motor that is to remain on a boat should be tilted out of the water. Always disconnect the negative battery terminal when in dock or in storage for any period of time.

Lubricate the swivel bracket frequently and other moving parts regularly. Grease the thumb screws on the clamps to insure smooth operation. Grease the propeller shaft splines occasionally with a waterproof-type lubricant, thus enabling the propeller to be removed easily.

Spray the entire powerhead with a coating of a rust preventive to protect the finish of all parts beneath the cowl. The exterior of the engine also can be sprayed with rust preventive to keep corrosion from dulling the finish.

Attach a flushing hose and turn on the water tap. Operate the manual starter to facilitate the flow of water through the pump. **CAUTION: Do not use full pressure from a city water tap. CAUTION: During and after flushing, keep the motor in an upright position, resting on the skeg, until all water has been drained from the driveshaft housing in order to prevent water from entering the powerhead through the exhaust ports.**

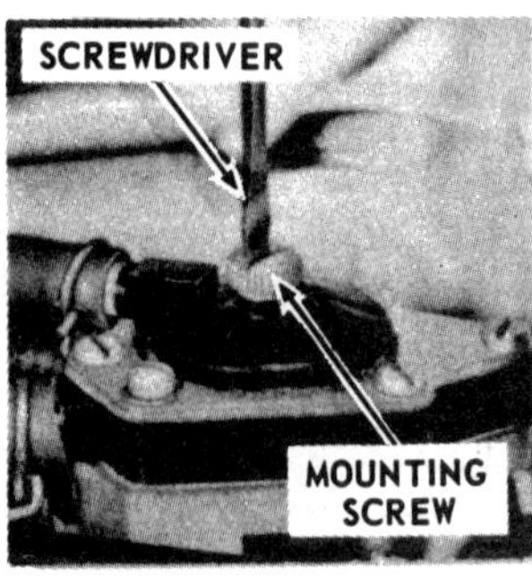

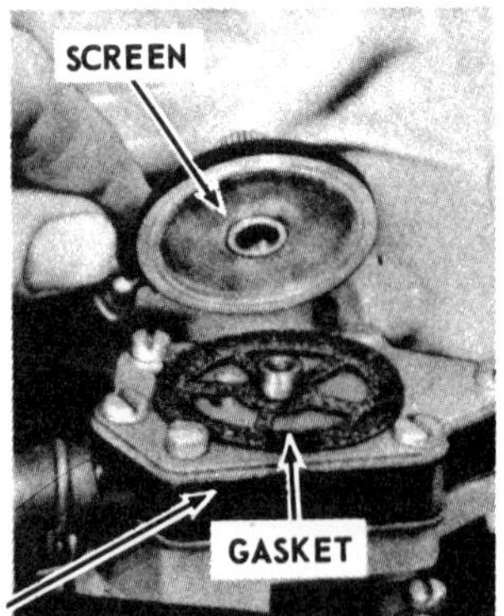

The fuel filter on top of the fuel pump should be cleaned periodically. Always use a new gasket to prevent leaks.

AFTER SUBMERSION

An engine which has been submerged must be disassembled completely for cleaning and inspecting. This should be done as soon as possible after recovery. Delayed action will encourage rust and corrosion of internal parts. Emergency treatment may be accomplished by following the instructions below. This temporarily will retard rust and corrosion. Basically, the points to remember are these: (1) Recover the engine as quickly as possible. (2) Wash the entire unit with fresh, clean water to remove mud, weeds, etc. (3) Get as much water as possible out of the powerhead. Most of the water can be eliminated by removing the spark plugs and operating the starter with the spark plug holes facing downward. **CAUTION: If the engine does not turn freely when the starter is operated, do not force it. This may be an indication of internal damage, such as a bent connecting rod or a broken piston.** (4) Pour alcohol into the cylinders because it will dissolve water, and then lubricate all the internal parts that are accessible. This can be accomplished by injecting oil into the spark plug holes, installing the spark plugs, and then operating the starter to distribute the oil. If alcohol and oil are not available, insert a rod into the fuel check unit to open the check valve, and then actuate the primer bulb, thus forcing the oil-fuel mixture into the cylinders. (5) Disassemble and clean the engine as soon as psosible.

STORAGE

When storing an outboard motor for the winter, be sure that all water drain holes in the gear housing are open and that the flushing plug is removed so that the water will drain out. Trapped water may freeze and expand, thus cracking the gear housing and/or the water pump housing. Check and refill the lower unit with gear lubricant before storage to protect against possible water leakage into the gear housing, caused by a loose air vent or grease filler plug. Be sure to replace the gaskets under the vent screws.

Prior to packing at the factory, new engines are "fogged out" at the final test by injecting approximately 2 oz. of rust preventive oil through the carburetor air intake. This practice is desirable when engines are stored in a damp place, or when they are expected to stand idle for a long period of time. When an engine is started after fogging, the spark plugs should be checked and replaced, if necessary, as they may have become fouled from the rust preventive oil.

Before storage, disconnect the fuel line or turn off the fuel shut-off valve, and then allow the engine to run at idling speed until it stops of its own accord. Position some rags under the carburetor, and then take out the drain plug. Drain the fuel tank and the fuel lines. If the storage is not for a long period of time, you can pour some Sta-Bil additive into the last tankful of gasoline to prevent its decomposition. If an outboard motor is to remain on the boat, it should be tilted out of the water.

USING A CLEANER

Several chemical cleaners have been developed to remove the carbon deposits which reduce the power of an outboard motor. To use the cleaner, run the engine until normal operating temperature is reached. On engines with one carburetor, slowly pour about 10 oz. of the cleaner through the carburetor throat while the engine is running at a fast idle of 1,200 rpm. Use a pump-type oil can or pressure sprayer. Increase the speed and stall the engine with the balance of the cleaner. Let the engine stand for at least 30 minutes. Start the engine and run it at full throttle for 5 minutes.

On models with more than one carburetor with the engine operating at its lowest rpm above stalling, feed a sufficient quantity of the cleaner into the throat of one carburetor. Let the engine run until it is firing on all cylinders again, and then repeat the process for the other carburetors. Next, flood the entire engine through all of the carburetors and allow it to stand for 1/2 hour.

To clean a severely carbonized engine, tilt it to a horizontal position and close as many intake and exhaust ports as possible by turning the flywheel so that the pistons cover the ports. Pour the cleaner through the spark plug holes. Let it set overnight, position the engine vertically, and then pull the starter rope several times to remove the excess cleaner. Prepare the engine for running and repeat the regular cleaning process as discussed above.

WATER WISDOM

Coast Guard Regulations

To enjoy the waterways safely, it is advisable to check with authorities in regard to local, state, and federal boating regulations and restrictions. In addition, here are a few suggestions: (1) Carry one approved life jacket or buoyant cushion per person, (2) one approved fire extinguisher, (3) a flashlight or lantern, (4) an anchor, (5) a first aid kit, (6) a compass, (7) an extra propeller, (8) enough fuel, and (9) a blowhorn.

Rules of the Waterways

Keep practicing water safety by observing the following simple rules: (1) Do not operate your boat near swimmers, skin-divers, or fishermen. (2) Keep clear of sailing craft and rowboats, yielding the right-of-way to them. (3) Always keep to the right; show respect and courtesy at all times.

Signposts

Know the channel markers to follow a safe and confident course. When returning, keep the red buoys on your right; black buoys on your left. Black-and-white, vertically striped buoys indicate the middle of a channel; always pass as close as possible to them, on either side. Black-and-red, horizontally striped buoys indicate obstruction; give them a wide berth.

SEAMANSHIP FOR SAFETY

Stepping into the Boat

Step into the *center* of the boat. Don't carry equip-

Always carry enough approved equipment to ensure your safety.

Never carry equipment aboard. Equipment should be placed on the edge of the dock, and then lifted into the boat.

ment aboard; keep your hands free for steadying yourself. Equipment should be placed on the edge of the dock, and then lifted into the boat.

Casting Off
Back away *slowly* in reverse gear.

Weather Signals
Any flag or light which is all or part red is a warning that bad weather is developing or exists.

Rough Water
When heading into rough water, *decrease* speed but maintain plane to prevent water from entering the boat. Alter the direction of attack on the waves until it feels right.

Danger Zone
The danger zone is a 112-1/2° arc which is measured from dead ahead to off the starboard, or right-hand, side. A boat *must yield* the right-of-way to any other craft which approaches it within the danger zone.

Overtaking
A boat which is being overtaken has the right-of-way.

Turns
Practice boat turns in order to test for the amount of stern swing of your boat.

Reverse Gear
When reversing, the stern will dip; move your pas-

Buoys are the signposts of the waterways. When returning, keep the red buoys on your right, black buoys on your left. The black-and-white, vertically striped buoys indicate the middle of the channel; always pass close to them, on either side. The black-and-red horizontally striped buoys indicate obstructions; give them a wide berth.

sengers forward to guard against swamping the boat. When reversing, the motor will not tilt up when striking a submerged object; therefore, be alert so that the transom will not be damaged.

Skiing

The recommended procedures are: (1) Check the equipment for safe, smooth operation. (2) Know the skier's hand signals. (3) Carry an observer in the boat.

Stopping

Practice for stopping distance at various boat speeds in order to be prepared for any unusual situation.

Docking

Approach a dock slowly and, if possible, into the wind, waves, or current. Avoid buffeting by securing the boat to the dock, as shown.

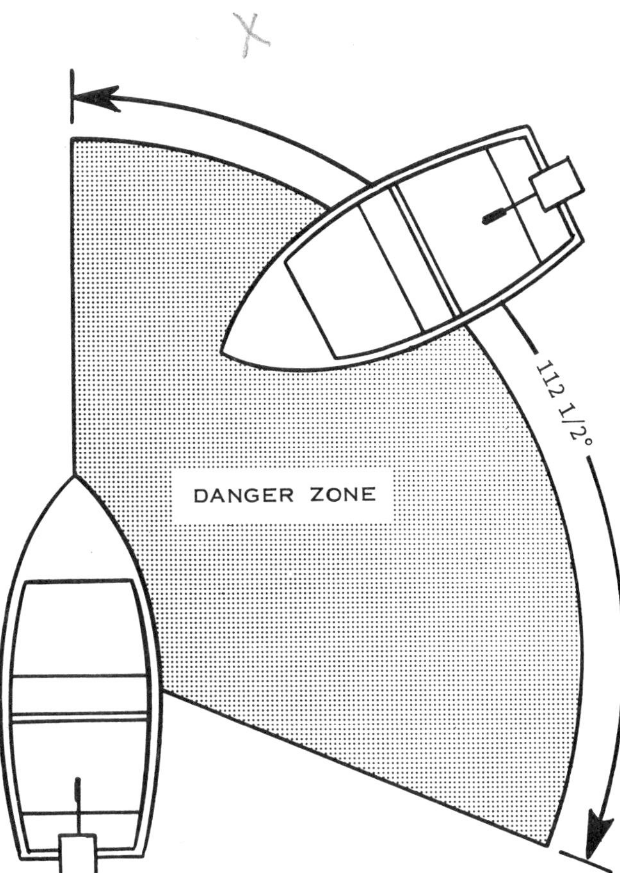

You must yield the right-of-way to any boat approaching within the danger zone.

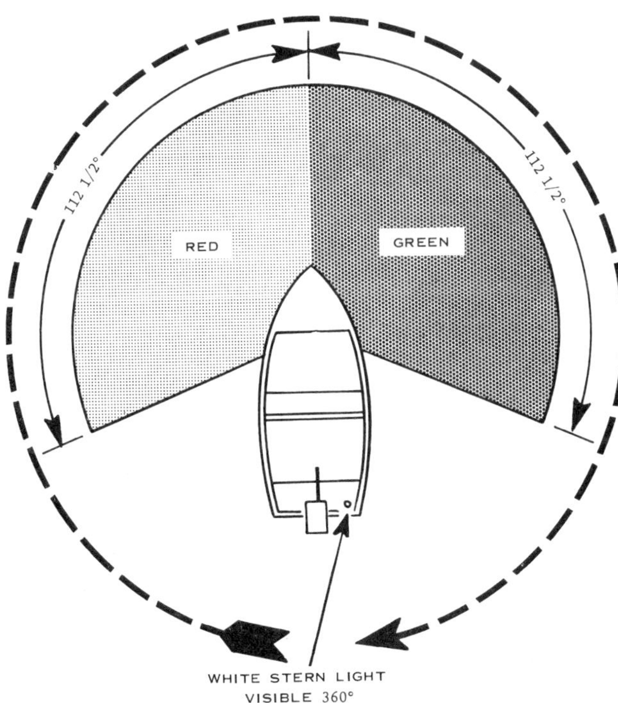

This diagram shows the direction and color of the lights that should be visible when you use the boat at night.

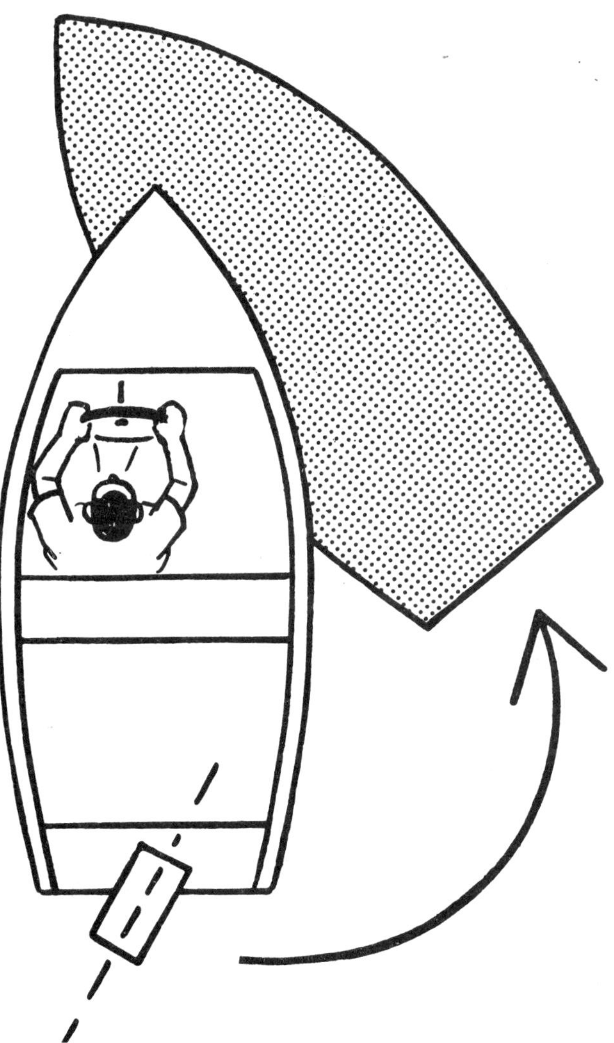

Practice turns to get used to the stern swing so that you can become an expert.

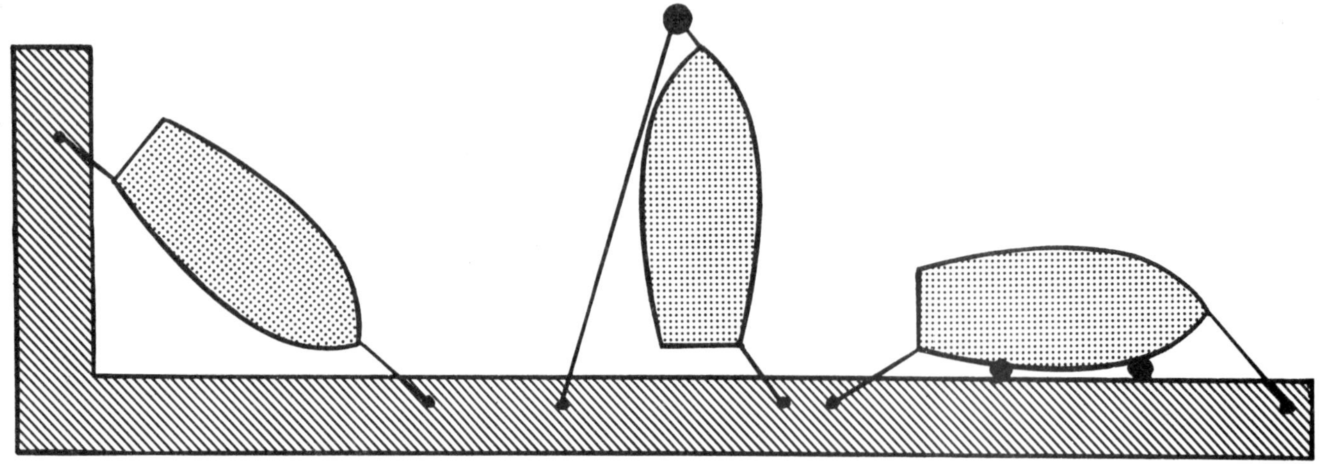

Secure your boat to the dock properly to avoid buffeting by the wind.

Learn all Coast Guard regulations and develop skill in handling your boat so that you will enjoy your vacation.

3

TUNING FOR PERFORMANCE

The material in this chapter is divided into two basic sections, the first of which covers the general procedures that are required for servicing all ignition systems. The second section deals with each type of engine according to the number of cylinders. Each of the engine-type sections is a complete unit, covering the timing, linkage, and carburetor adjustments that are necessary to make the engine perform to its designed power potential.

GENERAL IGNITION SERVICE PROCEDURES

SPARK PLUGS

Spark plugs are a small but vitally important component of modern gasoline engines. Without proper spark plug operation, satisfactory engine performance cannot be obtained. Outboard motors are equipped with spark plugs of a special electrode gap design. Surface-gap spark plugs are used with late-model CD ignition systems.

Spark plugs are made in a number of heat ranges to satisfy a variety of possible operating conditions. Some types, having a long insulator firing end, transfer heat slowly and are used where combustion chamber temperatures are relatively low. Sustained idling, stop-and-start, and light-load operation produce this condition. The short insulator plug remains cool enough to avoid pre-ignition and excessive gap erosion.

The appearance of spark plugs will indicate whether they are too hot or too cold for the engine. The end of the spark plug is subjected to intense heat from the burning of the fuel mixture, and this heat is dissipated by conduction along the porcelain end of the spark plug and thus to the cylinder jacket. If the porcelain part, which extends into the cylinder, is comparatively long, the heat cannot be dissipated rapidly, and the spark plug will run hot. If the porcelain is short, the heat can pass through it more quickly, and the spark plug will run cold.

The spark plug which is installed originally in the engine is the one that will give best service under normal operating conditions; however, if the speed is increased by placing the engine on a lighter hull, it may be necessary to substitute a colder spark plug. If the engine is placed on a heavier boat and the speed is decreased, a hotter spark plug may be required. If trouble arises with spark plugs fouling while trolling, changing to a hotter type of spark plug may help.

If the spark plug is operating at its most efficient temperature, the porcelain part, which projects inside of the cylinder, will be dark brown, chestnut, or coffee-colored. If the porcelain is chalky white or has flaky blisters, the spark plug is too hot. When an engine is operating at high speed with a spark plug that is too hot, it will run along evenly for a while, slow down, pick up speed again, and repeat this balking over and over. If a smutty or oily coating appears on the spark plug, it shows that there is incomplete fuel combustion because the plug is too cold. Hard starting generally is caused by too cold a spark plug.

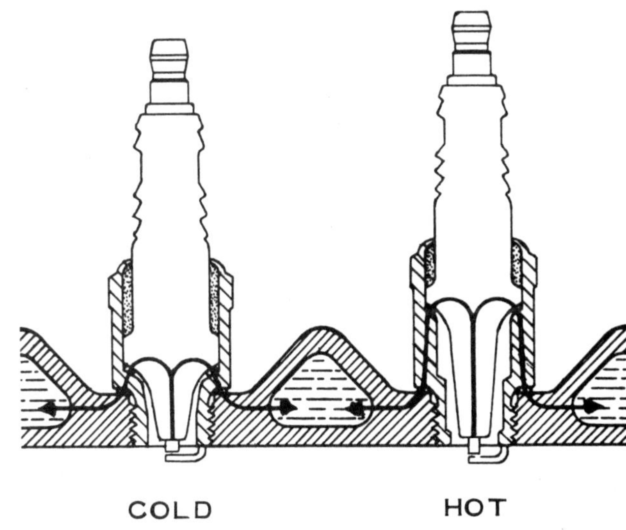

The heat range of a spark plug is determined by the length of the heat path from the tip of the insulator to the coolant or, in the case of an air-cooled engine, to the metal of the cylinder head.

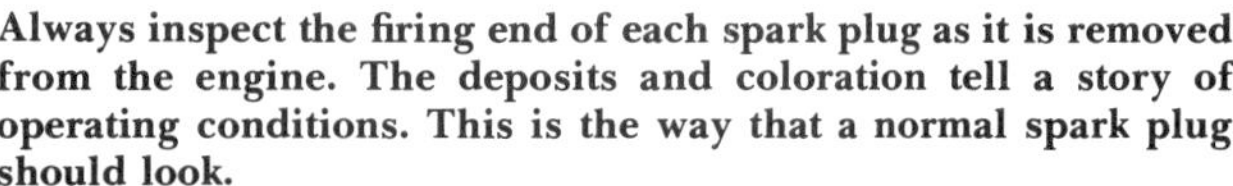

Always inspect the firing end of each spark plug as it is removed from the engine. The deposits and coloration tell a story of operating conditions. This is the way that a normal spark plug should look.

This spark plug is operating too hot. Either it is of an incorrect heat range, or the engine is running too hot.

The electrodes are shorted out by core bridging, the result of using the wrong oil.

Wet fouling can be caused by too much oil in the mixture or by a defective spark plug. This spark plug was not firing.

This spark plug is shorted by aluminum throw-off, which means that particles of the piston are being deposited on the hot insulator of the spark plug.

Core bridging is caused by using the wrong type of motor oil.

The spark plug's main job is to transfer the ignition system's energy into the cylinder in the form of a spark. If a normal fuel charge fails to ignite, the spark plug is misfiring. Most misfirings result from shorting through deposits on the insulator nose surface. When these are removed either by cleaning or, in some cases, by burning them off at high speeds, the spark plug's firing ability is restored. This type of shorting is troublesome in that it can occur long before it is noticed. An owner is not always aware of a slow decrease in performance and economy because one or more cylinders are misfiring.

Spark Plug Troubles

Extensive tests have shown that spark plug life is directly related to the gasoline used in the engine. Much of the spark plug trouble is simply lead fouling, resulting from the use of automotive gasolines with tetraethyl lead. There is no practical way of removing this lead from the fuel in the field. Lead fouling may be identified by the presence of small yellow or brown globules on the plug.

Some spark plug trouble is caused by excessive carbon formation in the combustion chamber, with eventual fouling of the plug by the carbon particles. It is natural for all internal combustion engines to form some carbon during operation, but excessive amounts are caused by use of fuels which burn to a gummy residue rather than to a fluffy carbon that can pass out with the exhaust. Cracked gasolines result in fuels which give gummy deposits that remain in the combustion chamber, while straight-run gasolines are cleaner in this respect.

The use of a marine white gasoline virtually will eliminate problems with the spark plug and the carbon or varnish formation. Marine white gasolines are straight-run fuels which contain no tetraethyl lead or other metallic additives and are excellent from the standpoint of engine cleanliness. They generally have an octane rating of 75 to 80 and should not be confused with the nonmarine "whites" sold for use in gasoline lamps and cook stoves. The 90 octaine aviation gasolines, as used in light aircraft, are limited to 0.5cc of lead and are suitable for outboard use.

In cases where spark plug or carbon difficulties are being encountered, it is suggested that a change be made to another fuel. If excessive carbon has already formed in the engine, it should be removed by dis-

The spark plug insulator should be cleaned of all foreign matter, because this could become a leakage path for the high-tension voltage.

When the dirty insulator of a spark plug gets wet, flash-over occurs, and the cylinder misfires.

assembly or with an engine cleaner.

Many so-called spark plug troubles in reality are not traceable to faulty spark plugs. Instead, they result from poor spark plug installation, abnormal operating conditions, ignition defects, over-rich fuel mixtures, fuel mixtures with too much oil, or engines in need of an overhaul.

Used spark plugs are generally the best guide to the type and source of trouble. Therefore, it is good practice to inspect each spark plug as it is removed from the engine. A gasket which is compressed to about 3/4 of its original thickness, with smooth, parallel surfaces, indicates that the spark plug was properly installed and tightened. Gaskets which are

Normal spark plug. The deposits are light tan or gray, indicating good engine and ignition system conditions. The electrode wear indicates normal spark rotation.

Worn out spark plug. This amount of electrode wear can cause misfire during acceleration or hard starting.

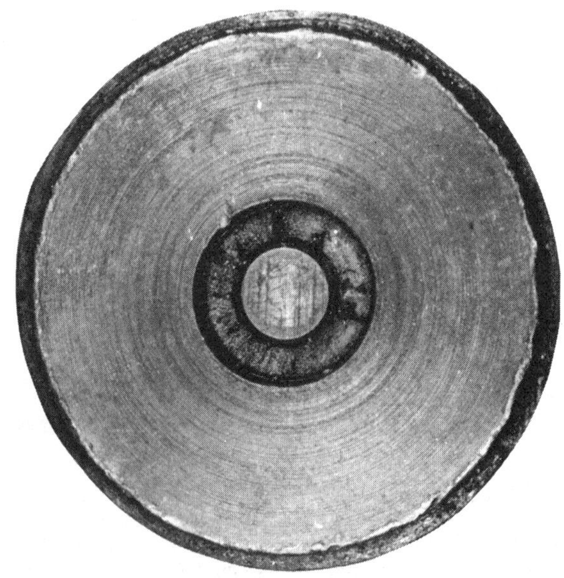

Channeling. This is sometimes incorrectly diagnosed as cracking. It is generally caused by extreme heat. When the deposits cover the shallow channels, the rate of insulation erosion is aggravated; the spark plug is masked, and misfire can occur.

Concentrated arc. The multi-colored appearance is a normal condition. It is caused by electrical energy consistantly following the same firing path. The arc path will generally change with deposit conductivity and gap errosion. This spark plug does not need to be replaced.

Surface-gap spark plug conditions.

compressed too much or too little reveal improper tightening. Rough and corroded surfaces indicate that the gasket seats were not cleaned before installation. In some cases, the resulting compression leakage may have overheated the spark plugs to cause excessive electrode erosion. *NOTE: Some spark plugs have conical seats and, therefore, do not use a gasket.* **CAUTION: Where a gasket is required, always use a new one to maintain the correct heat transfer path.**

Spark plugs that are not tightened securely will cause fast electrode burning, and they may burn the piston due to detonation. Torque spark plugs to 20 ft-lbs. for a good seat. In the event a torque wrench is not available, tighten the spark plug (with a new gasket) finger-tight, and then tighten it an additional half (1/2) turn.

Carbon tracking. The electrically conductive deposits on the firing end provide a low-resistance path for the high voltage. Carbon tracks are formed, and misfire generally occurs.

Cold-fouled spark plug. These wet fuel/oil deposits can be caused by "drowning" the spark plug with raw fuel during cranking, an excessively rich fuel/air mixture, or a weak ignition system.

Low-temperature fouling. The soft, sooty deposits indicate incomplete combustion. Possible causes are rich carburetion, weak ignition, retarded timing, or low compression.

Aluminum throw-off. This is an indication of preignition. Check the engine to determine the extent of damage. Replace the plugs.

Surface-gap spark plug conditions.

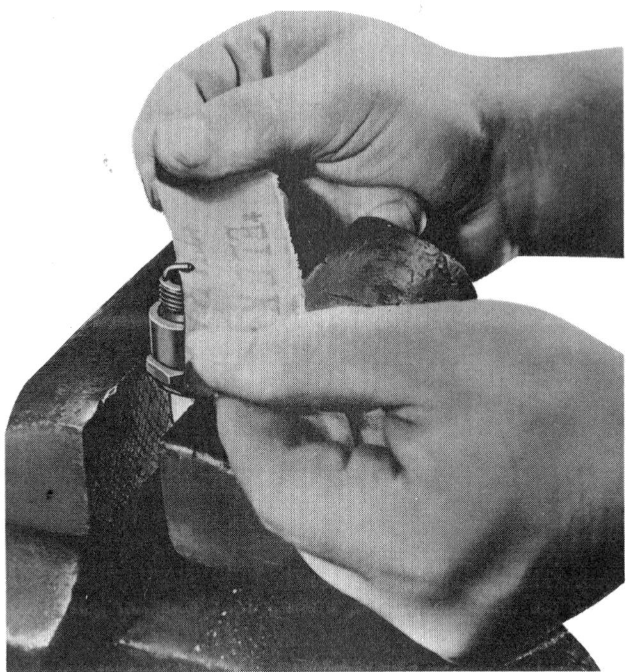

One of the most important spark plug service procedures is to file the electrodes to remove the corrosion. This mechanic is passing a piece of emery cloth between the electrodes to clean the metal.

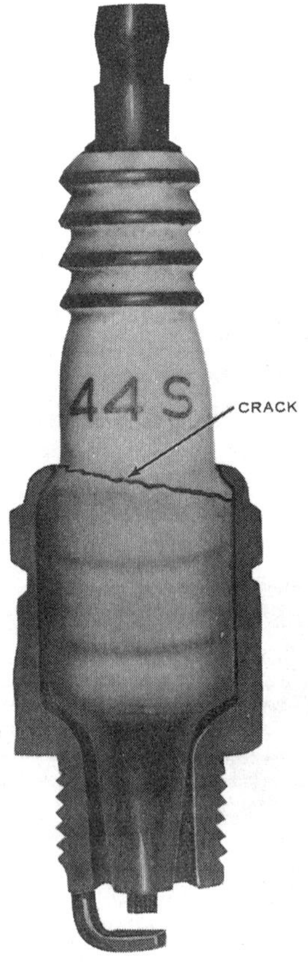

A cracked insulator can be caused only by tilting the spark plug socket.

Fuel fouling can be identified by wet, black deposits covering the entire firing end of the spark plug. These deposits result from incomplete combustion, which is traceable to an over-rich air-fuel mixture.

A crack in the insulator is sufficient cause for discarding the spark plug. Cracks in the upper portion of the insulator are caused by dropping the plug or by hitting the insulator with a wrench. For this reason, always use a deep-socket wrench of the proper size when removing or installing the spark plugs, and support the upper end with the palm of your hand to keep it from tilting enough to touch the insulator. Cracked or broken insulator firing ends result from bending the center electrode while setting the spark plug gap. To avoid damaging the insulator, bend only the side electrode.

Other engine conditions can cause spark plug troubles. In general, ignition timing advanced beyond specifications will encourage overheating, thus leading to shorter spark plug life and burned pistons. Burned, pitted, or improperly set breaker points and frayed ignition cables also are sources of spark plug trouble.

It is important to keep the upper portion of the spark plug insulators free from moisture, grease, dirt, and paint. Such deposits on the outside of a spark plug can cause surface shorting or flashover from the terminal to the shell, with resulting misfire and hard starting. Spark plug insulators should be wiped off periodically with a clean rag.

Surface-Gap Spark Plugs

Spark plugs used with CD ignition systems are not adjustable with regard to gap setting. These spark plugs must be replaced when the center electrode is worn 1/32" below the insulator. Spark plugs that are carbonized need not be cleaned as they will fire properly. Replace any spark plug with a cracked insulator.

Spark Plug Protectors

When installing a new set of spark plugs, inspect the spark plug protectors carefully for possible damage. No rubber will withstand indefinitely the heat of a spark plug operating under modern conditions, particularly with the high-temperature fuels now being used. When this rubber is stretched tight around the hot porcelain, the effect is to cause the rubber to dry out and crack. Once this has happened, the effectiveness of the spark plug protector as a waterproof seal is seriously impaired.

The sensitive area, where heat and stretch are greatest, is the inside bottom rim where it touches the porcelain. When this edge becomes hard, it loses its strength. The next phase is a series of fine cracks in the surface of the rubber along this same edge. It is safest to replace the spark plug protector when this edge gets hard, before it has a chance to start cracking.

The spark plug protector is not meant to be taken apart. Doing so will usually bend the prong in the spring, making it all but impossible to reassemble correctly. Don't pull the cable out of the spark plug protector except when the protector and spring are to be replaced.

When assembling a spark plug protector to a cable, make sure that the prong of the spring goes through the center of the cable to make solid contact with the ignition wire. If this is not a good electrical contact, a weak spark may result. Also, the point on this prong should always face down toward the spark plug. If it is assembled upside down, the spark plug protector may have a tendency to shake loose.

MAGNETO SERVICE PROCEDURES FOR ONE- AND TWO-CYLINDER ENGINES

The magneto consists of breaker points, condensers, and coils. These ignition parts are located under the flywheel; therefore, to service the ignition system of these smaller engines, it is necessary to remove the flywheel. Use tool no. 378103 to pull off the flywheel.

Generally, it is best to replace the breaker points before tuning an engine because of the load that they carry and the effect that they have on the operating efficiency of the engine. If new breaker points are not available, they can be cleaned in an emergency by folding a small strip of 320-grit emery cloth and inserting it between the points. Hold the points closed and rotate the emery cloth, using the points as a pivot. Open the points to remove the emery cloth. **CAUTION: Don't pull the cloth from between the points, or you will scrape off emery particles, which are an insulator.** Remove all traces of emery by inserting a clean piece of cardboard between the breaker points, and then (holding the points closed on the cardboard) rotate the cardboard, using the breaker points as a pivot, in order to remove the oxide and other foreign matter loosened by the emery cloth. The cardboard should be used in several spots until no further dirt can be removed.

To adjust the breaker point gap, move the throttle to the wide-open position to establish a common stationary location for setting the breaker points. Reinstall the flywheel nut so that you can turn the crankshaft with a box wrench. Rotate the crankshaft clockwise at least two full turns to establish a uniform grease film, and then rotate it enough to bring the breaker point cam follower to the high point of the cam (index line). **CAUTION: If the crankshaft is turned too far, it must be rotated an additional turn clockwise to reach the mark. Never turn the crankshaft in a counterclockwise direction to correct or you could damage the water pump impeller.**

Adjust the breaker point gap to specifications. **CAUTION: Always use a wire gauge or smooth, unworn feeler gauge blade and always make sure that the gaps are identical on two-cylinder engines so that the points will be synchronized. An error of 0.0015″ will change the ignition timing as much as 1°. CAUTION: Always clean the feeler gauge blade before inserting it between the points to prevent depositing a layer of oil, which will cause operating difficulties later on.**

Lubricate the breaker cam, breaker plate pilot bore, cam wiper felt, and all friction surfaces of the ignition

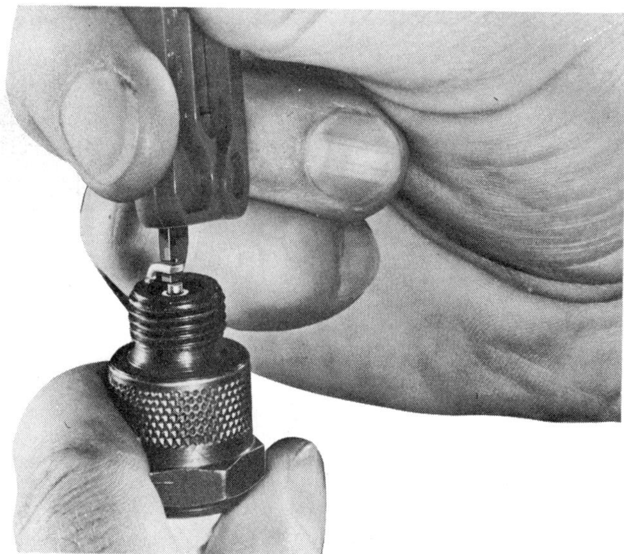

Always bend the ground electrode to adjust the gap. If you bend the center electrode, you will crack the porcelain.

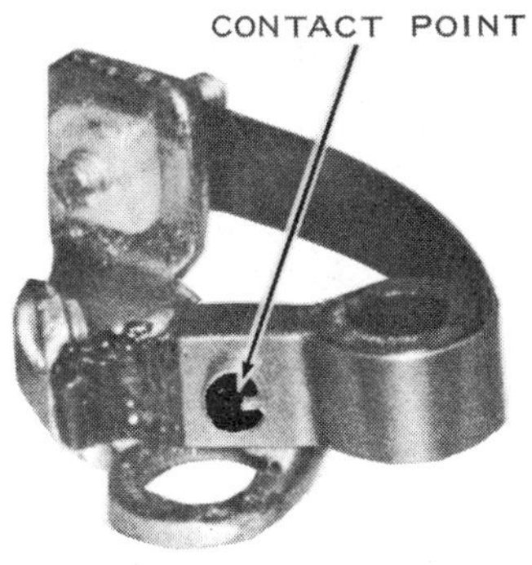

This black, pitted breaker point shows evidence of oil on the contact surface, which burned into an insulator. The oil can be placed on the contact point surface with your fingers or by using a dirty feeler gauge to measure the gap.

system with Rykon No. 2EP. Other types of lubricants will cause ignition troubles and operating difficulties.

BREAKER POINT SYNCHRONIZATION

On the larger two-cylinder engines, point synchronization is an important adjustment. Its purpose is to make sure that the spark occurs at precisely the same instant for each cylinder. Generally, the gap of the second set of breaker points is varied from the initial setting to obtain synchronization.

Breaker point cleaning and gapping must always precede synchronization. Changing the gap of either set of points will change both the timing and synchronization. After the breaker points are cleaned and gapped, the first set of breaker points should be timed to the top piston. Then, without moving the stator plate, the timing gauge should be transferred to the bottom cylinder and the gap of the second set of breaker points adjusted so that the spark will occur at the same position of the second piston.

Smaller engines are not sensitive to breaker point synchronization, and the manufacturer generally specifies that it is only necessary to gap the breaker points evenly. If the gaps are even, synchronization is close enough for all practical purposes. For engines on which breaker point synchronization is called for by the manufacturer, this adjustment will be covered in the second section of this chapter, under the tuning instructions for the individual engines.

IGNITION TIMING

The ignition spark must occur at precisely the instant it will do the most good. This means that the spark must occur close to TDC at idle speed and about 30° before TDC at high rpms. This ignition advance is required to compensate for the time lag between the start of combustion and the development of maximum pressure. At high engine speeds, it is necessary to start combustion about 30° BTDC so that maximum combustion chamber pressure will be reached when the piston reaches the top of the stroke.

The method of timing the engine varies, but most of the larger engines have the flywheel marked at the TDC position. In addition, some are marked at the specified Maximum Spark Advance point for setting the timing with the throttle at the wide-open position. These instructions vary with engine types and will be discussed in detail under each of the engine headings.

CARBURETOR THROTTLE PICKUP ADJUSTMENT

The throttle control of small outboard motors is connected to the magneto stator plate. Opening the throttle advances the stator plate (and the ignition timing). The stator plate is linked to the carburetor throttle, so that opening the throttle and advancing the stator plate opens the carburetor throttle valves at the same time. One of the most important tuning procedures is the throttle pickup adjustment; the point of spark advance at which the throttle valves begin to open.

ONE-CYLINDER ENGINE TUNE-UP PROCEDURES

A flywheel-type magneto furnishes the ignition spark for these engines. Moving the speed-control lever shifts the entire magneto stator plate, thereby affecting the ignition timing. A throttle-actuating cam, attached to the speed-control lever, synchronizes throttle valve opening to ignition timing.

① To remove the flywheel, take off the nut. Attach a puller, Tool No. 378103, to the flywheel, and then pull the flywheel from the crankshaft.

② Turn the crankshaft clockwise to position the breaker arm of the high point of the cam. **CAUTION: Always rotate the crankshaft clockwise to avoid**

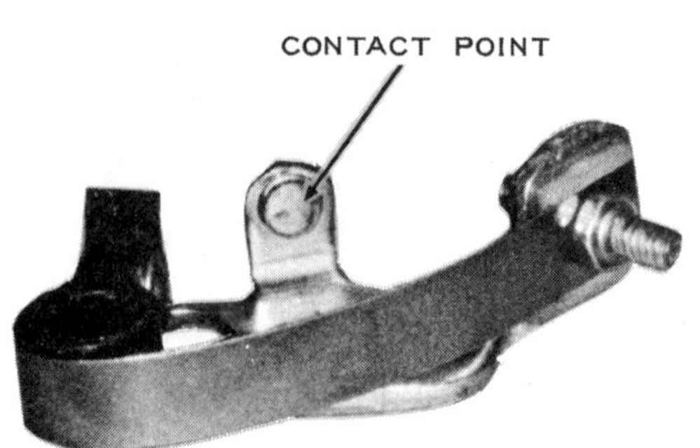

The frosted appearance of this breaker point is an indication that the ignition system was operating properly.

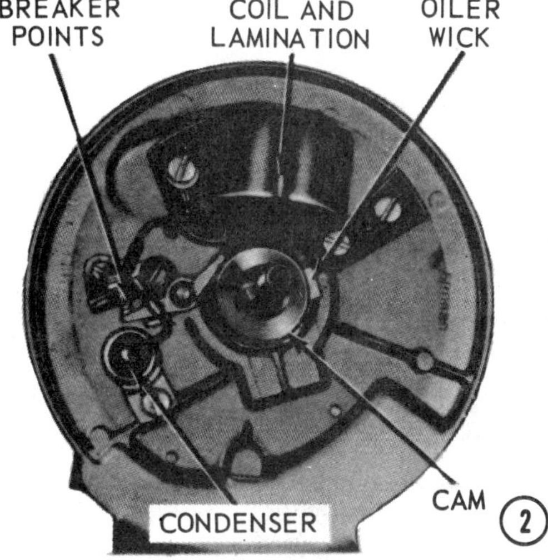

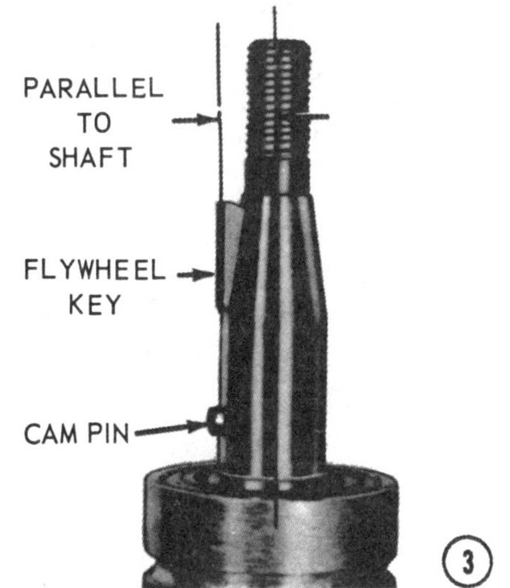

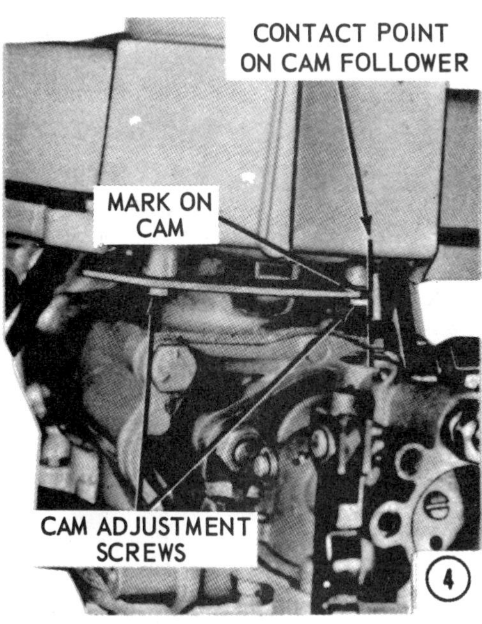

damaging the water pump impeller. Loosen the locking screw, and then turn the eccentric screw to obtain a gap of 0.020″. Tighten the locking screw, and then recheck the gap, which may change as you tighten the screw. *NOTE: New breaker points should be gapped to 0.022″ to compensate for initial rubbing block wear.* Lubricate the cam and wick with OMC Type "A" lubricant.

③ Check the crankshaft and flywheel tapers for traces of oil, which must be removed with solvent. **CAUTION: The assembly must be perfectly dry. CAUTION: Don't allow solvent to wash the oil out of the oiler wick.** The flywheel key must be installed so that it is parallel to the shaft. Replace the flywheel and nut, tightening it to 22-25 ft-lbs. of torque.

④ *To make the throttle cam synchronization,* set the speed control lever to the STOP position. Slowly advance the control until the cam follower just begins to open the throttle. The mark on the cam and the point of contact on the cam follower should now be aligned. If an adjustment is necessary, loosen the cam adjustment screws, and then position the cam so that, with all play removed from the linkage, the throttle valve is closed. The mark on the throttle cam must now align with the flat port side of the cam follower, just as it makes contact with the cam. Tighten the cam screws.

⑤ *To make the carburetor adjustments,* seat the high- and low-speed adjusting needles gently, and then back them out for a preliminary adjustment. **CAUTION: Don't force them into their seats, or you will dam-**

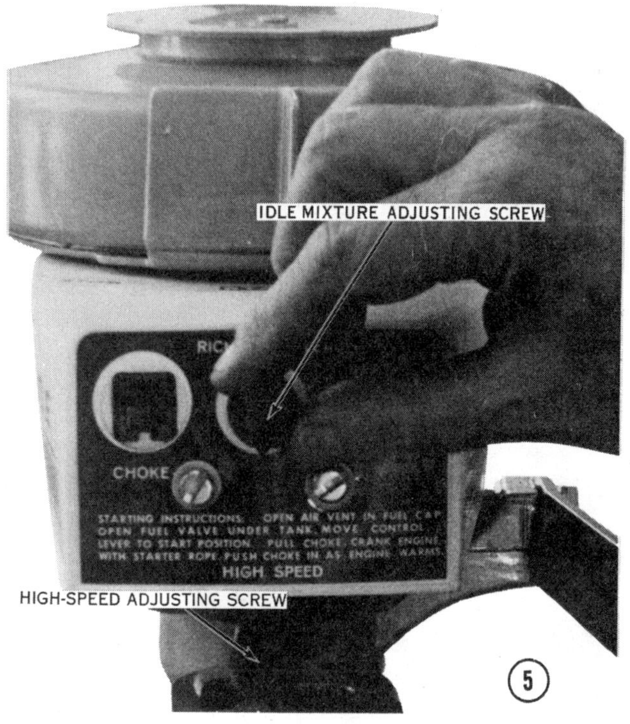

age the taper, making an accurate adjustment difficult. Back out the high-speed adjusting needle 1/2 turn and the low-speed needle 1-1/4 turns. Start the engine and allow it to reach normal operating temperature. Run the engine at full throttle, and then adjust the high-speed needle for maximum rpm. Adjust the low-speed needle until the highest rpm consistent with smooth performance is reached. *NOTE: Allow 15 seconds for the engine to respond after each adjustment.* After making the low-speed adjustment, recheck the high-speed adjustment. Install the adjustment knobs with each boss pointing straight up.

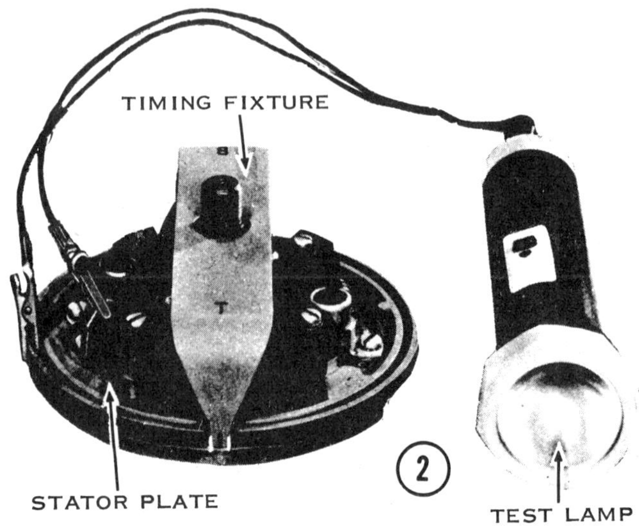

TWO-CYLINDER ENGINE TUNE-UP PROCEDURES (WITH FLYWHEEL MAGNETO)—THROUGH 1975

A flywheel-type magneto furnishes the ignition spark for these engines. Moving the speed-control lever shifts the entire magneto stator plate, thereby affecting the ignition timing. A throttle-actuating cam, attached to the magneto stator plate, synchronizes throttle valve opening to ignition timing.

① To remove the flywheel, take off the nut. Attach a puller, Tool No. 378103, to the flywheel, and then lift the flywheel from the crankshaft.

② Install new breaker points and adjust the gaps to 0.020″ (0.022″ for new points). **CAUTION: Keep the locking screw tight during the adjustment to prevent changing the gap which would occur if the screw were tightened later.** Disconnect all leads from the breaker point assemblies. Connect a self-powered test lamp between the breaker plate and the forward breaker point terminal screw. Install a timing fixture, Tool No. 304667, on the crankshaft.

③ Rotate the crankshaft so that the side of the fixture marked "T" (for top) is aligned with the first projection on the stator plate. **CAUTION: To avoid damaging the water pump impeller, rotate the crankshaft only in a clockwise direction.** Move the timing fixture or the stator plate slowly back and forth until the exact instant at which the points open is determined, this being indicated by the test lamp going out. The breaker points should open just when the timing fixture is midway between the two projections on the stator plate. If necessary, adjust the breaker point gap until the timing is correct. *NOTE: To compensate for initial rubbing block wear, adjust the gap of new breaker points so that they just open as the fixture passes the first mark.* Tighten the breaker point lock screws, and then recheck the timing.

④ Rotate the crankshaft clockwise a full turn, and then repeat the timing procedure for the second set of breaker points. *NOTE: If a test lamp or timing fixture is not available, adjust the breaker point gap to 0.020″ (0.022″ for new points) with the breaker arm on the high lobe of the cam, and the timing will be fairly accurate.*

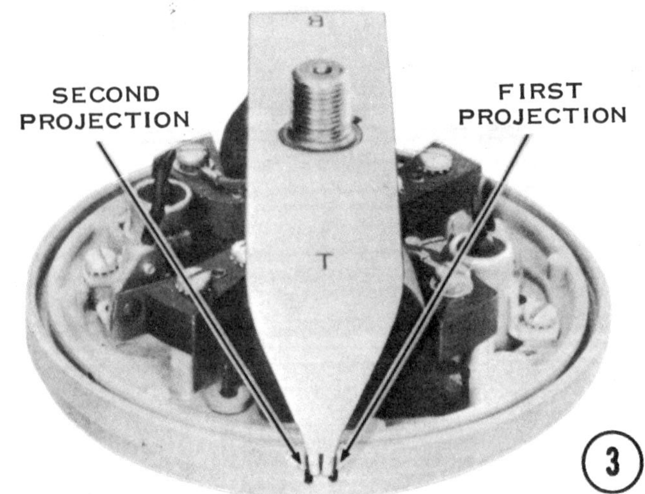

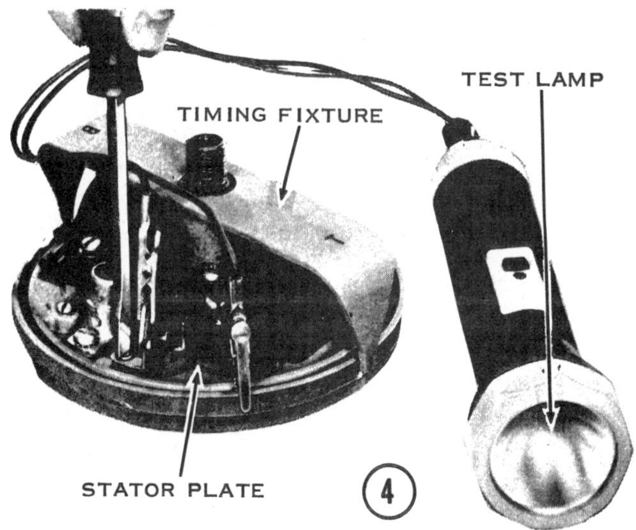

⑤ Check the crankshaft and flywheel tapers for traces of oil, which must be removed with solvent. **CAUTION: The assembly must be perfectly dry. CAUTION: Don't allow solvent to wash the oil out of the oiler wick.** The flywheel key must be installed so that it is parallel to the crankshaft and with the upset mark facing down. **CAUTION: Incorrect installation will adversely affect the ignition timing.** Replace the flywheel and nut, torquing it to specifications according to the model.

THROTTLE CAM SYNCHRONIZATION

3.0, 4.0, 5.0, 5.5 & 6.0 Hp Engines

⑥ Set the speed-control lever to the STOP position. Slowly advance the control until the cam follower

just begins to open the throttle. The timing mark on the cam and the contact point of the cam follower should now be aligned. If an adjustment is needed, loosen the cam mounting screws, and then position the cam so that, with all play removed from the linkage, the throttle valve is closed. The mark on the throttle cam must be aligned with the flat port side of the cam follower just as the follower makes contact with the cam. Tighten the cam retaining screws securely.

CRANKSHAFT
FLYWHEEL KEY
UPSET MARK
5

9.5 Hp Engine

⑦ Loosen the cam-follower adjustment screw. Move the cam follower so that it just contacts the throttle-control cam. Make sure that the throttle valve is fully closed, and then rotate the throttle-lever roller against the cam follower. Securely tighten the throttle lever to the throttle shaft. **CAUTION: Make sure that the adjustment setting is not disturbed when tightening the cam-follower screw.**

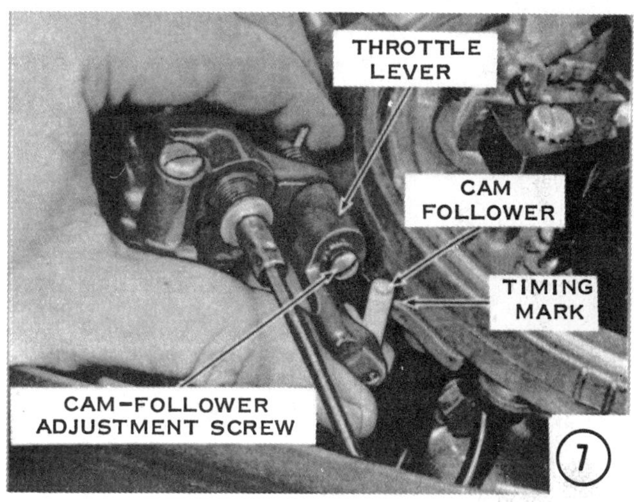

9.9, 15, 18, 20 & 25 Hp Engines

(8) Advance the throttle control to the position where the cam-follower roller is centered between the two marks on the throttle cam. The throttle valve must be closed at this point. If it is not, adjust it by advancing the throttle control to the position where the cam-follower roller is centered between the two marks. Loosen the two hex-headed screws holding the cam to the magneto stator base, and then push the cam back toward the rear of the engine. Now, pull the cam forward until it just contacts the cam-follower roller. The throttle valve must just begin to open after the edge of the roller passes the second mark on the cam. If necessary, either change the position of the cam or remove all unnecessary slack in the linkage. **CAUTION: The choke knob must be all the way in.**

33 Hp Engine

(9) Advance the throttle control so that the mark on the throttle cam is in line with the projection on the intake manifold. At this point, the throttle valve should be closed and the cam-follower roller must touch the cam. If the throttle valve is not closed, adjust it by advancing the throttle control until the mark on the stator plate cam is in line with the raised projection on the carburetor manifold. Loosen the throttle arm clamp screw. Make sure that the throttle valve is in the closed position and that the cam-follower roller touches the cam. Tighten the screw securely. *NOTE: As the throttle is advanced, the throttle valve must just begin to open after the mark on the cam passes the projection on the intake manifold.*

(10) *To make the fuel economy adjustment,* move the magneto stator plate by hand (without touching the throttle control) to the Maximum Spark Advance position. Adjust the control rod collar for 1/32″ clearance from the pivot pin, as shown in the insert.

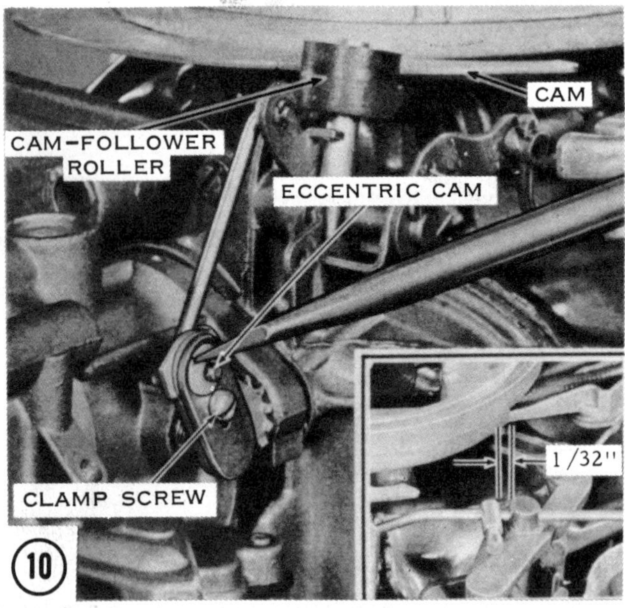

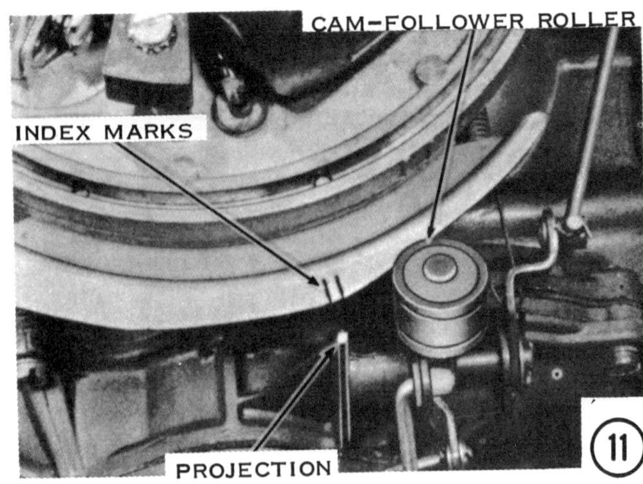

40 Hp Engine

⑪ Advance the throttle control so that the marks on the throttle cam are in line with the projection on the intake manifold. At this point, the throttle valve must be closed and the cam-follower roller must just touch the cam. If an adjustment is needed, advance the throttle control until the two marks on the throttle cam are aligned with the projection on the intake manifold. The cam-follower roller must just touch the cam at this point.

⑫ Loosen the throttle arm clamp screw. With the throttle valve closed, push the cam-follower roller so that it touches the cam, and then tighten the clamp screw. *To make the fuel economy adjustment,* move the magneto stator plate by hand (without touching the throttle control) to the Maximum Spark Advance position. Adjust the control rod collar for 1/32" clearance from the pivot pin, as shown in the insert.

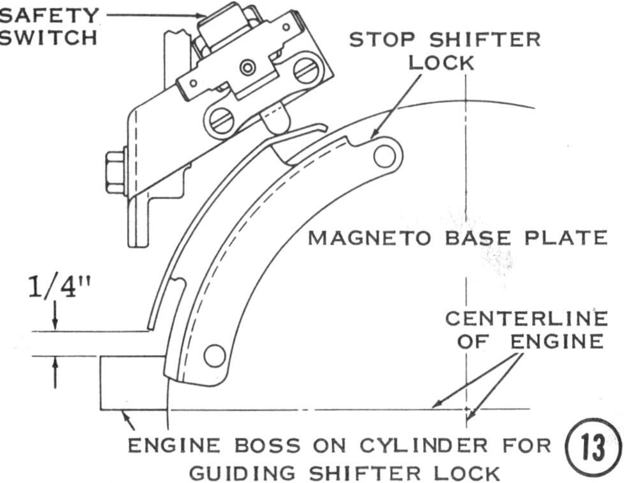

ADJUSTING THE VACUUM CUTOUT AND SAFETY SWITCHES

33 & 40 Hp Engines

⑬ The safety switch completes the cutout switch circuit and prevents it from operating at full throttle. The safety switch also prevents the starter from being engaged with the throttle advanced too far. *To make an adjustment to the safety switch,* connect a test lamp across the terminal screws, and then adjust the position of the switch on its bracket so that the circuit opens when the plunger reaches the midpoint on the slope of the shifter lock stop.

⑭ *To test the vacuum cutout switch,* connect a test lamp to the switch terminal and ground. Alternately apply oral suction and pressure at the switch vacuum

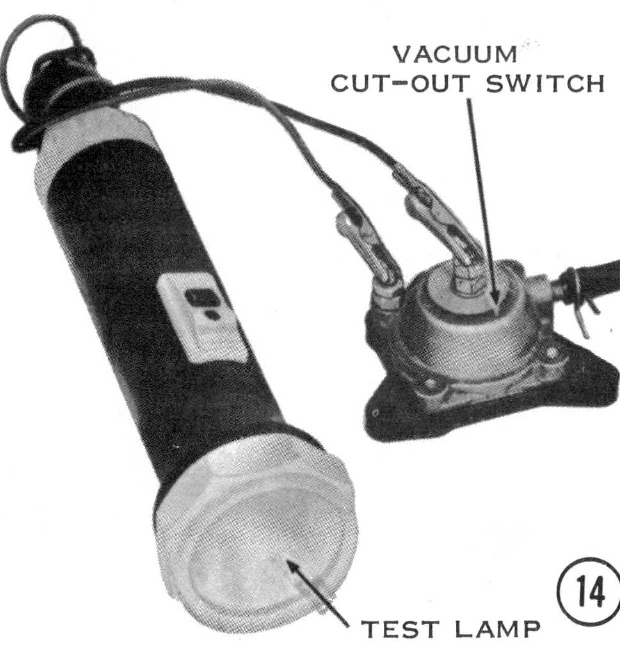

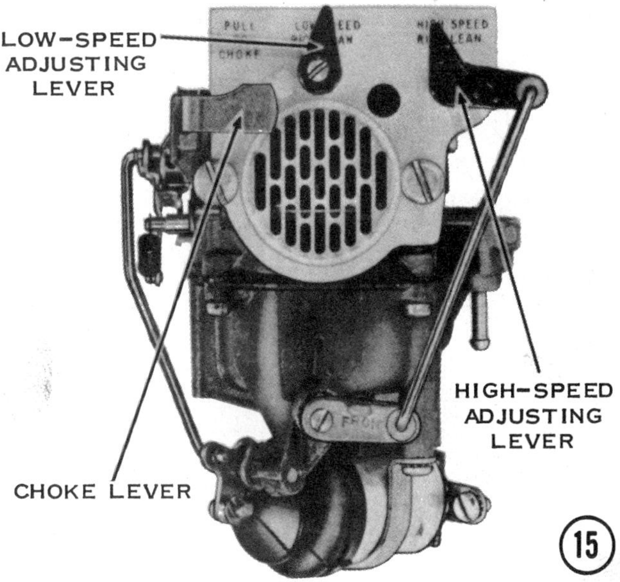

hose connector; the light should go on and off. Check the hole in the intake manifold with a #76 drill to make sure that it is free. Check the manifold vacuum hose for a leak, which would adversely affect the operation of the switch.

ADJUSTING THE CARBURETOR

(15) Seat the high- and low-speed adjusting needles gently, and then back them out for a preliminary adjustment. **CAUTION: Don't force them into their seats, or you will damage the taper, making an accurate adjustment difficult.** Back out the low-speed adjusting needle as follows: 1/2 turn for the 6 Hp engine; 3/4 turn for the 9.5 and 40 Hp engines; 1-1/4 turns for the 3, 5, and 33 Hp engines; and 2 turns for the 18/20 Hp models. Back out the high-speed adjusting needle 3/4 turn for all models. Start the engine and allow it to reach operating temperature. Run the engine at full throttle, and then adjust the high-speed needle for maximum rpm. **CAUTION: The prop must be in water when you run an engine at top speed, or you will throw a connecting rod.** Adjust the low-speed needle until the highest rpm consistent with smooth performance is reached. *NOTE: Allow 15 seconds for the engine to respond after each adjustment.*

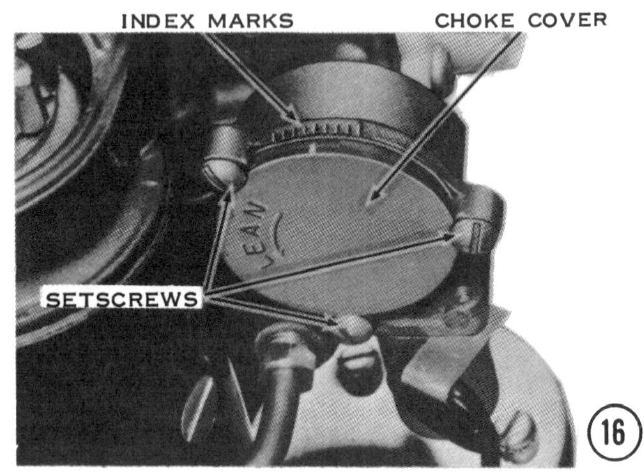

After making the low-speed adjustment, recheck the high-speed adjustment. Install the adjustment knobs.

(16) If starting is difficult in hot or cold weather, it may be necessary to adjust the automatic choke. Before disturbing the original factory setting, scribe a mark on the choke housing to serve as a reference point. To make an adjustment, loosen the setscrews, and then turn the cover one or two notches, as needed. Tighten the setscrews.

The idle speed adjustment for the larger two-cylinder engines is located at the base of the steering handle.

The idle speed adjusting screw for the 9.5 Hp engine is located at the base of the steering handle.

TWO-CYLINDER 50 HP ENGINE TUNE-UP PROCEDURES (WITH MAG-FLASH CD IGNITION)—SINCE 1971

This engine is equipped with a "Mag-Flash" (breakerless-type) ignition system. All parts of the ignition system (with the exception of the coils and amplifier) are under the flywheel: sensor, charge coils, and timer. The amplifier and ignition coils are mounted on the side of the engine and the connections to them can be used for testing the parts which are under the flywheel, as discussed in Chapter 7.

A safety switch is mounted on the engine, to the rear of the advance arm; its purpose is to prevent engaging the cranking motor when the throttle is advanced too far. An ohmmeter can be used to check the safety switch, which must show continuity with the throttle at idle and an open circuit when the throttle is advanced.

There are four tuning adjustments to be made: throttle pickup, maximum spark advance, idle speed, and idle mixture.

① *To synchronize the carburetor throttle valves,* loosen the throttle link fastener screw. Hold the throttle valves closed by applying light finger pressure to both the upper and lower throttle shaft levers, and then tighten the fastener screws. Repeat for the choke valves.

② *To check the throttle cam adjustment,* close the throttle; the scribe mark on the cam must be aligned with the cam follower roller. If it isn't, loosen the carburetor throttle arm screw and move the arm to close the throttle valves; tighten the screw.

③ *To check the throttle linkage clearance,* move the throttle lever to the wide-open position. The clearance between the cam and roller should be 0.000-0.020".

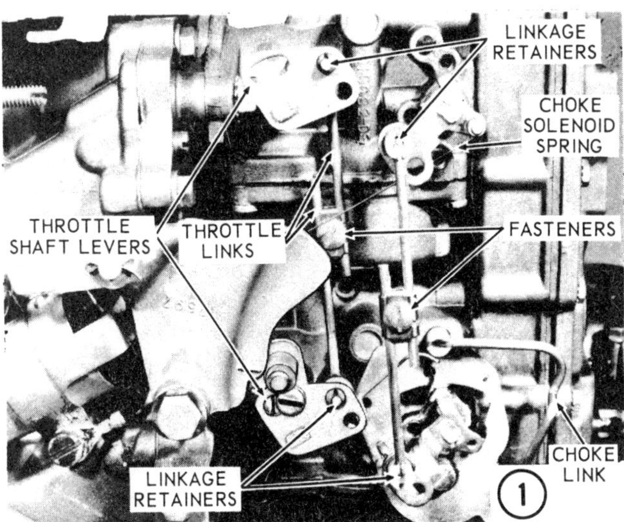

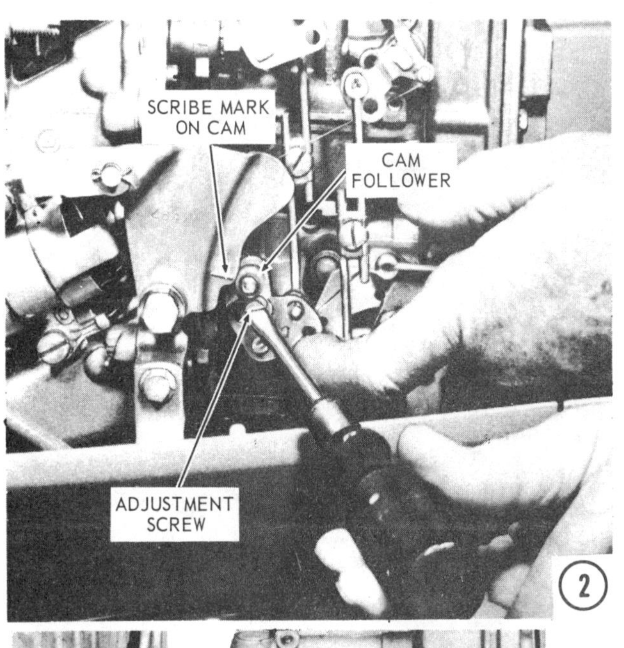

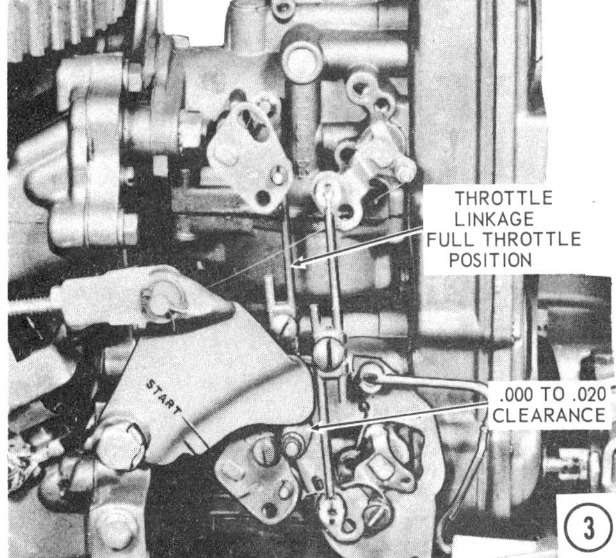

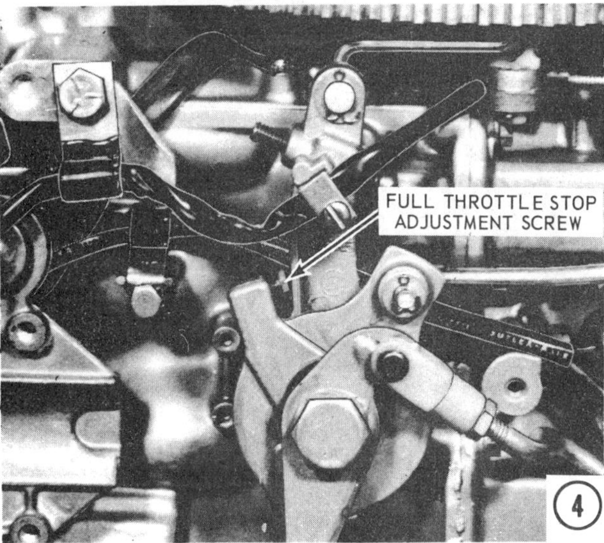

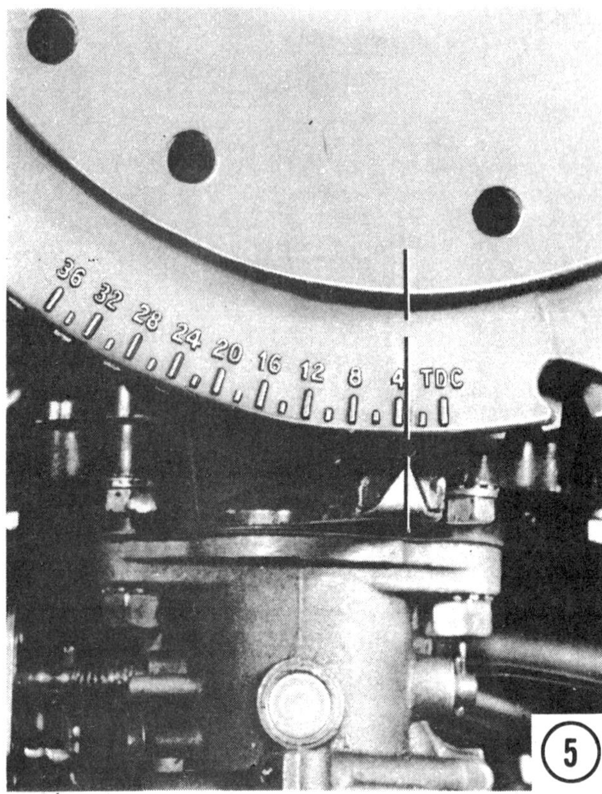

④ *To adjust the throttle linkage clearance,* turn the full-throttle stop screw to obtain up to 0.020″ clearance.

⑤ *To make the primary throttle pickup adjustment,* connect a timing light to No. 1 spark plug, which is the top one, and then start the motor. Turn the idle speed adjusting screw to obtain 3±1° advance timing, as shown, and then stop the motor.

⑥ Turn the throttle cam yoke to align the embossed mark on the throttle cam with the center of the throttle cam roller.

⑦ *To make the maximum spark advance adjustment,* rev the motor to at least 2500 rpm with a test wheel or the propeller in water, and then adjust the full-spark advance stop screw to obtain 19±1° BTDC. One full turn of the screw will change the timing about 1°. Tighten the locknut securely after making the adjustment.

⑧ *To make the low-speed adjustment,* back each low-speed adjusting needle out 3/4 turn from a lightly seated position, and then start the motor. Warm the motor to operating temperature with the propeller

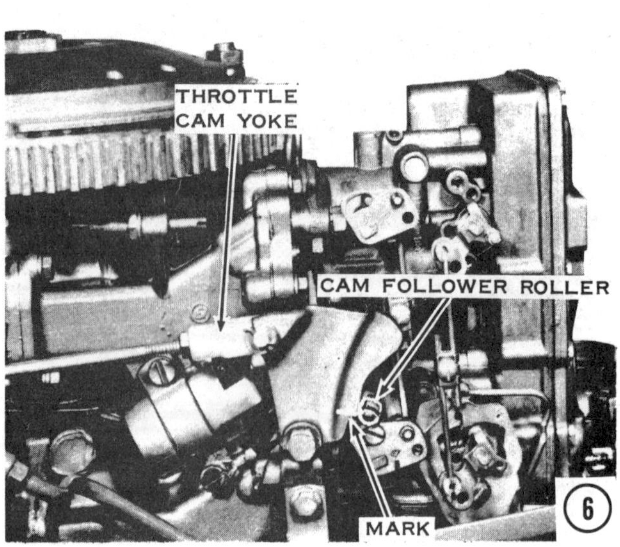

turning in water, and then adjust each low-speed needle to obtain the highest rpm and smoothest performance. Allow ample time for the motor to respond before changing the adjustment.

⑨ Turn the idle-speed adjustment screw to obtain 750-800 rpm in reverse gear. Install the air silencer and cover.

4

FUEL SYSTEM SERVICE

The fuel systems of the smaller engines are gravity fed, while the larger engines use a single-stage fuel pump to lift the fuel from a remote gas tank.

The carburetors of the two-cylinder engines are basically alike in construction details, except that some of the larger models have a fixed high-speed jet and some have an automatic choke.

Service procedures for these similar models will be grouped, using exploded views as a guide. Service procedures for the carburetors of the larger engines will be covered through step-by-step illustrated instructions.

FUEL PUMP

The fuel pump is of the single-stage, diaphragm-displacement type; it is operated by changes in crankcase pressure. Alternate suction and pressure pulses in the crankcase are transmitted to the fuel pump diaphragm through a flexible hose. Fuel is drawn through a fine-mesh filter before entering the pump.

The fuel pump is attached to the powerhead with two screws and is serviced only as an assembly. The filter screen can be serviced by taking out the cover retaining screw.

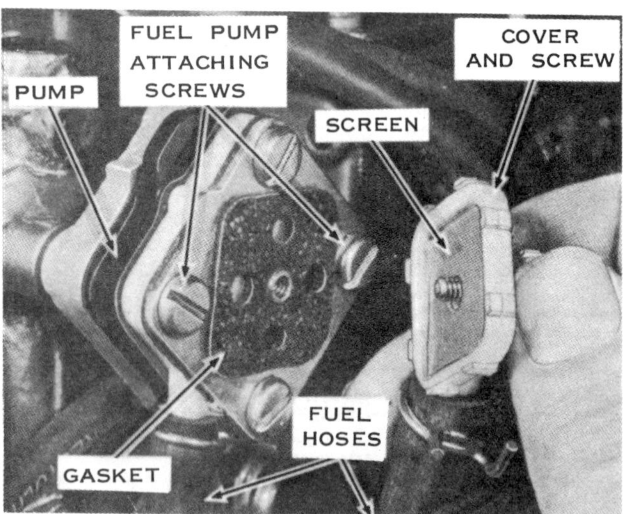

The fuel pump is serviced as an assembly. The filter screen can be cleaned or replaced by taking off the fuel pump cover.

REMOVING THE CARBURETOR

1.5, 2.0, 3, 4, 5, 6, 9.5, 18 & 20 Hp Engines

① Shut off the fuel supply at the shut-off valve. Remove the low-speed needle adjusting knob. Disconnect the choke retaining pin and control shaft. Disconnect the fuel hose at the carburetor. Keep the free end above the level of the carburetor to prevent fuel from leaking into the lower motor casing. Remove the two screws holding the manual starter in position, and then swing the starter aside for clearance. Remove the carburetor retaining nuts and lockwashers, and then lift off the carburetor. Discard the gasket.

② To remove the reed valve assembly, take out the manifold attaching bolts, and then lift out the intake manifold and valve block as an assembly.

9.9 & 15 Hp Engines (1974)

③ Remove the low-speed knobs. Take off the air silencer cover by removing the four screws (arrows). Take out the two screws holding the air silencer base to the cowl, and then lift off the base.

④ Remove the choke knob detent. Disengage the choke shaft from the choke lever, and then remove the choke knob and shaft from the lower motor cover. Remove the manual starter.

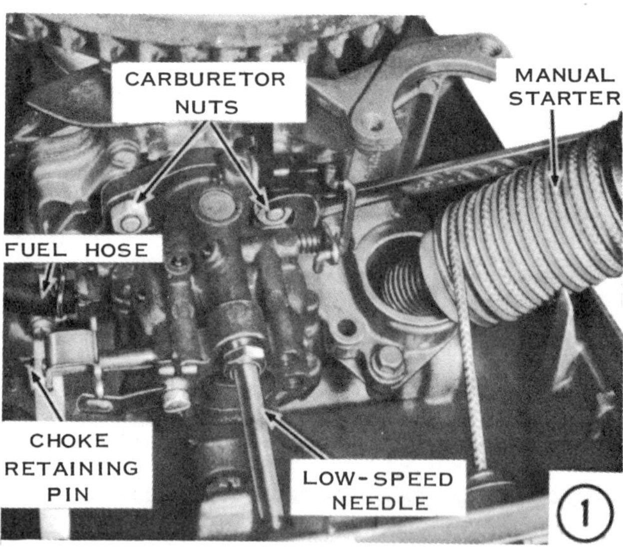

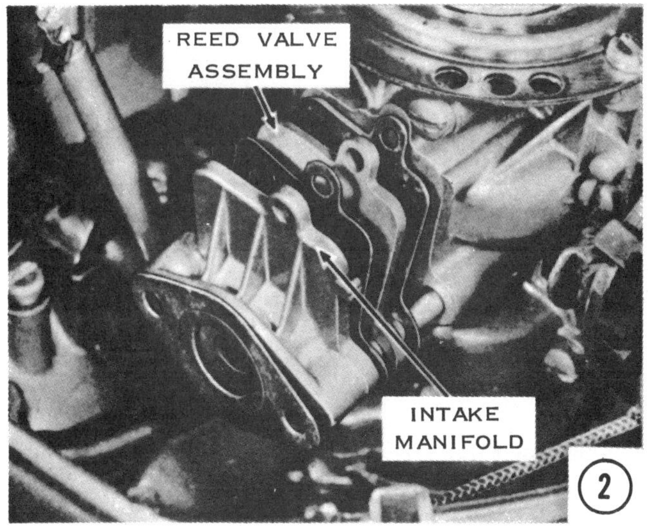

⑤ Take out the cam follower shoulder screw and washer, and then disengage the lever from the link. Remove the two nuts, carburetor, gasket, and link as an assembly from the intake manifold.

⑥ Observe the position of the link in the cam follower lever and on the throttle lever. The link must be installed in the throttle lever before installing the carburetor on the manifold because the manual starter lockout bracket prevents installing it after the carburetor is mounted on the manifold.

⑦ Remove the fuel hose tie strap, and then disconnect the fuel hose from the carburetor. Take out the six screws (arrows) holding the intake manifold to the engine. Remove the leaf plate and gasket from the crankcase.

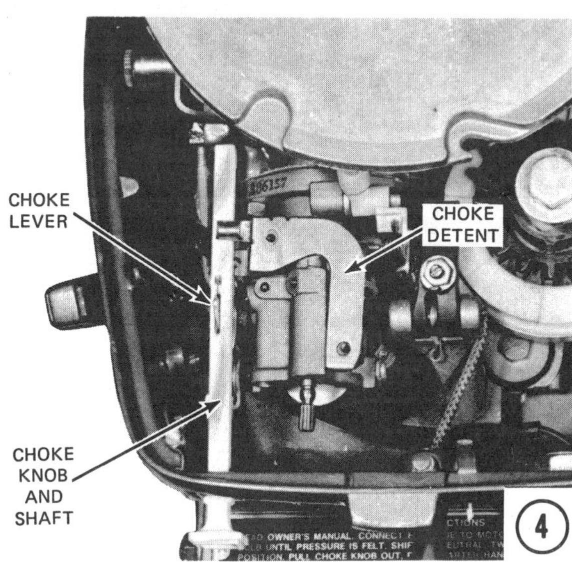

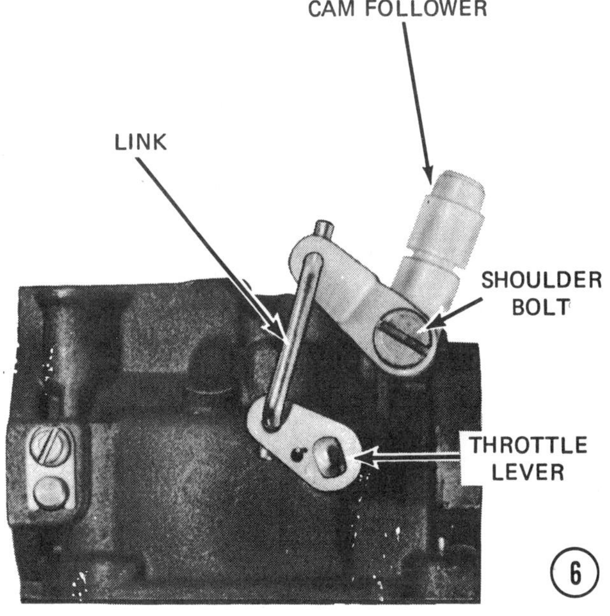

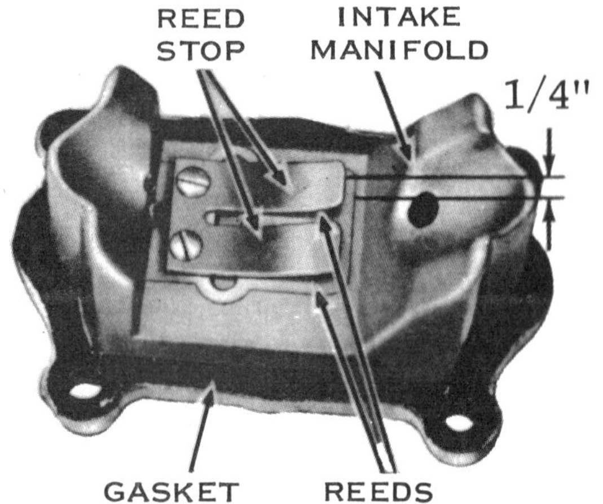

This picture shows the reed valves of the 1.5 and 2.0 Hp engines. The stop should be adjusted so that it extends 1/4" above the level of the base.

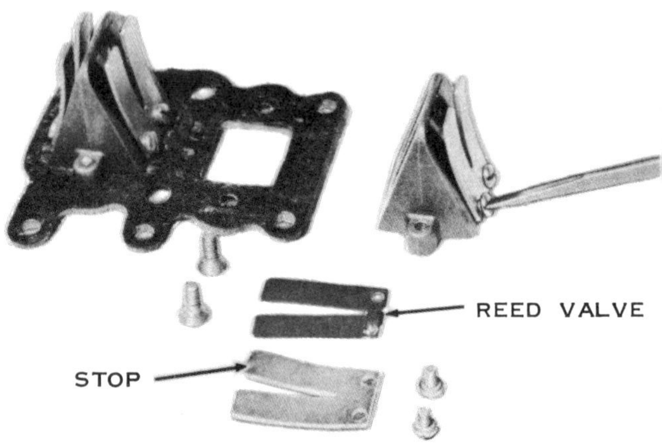

Details of the reed valve assembly used on the 9.5 Hp engine.

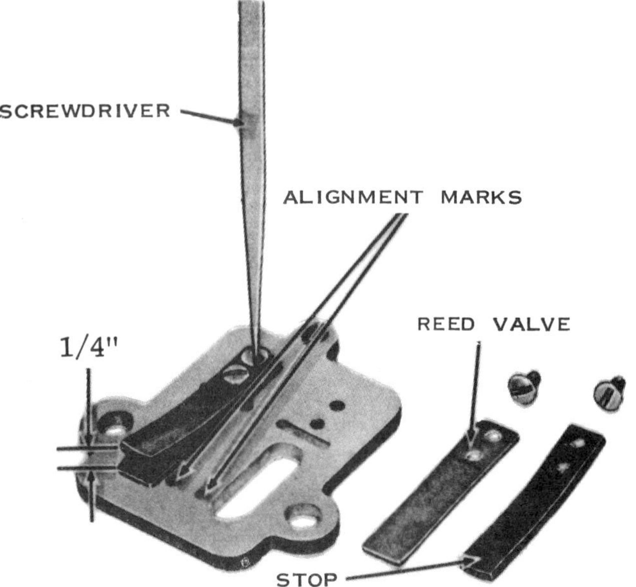

Details of the reed valve assembly used on the 3.0 Hp engine.

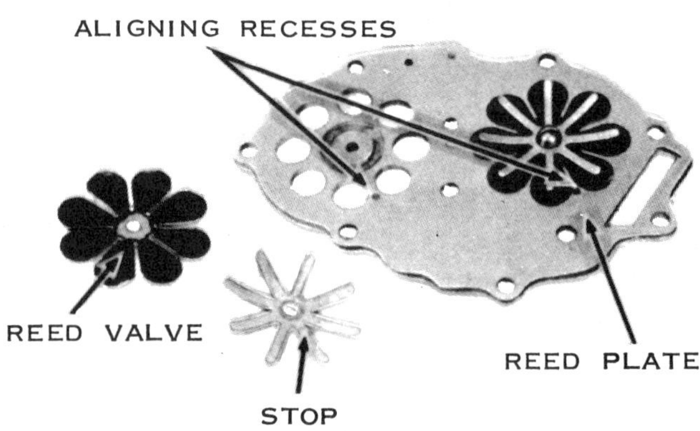

Reed valve plate details for the 20, 25, 33, and 40 Hp engines.

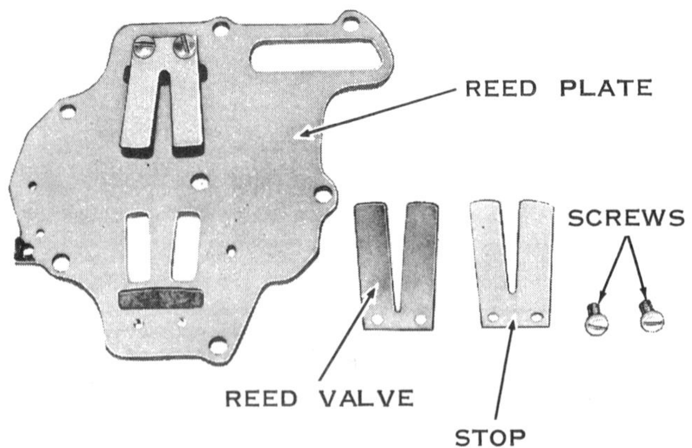

Details of the reed valve assembly used on the 5.0, 6.0, 9.9 and 15 Hp engines.

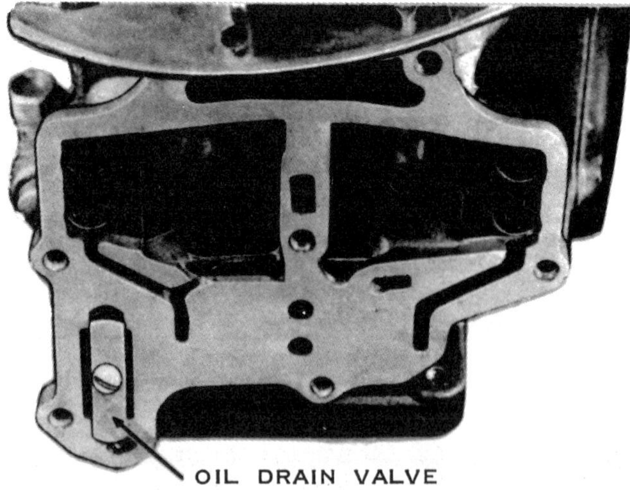

The oil drain valve normally does not require periodic service. However, it should be cleaned whenever the engine is disassembled for service.

(7)

25 Hp Engine

(8) Remove the shoulder screw and the choke lever. Lift up on the choke arm in order to remove the choke control knob from the carburetor.

(9) Remove the low-speed valve arm from the needle valve. Take out the two screws holding the silencer cover to the carburetor body. Remove the silencer cover. Disconnect the cam follower-to-throttle lever link. Disconnect the cam fuel line at the fuel pump, keeping the free end of the line above the carburetor to prevent fuel from spilling into the lower motor cover.

(10) Remove the two nuts and lockwashers attaching the carburetor to the intake manifold. Remove the carburetor and gasket. Take out the eight screws

CAM FOLLOWER ROLLER
SHOULDER SCREW
CAM FOLLOWER
CAM FOLLOWER LINK
WASHER
THROTTLE SHAFT AND LEVER
THROTTLE VALVE
GASKET
THROTTLE RETURN SPRING
THROTTLE ADVANCE LEVER
BEARING
RETAINER
SLOW SPEED NEEDLE
CHOKE LEVER
CHOKE VALVE
THROTTLE LEVER LINK
FLOAT VALVE AND SEAT ASSEMBLY
ORFICE PLUG
CHOKE SHAFT AND LEVER
GASKET
AIR SILENCER SEAL
FLOAT
FLOAT CHAMBER

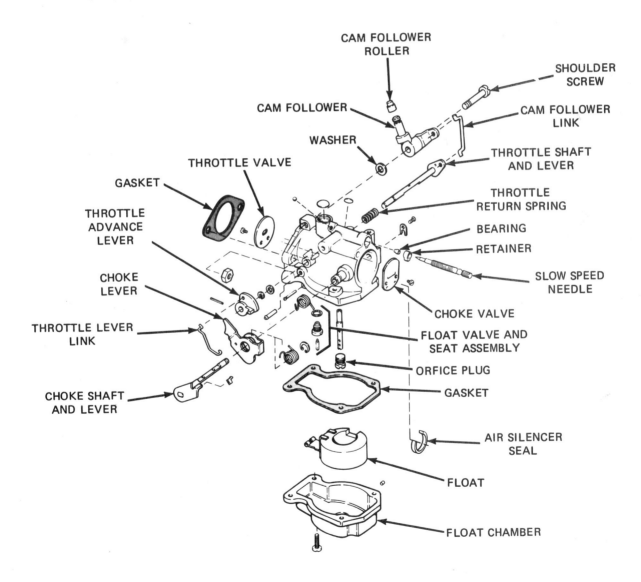

Exploded view of the carburetor used on the 1974 9.9 and 15 Hp engines.

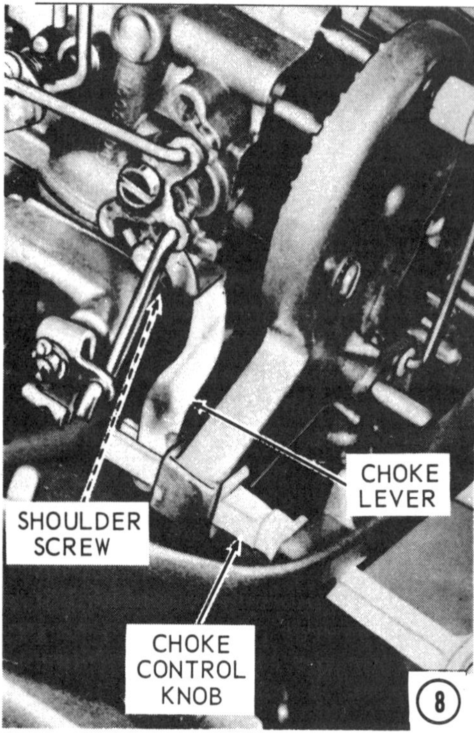

holding the intake manifold to the power head. Remove the screw (through the carburetor flange opening) holding the leaf plate to the crankcase. Remove the leaf valve assembly and the gasket.

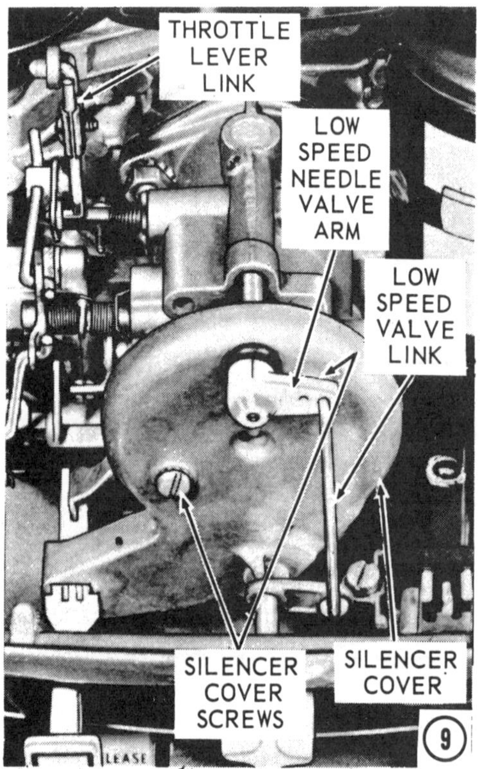

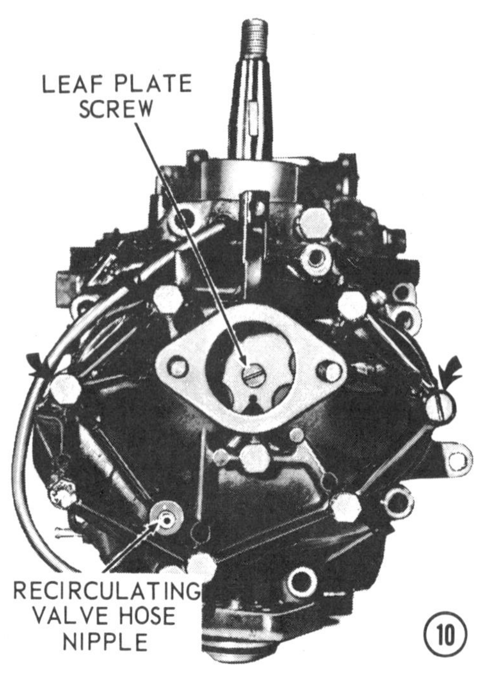

33 Hp Engine

⑪ Disconnect the fuel line at the carburetor. Remove the throttle lever link by taking out the lever pin at the throttle arm (on electric models).

⑫ Remove the cranking motor by disconnecting the main battery lead. Remove the three nuts and the five screws holding the starter bracket and mounting bracket to the crankcase. Lift the starter and bracket assembly off the bracket studs. Remove the two nuts and lockwashers holding the carburetor to the intake manifold. Disconnect the choke solenoid wire at the terminal. Remove the carburetor and gasket from the intake manifold.

⑬ Remove the cotter pin from the bottom end of the starter lever lock-out rod. Disconnect the rod

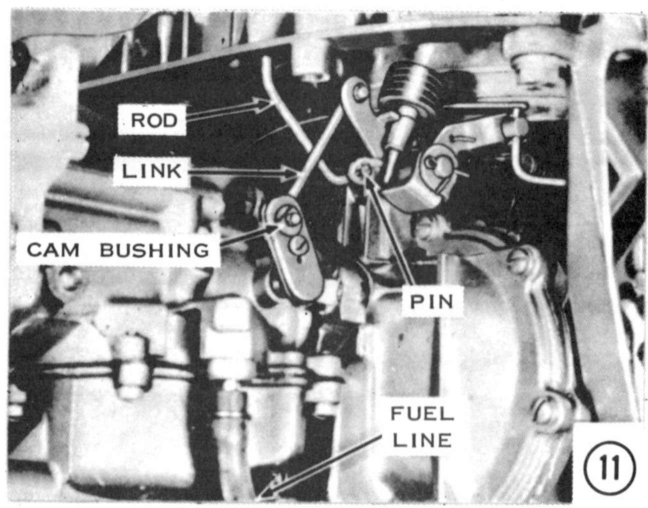

from the throttle lever. Remove the cut-out switch hose from the intake manifold. Take out the eleven screws holding the intake manifold to the powerhead, and then lift off the intake manifold. Remove the screw holding the reed valve plate to the crankcase, and then remove the valve and gasket assembly.

40 Hp Engine

⑭ To remove the manual starter from the powerhead, disconnect the locking lever by removing the screw and wave washer which holds the locking lever to the starter housing. Remove the three screws, and then lift the starter assembly from the powerhead.

⑮ Remove the heat tube shield and heat exchanger tubing (automatic choke models).

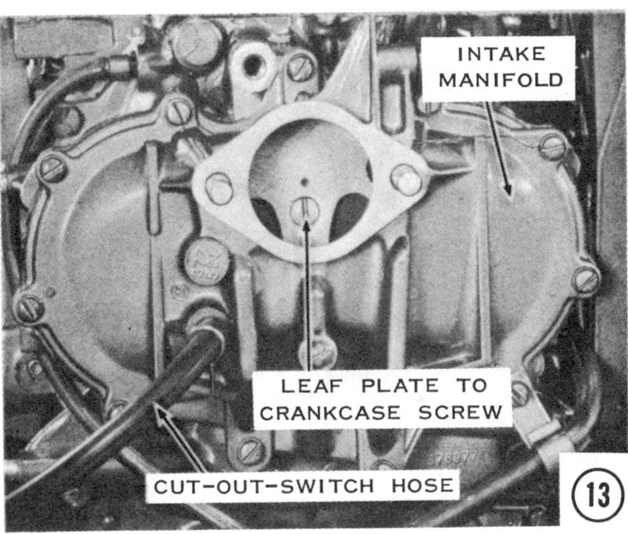

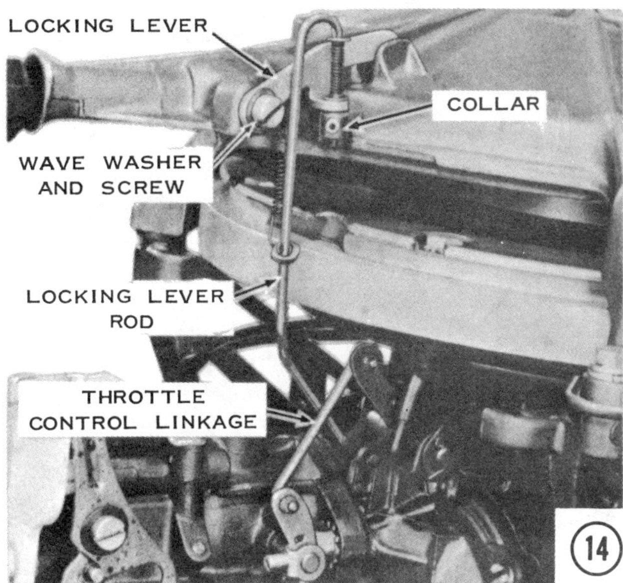

⑯ Disconnect the wires from the starter, generator, and choke solenoid. Remove the generator by taking off the pulley flange nut and lockwasher. Loosen the through-bolt nuts to permit releasing the

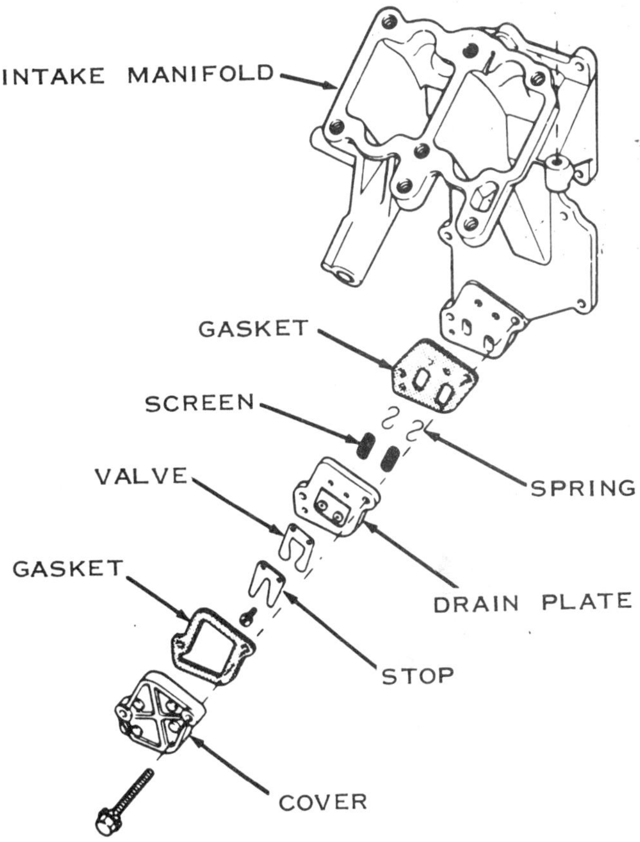

This is the oil drain valve used on the larger two-cylinder engines.

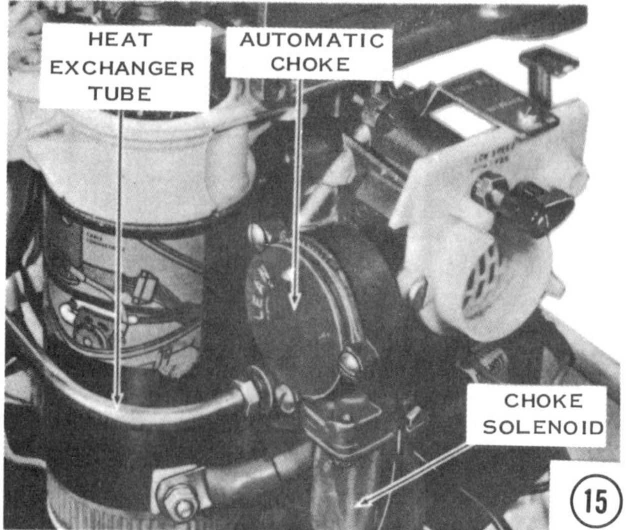

drive belt tension. Lift off the drive belt. Remove the nuts from the generator bracket studs. Remove the screw holding the ring guard to the generator bracket. Lift the bracket and generator from the powerhead as an assembly. Remove the starter by taking out the three nuts and five screws holding the starter motor bracket and mounting bracket to the crankcase. Lift the starter and brackets off the studs.

(17) Disconnect the fuel hose at the carburetor and the cam follower link at the throttle arm. Remove the two nuts and lockwashers holding the carburetor to the intake manifold. Remove the carburetor and discard the gasket.

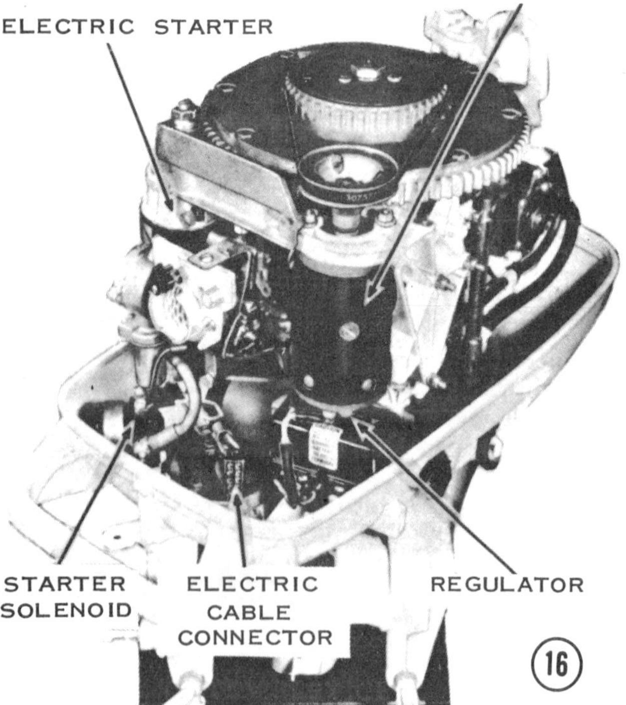

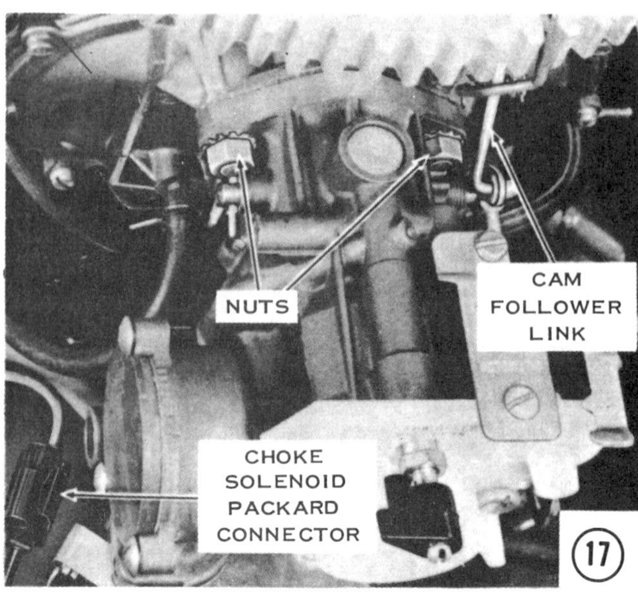

(18) Remove the intake manifold from the powerhead and discard the gasket. Remove the screw holding the reed valve plate assembly to the powerhead, lift out the plate, and discard the gasket.

50 Hp Engine

(19) Disconnect the fuel lines from the fuel pump. *NOTE: On electric-start models, the carburetors and air silencer can be removed as an assembly for servicing the leaf valve assembly or the powerhead without disturbing the carburetor linkage.* Manual-start models require removal of the starter rope guide.

(20) Remove the cotter pin holding the low-speed adjustment link, and then disconnect it from the low-speed shaft-and-arm assembly. Disconnect the choke link by pulling it out of the retainer. Remove the drain hose at the bottom of the intake manifold. Remove the pump-to-crankcase hose.

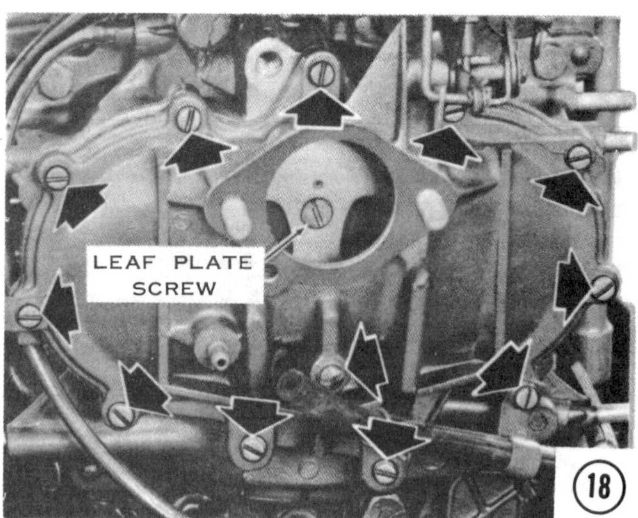

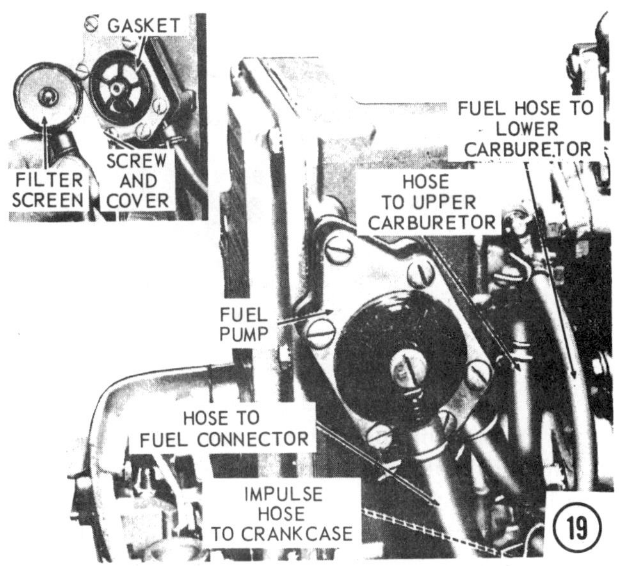

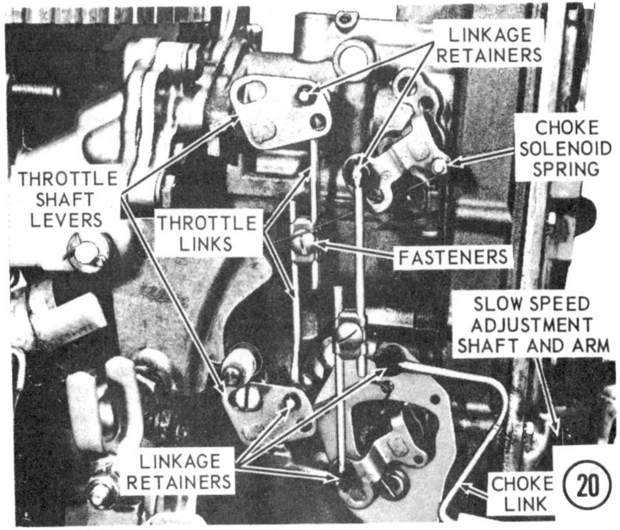

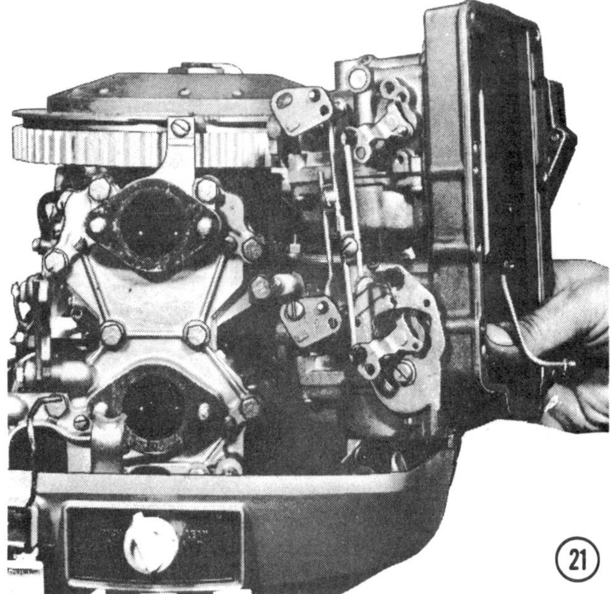

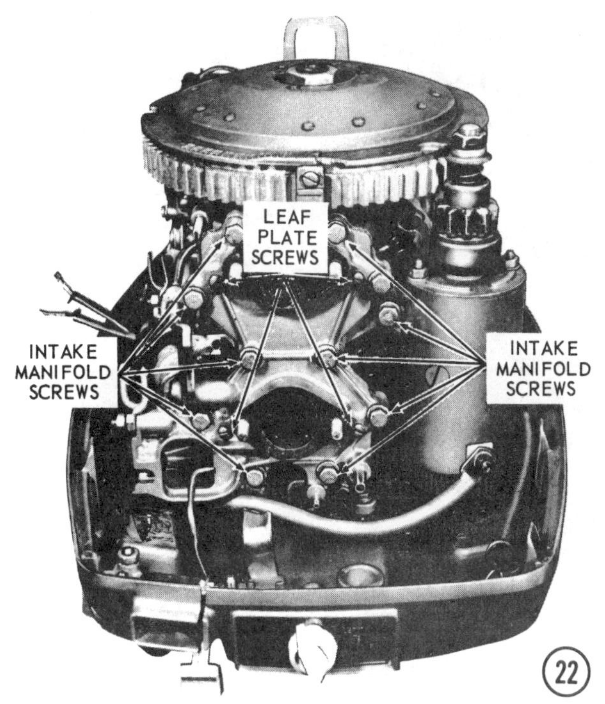

(21) Take out the eight screws holding the air silencer cover. Disconnect the choke solenoid spring. Remove the four carburetor mounting nuts, lockwashers, carburetor, and air silencer assembly. Discard the gaskets.

(22) Remove the 10 screws holding the intake manifold and leaf valve assembly. **CAUTION: Don't remove the four leaf plate screws.** Take out the leaf plate-and-base assembly, being careful not to damage it.

OVERHAULING THE CARBURETOR

There are three basic types of carburetors used on one- and two-cylinder engines; one being used on all models through 4 Hp, a special one for the 9.5 Hp engine, and a third type for all others.

DISASSEMBLING

(1) Drain the carburetor bowl by removing the high-speed metering needle or the drain plug. Re-

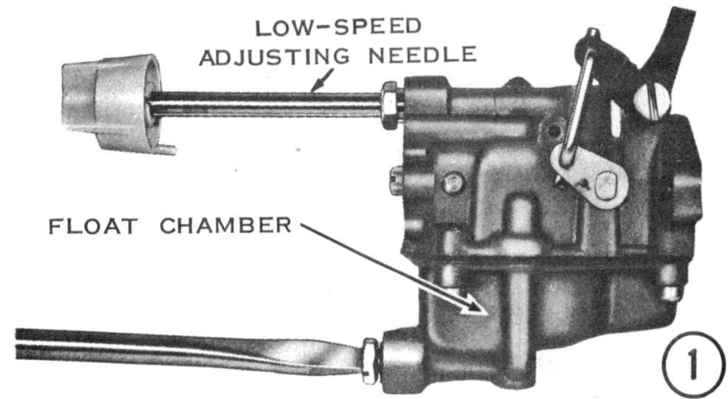

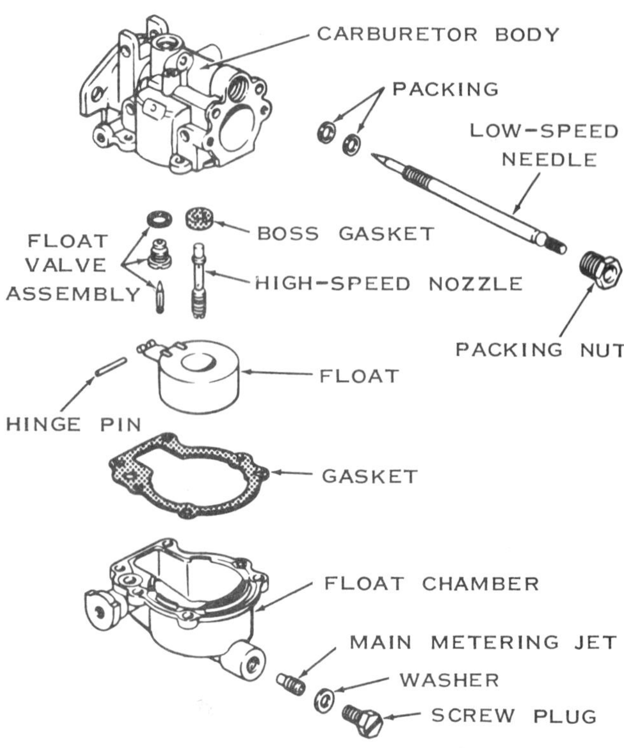

Exploded view of the carburetor used on the 5 through 50 Hp engines. It is similar to the other carburetors, except that it has a fixed main metering jet.

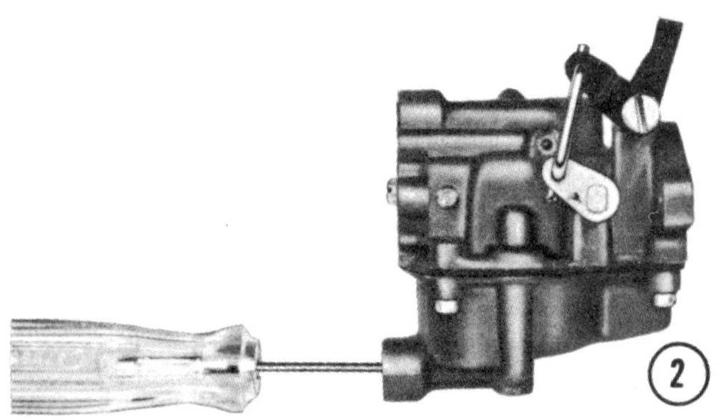

move the packing nut. Remove the low-speed adjusting needle nut, and then take out the adjusting needle. Remove the packing from the carburetor body and the float chamber; be careful not to damage the threads in the carburetor body.

② On models with a fixed high-speed jet, take out the main metering jet, using the illustrated tool to keep from damaging the threads. Take out the screws holding the float chamber to the carburetor body, and then separate the two castings. Discard the gasket. Remove the float hinge pin, float, and float valve. Unscrew the inlet needle valve seat and discard the gasket. Remove the high-speed nozzle.

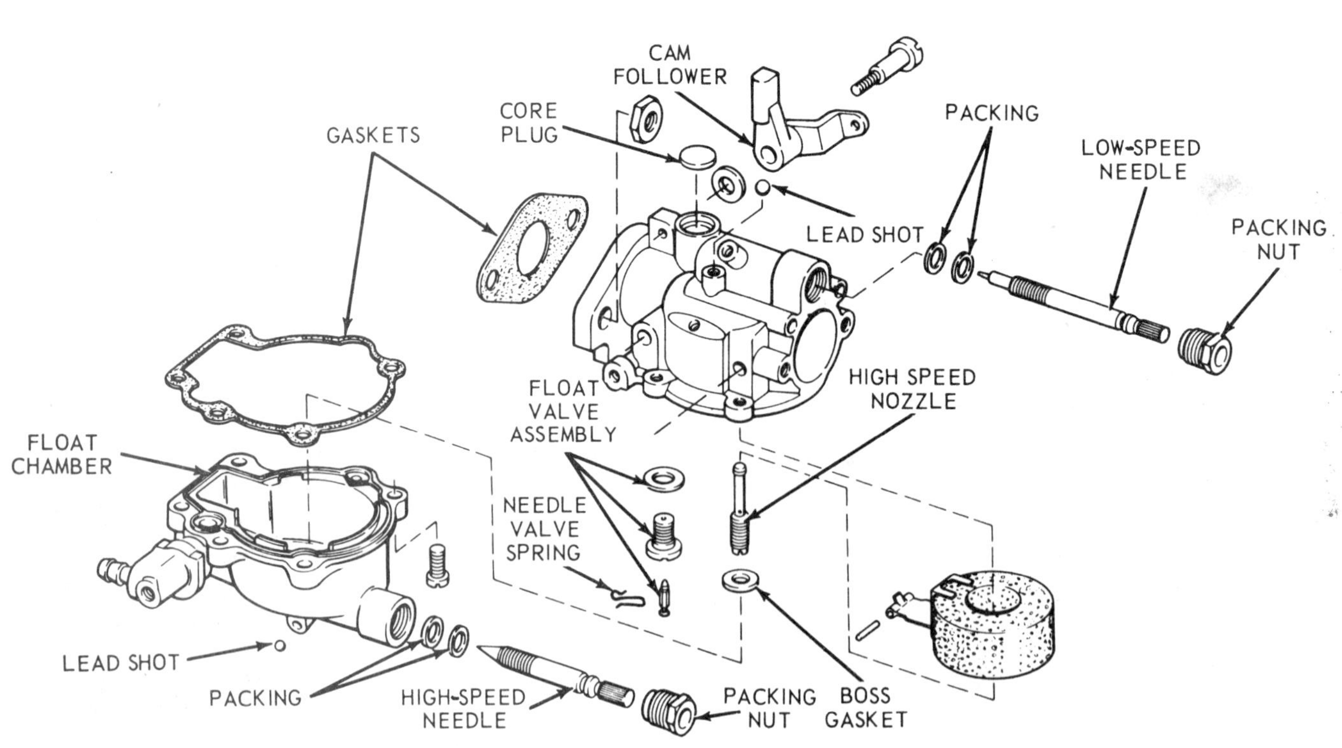

Exploded view of the carburetor used on the 1.5 through 4 Hp engines.

CLEANING AND INSPECTING

Clean all parts, except the cork float, in solvent and blow dry. **CAUTION: Don't use cloth to dry the parts because of the danger of leaving lint in one of the jets or passageways.** Be sure that all particles of gasket material are removed. Flush out all passageways in the carburetor body and float chamber with solvent. Remove any gummy deposits with OMC Accessory Engine Cleaner. *NOTE: Solvent will not remove the gum which accumulates in the float chamber and on the inlet needle valve seat.*

Check all gasket surfaces for nicks, scratches, or distortion. Slight irregularities can be corrected by using a surface plate and emery cloth.

Check the throttle shaft for excessive play. Check the operation of the choke and throttle valves to make sure that they shut off fully, yet move freely without binding. Replace the carburetor body if the valves or shafts are worn.

Inspect the float and arm for wear or damage. If the float is oil-soaked or leaks, replace it. Check the float arm for wear in the hinge pin hole and the needle valve contact area. Replace the float if it is heavy or damaged. Inspect the hinge pin for wear, which generally results from vibration. Replace the pin if it is grooved.

③ Always replace the needle valve and seat assembly as this is the part of the carburetor which wears the most. If this valve leaks, the fuel level will become too high and the fuel may leak. Always replace all O-ring seals and gaskets to prevent leaks.

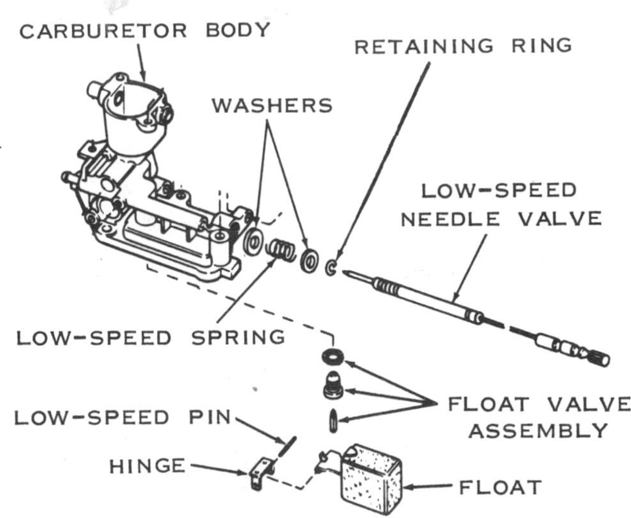

Exploded view of the carburetor body used on the 9.5 Hp engine. Note the washers at each end of the low-speed adjusting needle spring.

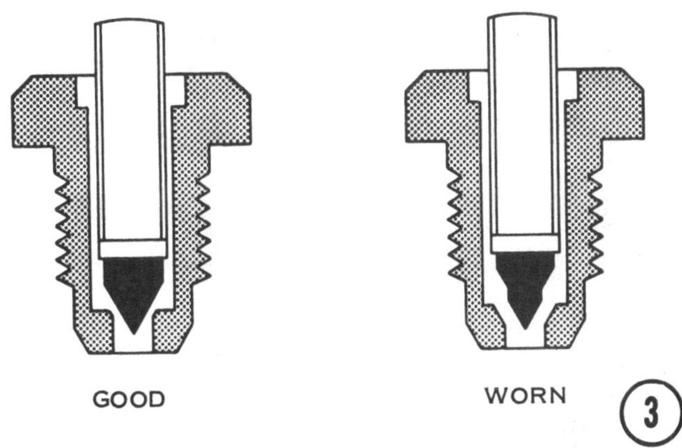

④ Inspect the tapered part of the adjusting needle valves to make sure that there are no grooves, nicks, or scratches, which would make an accurate adjustment difficult.

⑤ If necessary, remove the core plug to clean out the low-speed orifices. If leakage occurs at the core plug area, a smart tap with a hammer and a flat punch in the center of the core plug will correct the condition.

⑥ If leakage persists, drill a 1/8″ hole through the center of the core plug to a depth of not more than 1/16″ below the surface. Use a punch to pry out

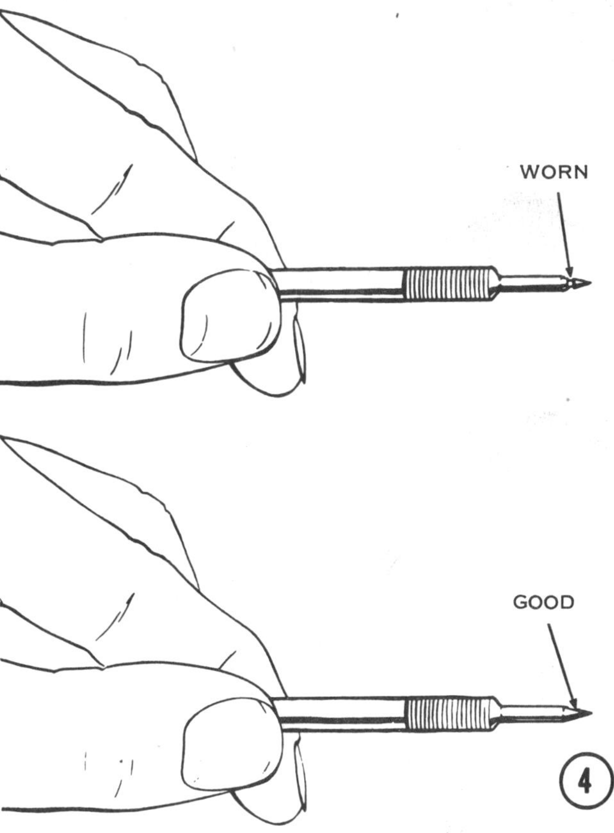

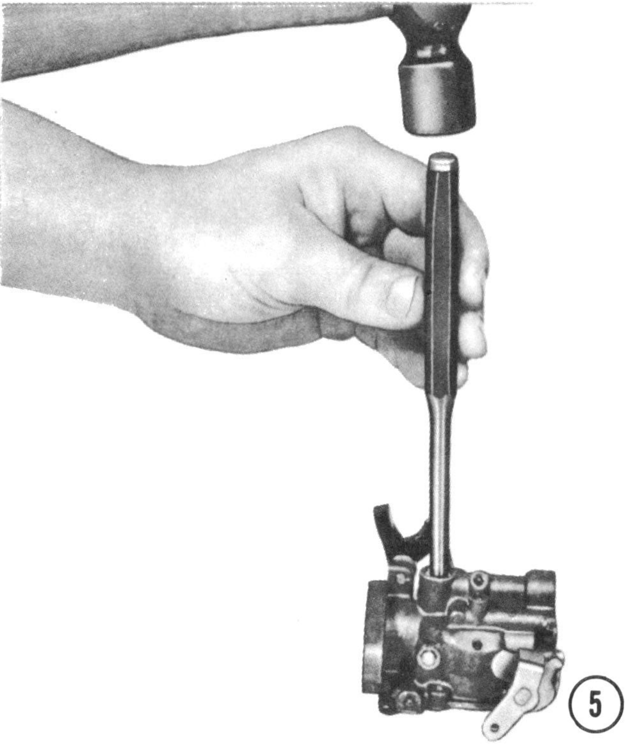

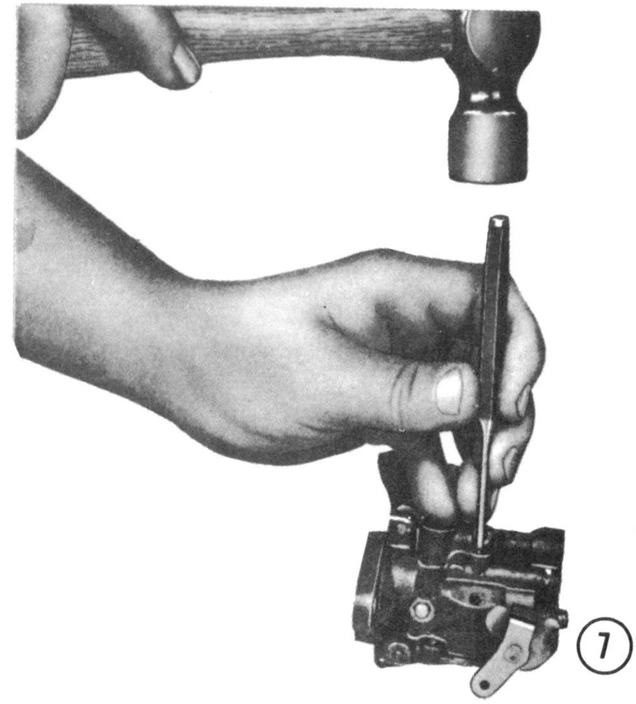

the core plug. Inspect and clean the casting contact area carefully. If nicks, scratches, or an out-of-round condition exists, the casting will have to be replaced. If the hole in the casting is normal, apply a bead of Sealer 1000 to the outer edge of a new core plug, and then place the plug in the casting, convex side facing up. Flatten the plug with a flat punch, and then recheck for leakage.

⑦ If leakage occurs around a lead shot area, tap the center of the lead shot with a hammer to correct the condition.

⑧ If necessary, remove the lead shot with a sharp-edged tool. Clean and inspect the casting opening. If it is normal, install a new lead shot and flatten it out with a light hammer tap. Recheck for leakage.

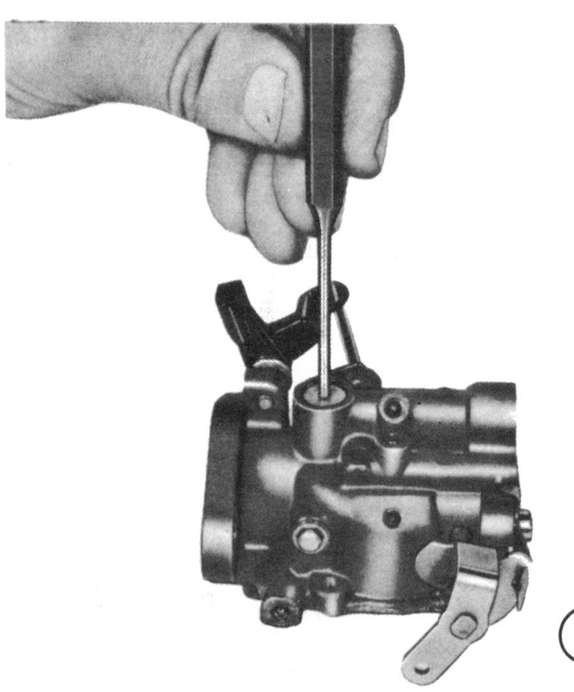

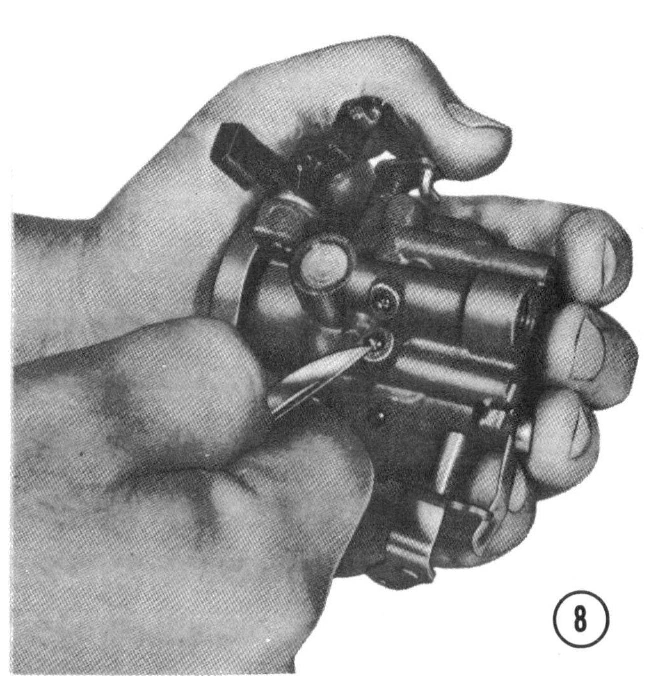

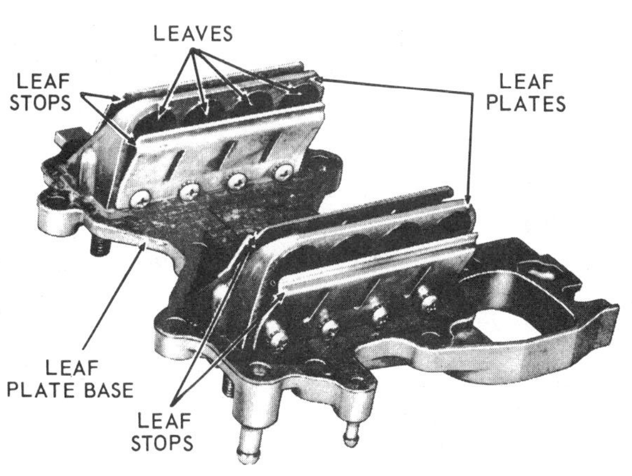

Details of the leaf valves used on the 50 HP engine.

ASSEMBLING

⑨ Replace the high-speed nozzle. Install a new needle valve seat using a new gasket. A drop of oil inside of the seat will keep the needle valve from sticking. Replace the needle valve, and then install the float and hinge pin in the carburetor body. Check the float level on all except the 9.5 Hp engine carburetor by turning the carburetor casting upside down so that the weight of the float closes the needle valve. The float must be parallel and flush with the edge of the casting. Install a new float chamber gasket, and then secure the float chamber to the carburetor body, tightening the screws securely.

⑩ On the 9.5 Hp engine carburetor, turn the carburetor casting upside down so that the weight of the float closes the needle valve. The float should be parallel with the face of the casting and 13/16″ from the flange.

⑪ To measure the float drop on the 9.5 model, turn the body upright, as shown, and the float should drop 1-7/16″ from the flange of the body.

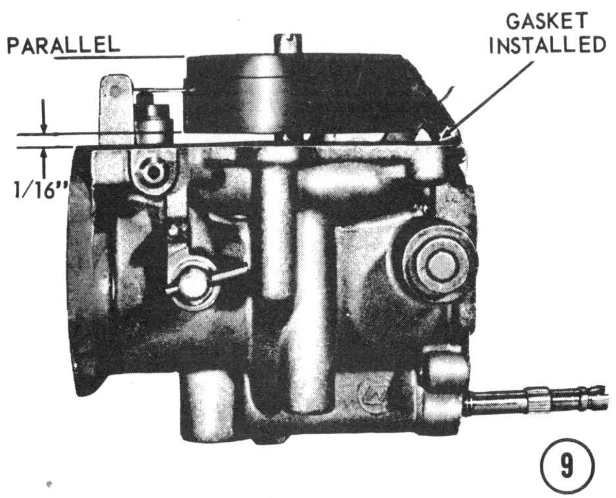

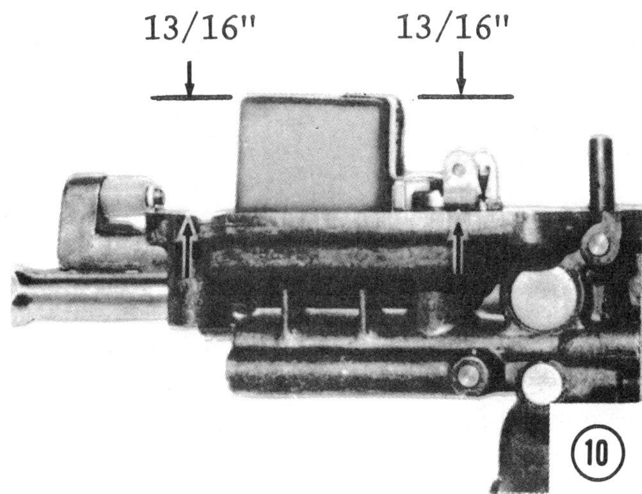

⑫ On all models, replace the packing on the low-speed adjusting needle gland, and then install the needle and packing nut, but do not tighten it. *NOTE: There are washers at each end of the spring on the 9.5 model only, as shown.* Replace the high-speed metering

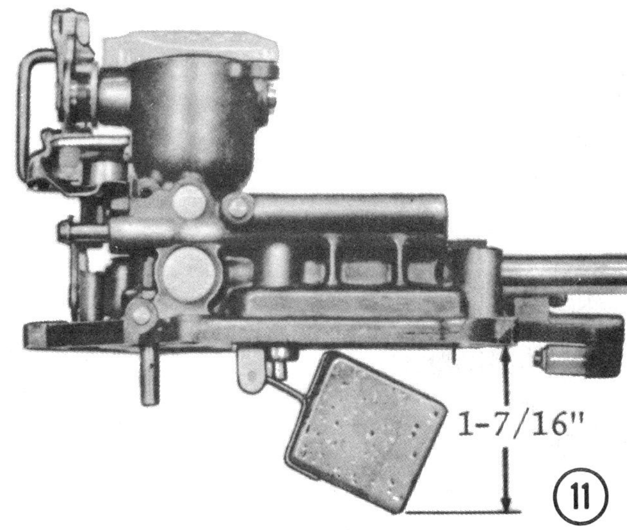

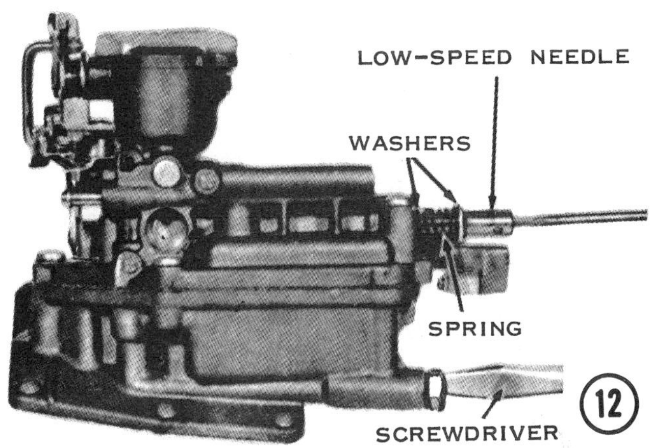

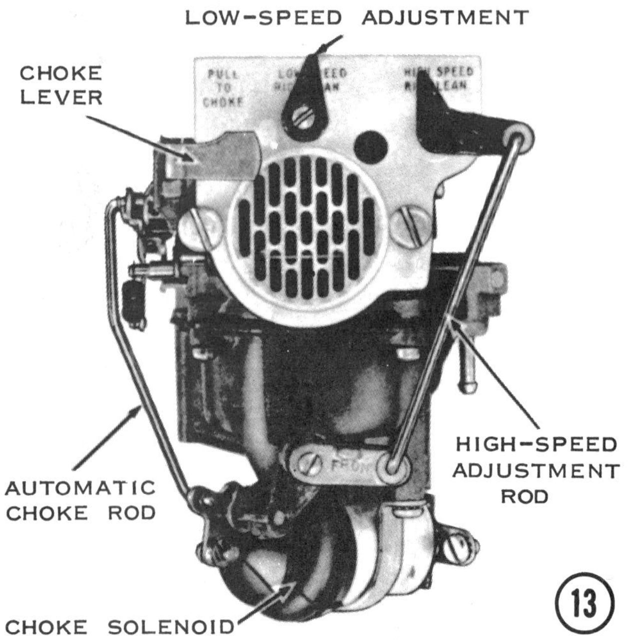

13

jet or adjusting needle, tightening the packing gland nut finger-tight. Turn each of the adjusting needles down until it seats lightly. **CAUTION: Don't turn the adjusting needle in tightly, or you will damage the taper, making an accurate adjustment difficult.** Back out the low-speed adjusting needle for a preliminary adjustment as follows: 1/2 turn for the 6 Hp engine; 3/4 turn for the 9.5; 1-1/4 turns for the 1.5, 3.0, and 5.0; and 2 turns for all other models. Back out the high-speed adjusting needle 3/4 turn for all models. Tighten the packing gland nuts until the adjusting needle can just be turned with your fingers.

33 Hp Engine

(13) This is the same basic carburetor used on the previous models with the addition of an automatic choke which is operated by a solenoid. To disassemble this carburetor, remove the screw in the end of the low-speed adjusting needle so that you can take off the adjusting knob. Remove the two screws to take off the control panel.

(14) This exploded view shows that the parts are installed in the same relative positions as on the carburetor just covered.

(15) After assembling the carburetor, check the choke valve for free operation, and then attach the choke arm to the choke shaft. Install the choke solenoid and spring. Pull out the manual choke lever to the fully choked position. Adjust the position of the choke solenoid in the bracket until the solenoid plunger has approximately 1/16″ free play. The closed end of the solenoid should be approximately flush with the edge of the boss, as shown. For a preliminary adjustment, the low-speed adjusting needle should be backed out 1-1/4 turns and the high-speed needle 3/8 turn.

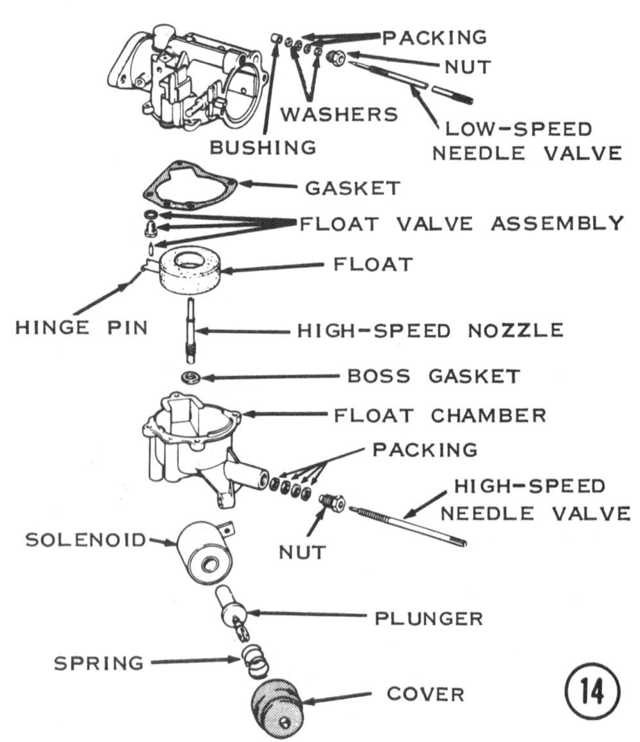

14

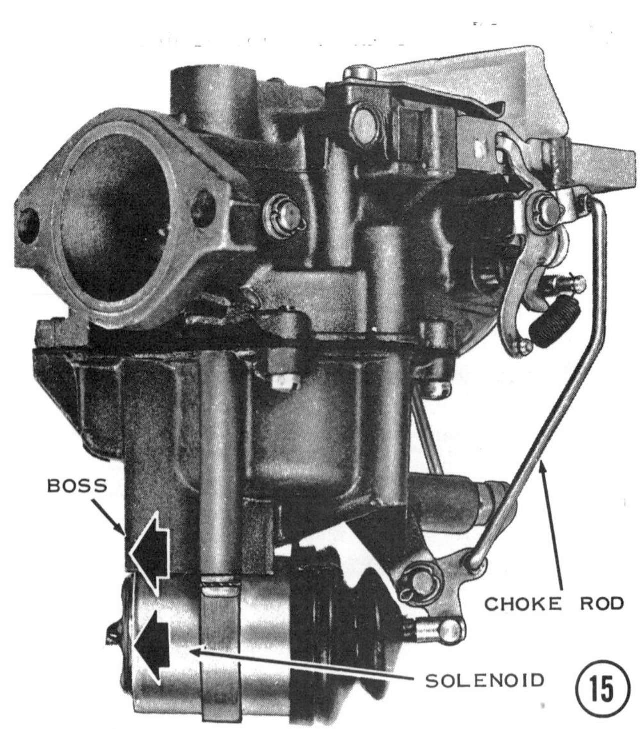

15

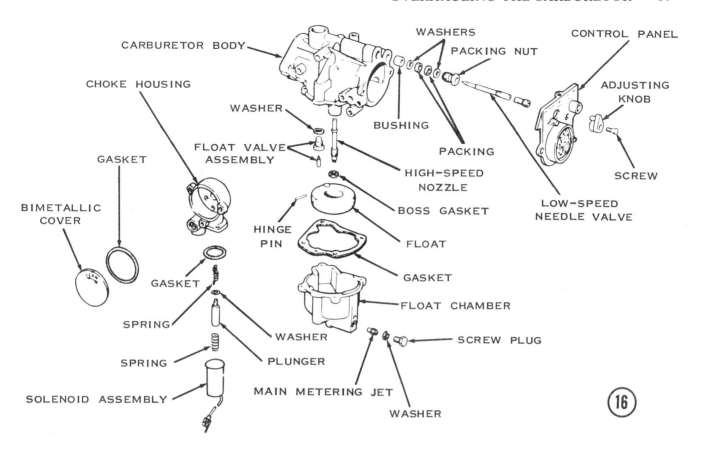

CARBURETOR BODY
WASHERS
PACKING NUT
CONTROL PANEL
CHOKE HOUSING
ADJUSTING KNOB
WASHER
BUSHING
FLOAT VALVE ASSEMBLY
PACKING
GASKET
HIGH-SPEED NOZZLE
SCREW
BIMETALLIC COVER
BOSS GASKET
LOW-SPEED NEEDLE VALVE
HINGE PIN
FLOAT
GASKET
GASKET
FLOAT CHAMBER
SPRING
WASHER
SCREW PLUG
SPRING
PLUNGER
SOLENOID ASSEMBLY
MAIN METERING JET
WASHER

16

40 Hp Engine

(16) The carburetor used on the 40 Hp engine is basically the same as the previous models; it has a fixed high-speed jet and an automatic choke, which is attached to the side of the carburetor casting. The high-speed jet is not adjustable. For a preliminary adjustment, back out the low-speed adjusting needle 1-1/4 turns.

50 Hp Engine

(17) This engine uses a single-barrel carburetor of similar design. As seen by the exploded view, the servicing instructions are the same as for those of the previous models. The top of the float should be parallel with the rim of the casting. The low-speed adjusting needle should be backed out 5/8 turn for a preliminary adjustment.

(18) If the spring was removed from the solenoid plunger, install it by twisting it onto the plunger 2-1/2 to 3-1/2 turns. Attach the solenoid to the intake manifold with the clamp and two screws. The solenoid should be positioned so that the shoulder of the rod extends out 3/16", as shown.

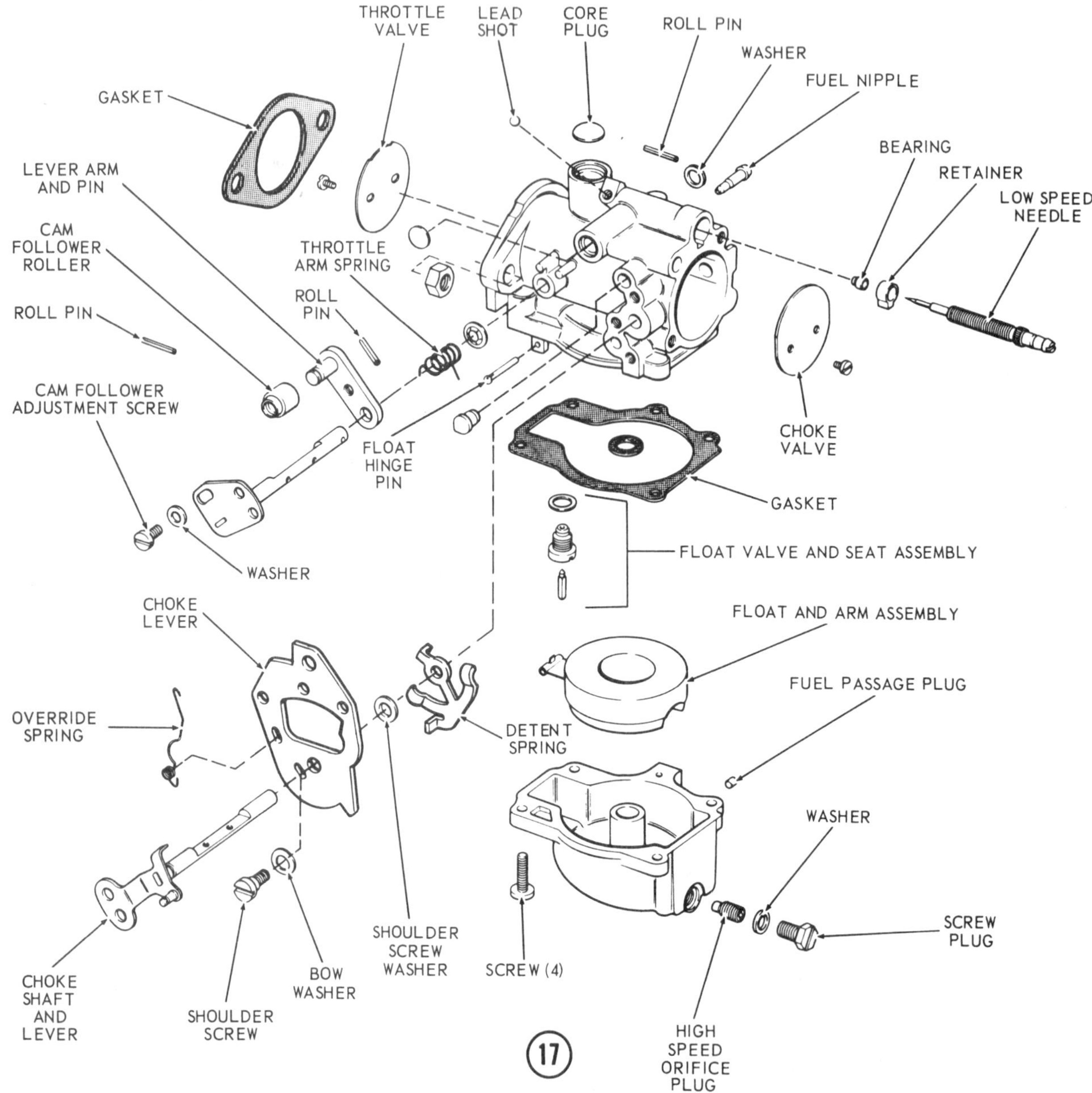
THROTTLE VALVE
LEAD SHOT
CORE PLUG
ROLL PIN
WASHER
FUEL NIPPLE
GASKET
BEARING
RETAINER
LOW SPEED NEEDLE
LEVER ARM AND PIN
CAM FOLLOWER ROLLER
THROTTLE ARM SPRING
ROLL PIN
ROLL PIN
CAM FOLLOWER ADJUSTMENT SCREW
FLOAT HINGE PIN
CHOKE VALVE
GASKET
FLOAT VALVE AND SEAT ASSEMBLY
WASHER
CHOKE LEVER
FLOAT AND ARM ASSEMBLY
FUEL PASSAGE PLUG
OVERRIDE SPRING
DETENT SPRING
WASHER
SCREW PLUG
SHOULDER SCREW WASHER
BOW WASHER
SCREW (4)
CHOKE SHAFT AND LEVER
SHOULDER SCREW
HIGH SPEED ORIFICE PLUG

17

5
ENGINE SERVICE

Outboard motors operate on the two-cycle principle. That is, they fire each time that the piston comes up. Most two-cycle motors have reed-type valves in place of the poppet-type used in a four-stroke cycle engine. Also, the oil must be pre-mixed with the fuel as both have to pass through the crankcase on the way to the combustion chamber.

PRINCIPLES OF OPERATION

The piston in a two-cycle motor acts as an inlet and exhaust valve. In starting a two-cycle motor, the crankshaft turns and the piston rises. Starting with the piston at its highest point of travel (and with the combustion chamber filled with a compressed mixture of air and fuel), a spark from the spark plug ignites the compressed mixture. The resulting explosion within the cylinder forces the piston down, delivering its energy to the crankshaft. During the upward stroke, the piston draws a fresh charge of fuel and air through the intake reed valve and into the crankcase. The crankcase, which is air-tight, contains the crankshaft and connecting rods. On the downward stroke, the charge of fuel and air, previously drawn in, is compressed in the crankcase and, when the piston approaches the bottom of the stroke, an exhaust port is uncovered on the side of the cylinder wall. The unburned gases escape through this port, and the combustion chamber pressure falls. An instant later, the piston uncovers an inlet port on the opposite side, and the fresh charge forces its way up from the crankcase to drive out the remainder of the exhaust gases. A projection on the top of the piston, on the intake side, deflects the fresh charge and prevents it from passing directly across the cylinder and out of the exhaust port.

Recently, a new system of loop scavenging the combustion chamber has come into use. This engine has an almost flat piston dome, with a slightly curved contour. Two intake ports are slanted upward and face each other. This has a directional effect on the two incoming charges so that they impinge on each other and flow upward and around the smooth dome-shape of the combustion chamber, and then down and out of the exhaust ports on the adjacent side of the cylinder wall. The flow pattern of the fresh incoming fuel-laden gases very effectively drives out the burned gases.

On alternate-firing, twin-cylinder outboard motors, the pistons are connected to the crankshaft at a 180° angle, and a power stroke is delivered every 180°, producing the reciprocating motion which is transferred to the shaft to create the rotary motion. The firing order is governed by the magneto, which is

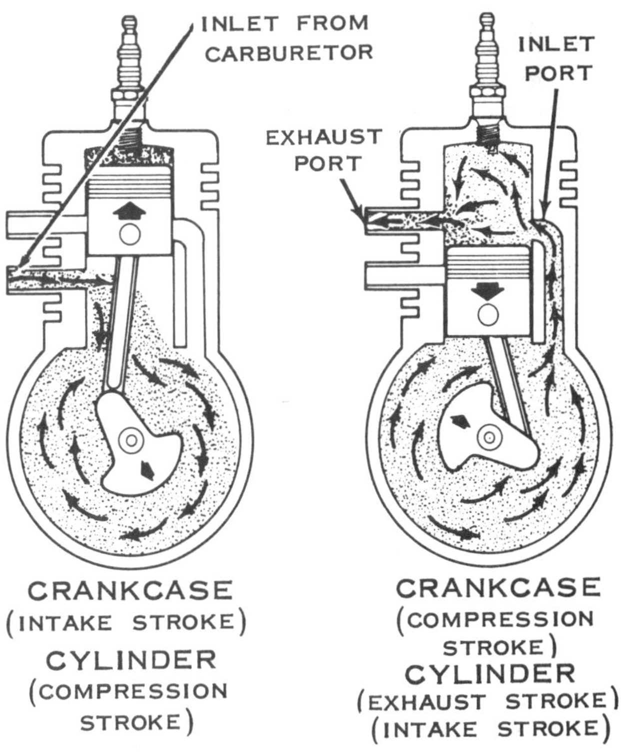

The two-stroke cylinder engine fires each time that the piston comes up. Because the crankcase acts as a transfer pump for the air-fuel mixture, lubrication of the engine depends on the addition of lubricating oil to the gasoline.

connected to one end of the crankshaft. At each 180° of rotation of the crankshaft, electrical sparks are generated and transmitted to the spark plugs to fire the charges alternately. A cam, mounted on the crankshaft within the magneto, opens and closes the breaker points to produce these sparks.

Reed-type inlet valves operate automatically, opening when the pressure in the crankcase is low enough so that the outside pressure can overcome the reed tension. The rate of speed at which the engine is operating varies the crankcase pressure and regulates the degree of opening of the reeds. This allows a satisfactory performance level throughout the entire speed range of the engine because the reeds open to the varying demands created by the different speeds.

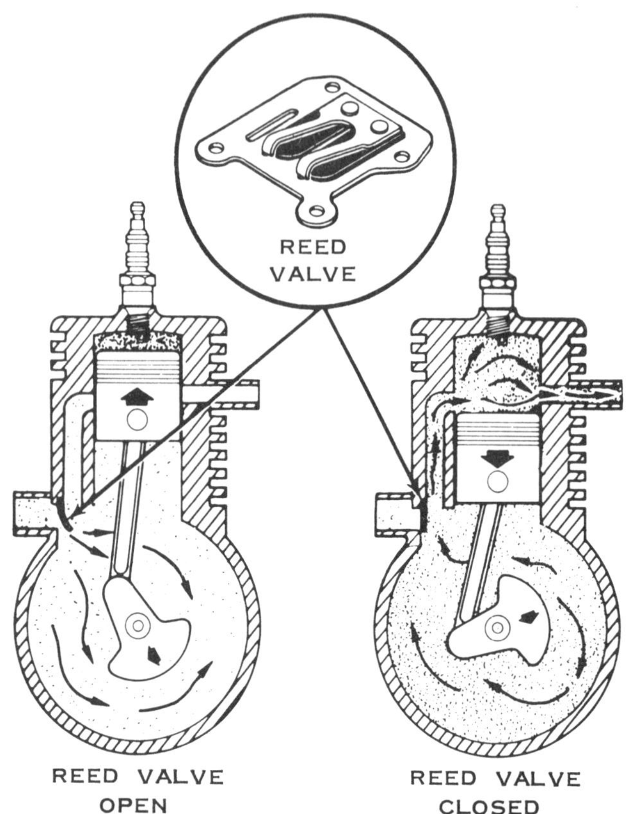

Reed valves are used to control the flow of fuel to the crankcase. As the piston moves upward in the cylinder, the resulting crankcase suction overcomes the spring tension of the reed, pulling the free end from its seat so that the air-fuel mixture can be sucked into the crankcase.

DETAILS OF THE ENGINE

All of the two-cylinder motors manufactured by the Outboard Marine Corporation are basically alike in construction details. Therefore, detailed repair instructions for the 18-40 Hp engines are covered through step-by-step illustrated sequences. The engineering design of the 50 Hp engine and that for the one-cylinder engine is similar to that for the other models, and the small differences are covered by exploded views and essential service notes.

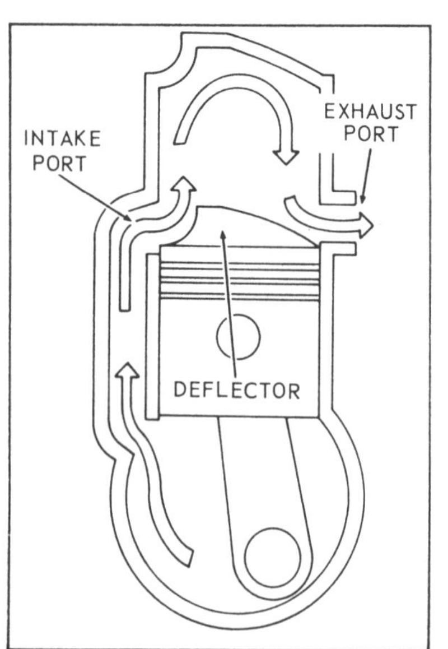

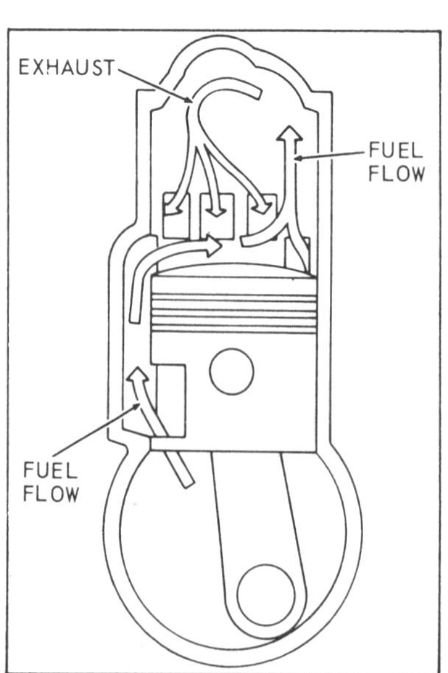

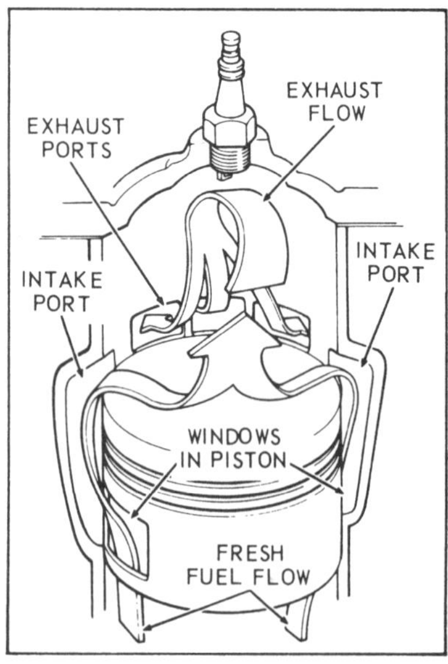

These drawings show the difference between a cross-flow type of combustion chamber (left) and the new loop-scavanged chamber (right two drawings). In the loop-scavenged system, the piston dome is rather flat. The incoming gases are deflected across the piston by the angular direction of the ports and drive out the exhaust gases, as shown at the right.

Before attempting to repair one of these engines, it is absolutely essential to invest in some special tools and equipment to do the job properly. Without the proper tools, some of the processes are exceedingly difficult, and the danger of damaging parts becomes greater.

GENERAL INSTRUCTIONS

Make sure that the work bench and surrounding areas are clean before starting to work. Use clean containers to hold the parts to keep them from being lost; biscuit tins do very nicely for screws, washers, nuts, and the other small parts. Use bread tins or coffee cans for the larger parts. Always keep replacement parts in their cartons or wrappers until ready for use. If parts are unwrapped, they are apt to get dirty, to be lost, or to be mixed with other parts which are similar.

When an engine comes into the shop for repair or overhaul, clean the exterior thoroughly. As the engine is disassembled, clean the parts in solvent and dry them with low-pressure compressed air.

ONE-CYLINDER ENGINE SERVICE NOTES

To disassemble the engine, remove the cover, carburetor, manifold, and fuel tank. Take off the flywheel, magneto cam, and magneto armature plate. Remove the spark plug. Remove the six screws hold-

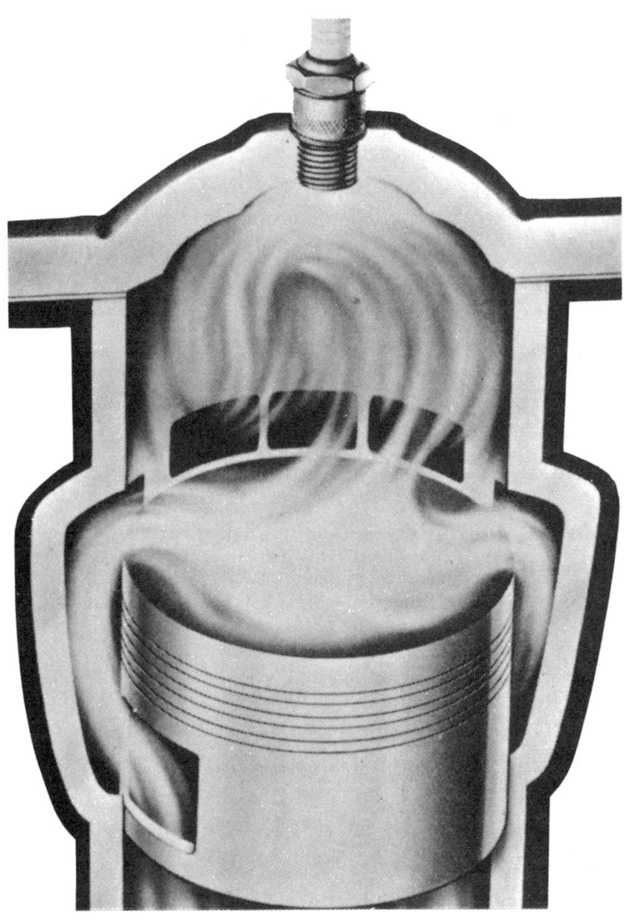

In the loop-scavenged engine, the intake gases are deflected across the top of the piston by the angle of the intake ports.

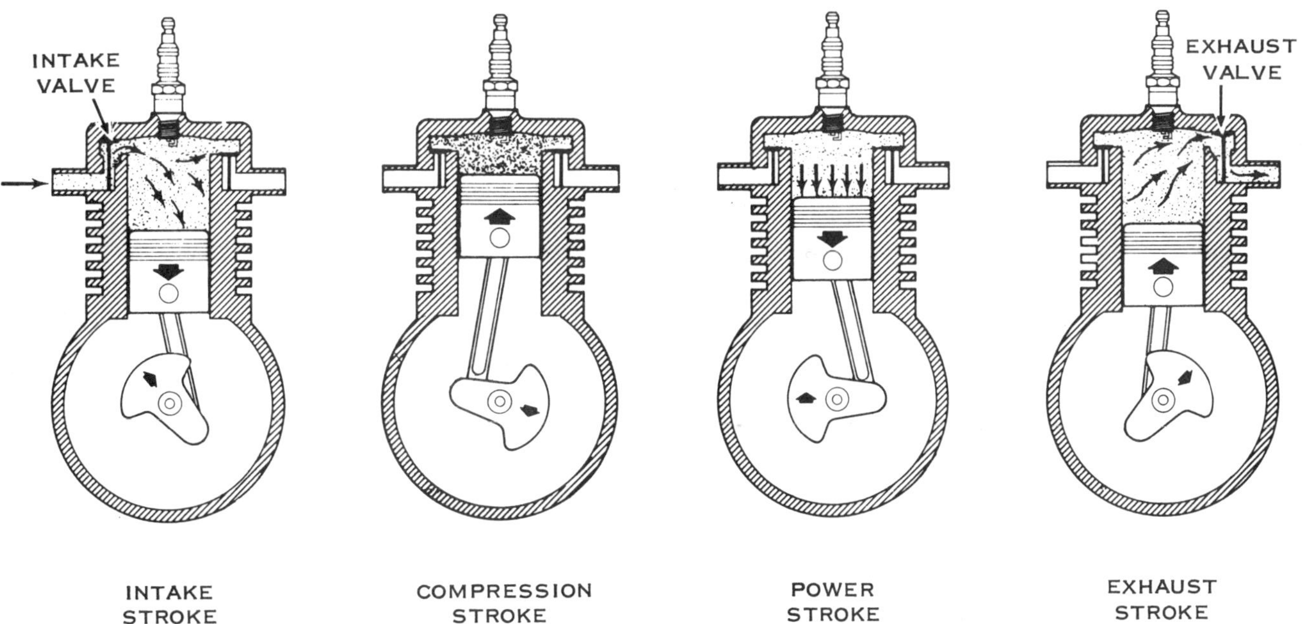

This diagram shows the four-stroke cycle gasoline engine, which fires every second time the piston reaches the top of its stroke. In other words, it takes four strokes of the piston to complete one entire cycle.

ing the powerhead to the exhaust housing, and then lift the powerhead to the bench for further work.

Use the exploded view to assist in disassembling the engine, making sure to note the special instructions which follow:

To remove the connecting rod screws, it is necessary first to bend back the lock plate tabs. If a tab is broken off, it is essential to find the piece so that it cannot remain in the engine to cause damage. Thirty (30) needle bearings are used in the connecting rod and cap. Be careful not to lose any needle bearings or the two connecting rod-to-cap dowels.

Measure the cylinder bore for wear, which must not exceed 0.002", or the cylinders should be rebored. A 0.020" oversize piston and ring set is available for service.

When installing a new wrist pin, it must be inserted through the slip-fit side of the piston (marked "L," for loose). The exhaust deflector side of the piston should be on the same side as the boss markings on the connecting rod and cap. When installed in the engine, the oil hole in the big end of the connecting rod must be facing up, and the exhaust deflector side of the piston should be facing the port side of the engine.

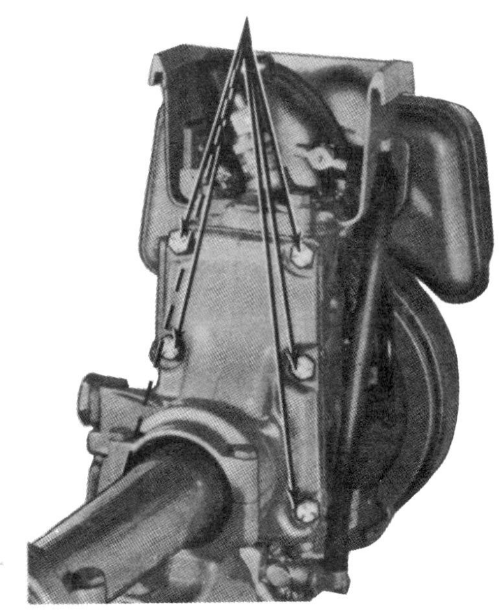

To remove the powerhead from the one-cylinder engine, take out the six screws from underneath, as shown.

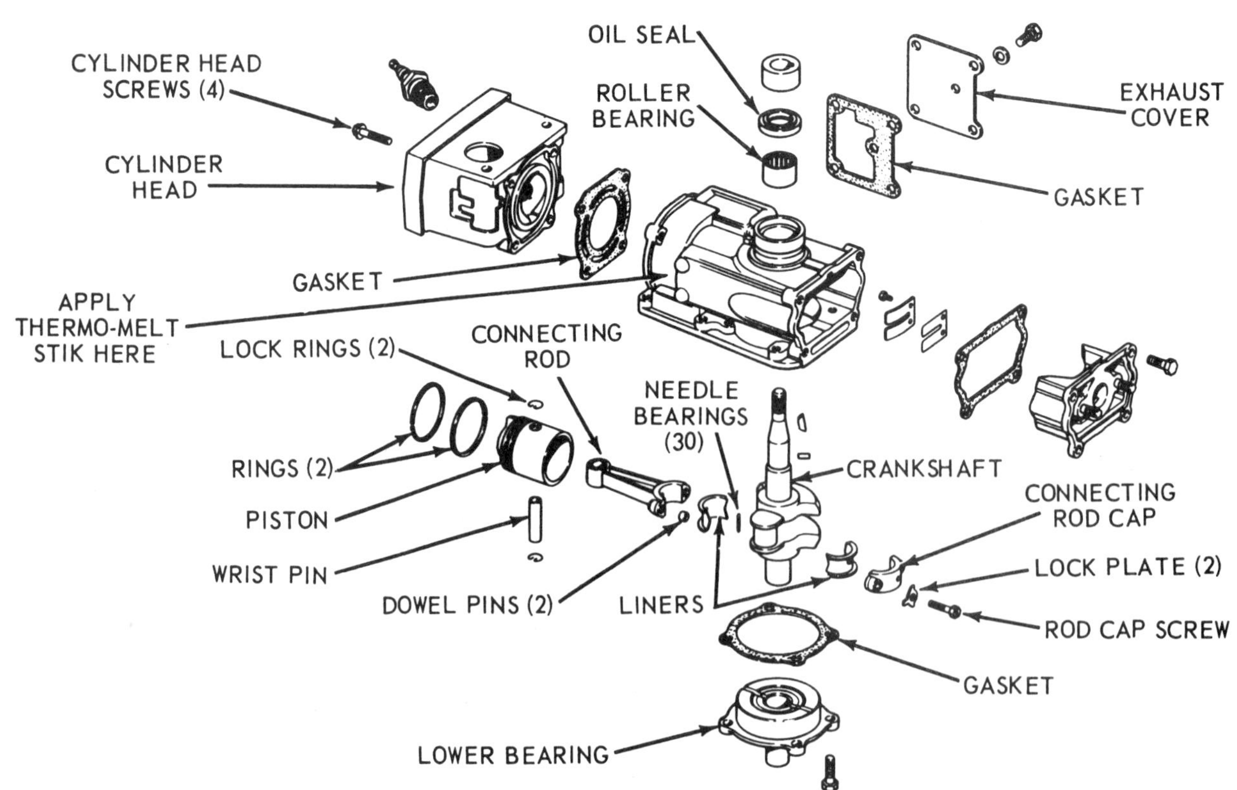

Exploded view of the parts of the powerhead of the one-cylinder engine.

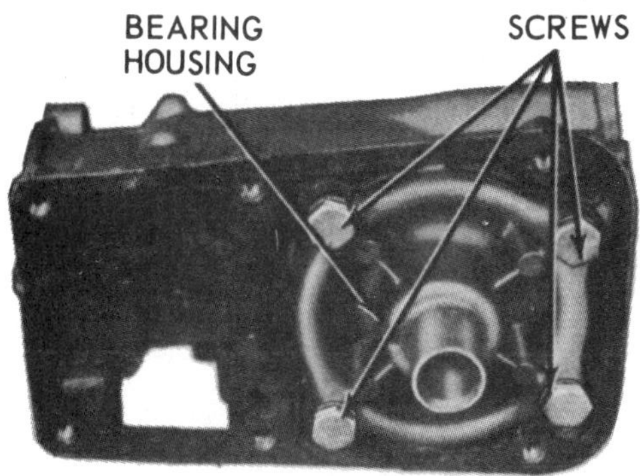

The crankshaft lower bearing is supported by four screws.

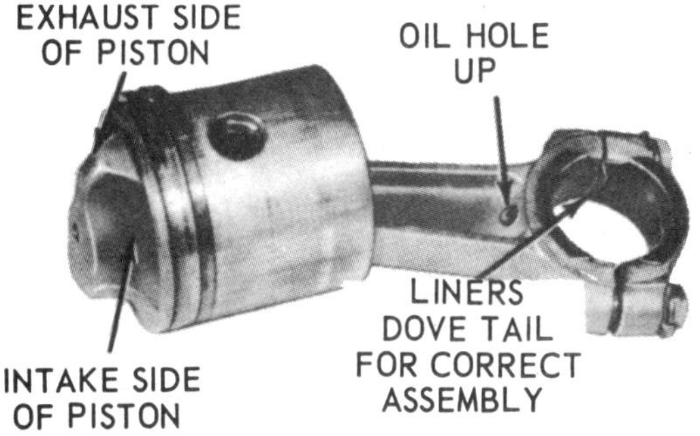

This picture shows how the piston should be assembled to the connecting rod.

When replacing the needle bearing inserts, make sure that the dovetail ends match when the connecting rod and cap are matched. When installing the connecting rod, position 14 needle bearings in the connecting rod, holding them in place with OMC

The slip-fit side of the piston is marked with an "L." The wrist pin must be installed from this side.

Needle Bearing Grease. Move the piston up so that the connecting rod bearings are against the crankpin. Apply some Needle Bearing Grease to the crankpin, and then install 16 needle bearings. Attach the cap, making sure that the dowel pins are in place. To check whether all of the needle bearings are in place, insert a small rod or piece of wire through the oil hole in the cap, as shown. It should not be possible to touch the crankpin with the wire, unless one of the needle bearings has been left out. Tighten the connecting rod screws to 60-66 in-lbs. of torque, and

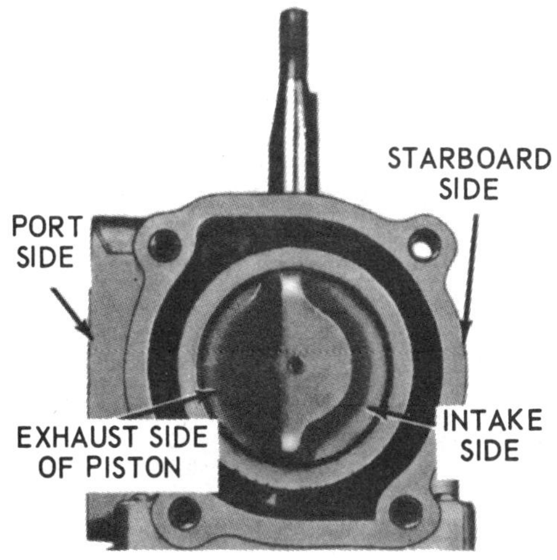

When installing the piston in the cylinder, make sure that the exhaust side of the piston is facing the port side of the engine.

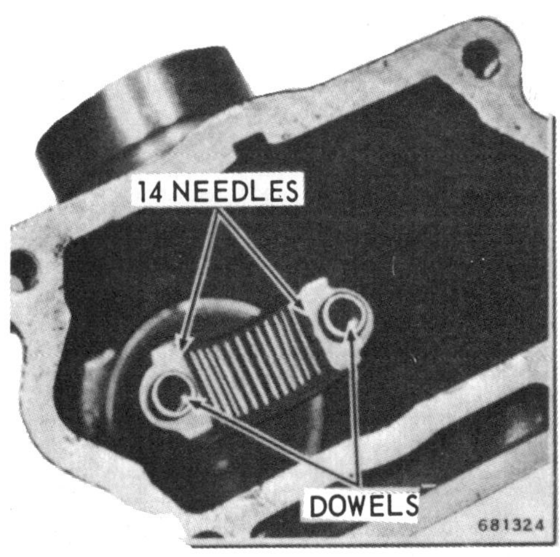

Install 14 needle bearings in the rod, holding them in place with OMC Needle Bearing Grease.

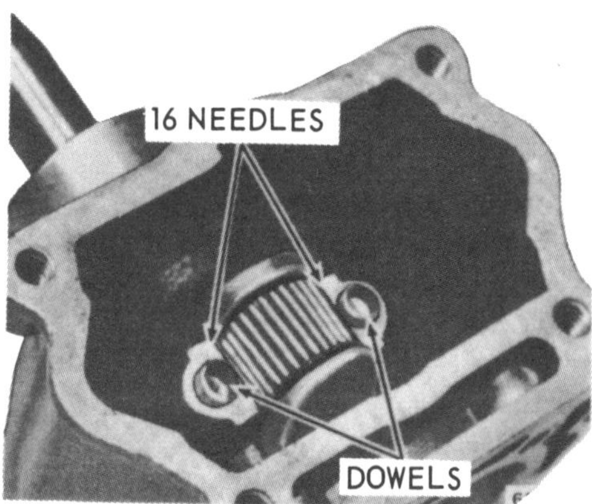

Position 16 needle bearings on the crankpin, as shown.

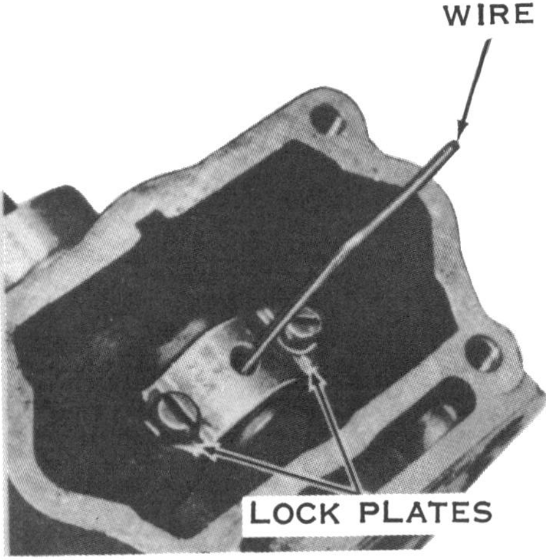

If the correct number of needle bearings has been installed, you should not be able to touch the crankpin with a piece of wire inserted through the oil hole.

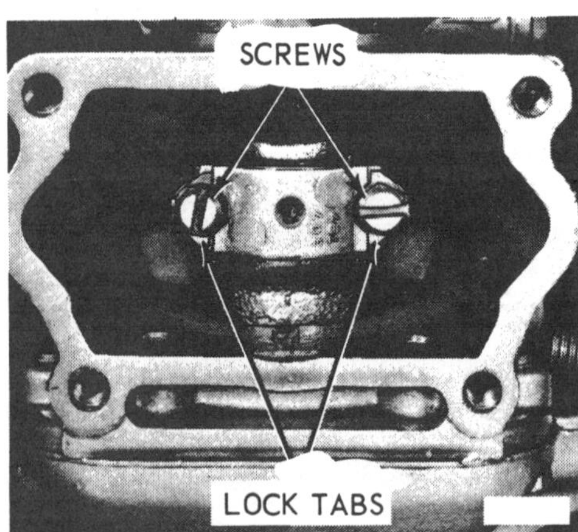

The locking tabs must be made to conform to the flat on the screw. CAUTION: Don't back off the screw to align the flat with the tab.

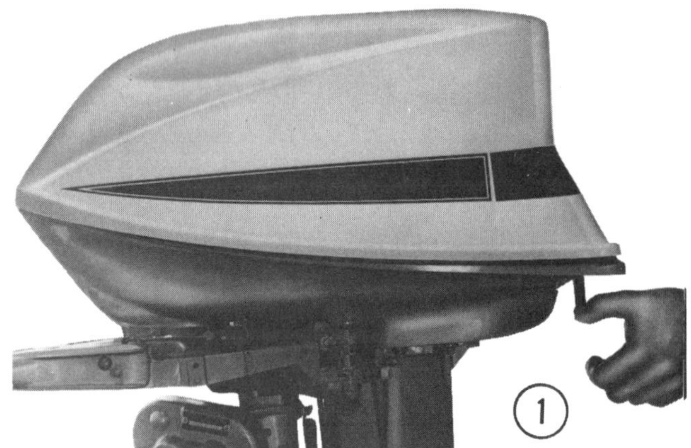

then bend up the locks. **CAUTION: Don't back off the screw if the locking tab does not fit against the flat on the screw. It is essential, instead, that the tab be made to conform to the flat on the screw.** Check the rod for binding; it must float freely over the full length of the crankpin.

When installing the magneto cam, make sure that the side marked TOP faces up.

Complete tuning instructions for the one-cylinder engine are covered in Chapter 3.

OVERHAULING A TWO-CYLINDER ENGINE

The following instructions specifically cover the 18/20 Hp engine, but they apply equally well to all two-cylinder engines. Specifications and tuning instructions may vary somewhat from the other engines; therefore, detailed specification charts for all engines are provided in this chapter. Tuning instructions for the other engines are covered in detail in Chapter 3.

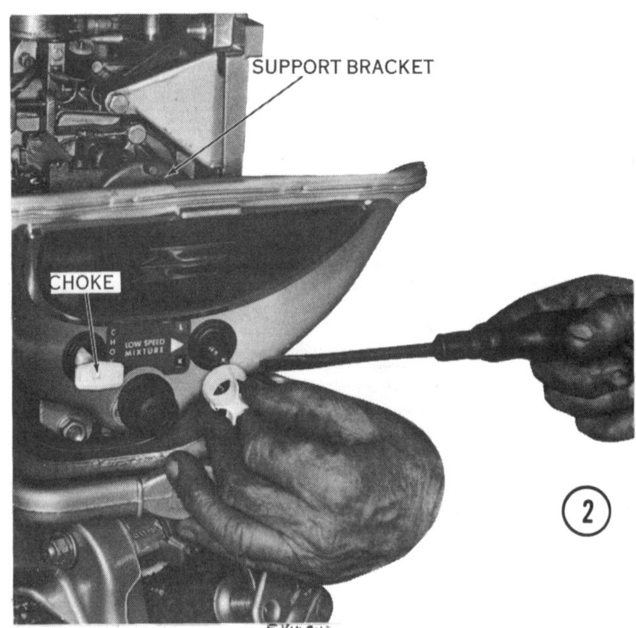

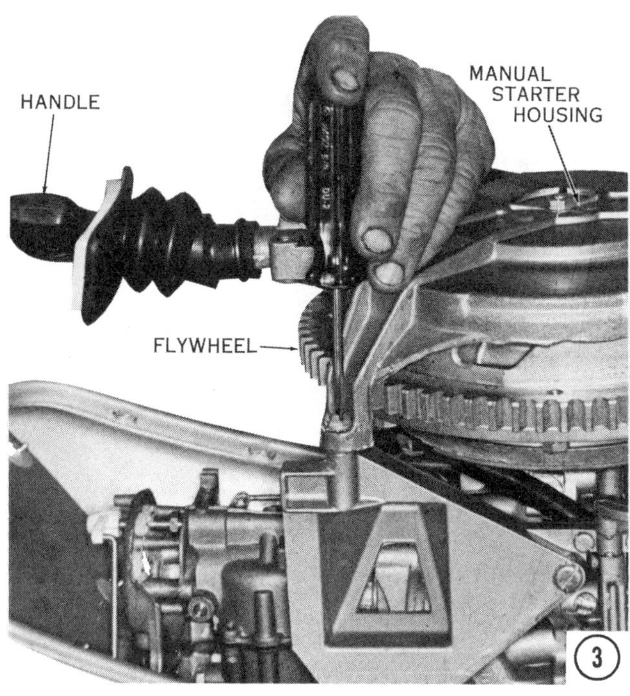

REMOVING THE POWERHEAD

① Remove the hood by depressing the latch and then lifting the hood from the front.

② Remove the low-speed mixture adjusting knob by prying it off with a screwdriver. Remove the arm from the low-speed adjusting needle valve. Lift up on the rear of the choke arm to disconnect the choke control shaft from the carburetor.

③ Remove the manual starter by taking out the three housing retaining screws and then lifting off the assembly.

④ Remove the flywheel nut. Keep the flywheel from turning with the special holding tool shown.

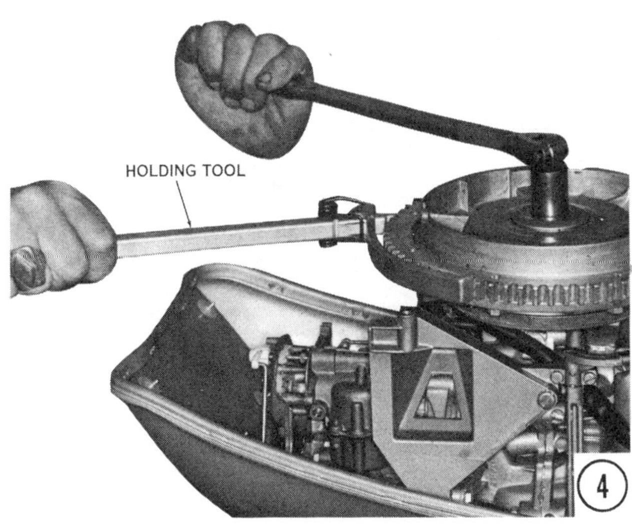

⑤ Attach a flywheel puller, Tool No. 378103, and then turn the center screw down until the flywheel is loosened. **CAUTION: Make sure that the screws holding the puller to the flywheel are tight, or you may pull out the threads.** *NOTE: It may be necessary to strike the center screw sharply with a medium weight hammer to break the taper fit, if it is tight.* Maintain upward pressure under the flywheel with your hands

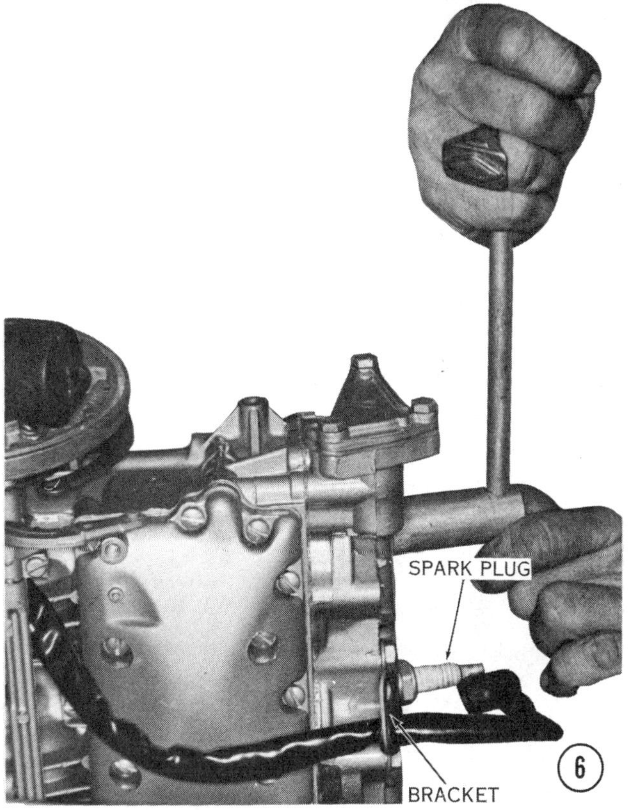

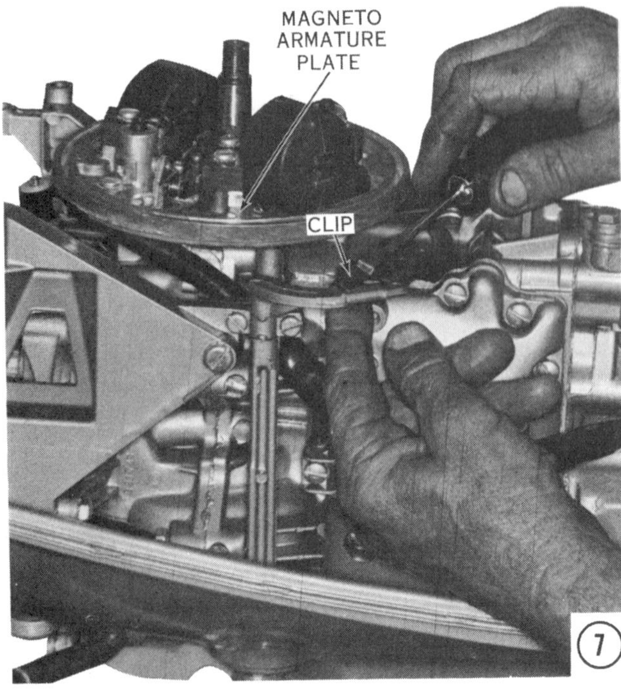

to keep the shock from being transferred to the crankshaft. Lift off the flywheel.

⑥ Twist the high-tension leads clockwise off the spark plugs. Remove the high-tension wire bracket on

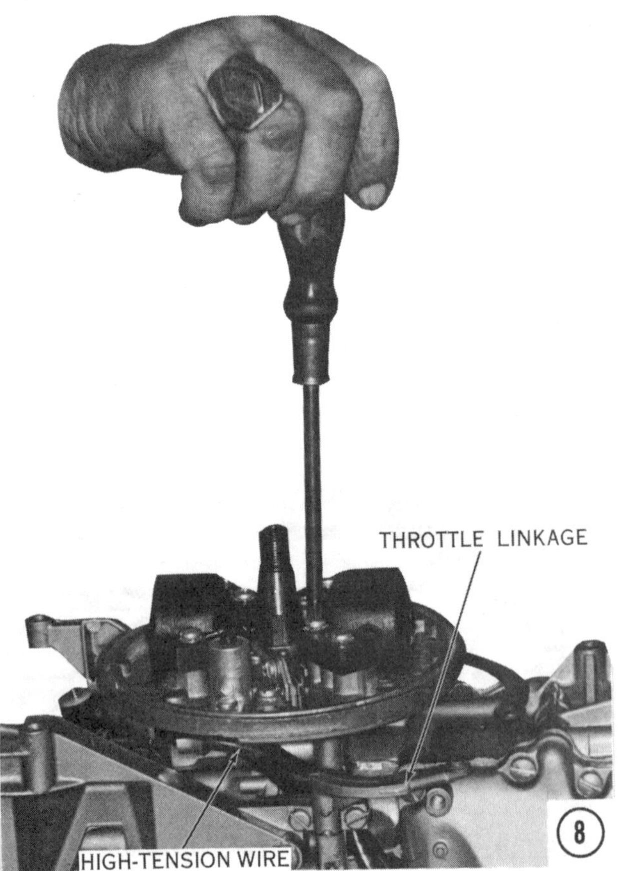

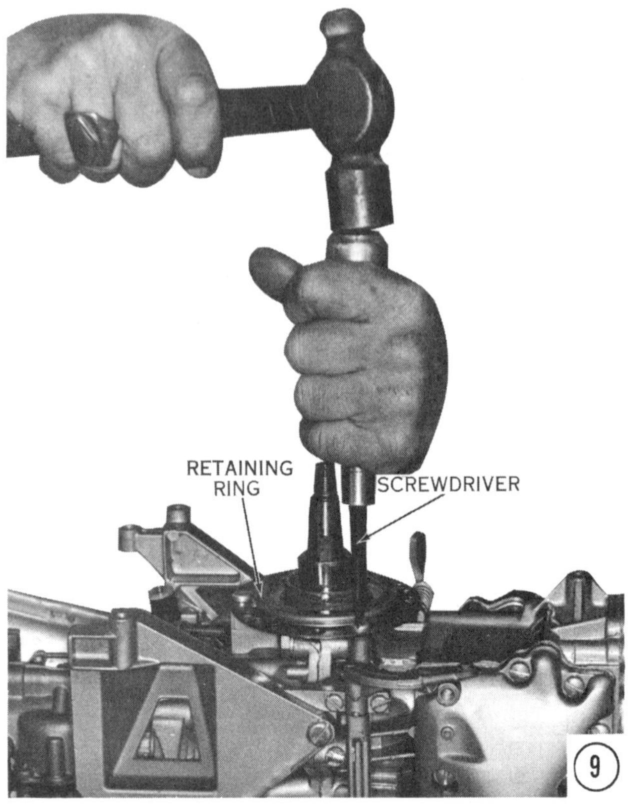

the cylinder head. Remove the spark plugs, supporting the end of the socket to keep it from tilting. **CAUTION: Unless the socket is properly supported, it may tilt and crack the porcelain.**

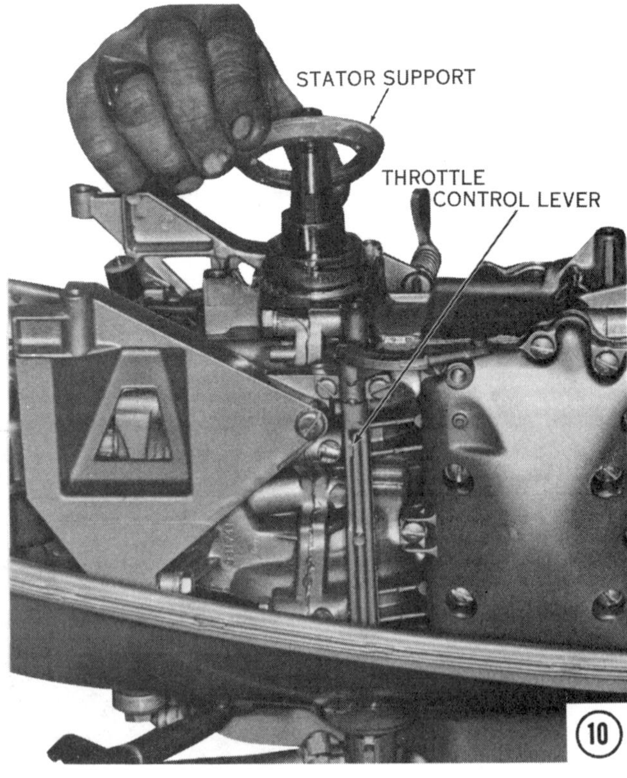

⑦ Remove the magneto armature plate link spring clip in order to disconnect the throttle linkage.

⑧ Take out the four Phillips-headed screws which hold the magneto armature plate to the powerhead. *NOTE: These screws have special split threads and it is necessary to lift them in order to engage a second set of threads after the first set of threads disengages.* Lift the magneto armature plate assembly from the powerhead by threading the wiring harness through the opening between the throttle linkage and the powerhead.

⑨ Remove the magneto armature plate support and the retaining ring. **CAUTION: It is necessary to use the special impact screwdriver shown in order to loosen the screws without damaging them.**

⑩ Take off the armature plate support. Note the way that the angled surface faces down. This is important when installing this plate because if it is installed in reverse, it is impossible to assemble the magneto armature plate properly.

⑪ Push the cam-follower roller forward so that you can remove the screw holding the throttle linkage to the cross-shaft. Disconnect the cam-follower spring which holds the roller in the retracted position.

⑫ Remove the two screws holding the linkage support to the carburetor, disconnect the linkage, and then lift out the support.

⑬ Remove the two nuts holding the carburetor to the powerhead, lift off the carburetor, and discard the gasket. Disconnect the fuel line at the carburetor. **CAUTION: Keep the free end of the line above**

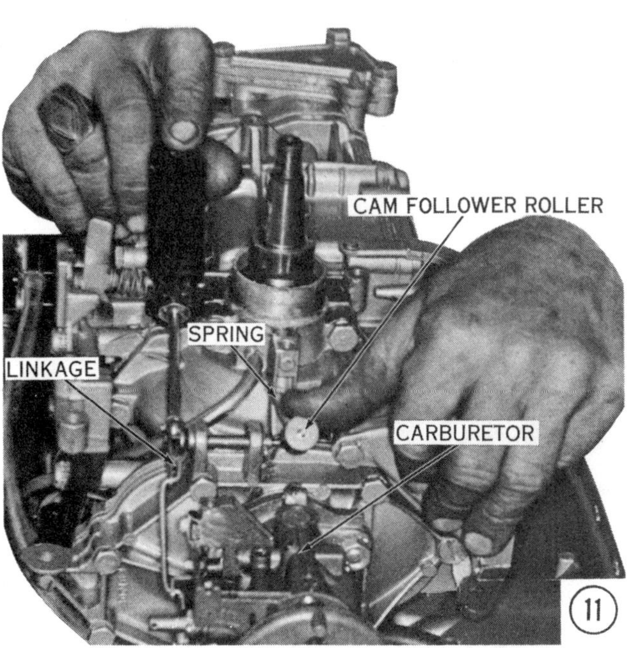

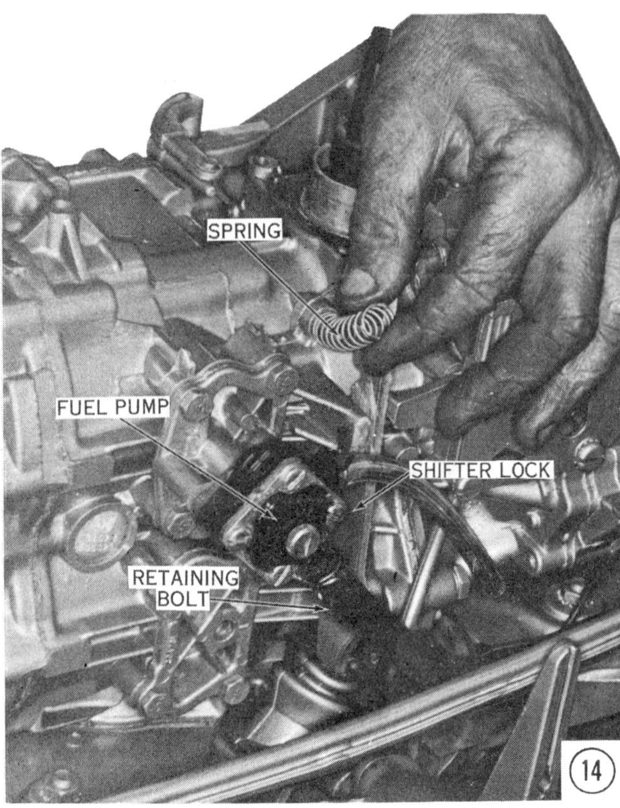

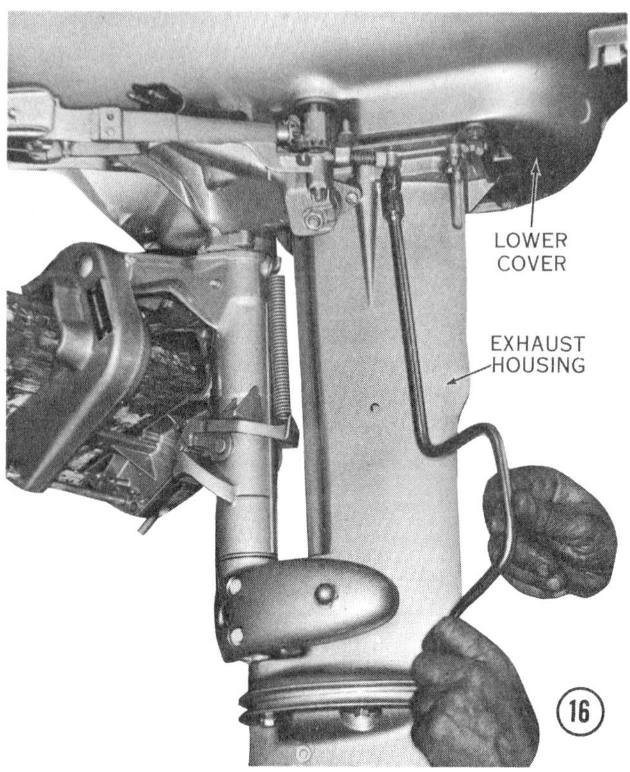

the level of the carburetor to prevent fuel from spilling into the lower cover.

⑭ Remove the shifter lock spring. Disconnect the two fuel lines to the fuel pump, and then remove the fuel pump in order to gain access to the shifter lock retaining bolt.

⑮ Remove the shifter lock retaining bolt. *NOTE: It is not necessary to detach the shifter lock from the rubber*

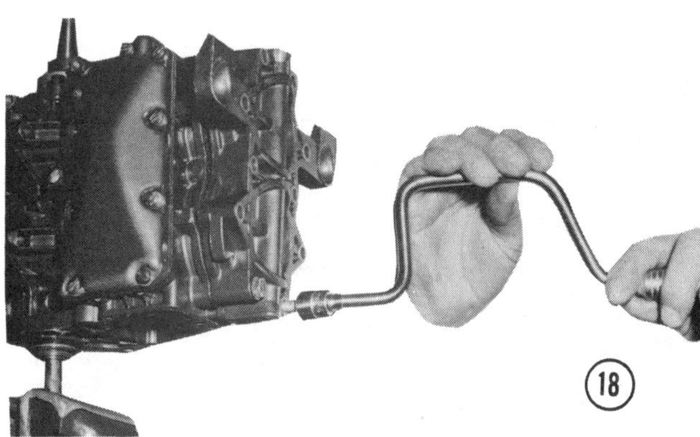

grommet. Remove the screws holding the port and starboard starter housing mounting brackets. The throttle control lever comes off with the port side starter housing mounting bracket.

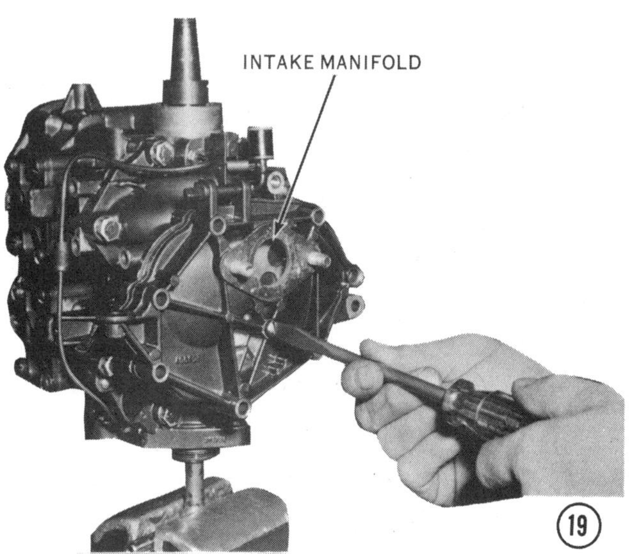

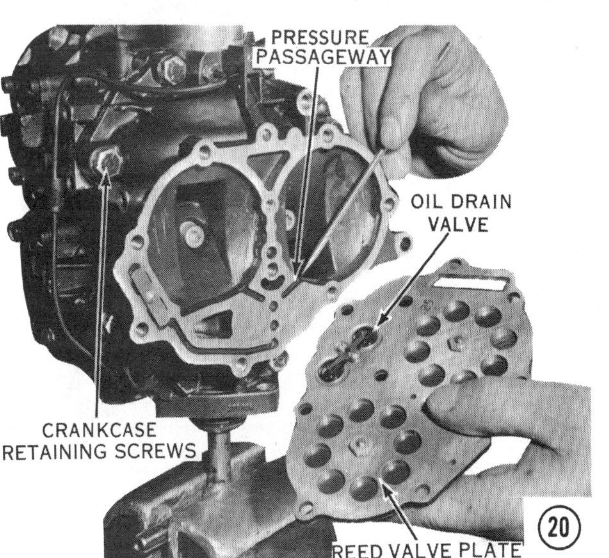

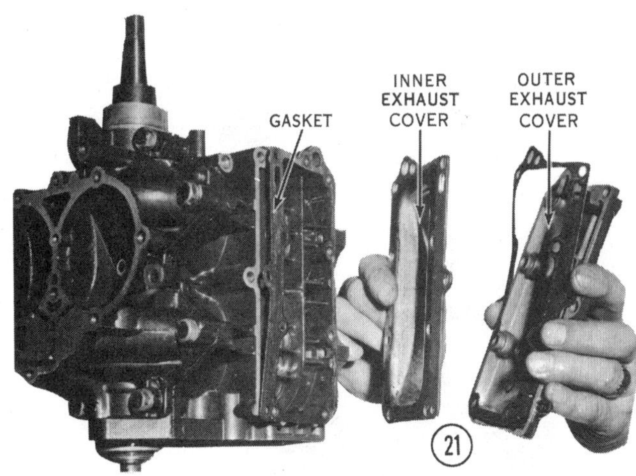

⑯ Remove the six hex-headed screws and one Phillips-headed screw which hold the powerhead to the exhaust housing. *NOTE: The Phillips-headed screw is located between the exhaust housing and the swivel bracket.*

⑰ Lift the powerhead up to disengage the crankshaft from the driveshaft splines, and then place the powerhead on a bench for disassembly.

DISASSEMBLING THE POWERHEAD

⑱ Take out the bolts holding the cylinder head, remove the head, and discard the gasket.

⑲ Remove the eight screws holding the intake manifold to the powerhead, and then lift off the manifold.

⑳ Take out the retaining screw, and then lift off the reed-valve plate assembly. Discard the gasket. Remove the drain valve.

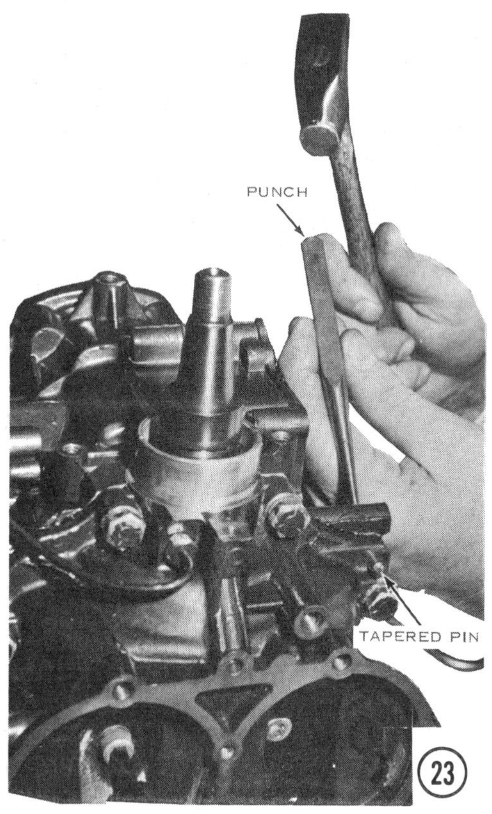

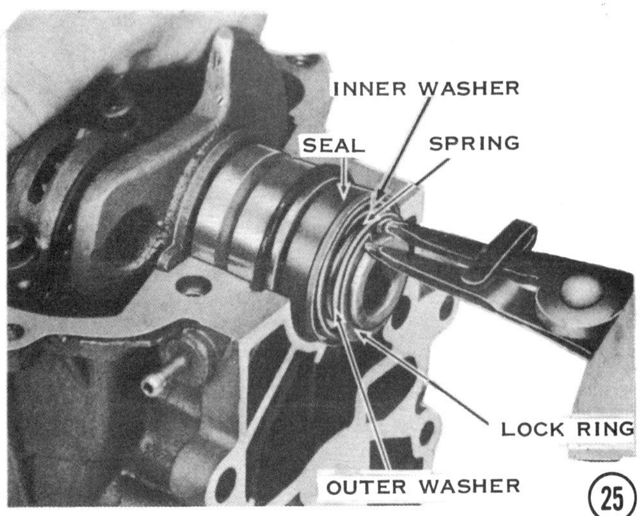

(21) Remove the bolts holding the exhaust cover, and then take off the outer and inner exhaust covers. Discard the gaskets. *NOTE: If pitting exists on the inner exhaust plate, install a new one.*

(22) Remove the bolts holding the two bypass covers to the powerhead. Take off the covers and discard the gaskets.

(23) Drive out the two tapered pins which align the crankcase halves. **CAUTION: Drive the pins out from the back of the crankcase.**

(24) Remove the two Allen-headed screws and the eight hex-headed screws holding the crankcase to the cylinder block. Tap the top side of the crankshaft with a rawhide mallet to break the seal between the crankcase and the cylinder block. Lift off the crankcase.

(25) Remove the carbon seal from the lower end

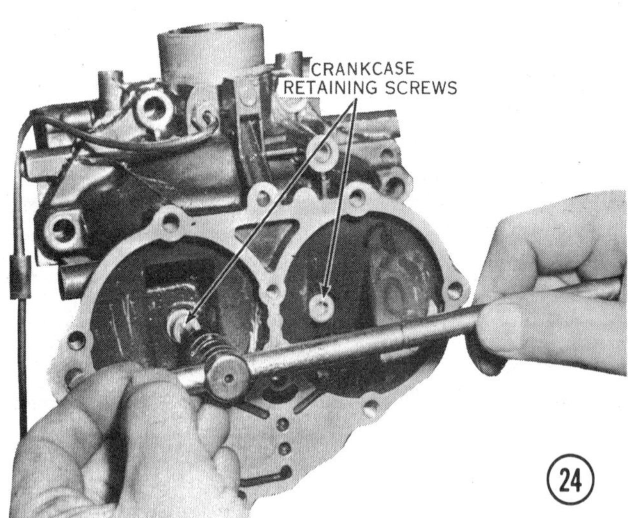

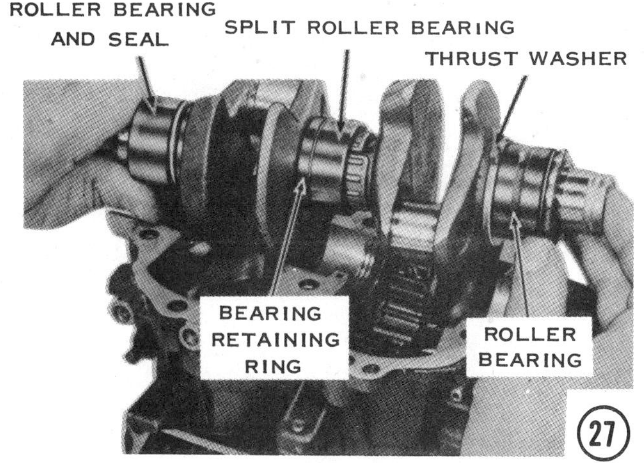

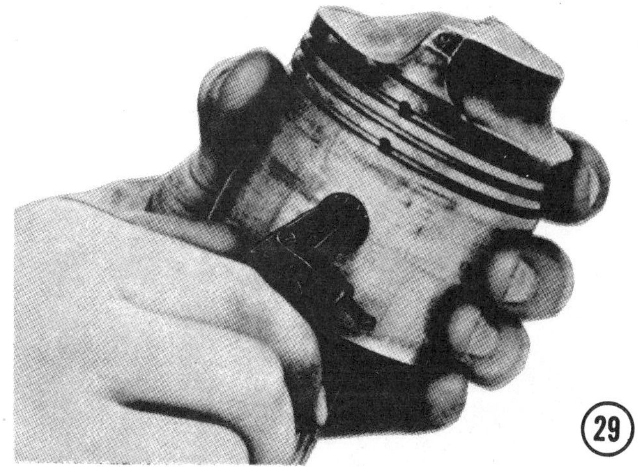

of the crankshaft by taking off the retaining ring with a pair of No. 2 Truarc pliers, Tool No. 303858. Remove the outer washer, spring, inner washer, and seal.

(26) Remove the connecting rod cap screws. Take off the caps and roller bearings. *NOTE: 15 rollers are used in each bearing.* **CAUTION: The pistons, connecting rods, caps, and bearing retainers are matched parts and seat with the operation of the engine. Because of this, it is essential to maintain their original positions during disassembly. Mark each connecting rod, cap, piston, and bearing component with tape to assure correct mating when they are assembled. Also mark the cylinders from which the parts are removed. CAUTION: Don't scribe the crown of the piston or you can start piston burning.**

(27) Lift the crankshaft from the cylinder block. Remove the crankshaft main bearings. Slide the center bearing retaining ring aside in order to be able to separate the center main bearing halves. Replace the matching caps on the proper connecting rods.

(28) Push the piston assemblies out of the bores. Remove the piston rings by prying the ends loose enough to grip them with pliers. Break the rings away from the pistons. **CAUTION: Don't try to save the old rings.** Always install a complete set of new piston rings during every powerhead overhaul.

(29) To detach the connecting rods from the pistons, use a pair of Truarc pliers, Tool No. 277152, to take out the retaining rings.

(30) Drive the wrist pin through the piston from the "loose" side (arrow). **CAUTION: When removing a wrist pin, the "loose" side of the piston must be facing up, and the driving tool must be applied through the "loose" side hole.**

PISTON RINGS

28

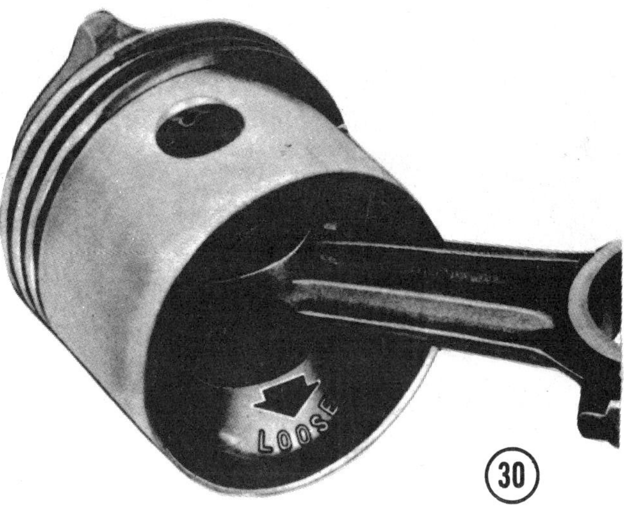

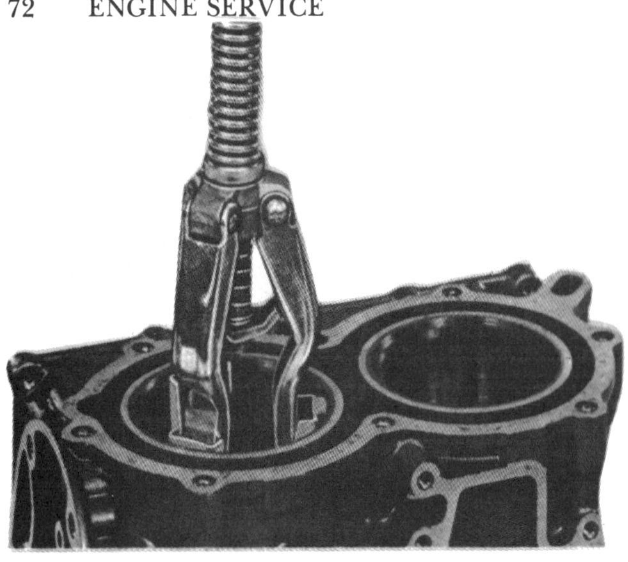

To remove the glaze, use a flexible hone. A few up-and-down strokes should provide the cross-hatched pattern so necessary for good ring break-in.

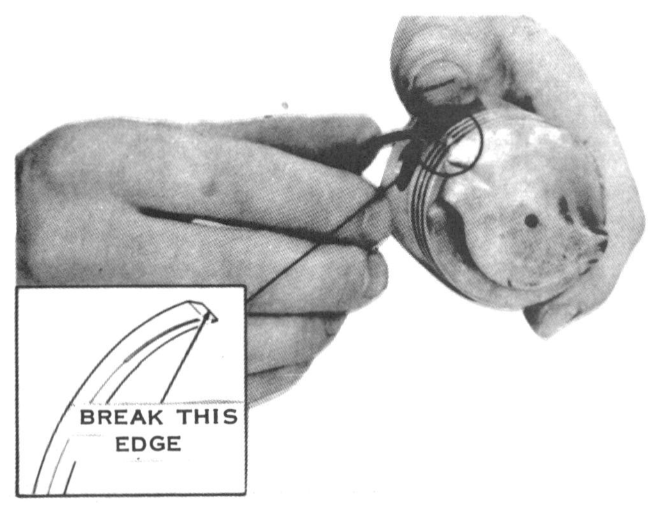

A piece of broken piston ring can be used as a scraper to remove the carbon from the ring grooves. CAUTION: The ring edges are very sharp. Use a rag to protect your hand against cuts.

CLEANING AND INSPECTING

Cylinder Block and Crankcase

Check the cylinder walls for excessive wear and the cylinder ports for carbon accumulation. The cylinder walls wear in varying degrees depending on lubrication and the conditions under which the engine is operated. Most wear is in the port area and the ring travel area. Check the cylinder for size and wall straightness by using an inside micrometer. If the wear is greater than 0.003″, replace the cylinder block or rebore it for oversize pistons. Piston and ring sets are available in 0.020″ and 0.040″ oversizes.

Carbon accumulations in the exhaust ports restrict the flow of exhaust gases and have a considerable effect on the performance of the engine. Carefully scrape the carbon from the cylinder heads and exhaust ports with a blunt instrument. The exhaust ports and all exhaust passages must be free of carbon deposits to insure maximum performance. **CAUTION: Avoid getting carbon particles in the water jackets. CAUTION: Don't scratch the gasket surfaces, or you will cause leaks.**

With continued engine operation, the cylinder walls take on a glaze which reduces the effectiveness of the seal between the piston rings and the cylinder walls. The result is reduced compression and a decrease in engine performance. Break the glaze by using a fine cylinder hone to refinish the walls. A few up-and-down motions of the tool should be sufficient to remove all cylinder wall glaze. Blow out all oil passages and drains.

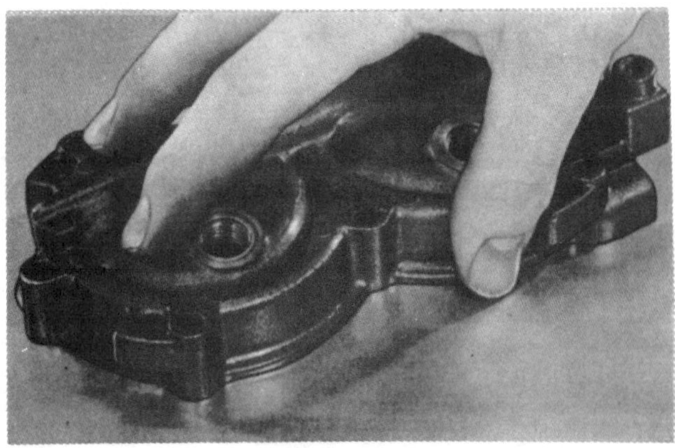

To dress the gasket surface of a cylinder head, move it over a piece of emery cloth on a surface plate.

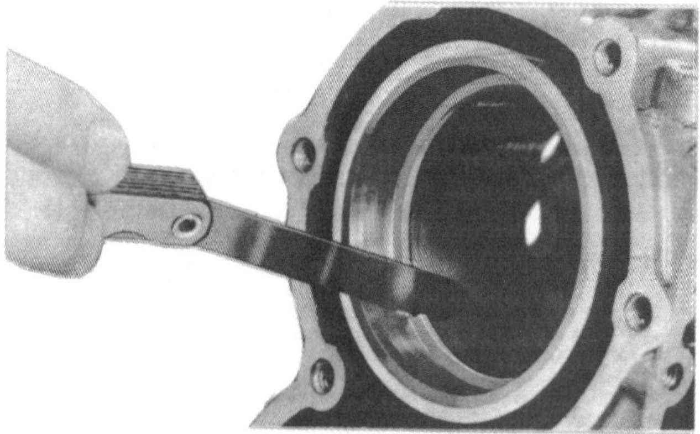

To measure the ring end gap, push the ring down into the cylinder bore with a piston to square it up.

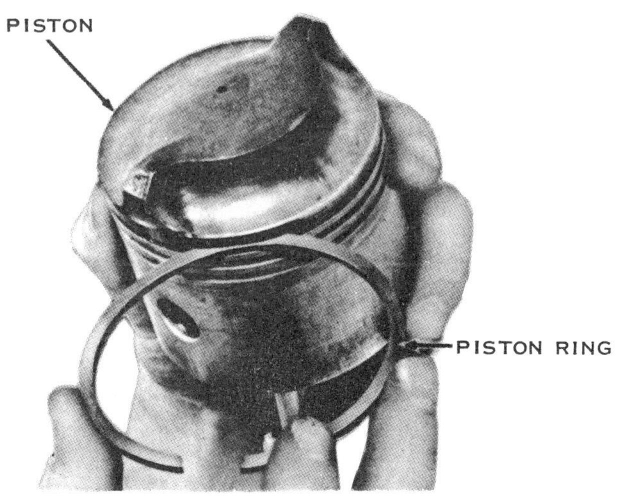

Make sure that the ring is free in the groove by rotating it around, as shown. Remove any burrs which restrict free movement of the ring.

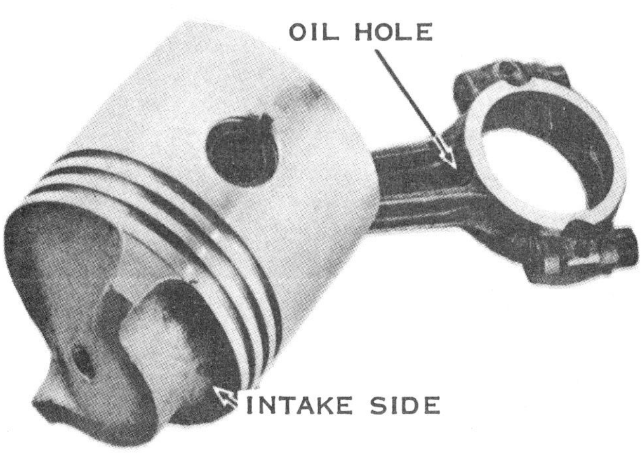

When assembling the piston to the connecting rod, make sure that the intake side of the piston is facing the direction shown when the oil hole in the rod is facing up.

Gasket Surfaces

Remove all traces of dried cement from the gasket surfaces, using lacquer thinner or trichloroethylene. Check all gasket faces for flatness. Under certain conditions, the faces may warp or spring, particularly where thin sections or flanges are employed and are subject to numerous temperature changes. To check for flatness, lay a sheet of No. 120 grit emery cloth on a surface plate or a piece of plate glass. Place the part to be surfaced on the emery cloth, and then move it slowly back and forth several times in a figure 8 motion, exerting light but evenly distributed pressure. If the surface is warped or sprung, the high spots making contact with the surface plate will take on a dull polish, while the low areas will retain their original state. To insure flatness, continue surfacing until the entire gasket surface is polished to a dull luster. Finish surfacing with 180 grit emery cloth.

Measure the side clearance of each new piston ring and check the measurement against specifications.

Bearings

All areas where bearings are to be serviced should be kept free from accumulations of oil and dirt to avoid contaminating the bearings. Place the bearings in a wire basket and immerse them in a solvent such as Solvasol. The tank should have a screened false bottom to prevent settlings from being stirred up. Agitate the basket frequently until the grease, oil and sludge are thoroughly loosened and can be flushed out. Bearings that contain especially heavy carbon deposits or hardened grease should be soaked in a separate container of solvent.

Use a spray gun with an air filter to apply the cleaning solvent. Use clean solvent to flush each bearing until all dirt and residue are removed. Since dry bearings rust rapidly, lubricate them at once with light, clean oil. After draining the excess oil, place them in a covered container until ready for assembly.

Discard bearings which show any of the following: (1) Rusted rollers or raceways. (2) A fractured ring. This may be caused by forcing a cocked bearing off a shaft or by too heavy a press-fit. (3) Worn, galled, or abraded surfaces. These may be caused by too loose a fit or a bearing locked by dirt and turning on the shaft or in the housing. (4) Badly discolored rollers and races. This is usually due to an inadequate supply of lubricant. Moderate discoloration is not a cause for rejection.

Carefully remove all carbon deposits from inside of the piston head. Inspect the ring grooves for carbon accumulation, excessive wear, or damage to the groove walls. Carefully scrape all carbon from the ring grooves, making certain that the carbon clinging to the bottom and sides of the grooves has been thoroughly removed. **CAUTION: Don't scratch the grooves.** A tool for cleaning the ring grooves can be made by breaking an old ring, grinding an angle on the edge, and then breaking the lower sharp edge to prevent damaging the lower ring land. **CAUTION: Care must be taken not to damage the lower ring lands, which are the ring sealing surfaces. CAUTION: The edges of a worn ring are very sharp and it should be handled with a rag to prevent cuts.**

Before installing new piston rings, check the gap between the ends of each ring by placing it in its cylinder bore and then pushing the ring down in the bore slightly with the bottom of a piston, which will square it up.

Check each ring and groove for side clearance with a feeler gauge.

Always replace all gaskets and O-ring seals.

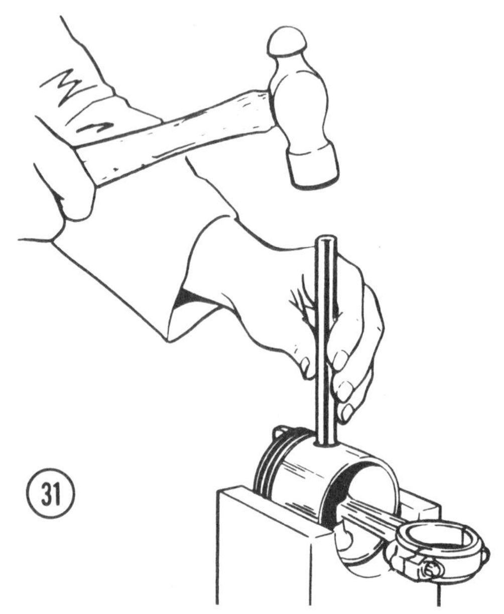

ASSEMBLING

(31) To assemble the connecting rod to its piston, lubricate the wrist pin, making sure that the surfaces are clean. Place a drop of oil in each pin hole. Posi-

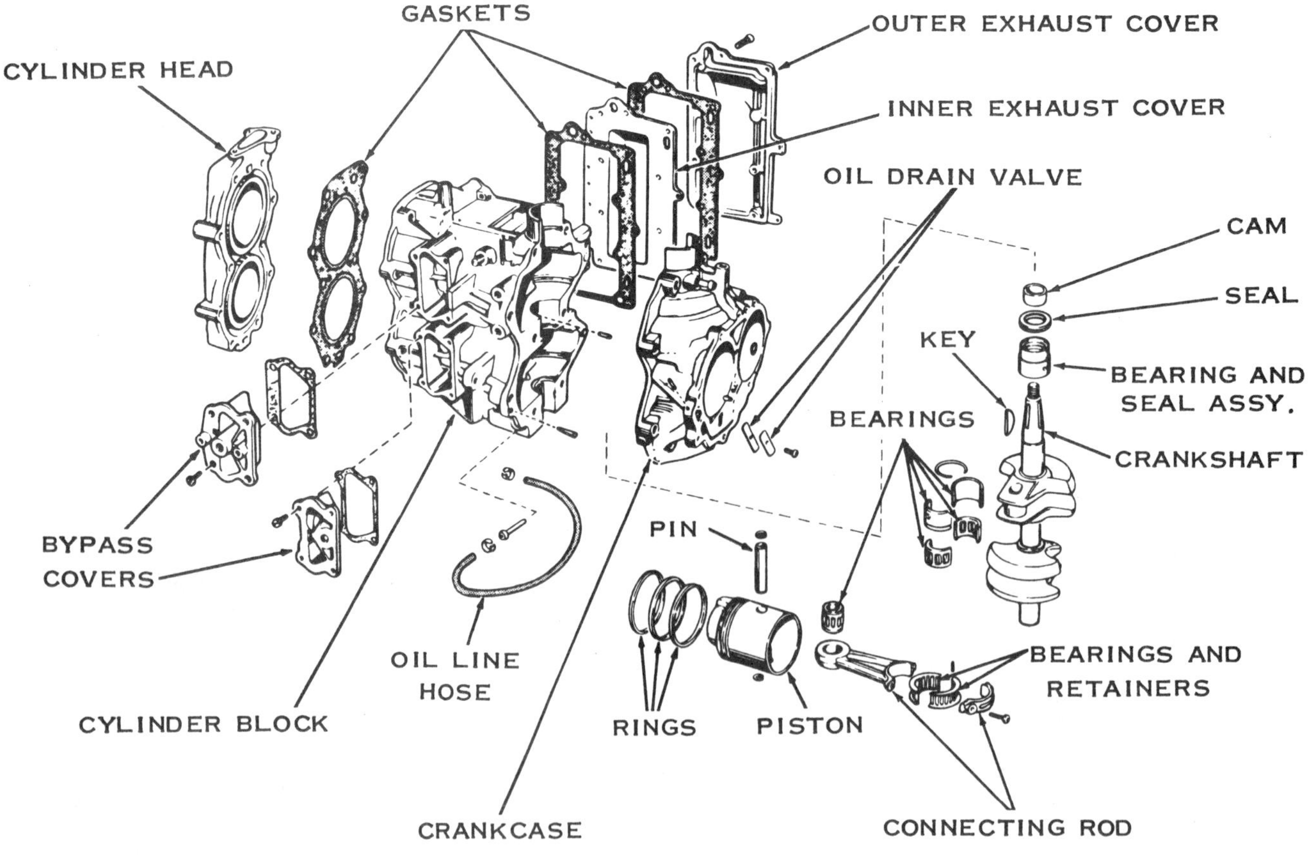

Exploded view of the parts of the 18-40 Hp engines.

tion the needle bearings in the small end of the connecting rod, and then insert the wrist pin through the "loose" side of the piston. Use a fixture to support the piston to guard against distortion or damage. Drive the pin through the hole. *NOTE: This can be accomplished easier if the piston is heated slightly to expand it.*

(32) Replace the lock rings, making sure that they seat securely in the grooves. **CAUTION: The square side of the lock ring must face out.**

(33) Check each piston with a micrometer to determine whether it has been distorted during assembly of the wrist pin. If necessary, tap the high side with a light mallet to restore the original roundness. **CAUTION: Don't use a steel hammer.**

(34) Install new piston rings on each piston. Spread each ring with a ring expander tool just enough to slip it over the head of the piston and down into place. Make sure that the rings fit freely in the ring grooves. *NOTE: The ring grooves are pinned to keep the rings from turning. This is done primarily to prevent the ends of the rings from catching on the edges of the ports in the cylinders; it also assures staggered ring gaps.* Coat the pistons and cylinder bores with oil, and then install each piston and connecting rod assembly, making sure to match each assembly to the cylinder from which it was removed. The deflector on the intake side of the piston must be facing toward the intake port, as shown. The piston rings must be compressed before the piston can be installed in the cylinder. **CAUTION: Make sure that the rings are correctly positioned with their gaps over the pins. CAUTION: Don't use an automotive-type ring compressor or the ring end could hang up on the pin and break. Use an approved compressor or start the rings into the cylinder with your fingers. CAUTION: Proceed slowly and don't force the piston into the cylinder. Also, make sure that the parts are free from dirt and grit.** Perfectly good cylinder walls, pistons, and rings can be ruined in a few minutes of engine operation when care is not exercised in keep-

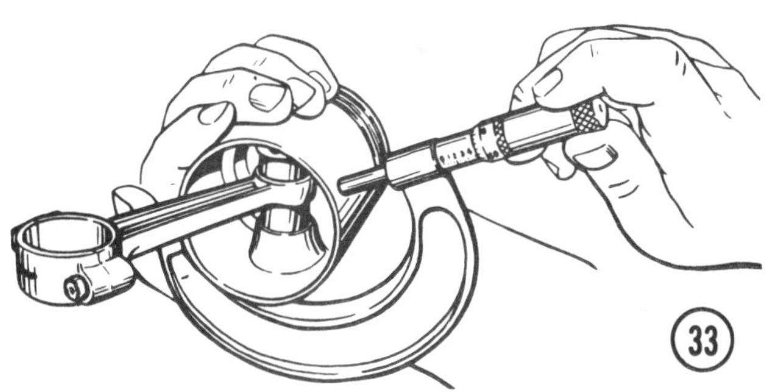

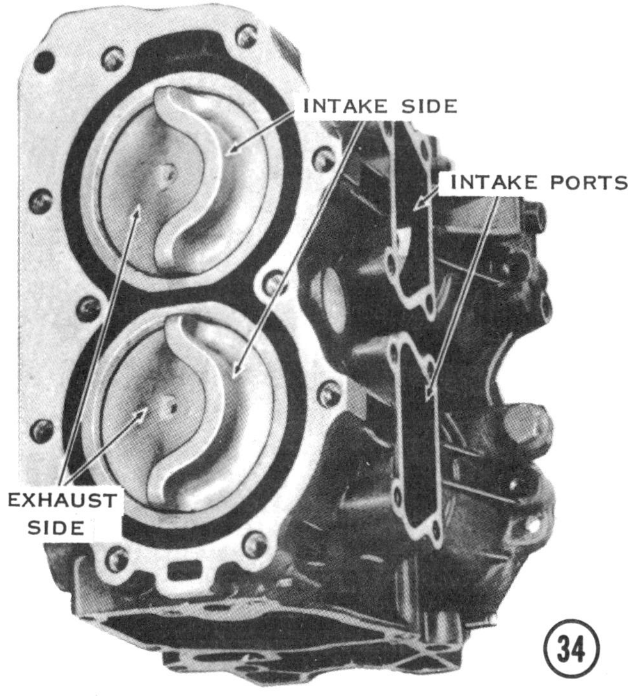

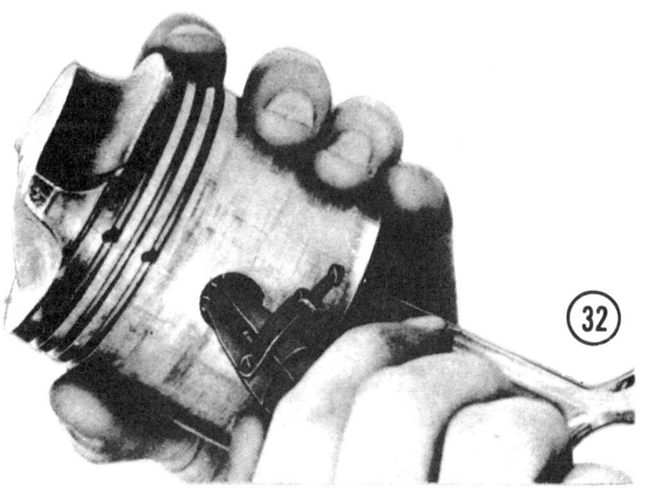

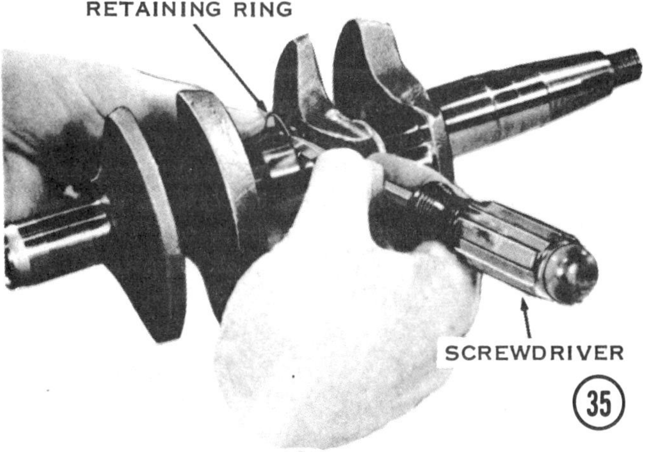

ing the parts clean. Work in clean surroundings and with reasonably clean hands. Coat all bearing surfaces, cylinder walls, and other parts with clean oil before assembling them.

(35) Install the center main bearing retainer halves, with the retaining ring groove toward the top end of the crankshaft. Secure the bearing halves with the retaining ring. Position the other main bearings on the crankshaft, and then install a new O-ring seal on the lower bearing.

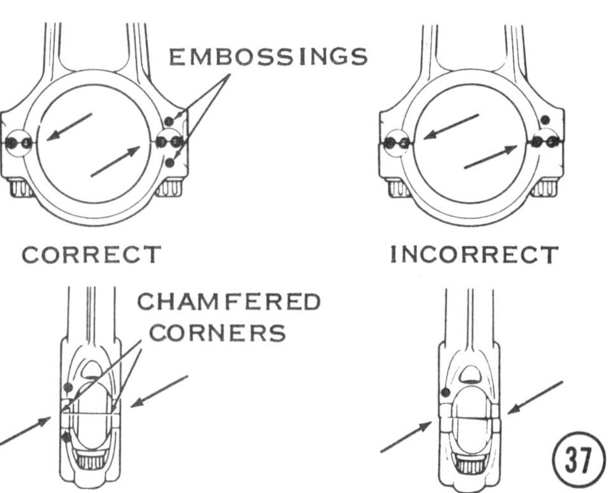

(36) Apply a coat of OMC Needle Bearing Grease or vaseline to both halves of the retainers to hold them in place, and then install the retainers in the connecting rods. **CAUTION: Heavier greases will cause bearing failure. CAUTION: The bearing retainer halves are matched. Don't interchange the retainer halves or turn them end for end. The notched ends must be facing each other.** Lower the crankshaft onto the cylinder block, aligning the connecting rods with the journals and the main bearings with the dowel pins in the block. **CAUTION: Make sure that each bearing shell is properly positioned over its dowel pin; otherwise, you could drive the pin into the block as you tighten the case screws, and this will ruin the block.**

(37) Position the smaller retainers, with roller bearings, over the crankshaft, and then install the connecting rod caps. **CAUTION: The rod caps are not interchangeable with those of other rods, nor should the caps be turned end for end.** To assist in correct assembly, small embossings are provided on the matching sides of each rod and cap. Draw a pencil over the chamfered corners on both sides to make sure that the cap and rod are aligned at the parting joint. If they are not properly matched, the extended edges can be felt with the pencil point. **CAUTION: Misalignment will affect the normal free action of the roller bearings, resulting in damage to the parts.**

(38) Tighten the connecting rod cap screws to 180-186 in-lbs. of torque. **CAUTION: The bearing retainers must rotate freely on the crankpins.**

(39) Apply a thin line of Sealer 1000 to the faces of the crankcase. **CAUTION: Don't use too much, or the excess will squeeze out and foul the oil channels.** Install the crankcase and tighten the screws finger-tight. Replace the taper pins, driving them in carefully with a hammer. Torque the upper and lower retaining screws to 110-130 in-lbs. and the center screws to 120-130 in-lbs. Check for binding by rotating the crankshaft clockwise from the flywheel end.

(40) Install a new carbon seal at the lower end of the crankshaft. Replace the inner washer, spring, and outer washer, securing the assembly with a new Truarc ring.

(41) Replace the oil drain valve, making sure that the valve seats properly and that the space between it and the stop is 0.040". If necessary, bend the stop as required.

(42) The proper operation of the reed valves is essential to good engine performance. The importance of keeping the reeds free from distortion cannot be overemphasized. Replace any reed or stop which shows evidence of distortion or damage. The reeds must maintain contact with the plate until a predetermined pressure is exerted by the vacuum in the crankcase. Reed travel is limited by the reed stop. When crankcase vacuum drops, spring action holds the reeds

40

39

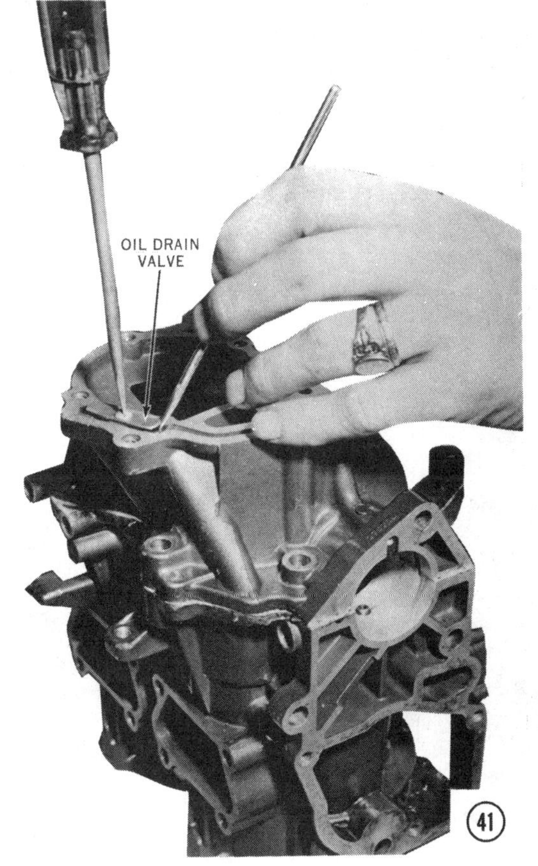

41

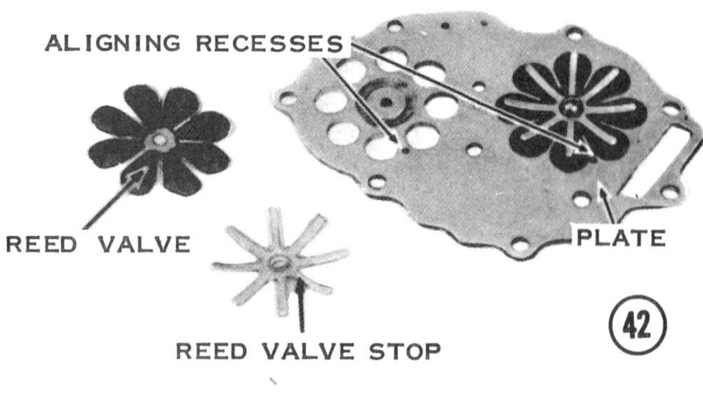

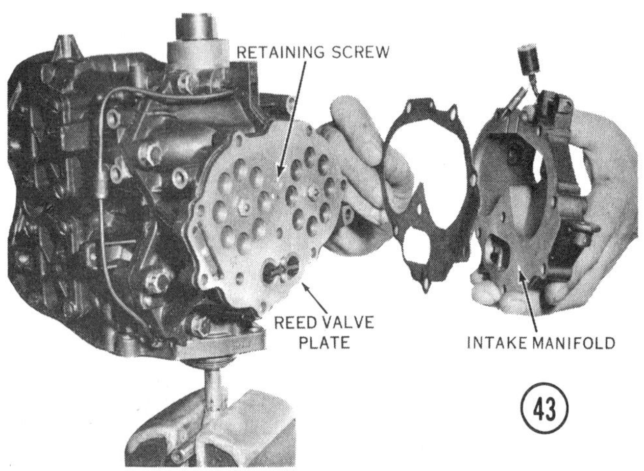

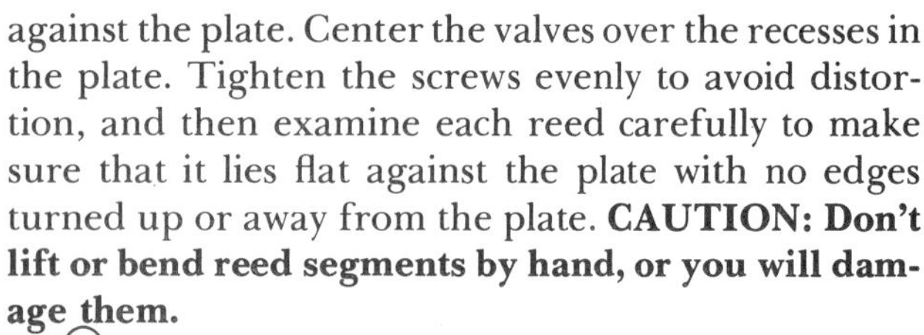
against the plate. Center the valves over the recesses in the plate. Tighten the screws evenly to avoid distortion, and then examine each reed carefully to make sure that it lies flat against the plate with no edges turned up or away from the plate. **CAUTION: Don't lift or bend reed segments by hand, or you will damage them.**

(43) Install the assembled reed-valve plate to the crankcase, using a new gasket. Tighten the retaining screw securely. Position a new intake manifold gasket on the reed-valve plate, and then install the intake manifold. Tighten the eight screws securely.

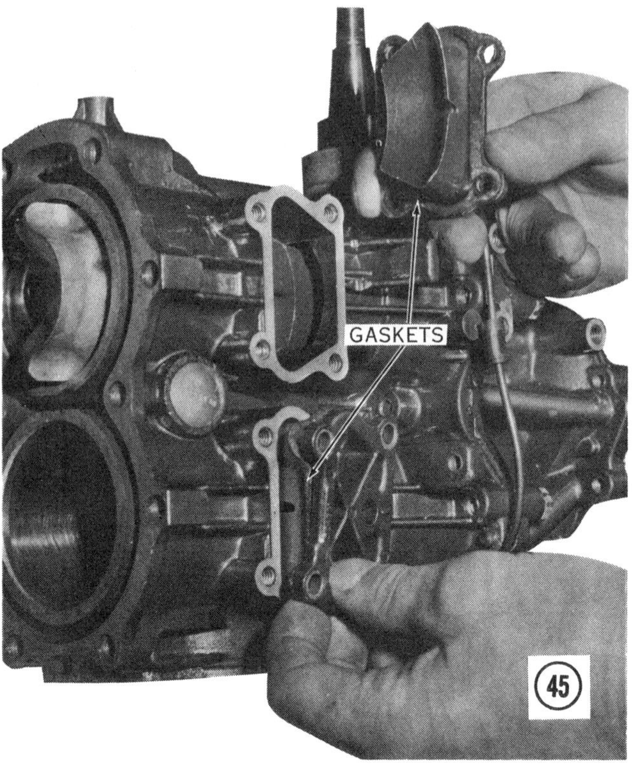

(44) Replace the inner and outer exhaust covers, using new gaskets. Install all screws finger-tight before tightening any of them.

(45) Replace the bypass covers, using new gaskets. Tighten the retaining screws securely.

(46) Install the cylinder head, using a new gasket. Tighten the head bolts to 96-120 in-lbs. of torque, following the sequence shown. *NOTE: The cylinder head screws must be torqued to the same specifications after the engine has been tested and has cooled off.*

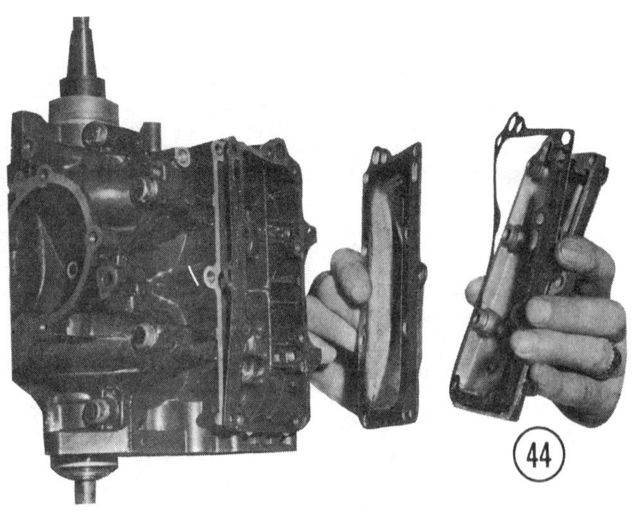

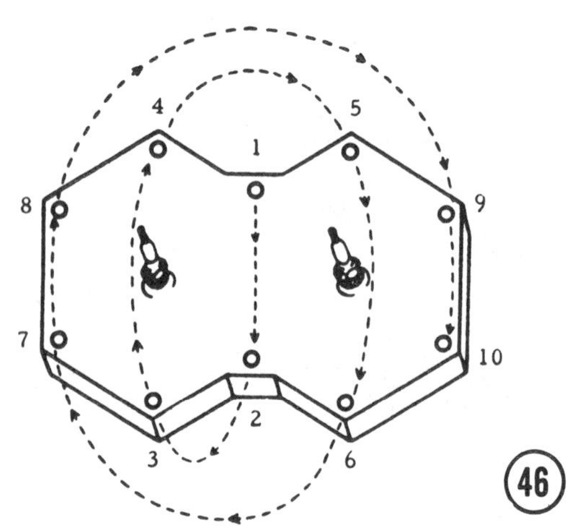

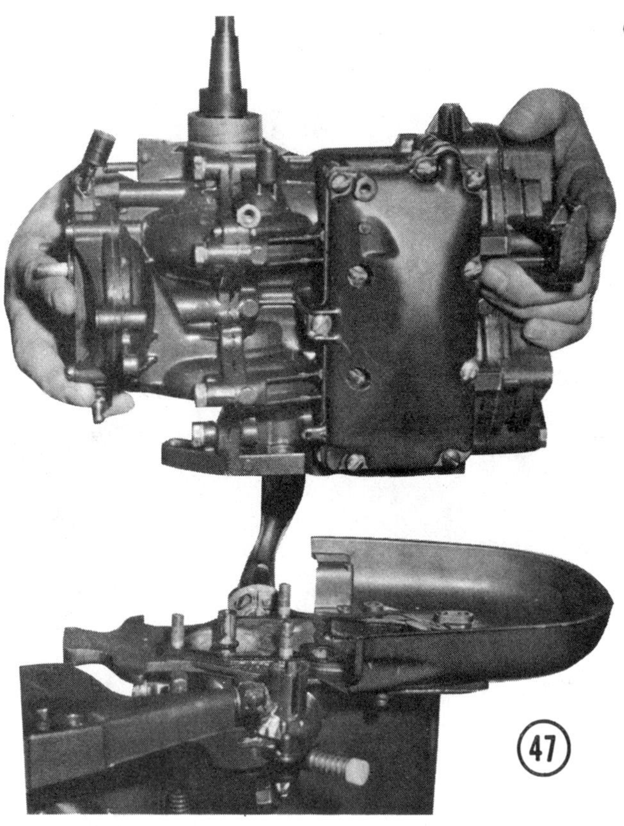

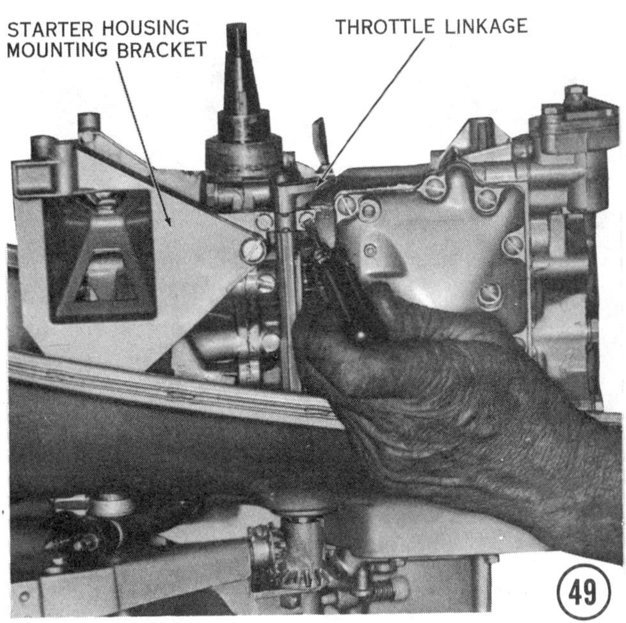

INSTALLING THE POWERHEAD

(47) Make sure that the gasket surfaces of the powerhead and the exhaust housing are clean. Position a new gasket on the exhaust housing, and then lower the powerhead onto the exhaust housing, taking care to avoid damaging the splined ends of the crankshaft and driveshaft. *NOTE: The splines can be engaged with ease if the crankshaft is rotated in a clockwise direction as the powerhead is lowered into position.* **CAUTION: Don't rotate the crankshaft counterclockwise, or you will damage the water pump impeller.**

(48) Install the seven screws holding the powerhead to the exhaust housing. *NOTE: The Phillips-headed screw should be installed between the exhaust housing and the swivel bracket.*

(49) Install the starter housing mounting brackets and the throttle linkage.

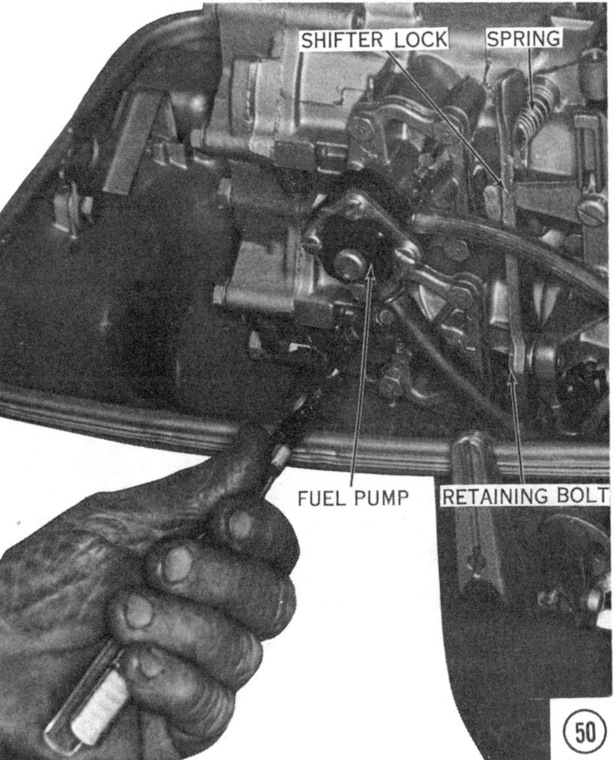

(50) Install the shifter lock retaining bolt, and then replace the spring. Install the fuel pump, using a new gasket. Attach both fuel lines.

(51) Attach the fuel line to the inlet fitting at the base of the carburetor, and then position a new gasket on the intake manifold flange. Install the carburetor, tightening the two nuts evenly. **CAUTION: Uneven tightening of these nuts can crack the casting.**

(52) Install the carburetor linkage support bracket, tightening the two retaining screws securely. Attach the throttle linkage to the cross-shaft.

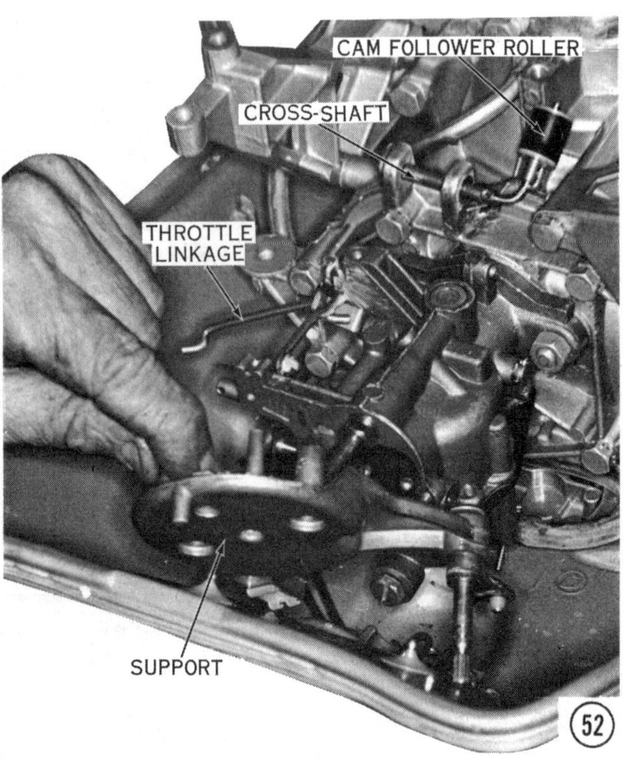

(53) Attach the cam-follower roller spring. Position the magneto plate support, with the tapered side facing down, as shown. **CAUTION: If installed upside down, it will be impossible to assemble the magneto armature plate properly.**

(54) Install the retaining ring, securing it with the three screws. Use an impact screwdriver to tighten them securely.

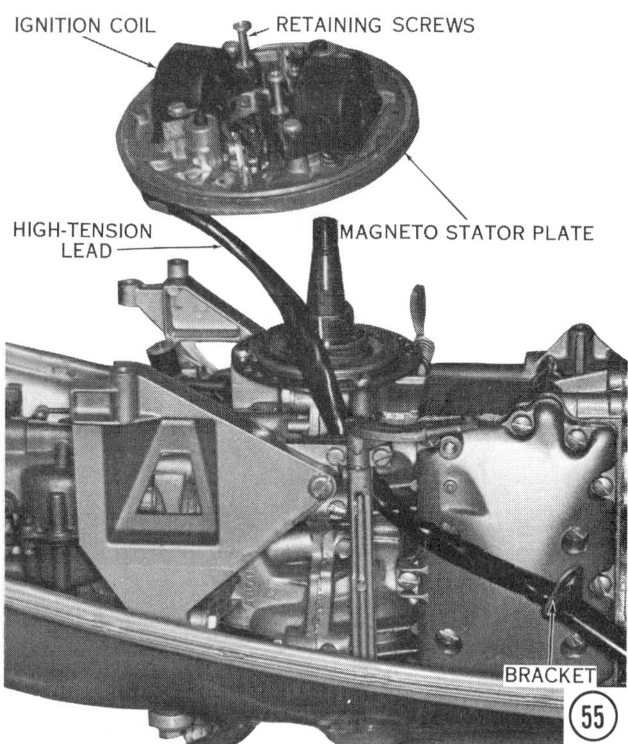

(55) Thread the high-tension wires through the opening between the powerhead and the throttle control linkage, and then lower the magneto armature plate over the crankshaft. Tighten the retaining screws securely. Install the throttle linkage clip. Replace the high-tension wire support bracket.

ADJUSTING THE IGNITION TIMING

(56) Disconnect all wires from the breaker point assemblies. Connect a self-powered test lamp between

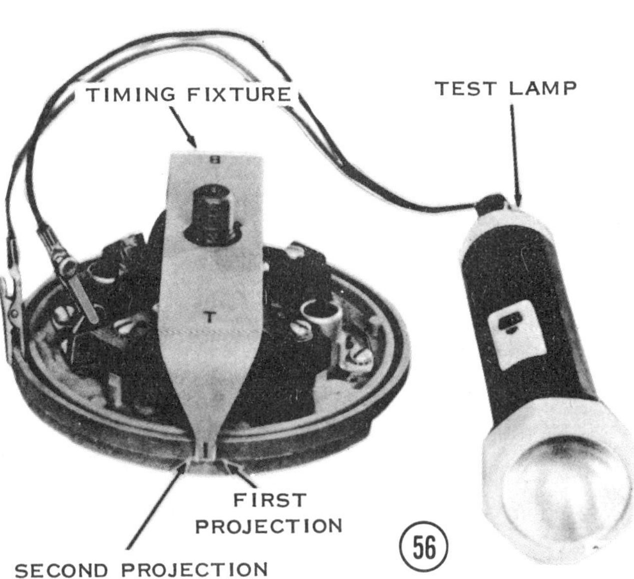

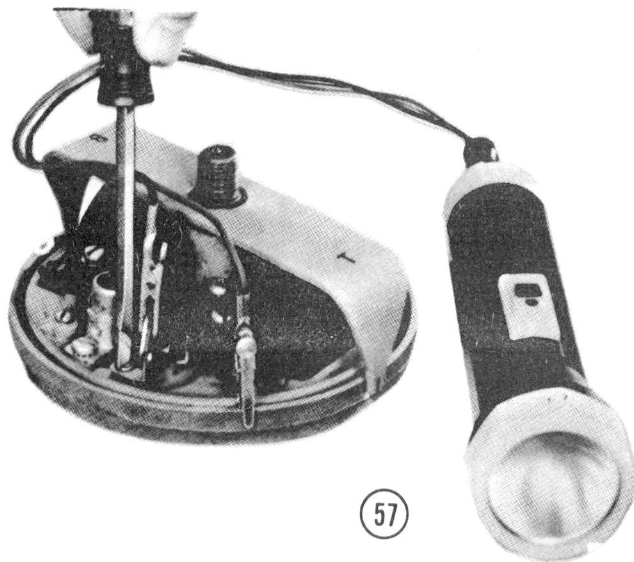

a good ground and the forward breaker point screw terminal. Position a timing fixture, Tool No. 304667, on the crankshaft. Rotate the crankshaft so that the side of the fixture marked "T" (top) is aligned with the first projection on the armature plate. **CAUTION: Always rotate the crankshaft in a clockwise direction to avoid damaging the water pump impeller.** The breaker points must just open when the timing fixture is midway between the two projections on the magneto armature plate. *NOTE: If new breaker points are installed, they must open as the timing fixture passes the first timing mark. This allows for seating of the breaker fiber block.* If a test lamp is not available, adjust both sets of breaker points to open exactly 0.020″ (0.022″ for new points) with the breaker arm on the high part of the cam lobe.

(57) Rotate the crankshaft 180° clockwise until the timing fixture is opposite the second set of timing marks on the magneto armature plate, and then repeat the timing procedure for the second set of breaker points. Disconnect the test lamp, and then reconnect the wires to the breaker point terminals.

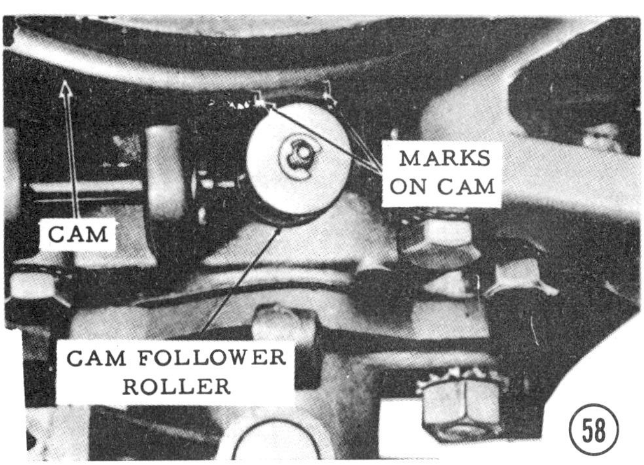

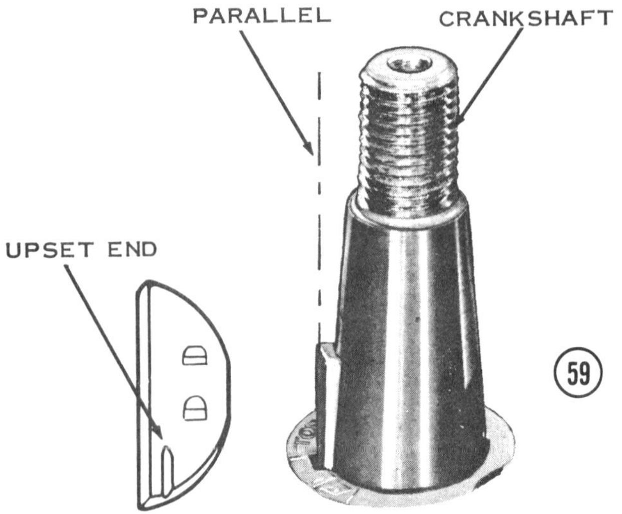

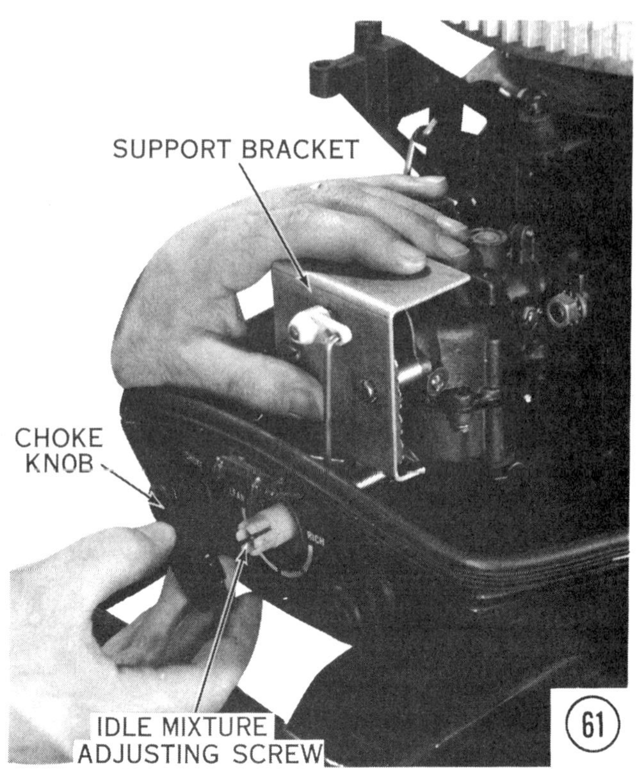

THROTTLE CAM SYNCHRONIZATION

(58) Advance the throttle control to the position where the cam-follower roller is centered between the two marks on the throttle cam. The throttle valve must be closed at this point. If necessary, loosen the two hex-headed screws holding the cam to the magneto armature plate, and then push the cam toward the rear of the engine. Now, pull the cam forward until it just contacts the cam-follower roller. The throttle valve must just begin to open after the edge of the roller passes the second mark on the cam. **CAUTION: The choke knob must be all the way in.**

(59) If the flywheel key has been removed, assemble it to the crankshaft with the outer edge vertical. Make sure that the single upset mark on the side of the key is facing down. **CAUTION: Incorrect installation of the key will so affect the cam position as to result in a retarded ignition timing.**

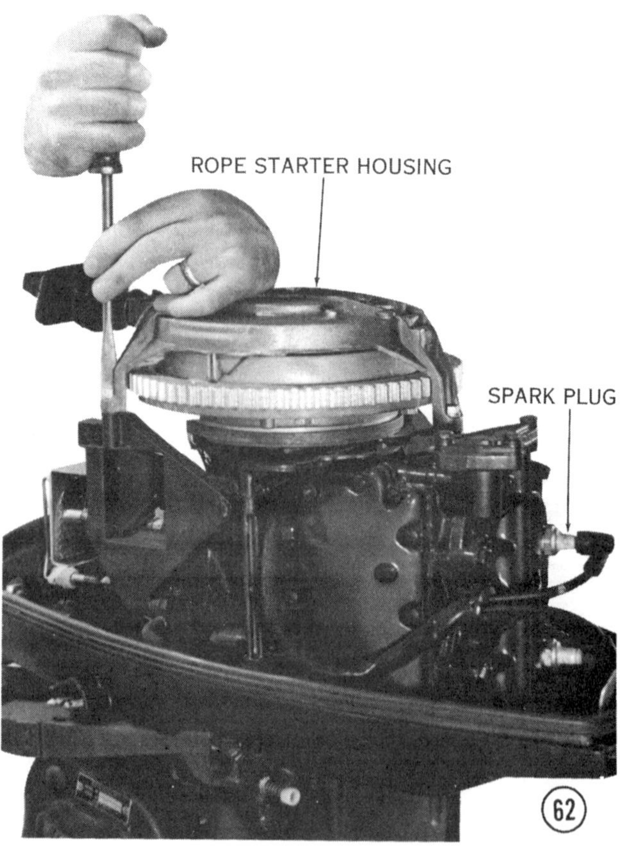

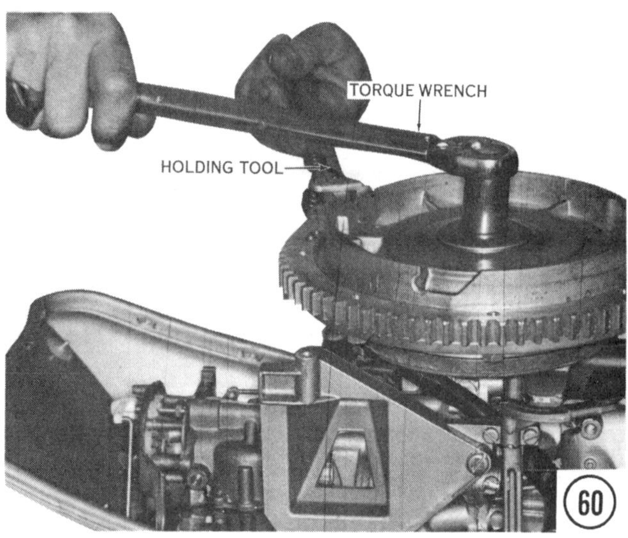

(60) Check the crankshaft and flywheel tapers for any traces of oil, which must be removed with solvent. **CAUTION: The assembly must be perfectly dry. CAUTION: Don't allow solvent to wash the oil out of the oiler wick.** Replace the flywheel and the nut, tightening it to 40-45 ft-lbs. of torque.

(61) Install the linkage support on the rear of the carburetor, tightening the two screws securely. Replace the low-speed adjusting valve arm. Lift up on the choke arm to install the choke control rod at the carburetor.

(62) Install new spark plugs, gapping them to 0.030″. If used spark plugs are to be reinstalled, use a new gasket to insure the proper heat transfer path. Torque the spark plugs to 17-20 ft-lbs. Connect the high-tension wires. Install the manual starter housing, tightening the three screws evenly.

(63) Install the hood, hooking it under the rear catch and then dropping it into position. Hook the front latch to secure the hood.

Additional tuning adjustments can be found in Chapter 3.

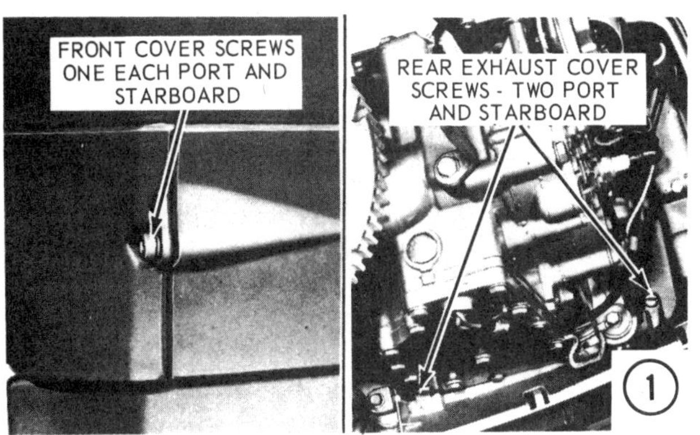

OVERHAULING A TWO-CYLINDER 50 HP ENGINE—SINCE 1971

REMOVING THE POWERHEAD

(1) Remove the front and rear exhaust cover screws.

(2) Slide back the insulating sleeve on each of the late-model shift cable wires so that the terminals between the shift cable and the motor cable can be disconnected. Remove the pivot screw from the shift rod.

(3) Remove the aft nut and washer from the stud in the powerhead. Remove the eight nuts holding the powerhead to the exhaust housing-and-adaptor assembly, and then lift the powerhead and lower motor cover assembly from the adaptor.

DISASSEMBLING

(4) Place the unit on a bench for disassembly, and then take out the four lower mount cover screws holding the powerhead to the motor cover. *NOTE: On*

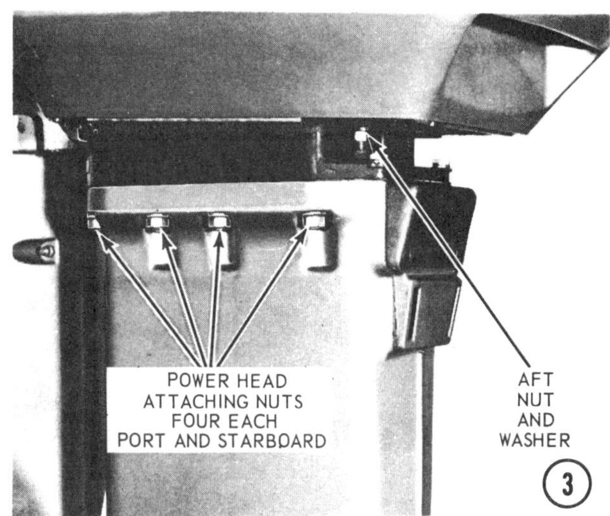

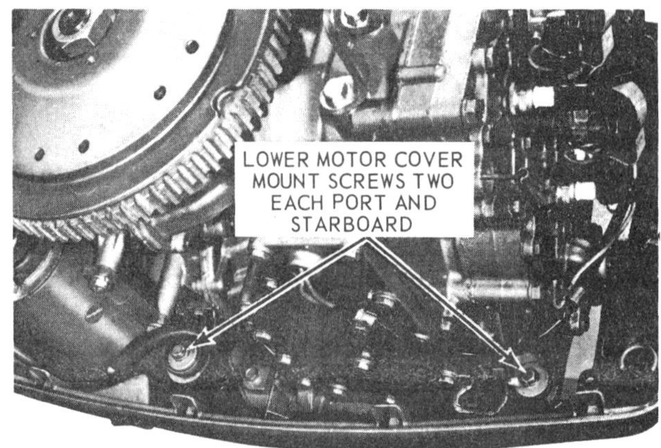

manual shift models, you should take off the shift handle. The shift lever cam, shaft, and bushings can be removed after removal of the lower motor cover.

⑤ On electric-start models, disconnect the lead from the cranking motor, and then remove the three starter mounting screws. On manual-start models, pull out the starter rope about one foot and lock the starter pinion gear to the flywheel with an open-end wrench. Remove the rope handle. Pull on the rope and remove the tool to unlock the starter. Allow the rope to unwind slowly on the spool. Remove the forward snap ring

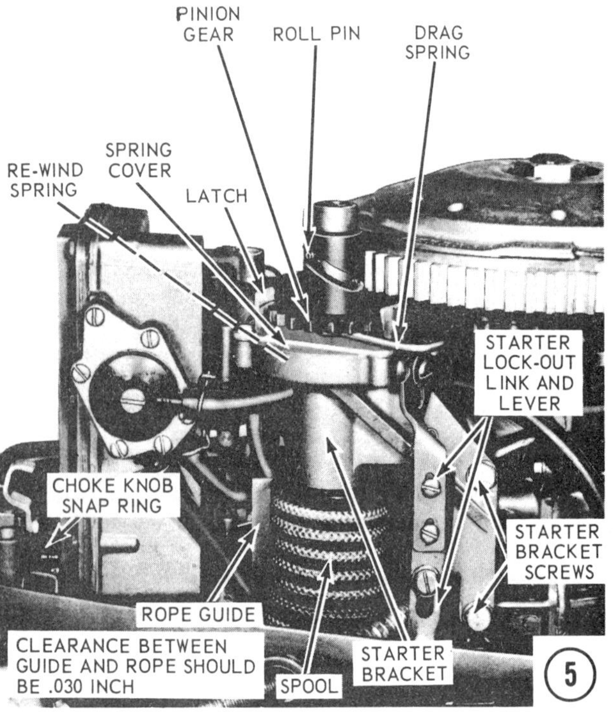

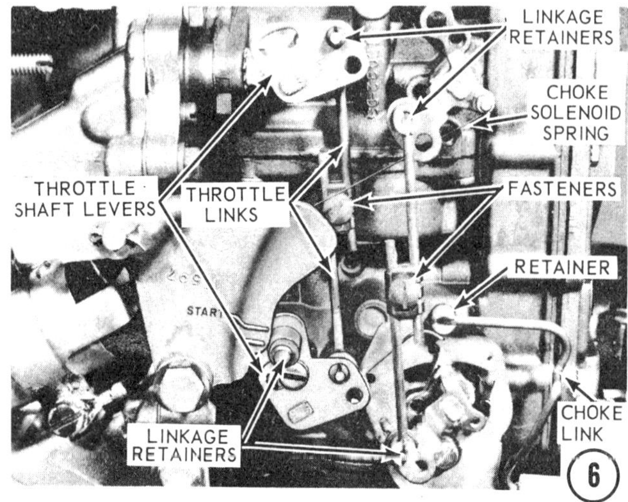

from the slow-speed adjustment knob and then pull the knob back. Remove the cotter pin to release the slow-speed needle adjustment link from the lever. Remove the seven hex head screws from the air intake cover, slide the cover away, and pull the needle valve arms off the shafts. Through the air intake, remove the two hex head screws and the large washers holding the starter rope guide, and then take off the guide. Remove the front starter bracket screw through the air intake and two on the port side. *NOTE: The front starter bracket screw has a thinner head to clear the rope guide.* Loosen the lower lockout linkage screw, and then release the clamp from the throttle cable. Remove the starter assembly from the motor.

⑥ Remove the carburetors and air silencer as an assembly, by disconnecting the choke link, fuel lines, drain hose at the bottom of the intake manifold, and the fuel pump-to-carburetor hose. Remove the seven screws holding the air silencer cover, disconnect the choke solenoid spring, and then take off the carburetor mounting nuts, and lockwashers. Remove the carburetor and air silencer as an assembly.

⑦ Remove the flywheel nut, blocking the flywheel with a holding fixture. Remove the flywheel using Tool No. 378103.

⑧ Disconnect the stator leads (yellow and yellow/gray) at the terminal board. Remove the four screws holding the stator in place, and then take off the stator. Remove the four timer retaining screws and clips, and then lift off the timer assembly.

⑨ Take off the electrical components bracket. Remove the throttle and timer advance linkage.

⑩ To disassemble the powerhead, remove the lower main bearing seal housing. Check the condition of the O-ring seal. Generally, it is best to replace it anytime it is taken apart to minimize the chance of an oil leak.

⑪ Remove the cylinder head bolts (arrows) and then lift off the cylinder head. To service the temperature switch, thermostat, or pressure-control valve, remove the cylinder head cover.

⑫ Drive out one taper pin from the back to the front of the crankcase. Remove the eight small and six large hex head screws holding the crankcase to the cylinder block. Note the length and location of the screws for assembly purposes. Tap the end of the crankshaft with a rawhide mallet to break the seal between the crankcase and cylinder. Lift the crankcase from the cylinder block. Use a 5/16" socket to remove the connecting rod screws, and then take off the rod caps and roller bearings. *NOTE: There are 16 roller bearings at each rod.* **CAUTION: Keep the parts together because they are matched and seat with the operation of the motor.** Because of this, it is essential to

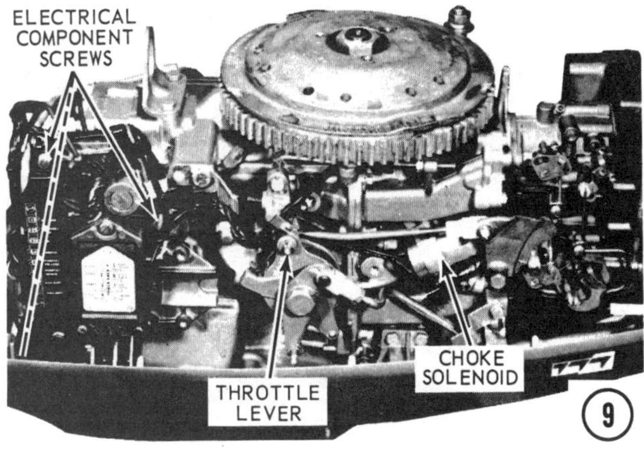

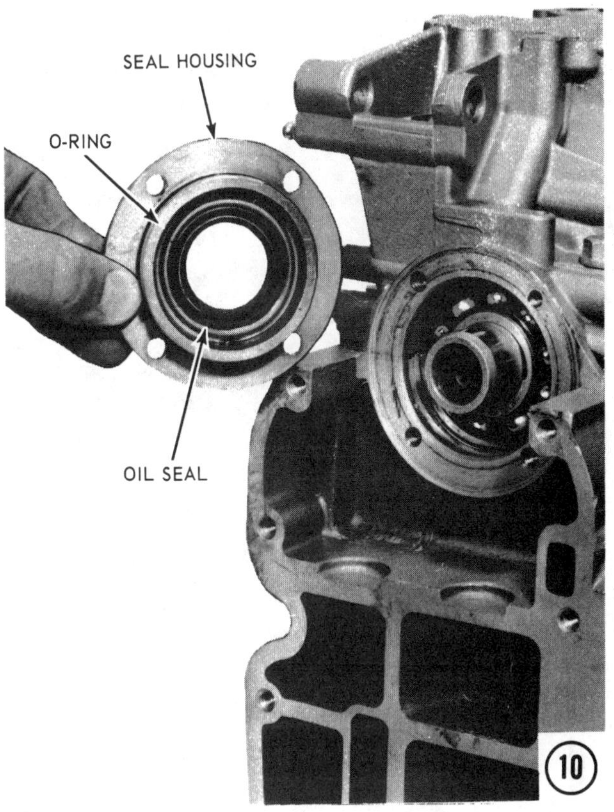

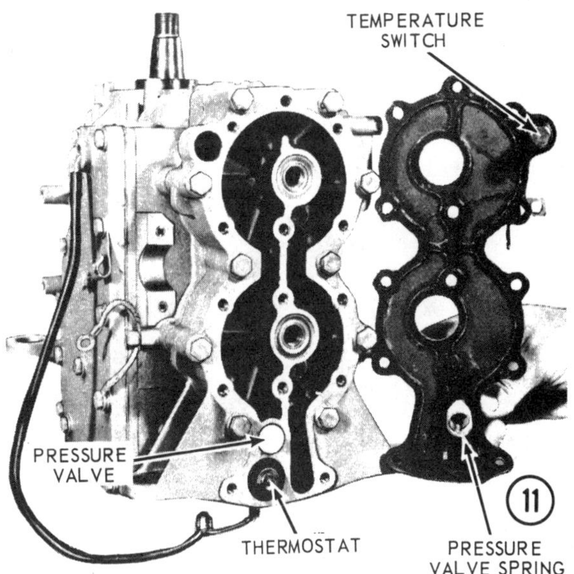

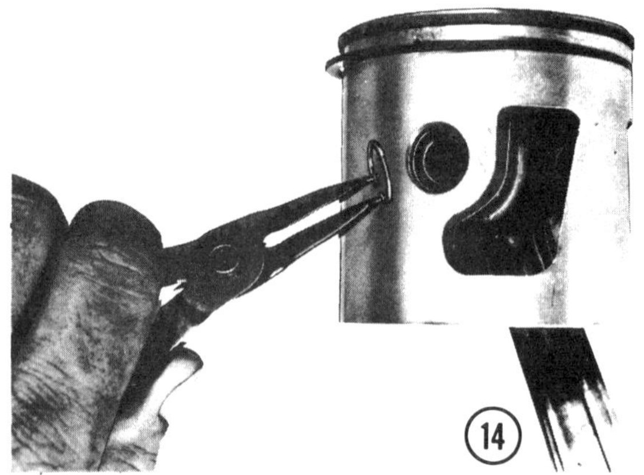

maintain their original positions for assembly purposes. Mark each connecting rod, cap, piston, and bearing component to assure correct mating when the parts are assembled. Also, mark the cylinder from which the pistons are removed.

(13) Lift the crankshaft from the cylinder block. Install the matched caps on the connecting rods, and then remove the pistons and rods from the cylinders. Lift the retaining ring out of the groove, and then slide it aside to remove the crankshaft center main roller bearing. The top main bearing and seal assembly will slide off. Use a bearing puller to take off the bottom main bearing.

(14) Remove the wrist pin retaining rings, using Truarc No. 1 pliers. The wrist pin is a press-fit in both piston bosses, and the piston must be heated in boiling water to remove the pin. **CAUTION: Don't remove the wrist pin completely. Leaving it in one side of the piston will assist in assembly.** Remove the piston rings by prying the ends loose enough to grip them with pliers and then breaking them away from the piston. **CAUTION: Don't reuse the old rings, or you will have power losses.**

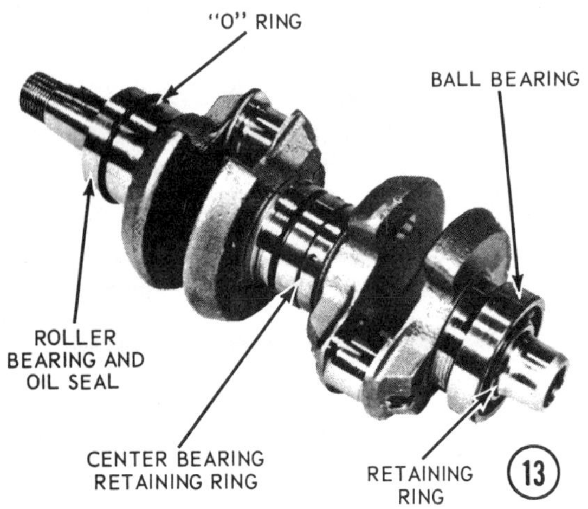

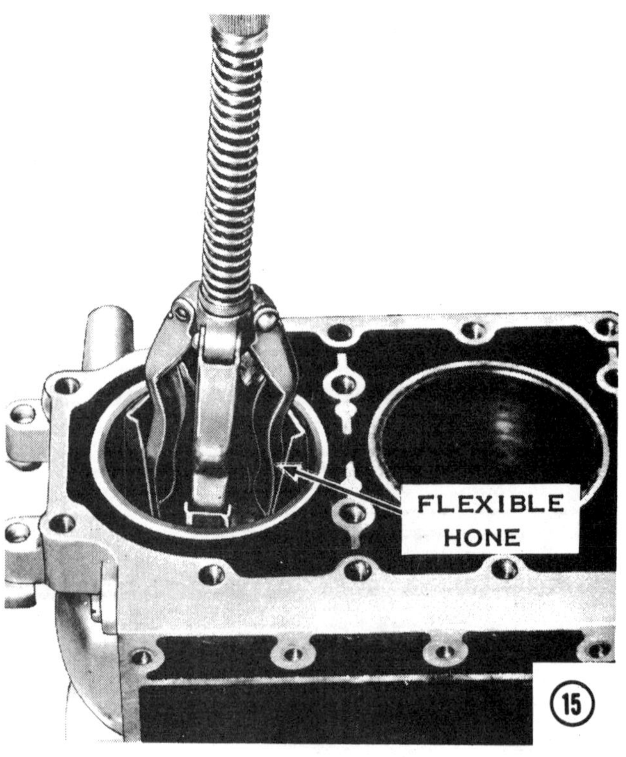

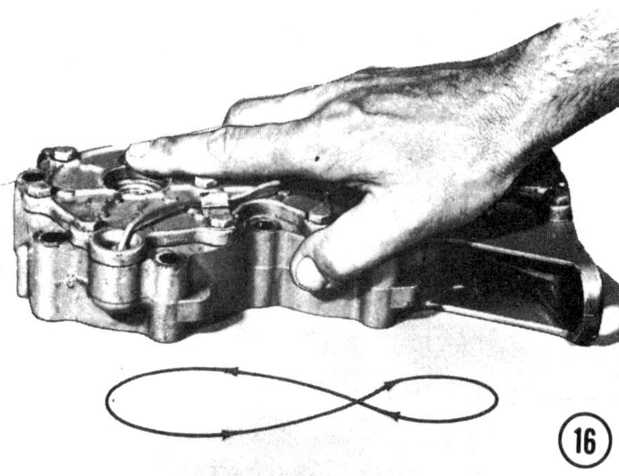
16

CLEANING AND INSPECTING

⑮ Check the cylinder walls for excessive wear. The cylinder walls wear in various degress, depending on lubrication and conditions under which the motor is operated. The major portion of the wear will be in the port and ring travel areas. Check the cylinder bore for straightness and wear with a micrometer. The bore should be 3.060", and the cylinder bores must be reconditioned by boring if the wear exceeds 0.003". If the bore is serviceable, the wall glaze must be removed with a fine hone. A few up-and-down motions of the rotating hone should be sufficient to remove the glaze so that new piston rings will seat properly. Clean the abrasives with a warm soap-and-water solution. Blow out all oil passageways. Scrape the carbon from the cylinder head and exhaust ports with a blunt instrument. **CAUTION: Carbon formation in the ports restricts the flow of exhaust gases and has a considerable effect on the operation of the motor.**

⑯ Use trichlorethylene or lacquer thinner to remove all traces of dried cement. Check all gasket surfaces for flatness. If any surface is warped, lay it on a sheet of No. 120 emery cloth on a surface or plate glass and dress it using a figurc 8 motion until all parts show a dull polish. Finish-surfacing with No. 180 emery cloth.

⑰ Soak all ball and roller bearings in a tank of Solvasol to clean them thoroughly. Flush each bearing to remove all loosened dirt and residue. Blow the solvent out of the bearings, using dry, filtered air. **CAUTION: Don't spin the dry bearings with compressed air or you will damage the races and balls.** Since dry bearings rust rapidly, lubricate them at once with clean oil. This illustration shows how the outer race of a cleaned ball bearing rusted from the moisture of a mechanics fingers. Always replace the top and lower bearing seals and O-rings to minimize the chances of leaks.

⑱ Check the pistons for roundness, wear, and scoring. Use a micrometer to determine the size at several points of the skirt. Remove the carbon deposits from inside of the piston head. Scrape the carbon from the ring grooves using the sharp edge of a broken piston ring. Hold the ring in a rag to prevent cutting your hand. **CAUTION: Don't scratch the side walls of the grooves, or you will damage the sealing surfaces.**

17

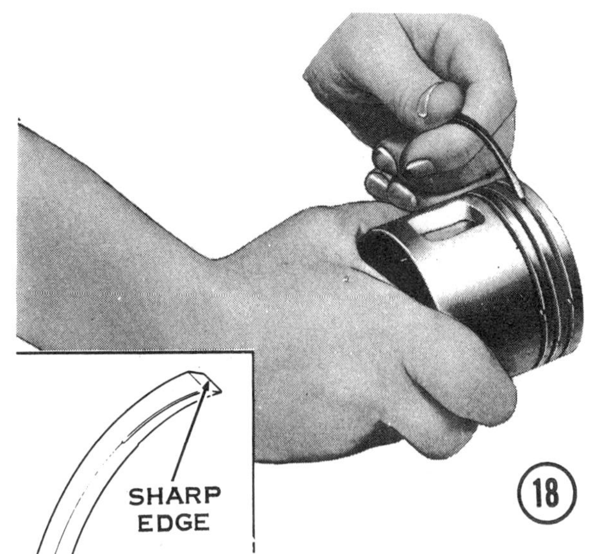

18

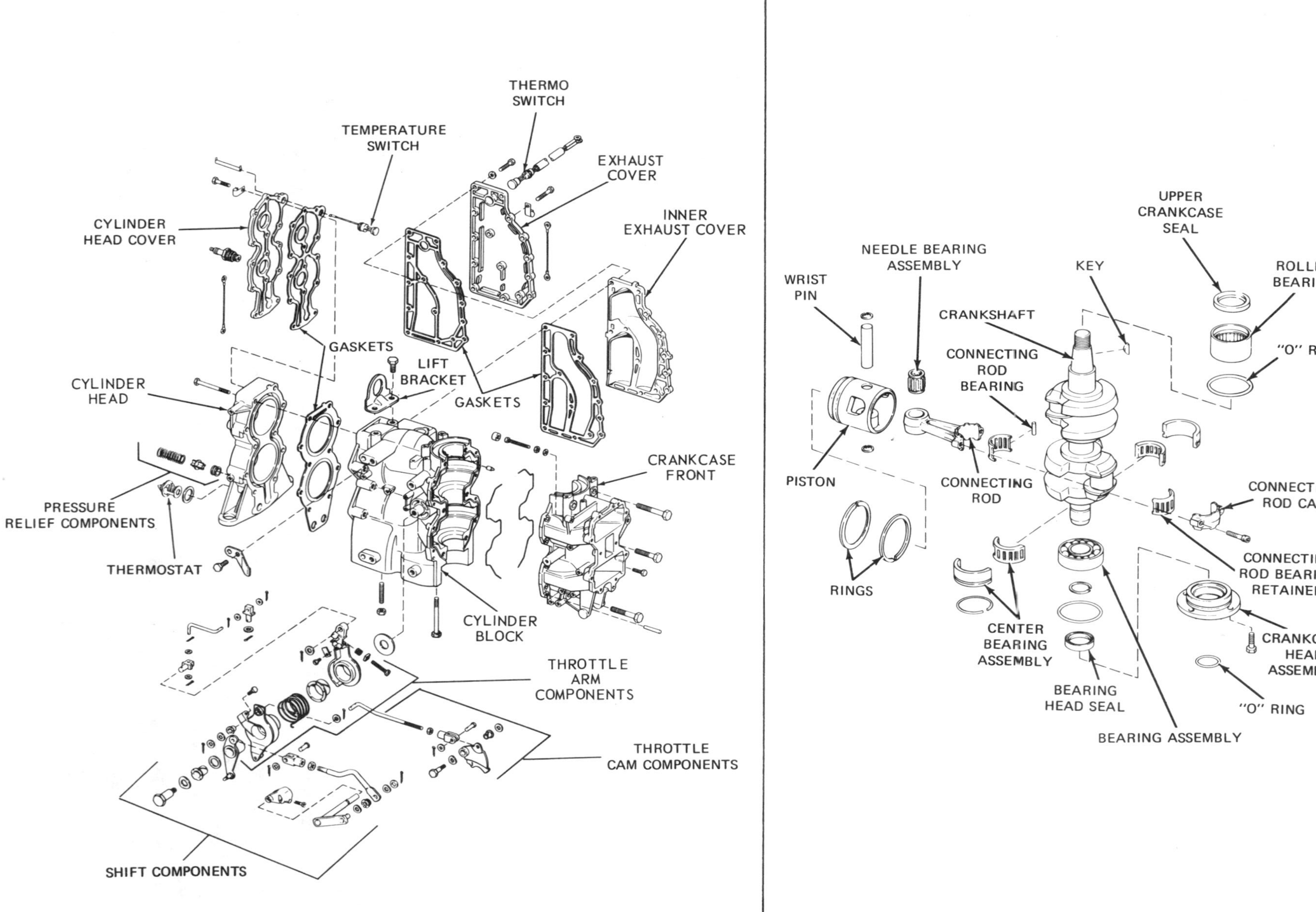

Exploded view of the 50 Hp engine.

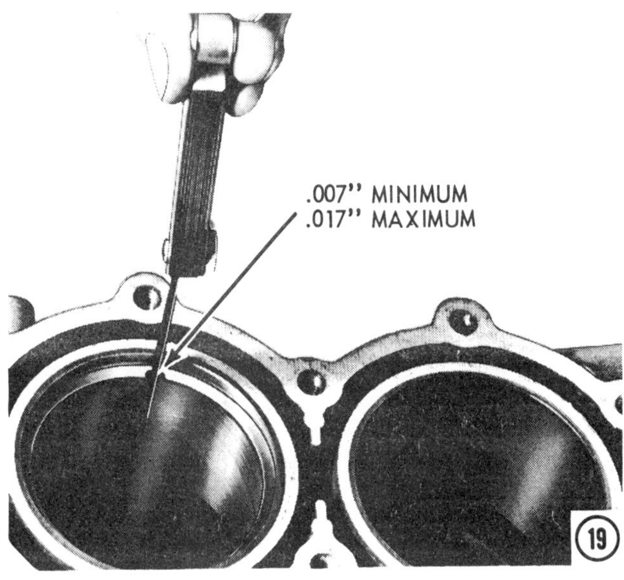

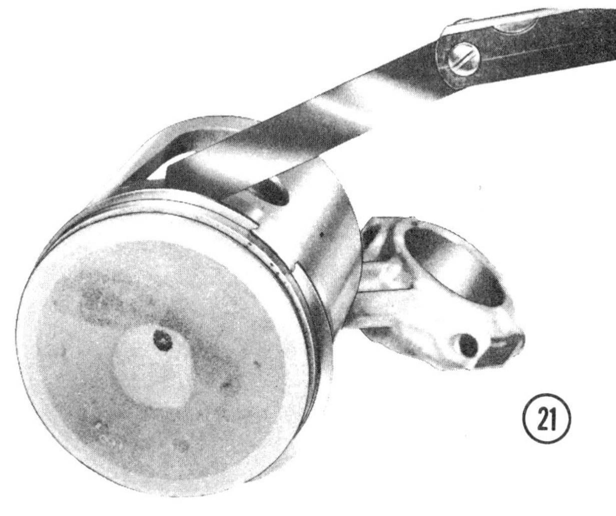

(19) Check the piston ring end gaps by placing each ring in its respective cylinder bore. Use a piston to push the ring down into the bore; this keeps the ring square with the walls. The end gap should be 0.007-0.017". File the ends of the rings to obtain this clearance.

(20) Check each ring in its respective ring groove by rolling the ring around, as shown. File off any burrs which might hinder the freedom of the ring.

(21) Measure the ring side clearance, which must be 0.0015-0.0040". Replace the piston and/or ring if the clearance is excessive.

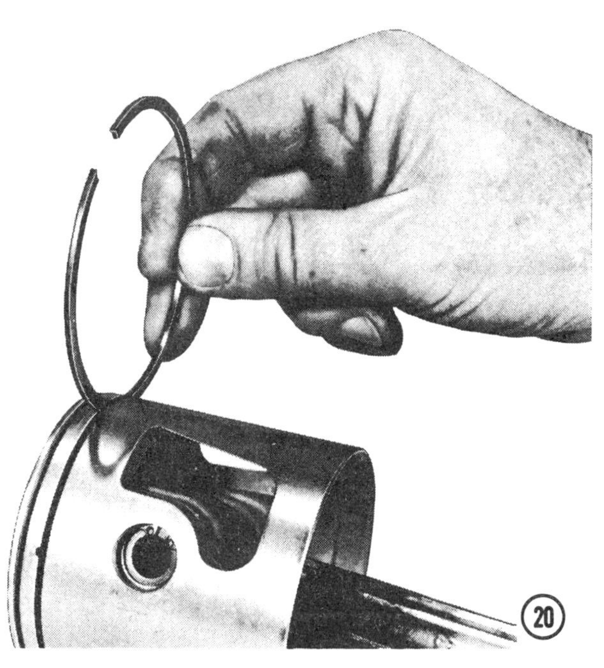

ASSEMBLING

(22) To assemble the pistons to the rods, apply OMC needle bearing grease to hold the 10 rollers in the wrist pin bearing retainer. Heat the piston in boiling water to expand the wrist pin bosses, and then assemble the piston to the rod so that the UP mark on the piston top corresponds with the oil hole, as shown. Press the wrist pin through the piston and connecting rod, and then check the piston for roundness with an outside micrometer. **CAUTION: Forcing the wrist pin into the piston can distort it.** Tap the high side of the piston skirt with a rawhide mallet to restore roundness. Replace the wrist pin retaining

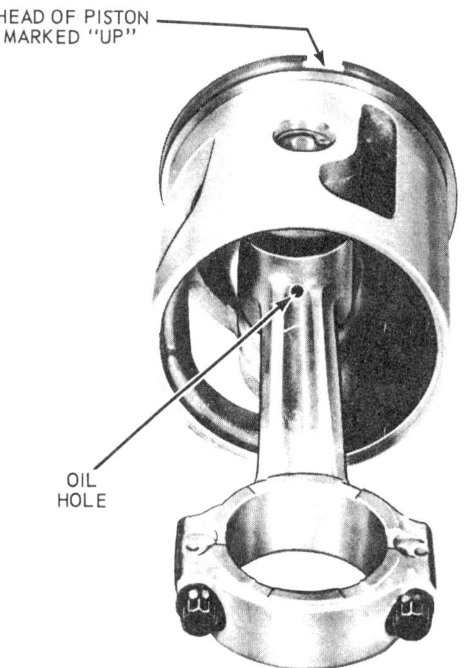

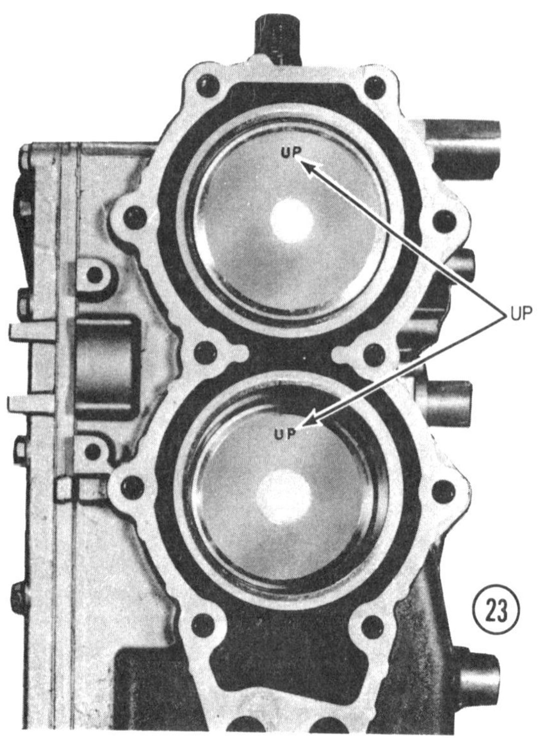

rings, with the lettered side facing out. **CAUTION: Make sure that they seat securely in the grooves.**

(23) Install the piston rings on each piston. Spread each ring with an expander just enough to slip it over the head of the piston and down into place. **CAUTION: Overstretching the rings will distort them and cause them to stick in the grooves of the pistons.** Note that the ring grooves are pinned. This is to prevent the ends of the rings from catching on the edges of the ports and it also assures staggered gaps to minimize compression losses. Coat the pistons and cylinder bores with oil, and then install each piston-and-rod assembly in the cylinder from which it was removed. The side of the piston marked UP must face the top of the powerhead. **CAUTION: Make sure that the ring gaps are centered over the pins in the grooves.** Use Tool No. 310673 to compress the rings for ease of installation. *NOTE: If this tool is not available, you can insert each ring on the piston, and then use a hose clamp tool to compress the ring as you push the piston down enough to cover the ring.* Then install the second ring, compress it, and push the piston down fully. **CAUTION: Never use an automotive-type piston ring compressor, or you will break off the ring ends.** Use one hand to push the piston into the cylinder and the other hand to guide the connecting rod into place and to align the rod with respect to the crankshaft.

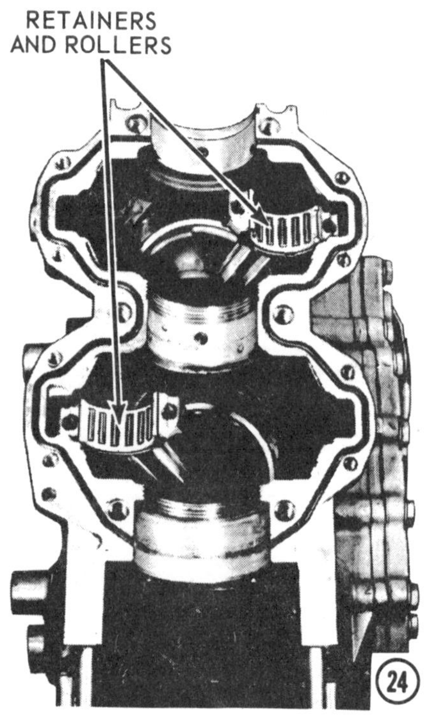

(24) Remove the rod caps from the connecting rods and apply a coat of OMC Needle Bearing Grease, Part No. 378642, to the connecting rod bearing areas. Place one retainer half and seven roller bearings on each rod, as shown.

(25) Install a new oil seal (with the lip facing toward the bearing) in the upper main bearing. Use Tool No. 316613 to assist you. Place the crankshaft in position on the cylinder block, aligning the top and center main bearing with the dowel pin in the cylinder block.

(26) Apply a coat of OMC Needle Bearing Grease to the crankpins. Install two roller bearings and the remaining retainer half on each crankpin. Place the seven roller bearings in each retainer. *NOTE: 16 rollers*

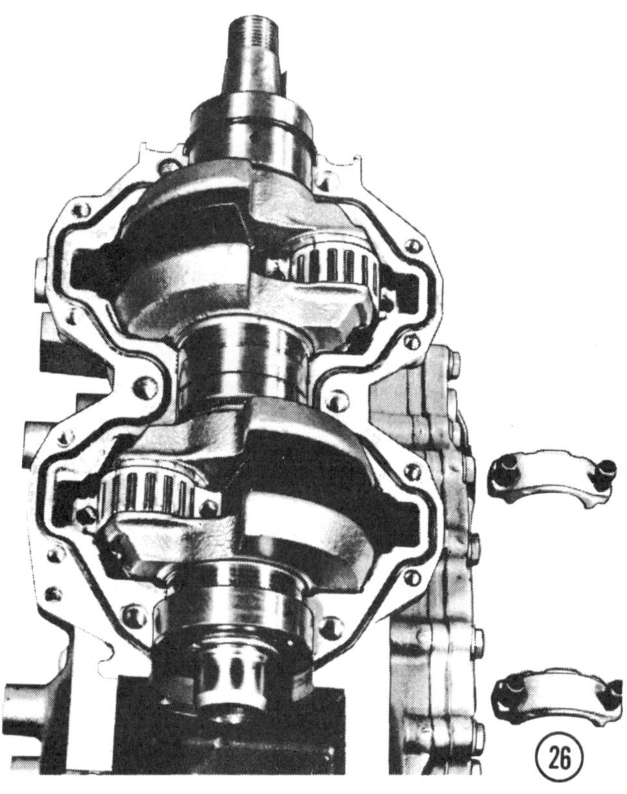

are used in each roller bearing. After the roller bearings are in place attach the rod caps.

㉗ To assist in correct assembly, small raised dots are provided on matching sides of the rod and cap. **CAUTION: The rod caps are not interchangeable with each other, neither can the cap on the same rod be turned end for end.** To check the alignment, draw a pencil over the chamfered corners on both sides of the rod to make certain that the cap and rod are aligned at this point. If they are not assembled properly, the

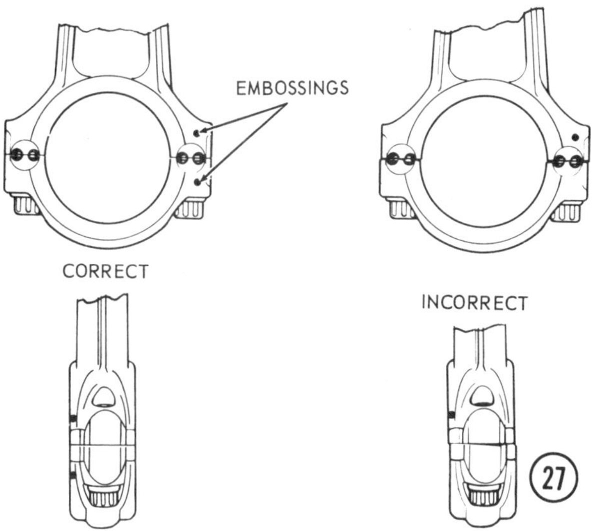

chamfered corners can be felt with the pencil point. **CAUTION: Misalignment will affect free action of the rollers, and this will result in major engine damage.** Tighten the rod screws to 348-372 in-lbs. of torque.

㉘ Install a new rubber seal into the groove of the crankcase face. **CAUTION: The new seal must be cut somewhat longer than the groove to obtain a good butt seal at both ends against the crankcase bearing, but not too long which might force it out of the groove.** Run a fine bead of Sealer 1000 in the groove to secure the seal while trimming. Force the seal into the outer edge of the groove with thumb pressure. After the sealer has set, trim the ends with a sharp knife, allowing approximately 1/32" of the seal to extend against each bearing for a butt or terminal seal. Apply a thin line of sealer to the crankcase face. **CAUTION: Too much sealer will squeeze out and block an oil channel, with disastrous results.**

㉙ Position the crankcase on the cylinder block and install the screws finger-tight. Replace the crankcase taper pin, driving it into place with a hammer. Rap the bottom end of the crankshaft with a mallet to seat the ball bearings and to center the crank throws in the crankcase. Check the motor for binding by installing the flywheel and rotating it. Now tighten all crankcase screws to 144-168 in-lbs. of torque.

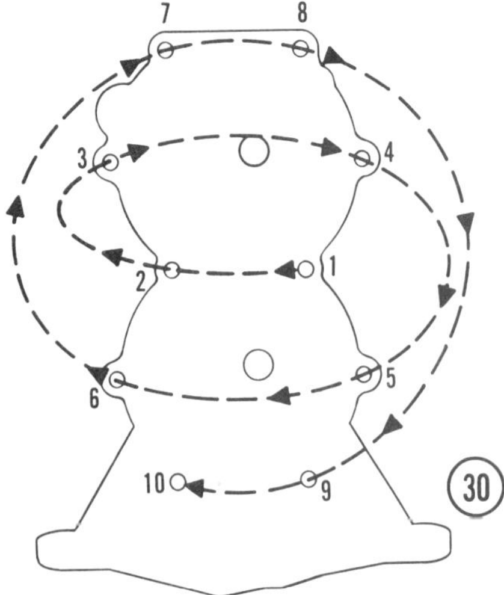

(30) Install the cylinder head, using a new gasket coated with OMC Gasket Sealing Compound. Recheck the motor crankshaft for binding by turning the flywheel. If the motor is free, tighten the head bolts to 168-192 in-lbs. of torque in the sequence shown. *NOTE: The cylinder head screws must be retorqued to 192-216 in-lbs. after the motor has been tuned and has cooled down enough to be comfortable to the touch.* Install the thermostat, pressure-control valve, spring, and temperature switch. Install the cylinder head cover, using a new gasket. Install the exhaust covers and the automatic choke thermo-switch assembly, using new gaskets.

(31) Install a new oil seal and a new O-ring seal in the lower main bearing housing, and then install the housing in the crankcase. On manual-start models, install the shift lever bushing, shaft, and cam. Lubricate the bushing with OMC Type C grease.

(32) Install the lower mount cover. **CAUTION: Make sure that the gasket surfaces of the powerhead and adaptor assembly are clean, and then place a new gasket in position.** Place the powerhead on the adaptor, using care not to damage the splines of the crankshaft and driveshaft. Rotating the crankshaft slightly clockwise as the powerhead is lowered onto the exhaust housing adaptor will assist in engaging the splines easier. **CAUTION: Make sure that the steering arm seal seats in the groove in the lower motor cover.** Replace the shift rod pivot screw.

(33) Replace the nine nuts and washers, tightening them securely. Install the front and rear exhaust covers.

(34) Replace the throttle-control arm and throttle cam. Replace the intake manifold, carburetor, and other components of the fuel system. Replace the timer assembly and other components of the ignition

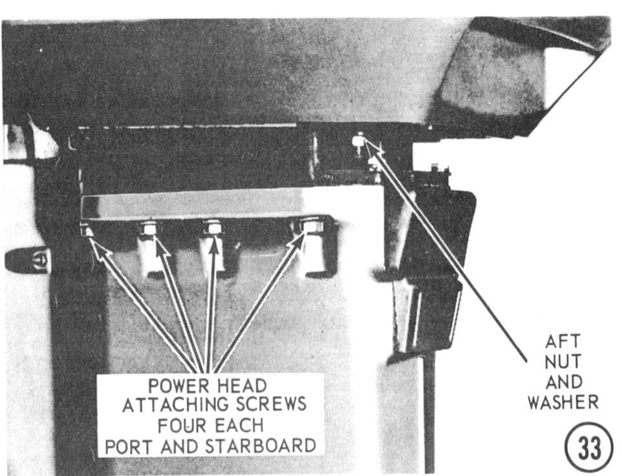

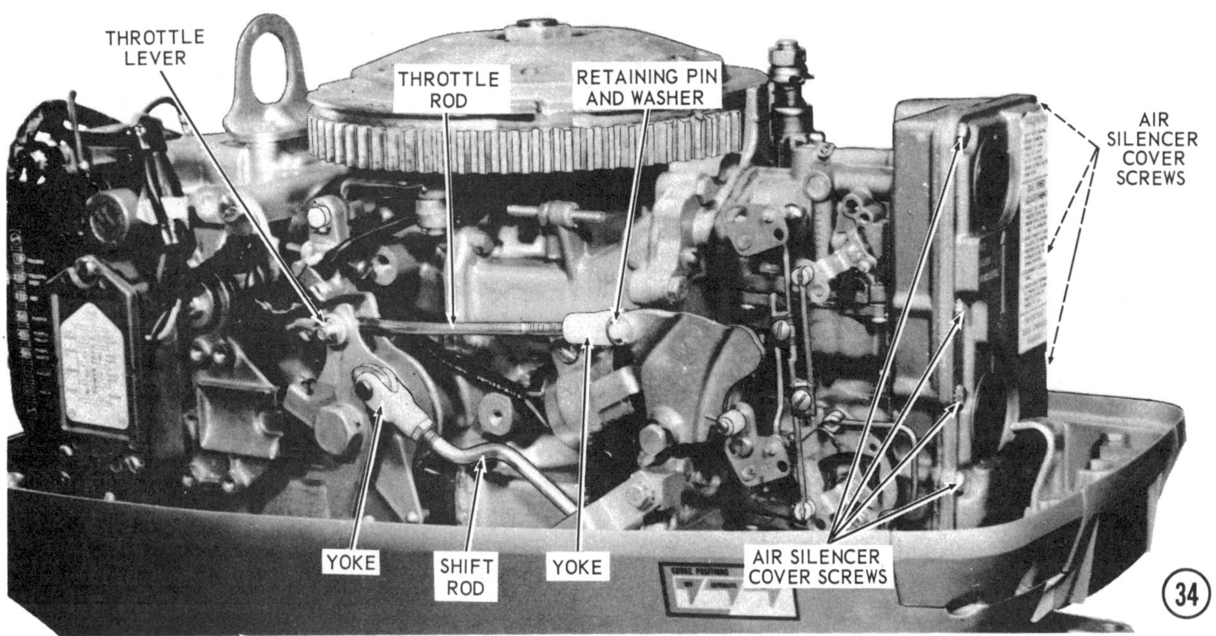

system, tightening the flywheel retaining nut to 100-105 ft-lbs. of torque. Install the electrical component bracket. Connect the powerhead ground wire.

(35) Install the starter and connect the cable. With the propeller in water, start the motor and operate it at a fast idle for about 10 minutes. **CAUTION: Check the operation of the water pump.** Run the engine at half throttle for the first hour to loosen it up. Tune the engine as described in Chapter 3, Tuning for Performance. After the engine has cooled down so that it is comfortable to touch, retorque the cylinder head screws to 192-216 in-lbs.

6

LOWER UNIT SERVICE

The lower unit of the 1.5, 2.0, 3.0, 4.0, and 5.0 Hp engines is a nonshift type; it is necessary to turn the entire unit 180° to obtain reverse. The lower unit of the 6 through 33 Hp engines is manually shifted, the operator being able to select forward, neutral, or reverse gear by moving a shift lever. The 40 Hp engine can be optionally equipped with either a manually shifted or an electrically shifted lower unit. The lower unit of the 50 Hp engine since 1971 utilizes hydraulic shifting. An oil pump, driven by the forward gear and using the lubricating oil in the gear case for shifting, is controlled by a solenoid; the solenoid operates a pump valve which forces the shifting dog clutch in the desired direction. Most of the larger engine sizes through 1968 can be shifted either mechanically or electrically.

All engines have a water pump, driven by the driveshaft, for cooling the engine and the lower unit.

EXHAUST RELIEF

Normally, exhaust gases are conducted down through the exhaust housing and out of the underwater outlet in the gear case. The siphoning action of the propeller and water provides an unrestricted escape for exhaust. In starting, however, water in the outlet creates back pressure that results in hard starting. Exhaust relief is provided by another outlet located in the water discharge passage above the water line. Since no water is discharged until after the engine is started, the exhaust gases will initially be discharged through the water outlet.

The water pump impeller forces water through the powerhead and the gear case for cooling. At low speed (left), the impeller works as a displacement pump. At higher speeds (right), the water resistance keeps the blades from flexing and the pump acts as a circulator.

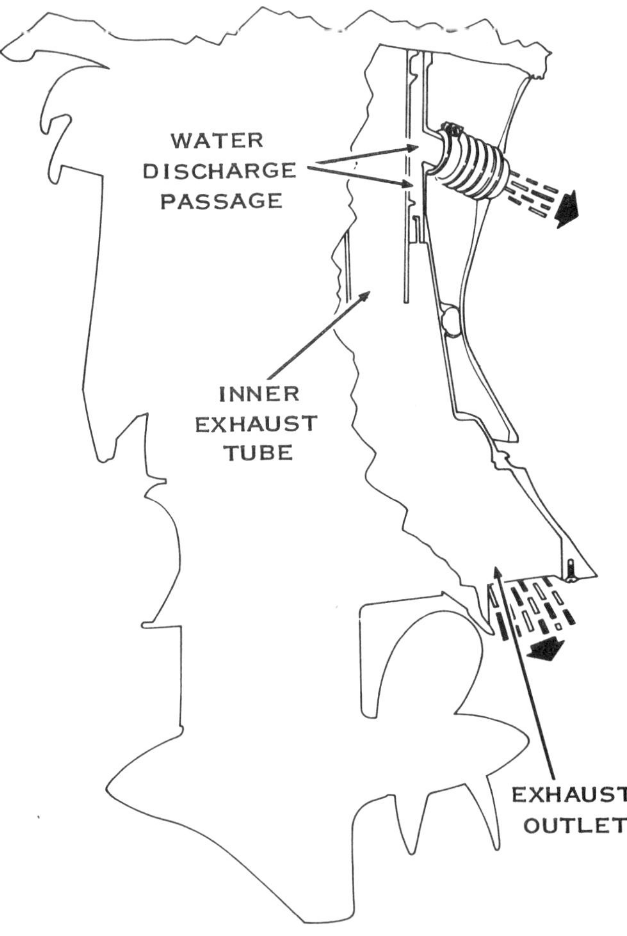

The water used for cooling the engine is discharged into the space between the exhaust housings and maintains a specified level when the engine is running. This chamber of water serves as an effective silencer, quiets the exhaust relief, and cools the outer housings. Normally, exhaust gases are conducted down through the inner exhaust tube and out through the underwater exhaust outlet. However, when starting the engine, the water in the exhaust housing creates back pressure which can cause hard starting. Exhaust relief is provided by an oulet in the water discharge passage above the water line. The initial flow of exhaust gases will pass out of this port until the water level rises to cut it off and force the exhaust out of the underwater outlet.

WATER PUMP

Water for cooling the powerhead is circulated by the water pump, located at the top of the gear case and driven directly by the driveshaft. The pump consists of a synthetic rubber impeller, which is keyed to the driveshaft, and the pump housing, which is offset from the center with respect to the driveshaft. Because the housing is offset, the impeller blades flex as they rotate, varying the space between them. The pump inlet port, located in the stainless steel plate which forms the lower part of the pump housing, is open to the blades when the space between them is increasing. The pump outlet port, in the impeller housing, is open to the blades when the space between them is decreasing. Thus, at low speeds the impeller works as a displacement pump. At higher speeds, water resistance keeps the blades from flexing, and the pump acts as a circulator, enough water being provided by the forward motion through the water.

ENGINE MOUNTS

To minimize engine and driveshaft vibrations and to prevent them from being transmitted to the stern bracket and the boat transom, all of the larger outboard motors are supported by rubber mounts. If a mount cracks, or if the rubber shears off its metal plate, several troubles typically occur: misalignment and shifting problems, excessive vibration, and related vibration-caused troubles.

SERVICE PROCEDURES

To check for a broken engine mount, push against the powerhead to see if it can be moved an excessive amount. Generally, a noise can be heard as the metal parts make contact.

To change an upper rubber mount on a two-cylinder engine, it is necessary to remove the front and rear exhaust covers. The lower mounts can be reached by taking off both lower mount covers.

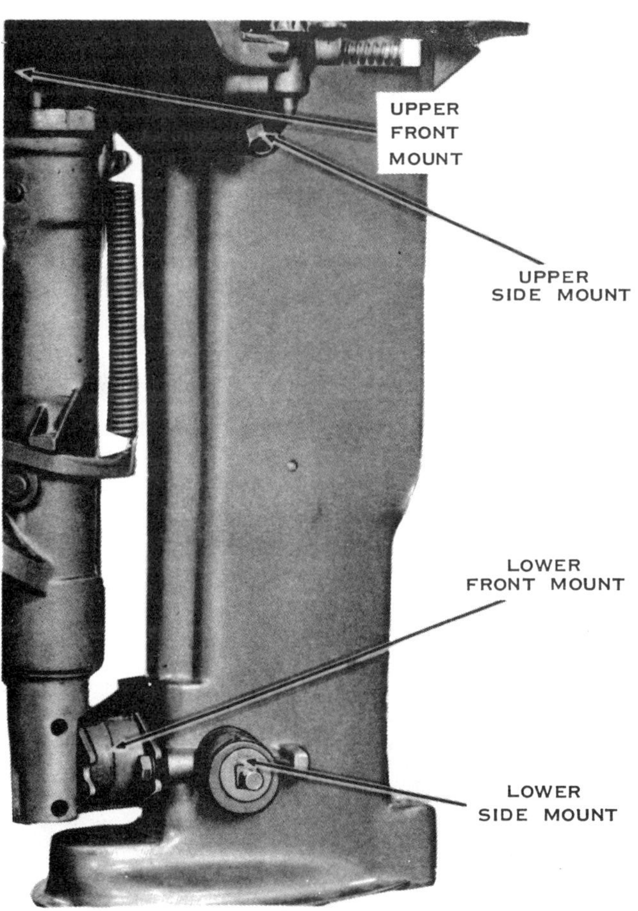

This illustration shows the locations of the rubber mounts used on the 18/20 Hp engines.

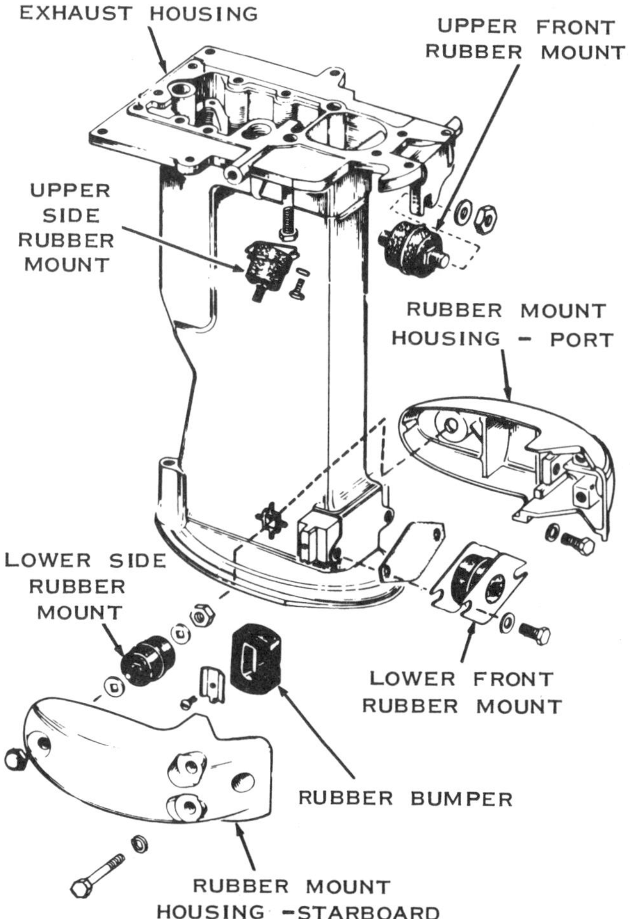

These are the positions of the rubber mounts on the 33 Hp engine.

GEAR SHIFT

The three functions of forward, neutral, and reverse operation are provided by the gear shift mechanism located in the lower gear case. The driveshaft pinion gear rotates constantly with the operation of the engine, driving two bevel gears which revolve freely on the propeller shaft. The shifter clutch dog is splined to the propeller shaft. In neutral, the shifter dog is centered between the two gears, which revolve in opposite directions. In forward or reverse operation, the shift lever causes the shifter dog to engage either gear. Power is then transmitted from the pinion gear, through the shifter clutch dog, to the propeller shaft and propeller.

LOWER UNIT SERVICE PROCEDURES

The service procedures for the five types of lower units will be covered in the order which follows: (1) nonshift types through 1974, (2) mechanical shift type through 1974, (3) electric shift type from 1963-68, (4) hydro-electric shift type from 1968-72, and (5) hydro-mechanical shift type since 1973.

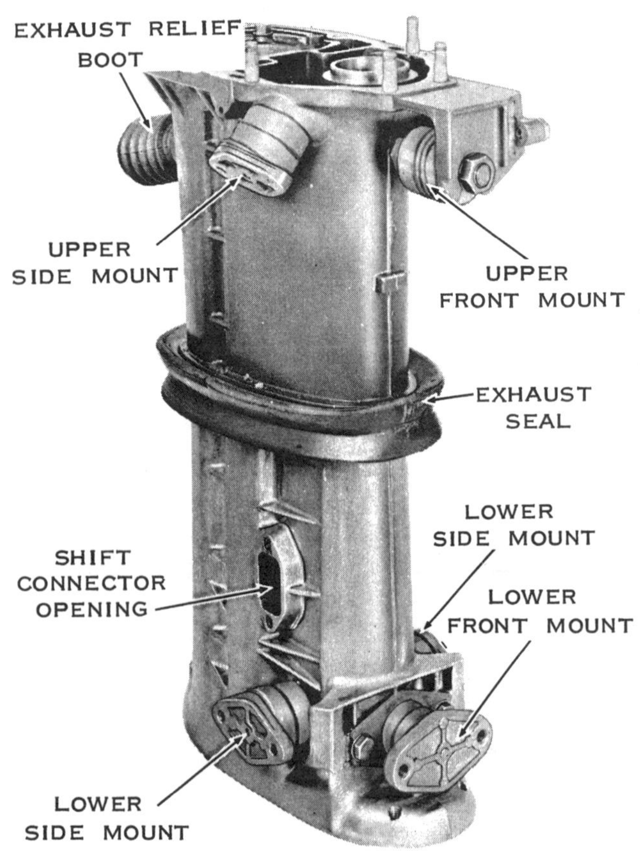

These are the locations of the rubber mounts on the 40 Hp engine.

SERVICING THE NONSHIFT-TYPE LOWER UNIT—THROUGH 1975

DISASSEMBLING

1.5, 2.0, 3.0, 4.0 & 5.0 Hp Engines

① It is possible to remove the gear case without removing the powerhead or the exhaust housing. Do this by taking out the bolts holding the gear case to the exhaust housing or extension. Most models have four retaining bolts. On the 5.0 Hp engine, the lower unit will drop about 3/4" after taking out the four bolts. It is then necessary to turn the propeller shaft to align the pin in the driveshaft with the slot in the exhaust housing. The washer and spring for the bottom seal of the powerhead will come off with the lower unit.

② Remove the propeller by taking out the cotter pin and then removing the propeller and drive pin. Drain the gear case.

③ Remove the water pump screws, and then lift the pump cover and driveshaft from the gear case. Take out the grommet from the water pump.

④ Remove the two screws holding the gear case head or bearing retainer to the case. Remove the head or bearing retainer by pulling on the propeller shaft. Slide the gear case head or bearing retainer from the propeller shaft, and then remove the seals. Remove the driveshaft seal from the top of the gear case, using puller No. 377565.

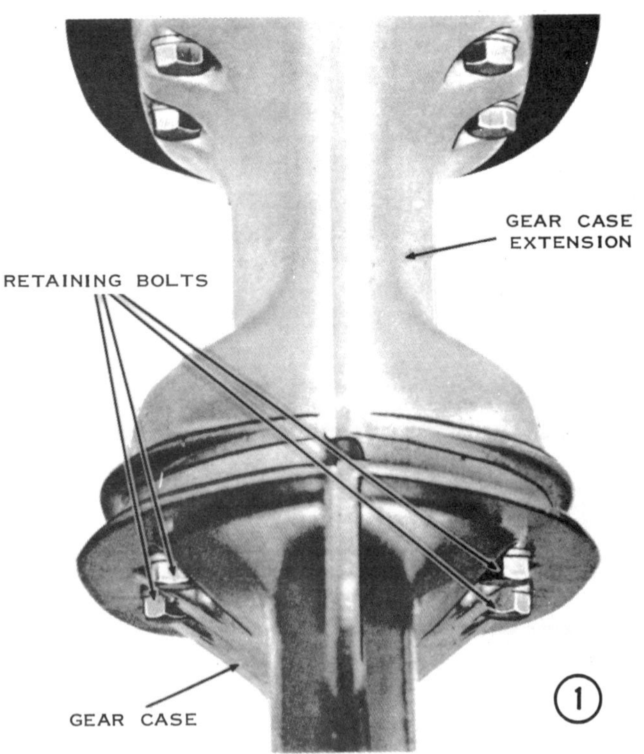

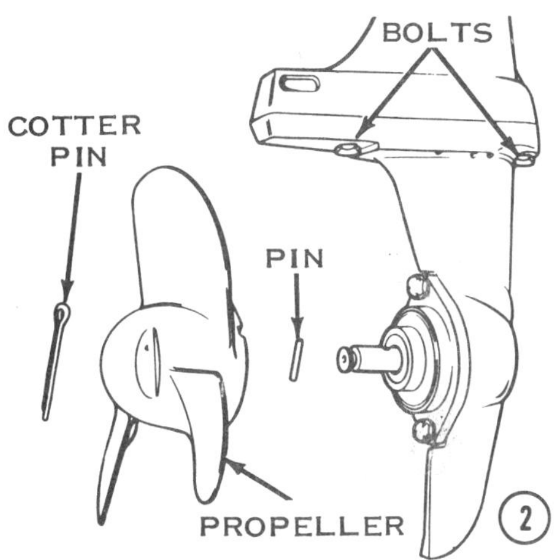

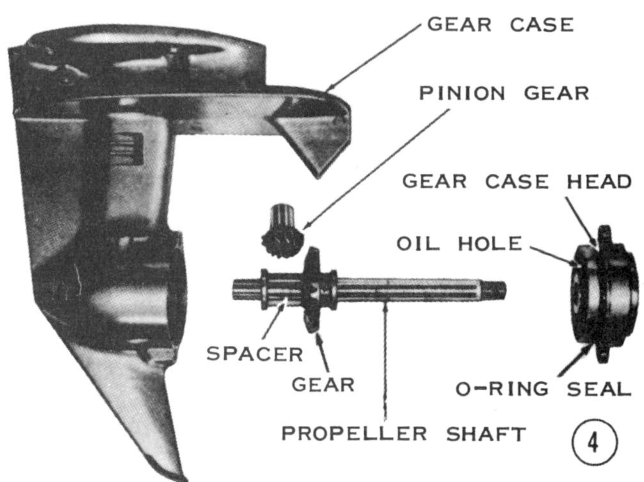

CLEANING AND INSPECTING

Clean all parts in solvent and dry with compressed air. Don't use rags to dry the parts because of the danger of leaving lint. Remove gasket particles and dried cement with trichloroethylene. Discard all gaskets, oil seals, and O-ring seals. Always use new ones during assembly.

⑤ Check the flatness of the gasket surfaces and the parallelism of machined faces of the exhaust housing and the gear case extension by using a surface plate and an indicator. **CAUTION: Don't attempt to straighten a bent housing; replace it.** Inspect the propeller shaft, pinion gear, and driveshaft splines for wear. A bent exhaust housing will cause excessive crankshaft spline wear. Inspect the bushings and thrust bearing for wear.

⑥ Inspect the impeller for wear or deterioration. Check the impeller drive pin on the driveshaft. Inspect the impeller chamber in the gear case for scoring, which will reduce the water output. Make sure that the air bleed hole in the cover is open. Inspect the water tube and the water intake holes for clogging or kinks, and clean them if necessary.

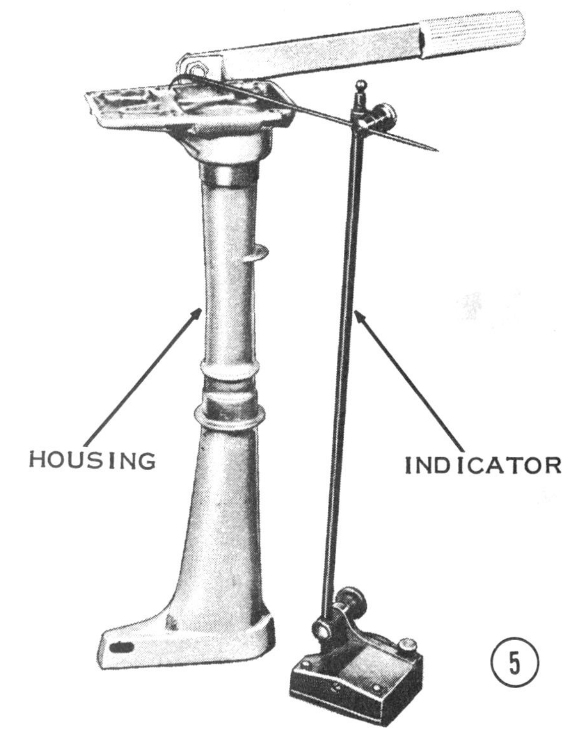

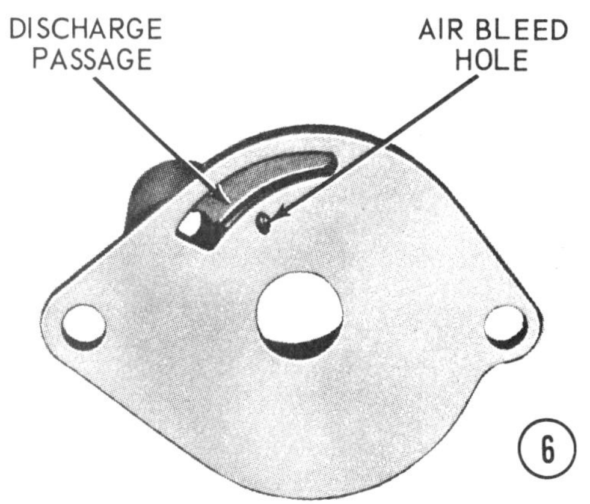

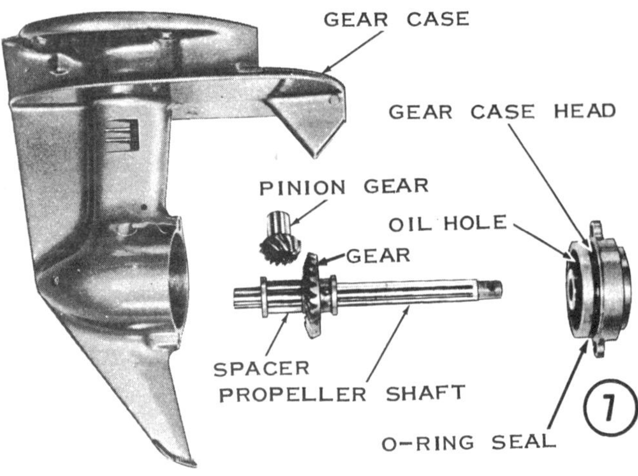

ASSEMBLING

⑦ Install a new seal on the top of the gear case. Press a new seal into the gear case head, and then place a new O-ring seal in position. *NOTE: Always lubricate new seals before assembling.* Oil the propeller shaft, and then slide the gear case head and spacer onto the shaft. Place the pinion gear in position in the gear case. Install the propeller shaft with the gear case head and spacer. **CAUTION: The gear case head has an oil hole which must face up. On the 1.5 Hp engine, the gear case head has a flat surface at the upper screw hole, which must face up.** Dip the gear case head screws in Perfect Seal #4, and then tighten them securely. Rotate the propeller shaft to check for binding.

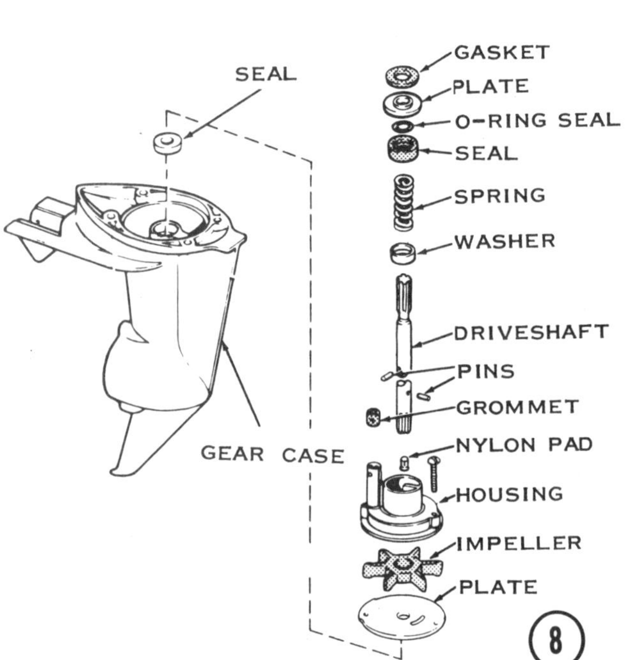

⑧ Apply a fine bead of Sealer 1000 to the gear case, and then place the impeller plate in position. Place the driveshaft, with the impeller and housing, in position in the gear case. Rotate the driveshaft to engage the pinion gear. Install the impeller pin. Oil the impeller, and then slide it down the driveshaft, aligning it with the drive pin. Install the housing, twisting the driveshaft clockwise (as viewed from the top) in order to seat the impeller vanes in the proper direction of rotation. Attach the impeller housing with the screws dipped in Perfect Seal #4, and then tighten them securely. Oil and install a new lower water tube grommet in the top of the water pump housing. Apply a light film of OMC Type A Grease to the propeller shaft, and then install the propeller, using a new drive pin and a new cotter pin to secure it.

SERVICING THE MECHANICAL-SHIFT TYPE LOWER UNIT—THROUGH 1975

5.5, 6.0, 9.5, 9.9, 15, 18, 20, 25, 33 & 40 Hp Two-Cylinder Engines

① It is possible to remove the lower gear case without removing the powerhead. However, if the exhaust housing is to be disassembled, it is necessary first to remove the powerhead. The gear case may be removed by taking off the upper engine cover and

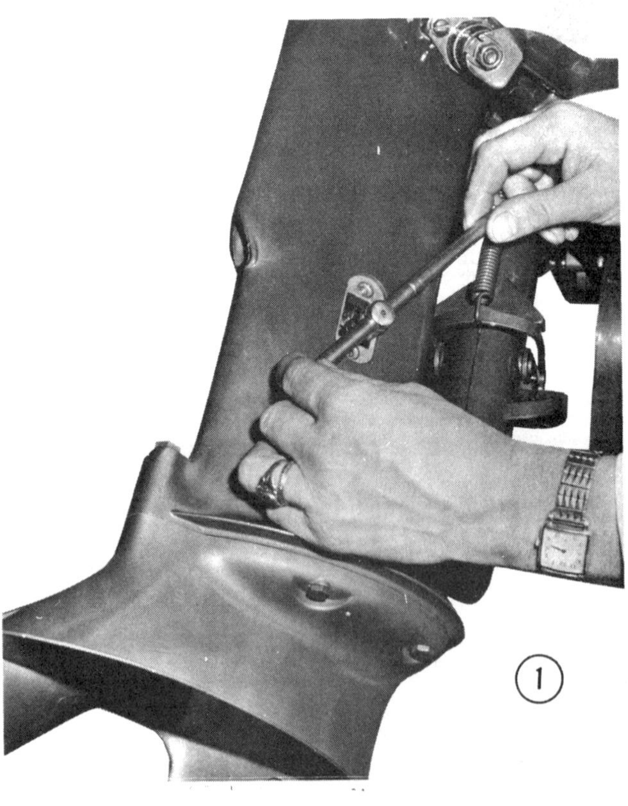

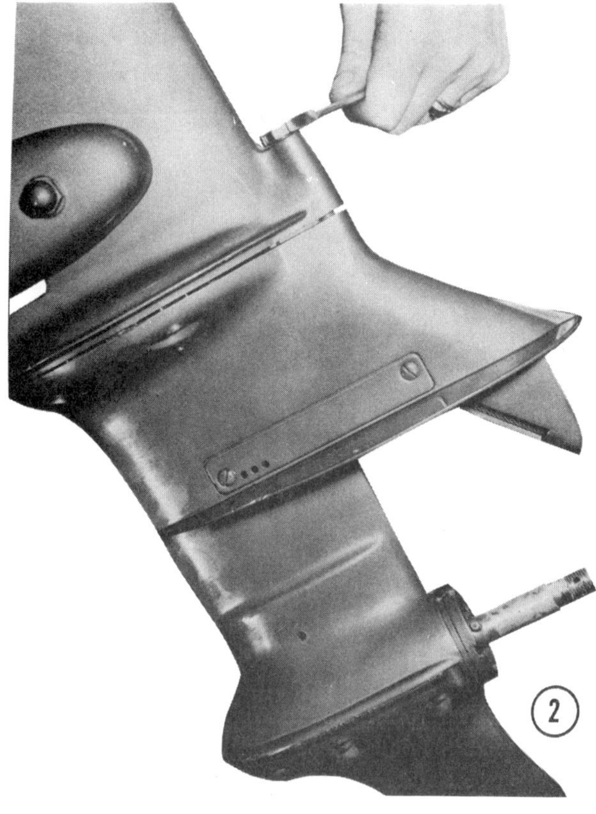

disconnecting the spark plug wires. Remove the exhaust housing cover plate to expose the shift rod connector. Take out the lower connector bolt. On the 5.5 and 6.0 engines, the lower unit will drop about 3/4" after taking out the bolt. It is then necessary to turn the propeller shaft to align the pin in the driveshaft with the slot in the exhaust housing. The washer and spring for the bottom seal of the powerhead will come off with the lower unit.

② Remove the propeller, and then take off the five bolts holding the gear case or extension case to the exhaust housing. *NOTE: One bolt is at the top of the case, as shown, and four are reached from the underside.* Remove the gear case extension, if desired.

DISASSEMBLING

③ Remove the three screws holding the water pump housing to the gear case, and then lift out the water pump assembly and driveshaft.

④ Remove the shift rod pivot pin and the six screws holding the gear case halves together. Separate the gear case halves.

⑤ Swing the shifter lever and cradle out of the way. Lift the propeller shaft assembly from the gear case, and then remove the parts. Remove the seal from the gear case head and discard the O-ring seal. Remove the pinion gear and thrust washer from the upper gear case. *NOTE: If the bushing in the gear case is worn excessively, the entire gear case must be replaced.*

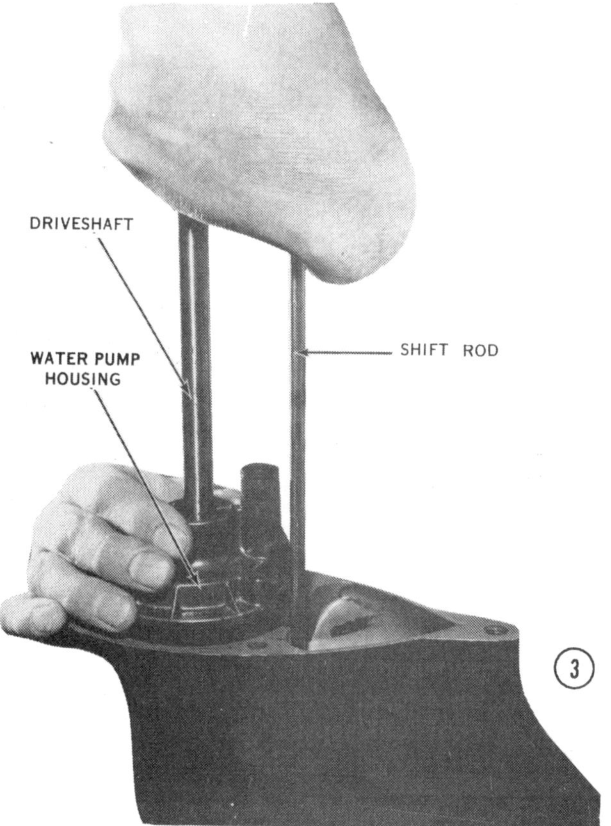

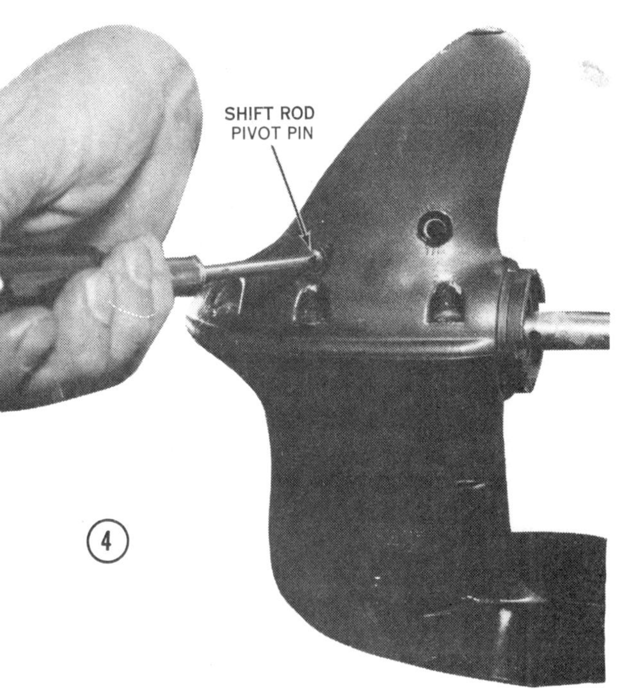

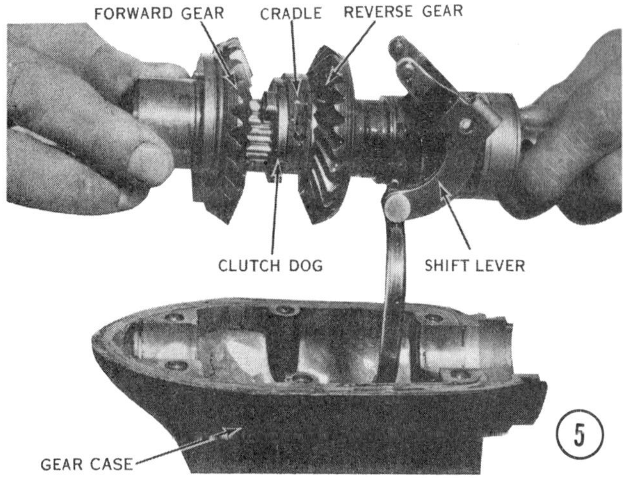

CLEANING AND INSPECTING

Clean all parts with solvent and dry with compressed air. Discard all oil seals, O-ring seals, and gaskets.

Inspect the driveshaft splines, drive gears, clutch dog, pinion gear, bearings, bushings, and thrust washers for wear or damage. Replace the clutch dog if the engagement surfaces are chipped or rounded.

Inspect the gear case and exhaust housing for nicks on the machined surfaces. Remove defects and resurface the faces on a surface plate, using No. 120 grit emery cloth and finishing with No. 180 grit cloth.

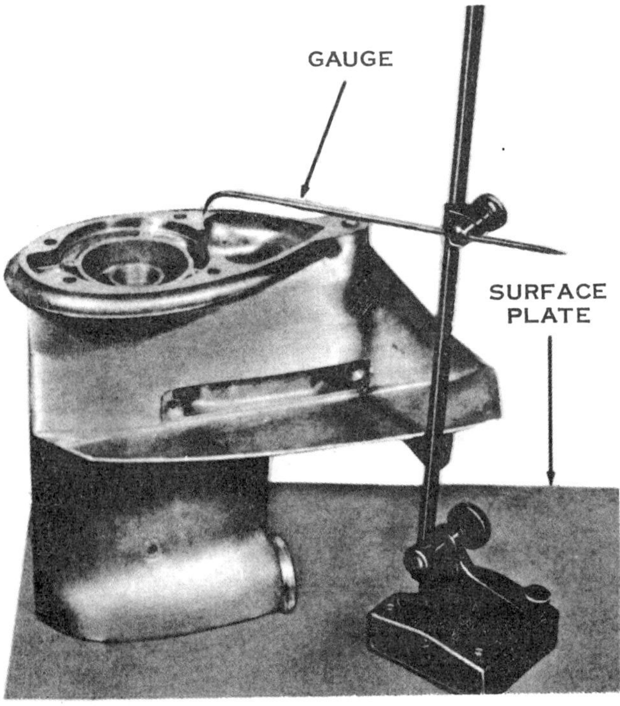

Check the parallelism of the gear case on a surface plate. If the gear case is bent, it must be replaced. Never try to straighten a bent gear case. Check the exhaust housing in the same manner.

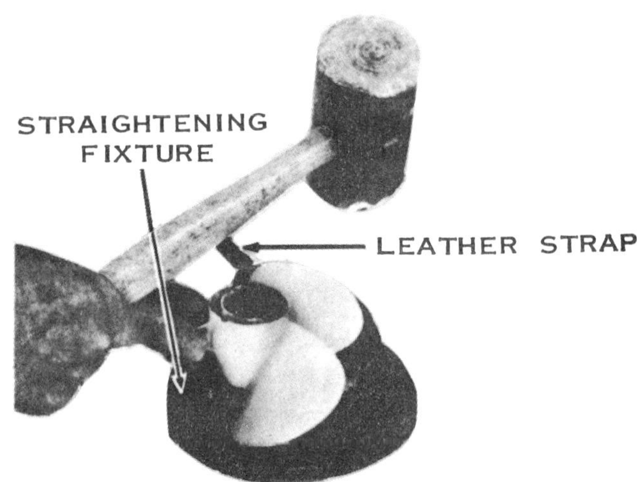

To straighten a bent propeller blade, use the special Tool No. 376934 and a piece of leather belting under the part of the blade that touches the fixture. Rap the high part of the blade smartly with a No. 3 rawhide mallet.

Check the parallelism on a surface plate, using a gauge, as shown. Don't attempt to straighten a bent gear case.

Inspect the water pump impeller and replace it if the vanes are damaged or worn. Inspect the pump housing and plate for scores and pits. Check the water intake tube and screen for clogging or obstructions.

Inspect the propeller for nicks, broken blades, and cracks. Remove minor nicks with a file. **CAUTION: Don't attempt to weld a cracked or broken blade.** Check the pitch on a propeller block, Tool No. 376934. To straighten a bent blade, use a piece of leather belting under the part of the blade that touches

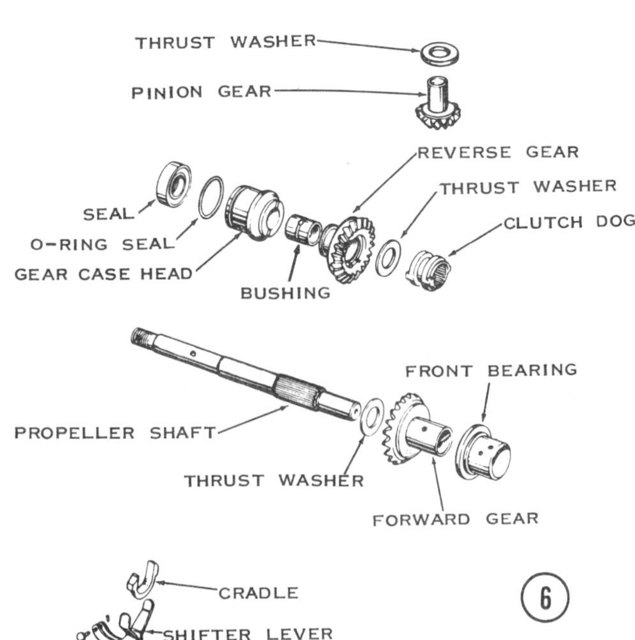

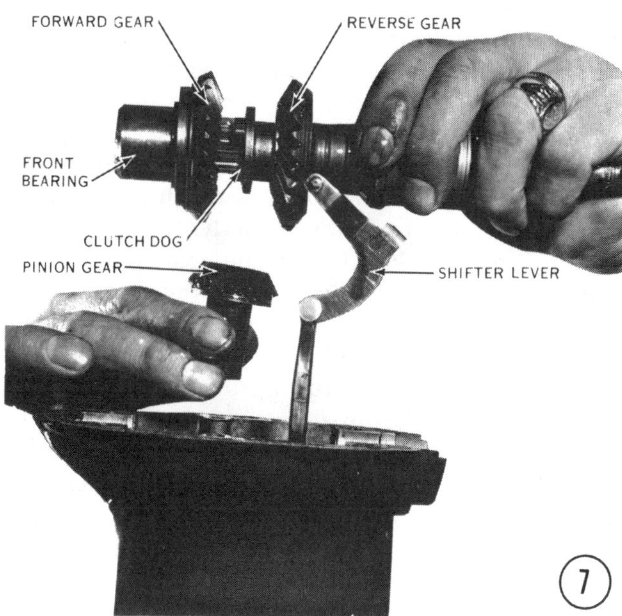

the fixture. Rap the high part of the blade smartly with a No. 3 rawhide mallet. The leather allows a slight overbend to correct for the blade's normal tendency to spring back.

Check the rubber slip clutch, using the special fixture, Tool No. 378448, and a torque wrench. The clutch should start to slip at 100-160 ft-lbs.

ASSEMBLING

⑥ Replace the shift rod bushing and O-ring seal, using the special tool, No. 304515, and then install a new driveshaft seal, pressing against the lettered side of the seal. Oil the end of the shift rod, and then insert it through the shift rod bushing.

⑦ Install a new seal in the gear case head and a new O-ring seal in the groove. Assemble the clutch dog, thrust washers, gears, bushing, front bearing, and gear case head to the propeller shaft. Install the propeller shaft assembly in the gear case so that the gear case head and front bearing are seated over the dowel pin and matching groove. Place the cradle in the shifter dog, and then swing the shifter lever into position in the cradle.

⑧ The propeller shaft for the 33 Hp engine varies in some details from the other engines' shafts, and these additional instructions are provided to assist in assembling the gear case for this model. Assemble the detent spring and the two detent balls to the propeller shaft, using OMC Needle Bearing Grease. Align the notches in the clutch dog with the detent balls in the propeller shaft as shown in the insert in the left corner. If the notches in the clutch dog appear to be off-center, rotate the clutch dog on the propeller shaft 180°. Slide the clutch dog forward onto the shaft and center it over the detent balls (which is the neutral position) as shown in the inset in the upper right corner. This will prevent accidental movement of the clutch dog during assembly and possible loss of the detent balls and spring. Assemble the oil retainer housing, washers, gears, and bearings to the propeller shaft in the sequence shown. **CAUTION: The bronze side**

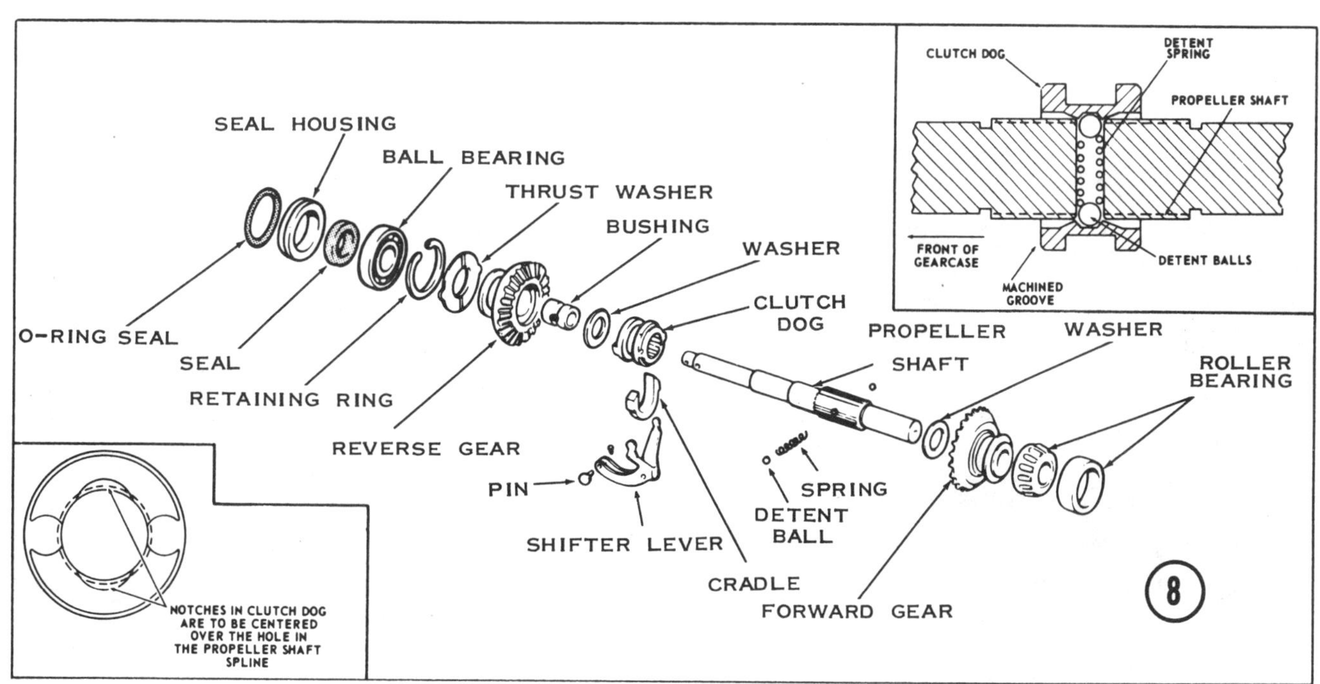

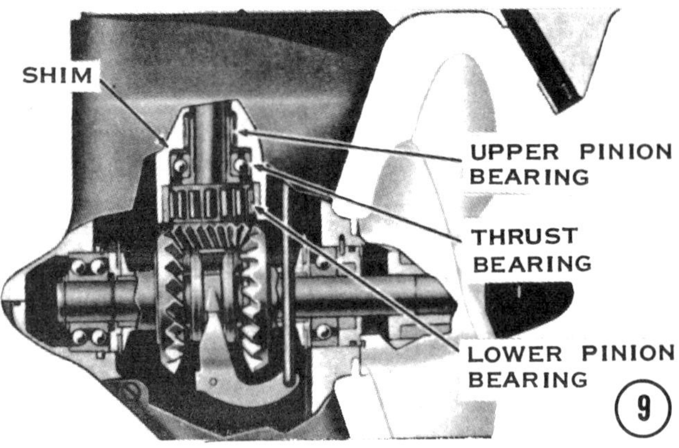

of the reverse gear thrust washer must face the gear. Install the assembled propeller shaft into the gear case, with the tabs on the thrust washer facing up and down. Place the cradle, shifter lever, and shift rod in position.

⑨ In the single-piece gear case, all parts of the larger units are basically like those of the 33 Hp model covered in the preceding step. This cutaway view is shown for comparison.

⑩ Wash the machined faces of the gear case halves. Apply Sealer 1000 to the machined faces, and then lay a sealing strip in each groove. Cut the ends of the seal square and allow 1/32″ to extend beyond the end of the groove in order to provide a tight butt seal against the gear case head. Add a little sealer to the ends of the sealing strip. Apply a thin line of Sealer 1000 to the machined surfaces of the upper gear case. Place the bottom half of the gear case on the upper half, and then install both pairs of end screws after dipping them in Perfect Seal #4. Tighten the end screws enough to draw the gear case halves together.

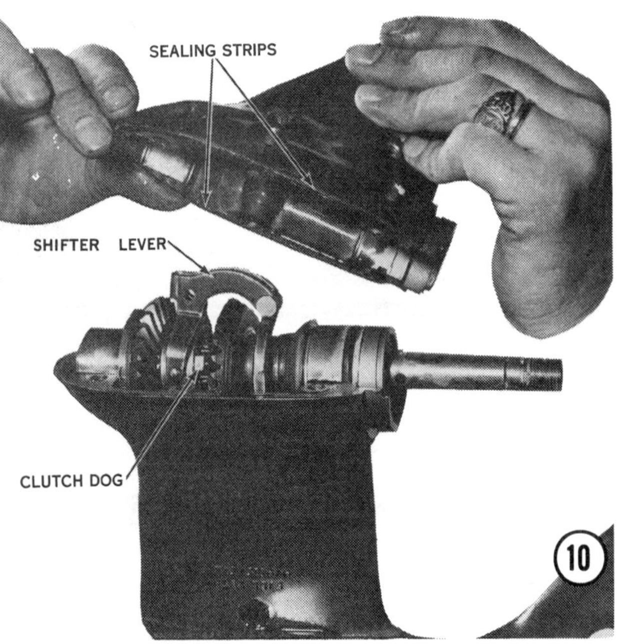

Install the shift lever pivot pin, using a new seal. Check the gear case seal for pinching between the gear case halves. Install the two center screws and gradually tighten all, alternating from side to side and working toward the end screws. Rotate the propeller shaft to check for free operation. Operate the shift mechanism to be sure that it operates properly.

⑪ Apply Sealer 1000 to the gear housing, and then position the impeller plate in the recess. Install the driveshaft, turning it to engage the pinion gear. Oil the impeller, and then slip it down over the drive pin. Install the water pump housing, turning the driveshaft clockwise so that the impeller blades slip into the housing in the proper direction. Dip the screws in Perfect Seal #4, and then tighten them securely. Install a new O-ring seal at the top of the driveshaft.

INSTALLING THE LOWER UNIT

⑫ Oil the upper end of the driveshaft and the lower end of the water tube. Place the shift lever in FORWARD gear. Bring the gear case into position under the exhaust housing, and then slide it up until the end of the driveshaft touches the crankshaft.

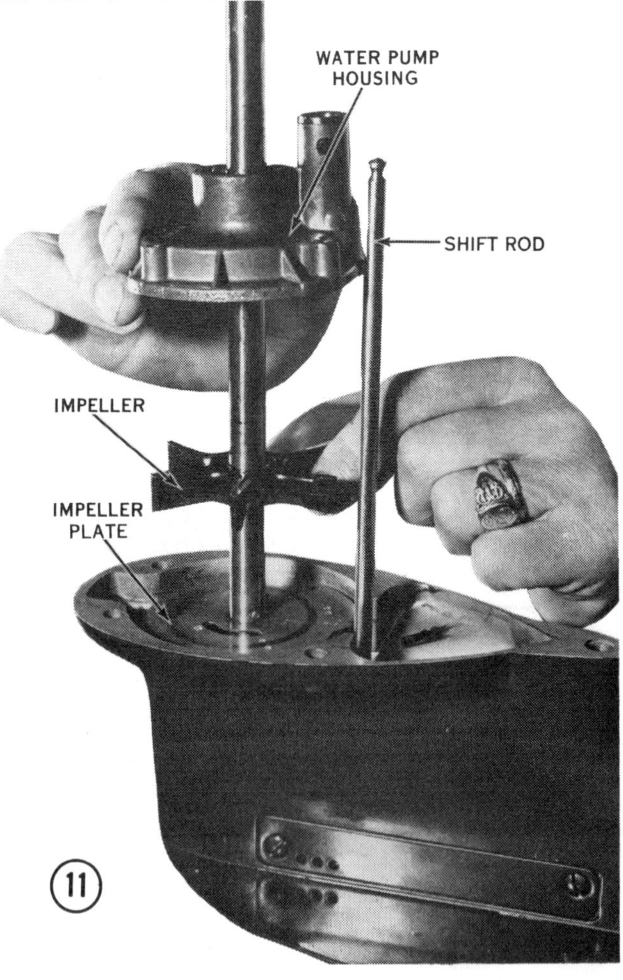

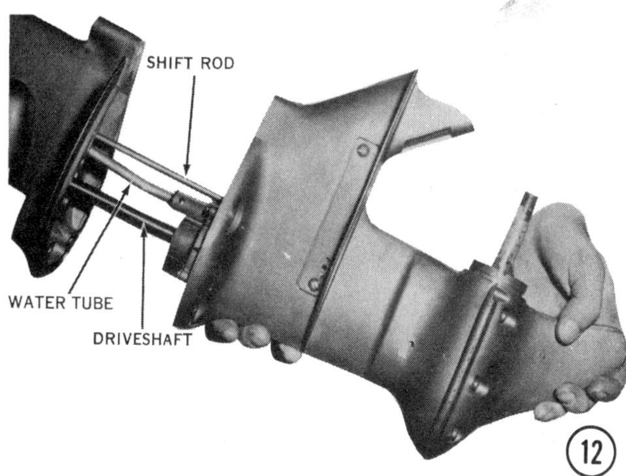

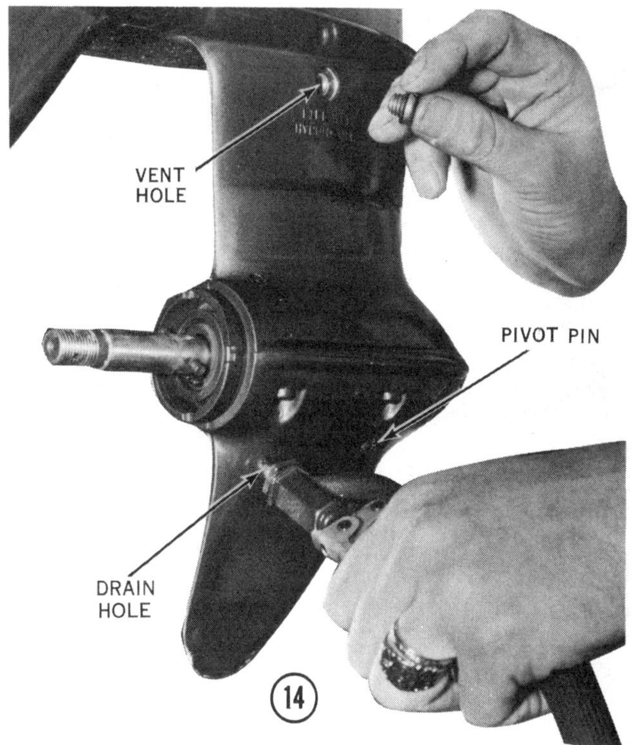

CAUTION: Alignment must be perfect to engage the driveshaft splines. Turn the flywheel slightly in a clockwise direction to help in engaging the splines. Look between the gear case and extension housing to make sure that the water tube enters the grommet on top of the pump housing.

(13) Attach the gear case to the exhaust housing with the bolts dipped in Perfect Seal #4. Four bolts are reached from the underside and one from the top. Replace the lower shift rod connector bolt. Replace the spark plug wires.

(14) Remove the vent screw, and then fill the gear case through the drain plug hole with OMC Type C Lubricant. Add lubricant until it runs out of the vent hole, replace the vent plug, and then replace the drain plug. **CAUTION: Don't remove the pivot pin.**

(15) Lubricate the propeller shaft with grease, and then install the propeller, shear pin, propeller nut, and cotter pin.

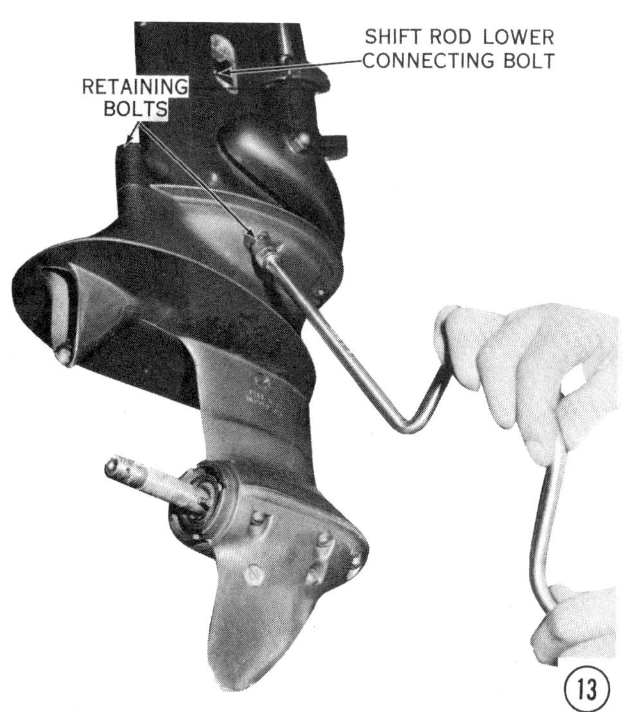

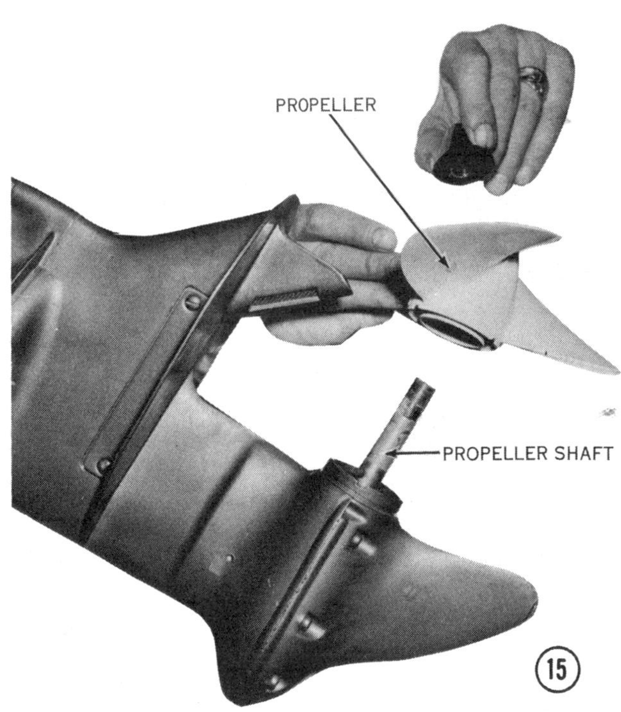

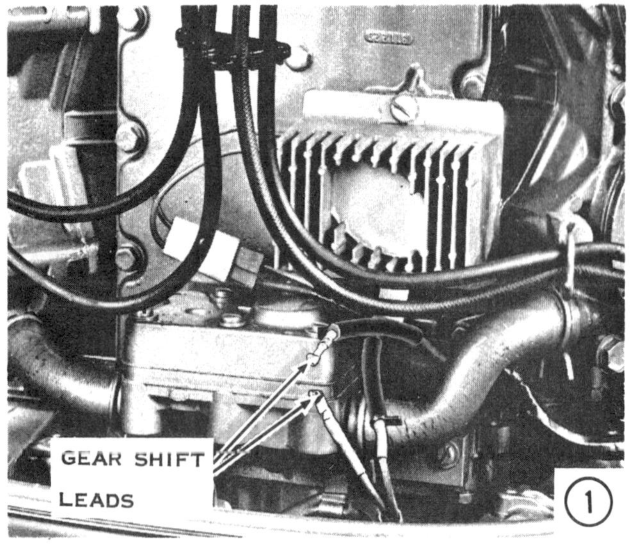

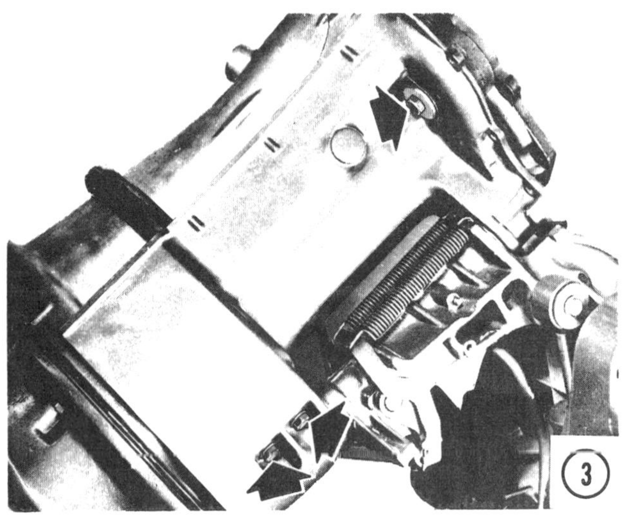

SERVICING THE ELECTRIC-SHIFT TYPE LOWER UNIT— 1963-68

40 Hp Engine

These models contain an electric-shift gear case in which an electromagnet attracts the free end of a spring to a clutch hub when the coil is energized. The revolving spring wraps itself tightly around the hub to establish a direct coupling with the propeller shaft. When the NEUTRAL button is depressed, the electromagnet is de-energized and the drive spring resumes its normal position, with the spring floating on the clutch hub.

It is possible to remove the upper and lower gear case without removing the powerhead. However, if it is necessary to disassemble the exhaust housing, the powerhead must be removed first.

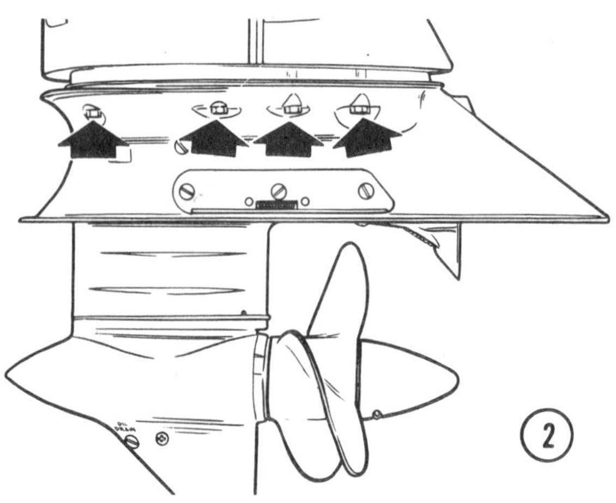

OVERHAULING THE LOWER UNIT

REMOVING THE GEARCASE

40 Hp Engine

① Disconnect the spark plug wires, drain the lubricant, and then take off the front exhaust housing cover plate and inner plate. Slide back the insulating sleeves on the shift cable wires so that the terminals can be disconnected. *NOTE: The terminals are located next to*

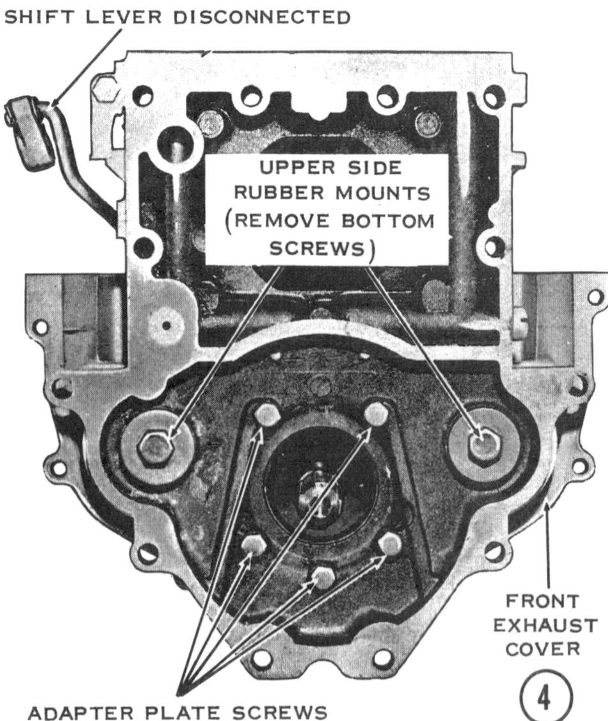

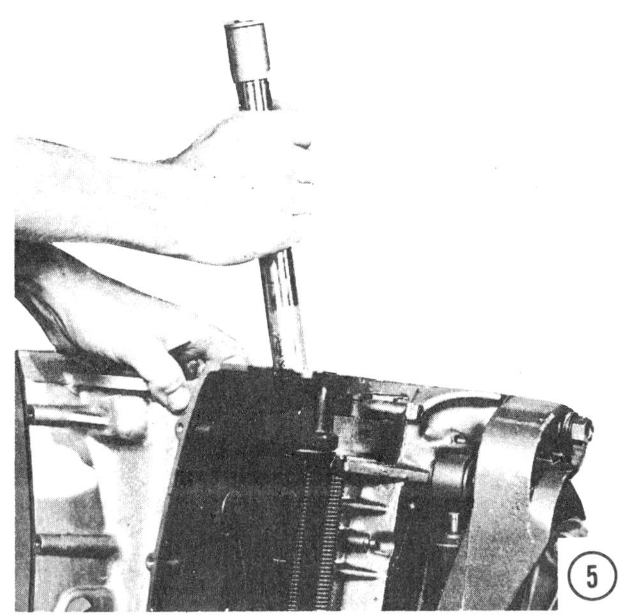

the exhaust cover. Attach a long piece of wire to the terminal at the lower end so that you can pull it back up during assembly. Apply liquid soap or oil to the cable, and then remove the inner cover and clamp. Then remove the bolts on the gear case. *NOTE: Some engines have a long bolt coming down through the exhaust housing.*

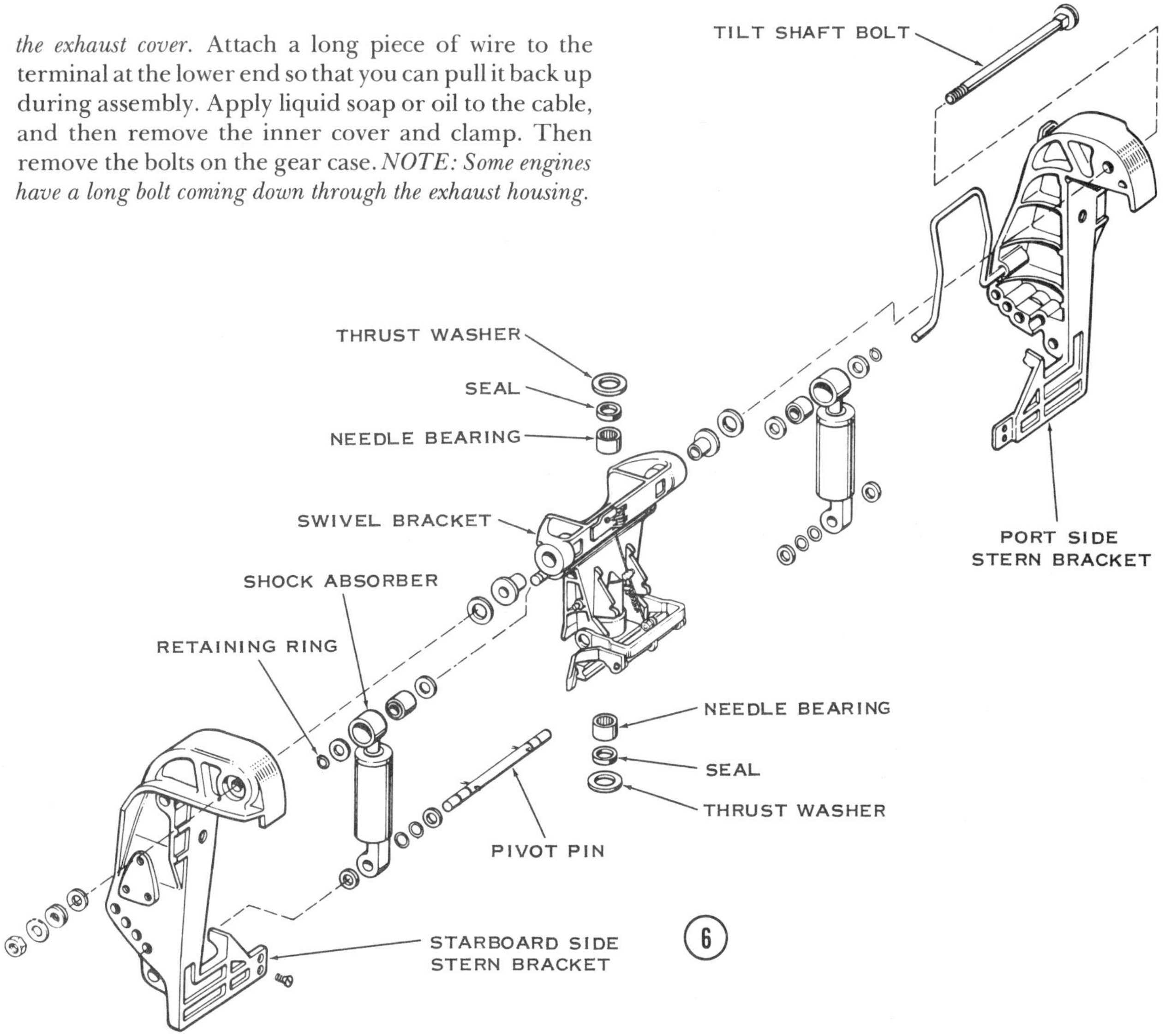

② Remove the eight screws holding the gear case to the exhaust housing, or to the gear case extension if one is used, and then pull the gear case straight away from the exhaust housing to disengage the driveshaft from the crankshaft and the water tubes from the grommets. **CAUTION: Avoid damaging the electric shift cables.**

③ Remove the screws holding the rear exhaust housing cover to the front exhaust housing cover. Lift the rear exhaust housing cover from the outer exhaust housing assembly. The exhaust housing and adapter plate, which carry the powerhead and thermostat, are rubber-mounted to the front exhaust cover. To release the exhaust housing disconnect the shift linkage, and then remove the two bottom screws from the upper side rubber mounts. Take out the four lower unit mount screws.

④ To remove the adapter plate, take out the five screws holding the plate to the outer exhaust housing.

TILT SHAFT BOLT
THRUST WASHER
SEAL
NEEDLE BEARING
SWIVEL BRACKET
PORT SIDE STERN BRACKET
SHOCK ABSORBER
RETAINING RING
NEEDLE BEARING
SEAL
THRUST WASHER
PIVOT PIN
STARBOARD SIDE STERN BRACKET

6

Remove the two upper rubber mounts-to-adapter screws. Lift the adapter plate, with the tubes, out of the outer exhaust housing, being careful not to damage the water tubes, grommets, and couplings. If damaged, remove the upper mounts from the front exhaust cover.

⑤ The front exhaust cover is hinged to the swivel bracket by a pivot shaft. Loosen the steering friction screws to release tension on the steering friction spring. Remove the screw and washer from the bottom of the pivot shaft. To detach the front exhaust cover from the swivel bracket, drive the pivot shaft up from the bottom, and then remove it from the top. Tag the upper and lower thrust washers to assure correct assembly.

⑥ Remove the thrust rod and retainer and the thrust rod spring from the stern bracket. Remove the two screws holding the port and starboard stern brackets. Remove the tilting shaft bolt, nut, spring, and washers from the top of the stern brackets. Remove the retaining rings and washers holding the shock absorbers to the swivel bracket. Pull the stern brackets and shock absorbers off the swivel bracket and pivot pin. **CAUTION: Each stern bracket and shock absorber must be removed together.** Remove the top and bottom seals from the swivel bracket. Replace damaged needle bearings.

⑦ To disassemble the water pump, remove the screws holding the water pump to the gear case, and then slide the impeller and housing off the driveshaft. **CAUTION: Don't lose the drive key.** Remove the impeller plate and gasket from the gear case. Remove the cover from the impeller housing, and then press out the seal. Remove the water tube grommet and seal from the top of the cover.

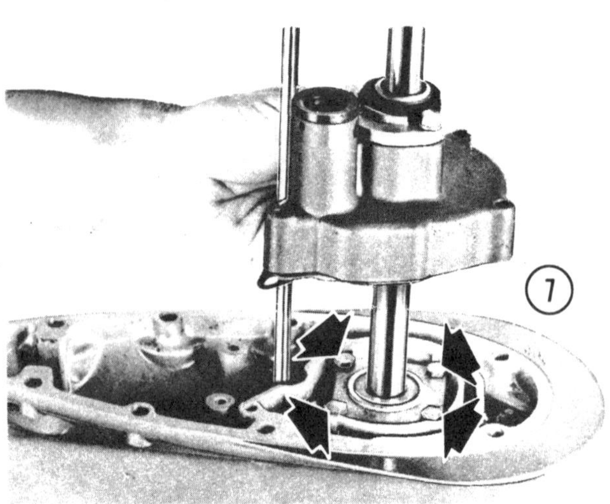

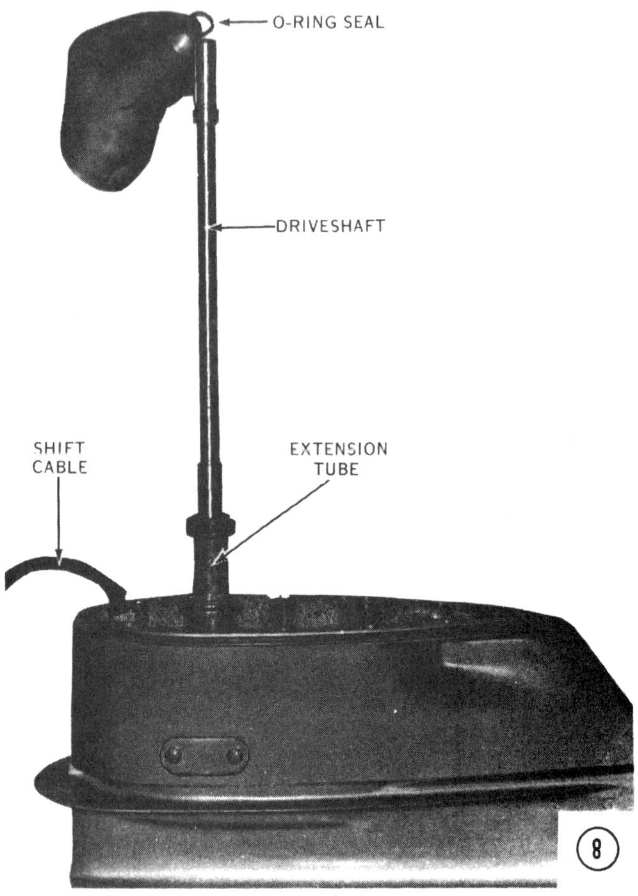

DISASSEMBLING

⑧ Remove the O-ring seal, the shim, and the extension tube.

(10)

⑨ Remove the water pump housing screws and the housing. Lift out the water tube and grommets. Take out the water pump impeller and the Woodruff key. Remove the short screw, and then take off the impeller plate and gasket from the gear case extension.

⑩ Remove the hex-headed bolts which hold the extension to the gear case. The lower one can be reached through the water intake opening.

⑪ Slide the extension away from the gear case to expose the shift cable connector sleeves, which must be slid back to expose the connectors. Remove the pilot ring.

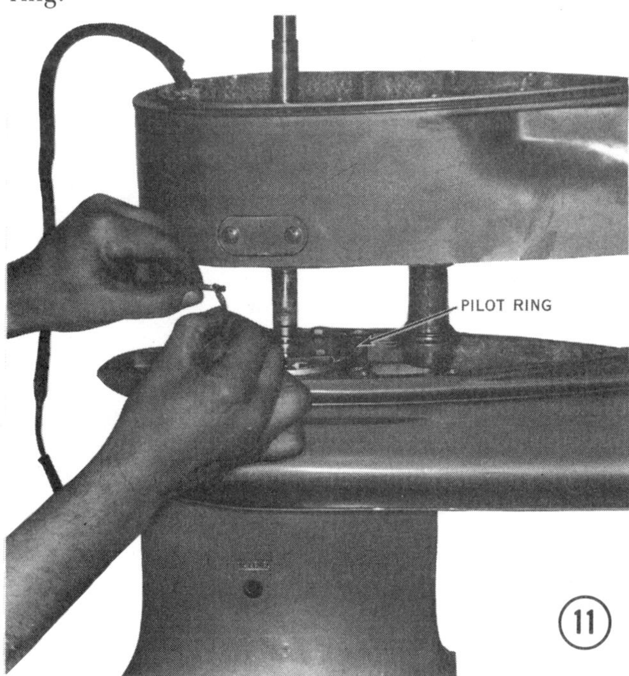

(11)

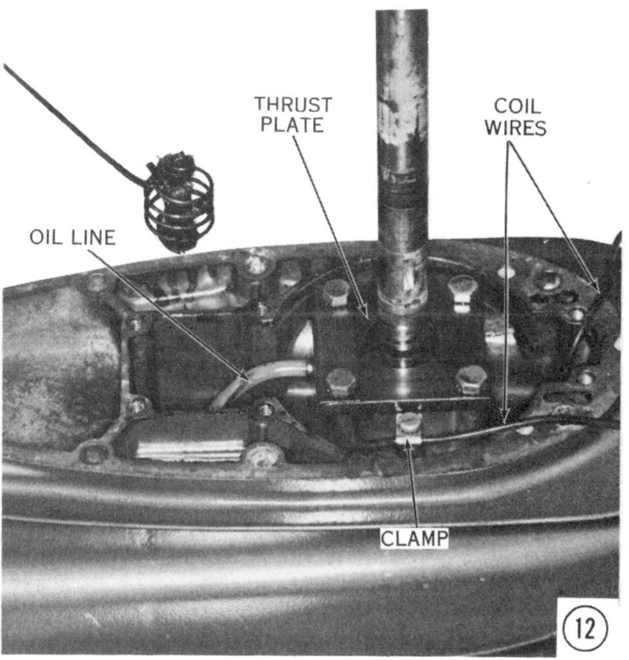

(12)

⑫ Reach in with a hook and pull out the two magnets, which are used to collect iron filings. Remove the clamp holding the blue reverse coil lead. Remove the thrust plate, bracket, and oil line. Lift out the thrust bearing.

⑬ Remove the gear case head by taking out the four bolts holding it in place. It may be necessary to use a puller if the gear case head is tight.

⑭ Remove the thrust bearing and thrust washers from the propeller shaft. Remove the Truarc retaining ring, using Tool No. 311879.

⑮ Feed the blue wire from the reverse coil down through its passageway before attempting to remove the coil and lead assembly. **CAUTION: Don't attempt to remove the reverse coil and lead assembly without first feeding this wire through its passageway, or you**

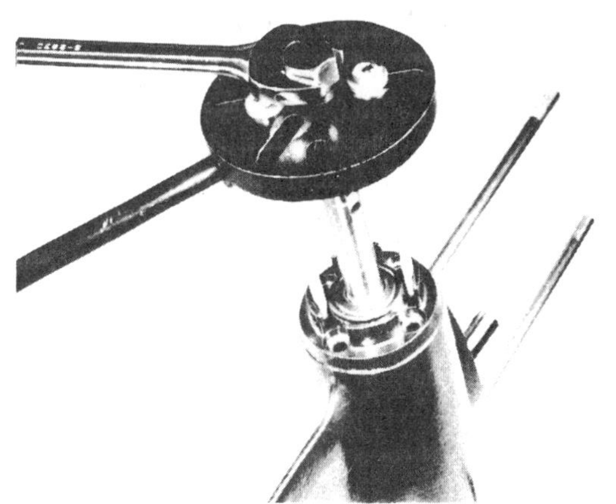
(13)

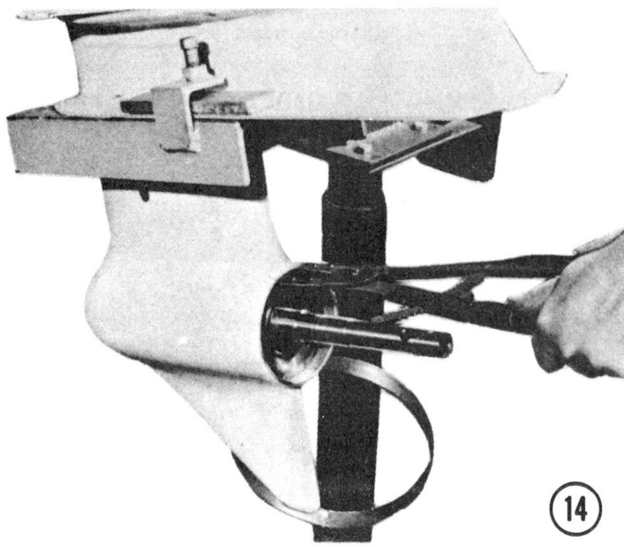

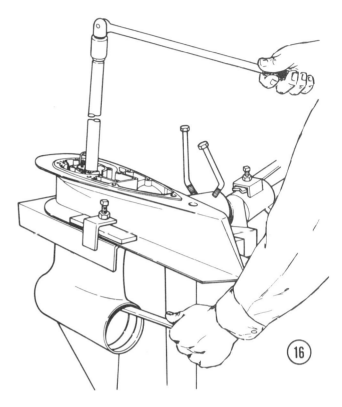

will cut the wire. After the coil wire is out, insert two gear case head screws into the opposite sides of the coil and carefully rock it out. Remove the propeller shaft, reverse gear, clutch hub cover, brass washer, and clutch spring as an assembly. **CAUTION: Make sure that the cam lobe on the shaft clears the oil pump plunger.** Remove the oil pump plunger, spring, and body assembly by lifting it straight up and out of its bore.

⑯ Remove the pinion locknut from the bottom of the driveshaft with a special holding socket, Tool No. 312752. Pull the driveshaft out of the case, and then remove the pinion gear.

⑰ Remove the forward gear, clutch hub, and spring as an assembly. Remove the forward coil and lead assembly, using the special remover, Tool No. 380658. After the coil is loose, make sure that the coil wire is free, and that the knife-disconnect does not get stuck in the passageway leading to the gear cavity. Remove the front propeller shaft bearing. Attach the bearing cup remover, Tool No. 380657, to the bearing cup, and then attach a slide hammer to the puller to remove the bearing cup.

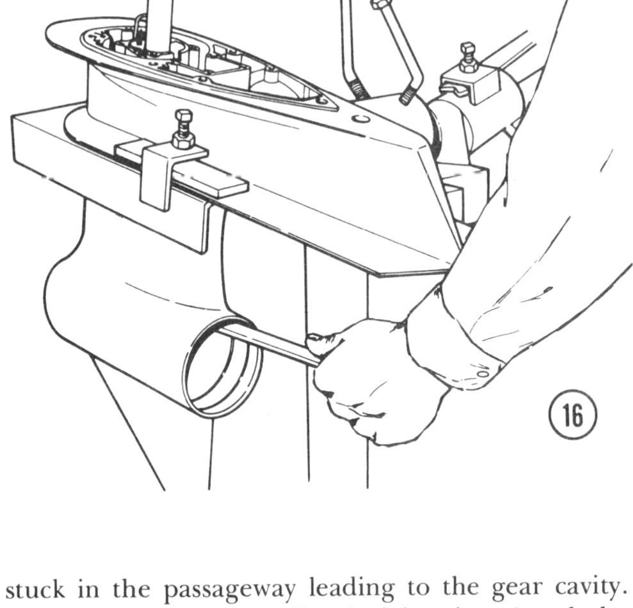

⑱ Attach a bearing remover, Tool No. 380657, to the upper needle bearing assembly. Next, attach a slide hammer and pull the needle bearing, as shown. Remove the oil deflector.

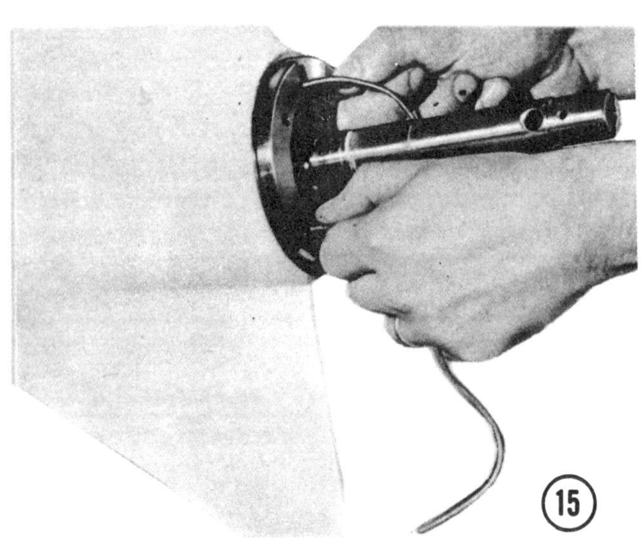

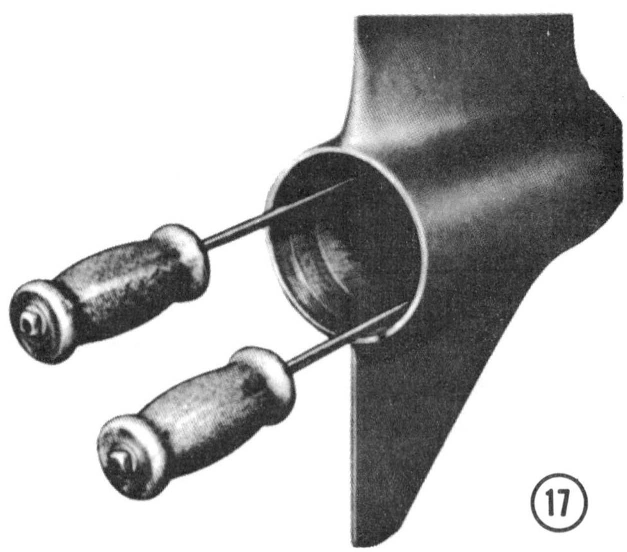

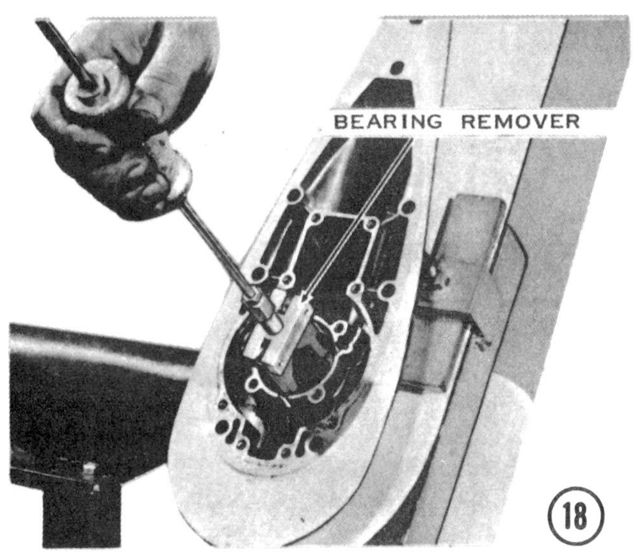

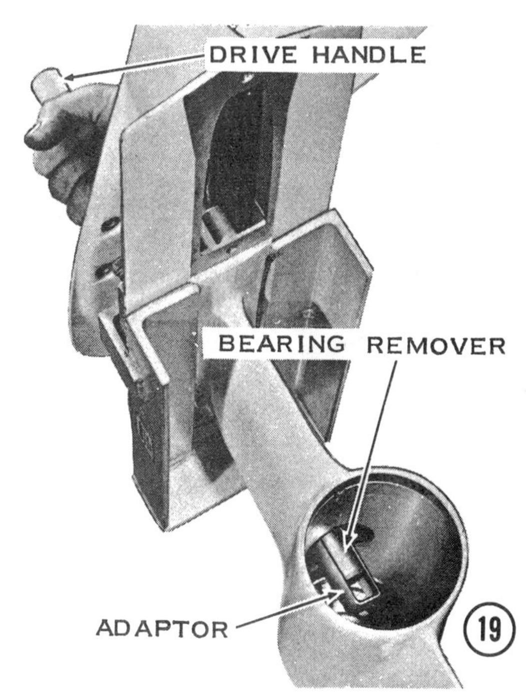

⑲ Place the adaptor, Tool No. 380659, on the roller bearing. Attach a remover, Tool No. 311885, to the handle of Tool No. 311880, and then drive the roller bearing out, as shown.

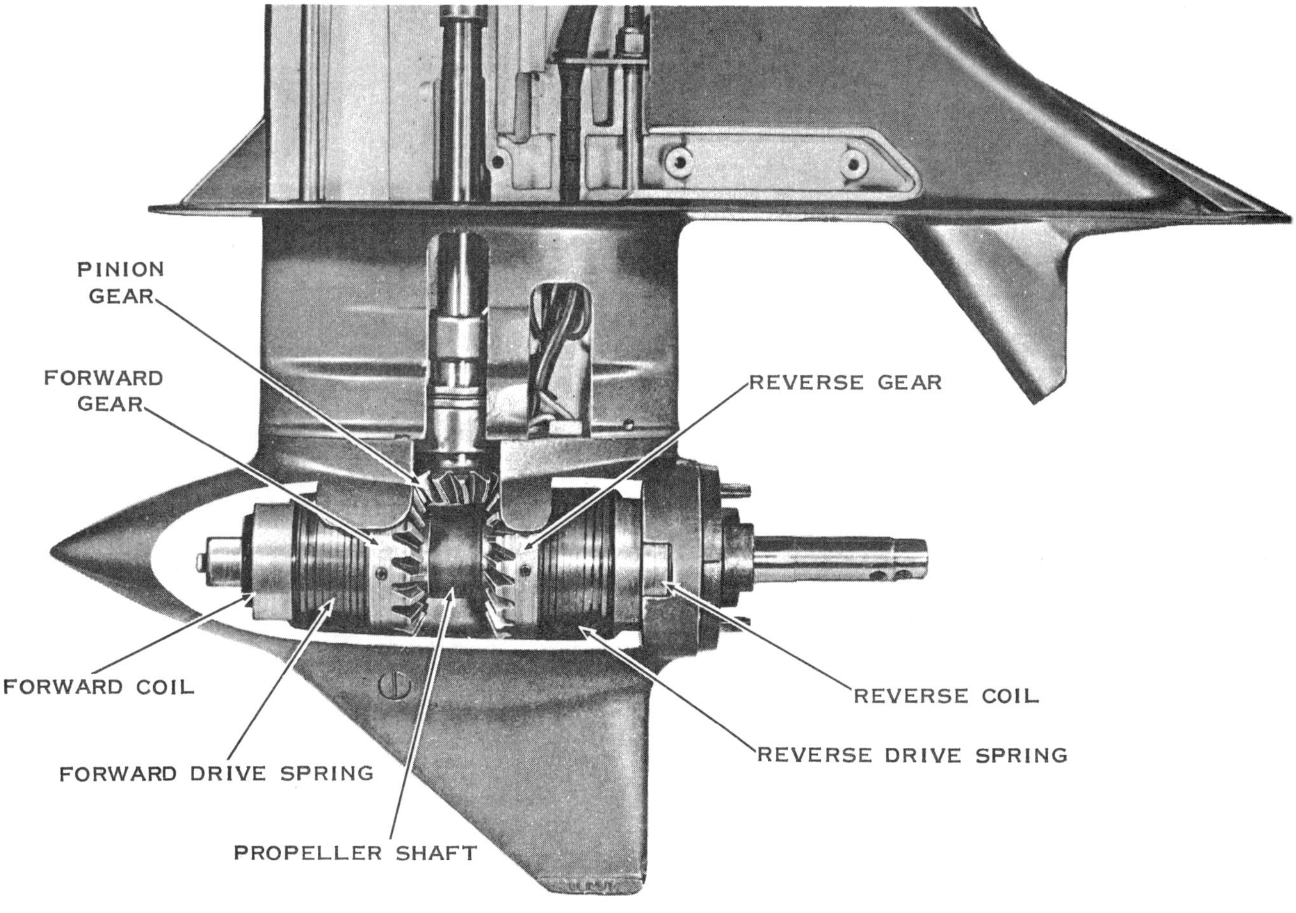

Cross-sectioned view of the electric-shift gear case. The drive spring is wrapped around the selected gear to lock it to the propeller shaft.

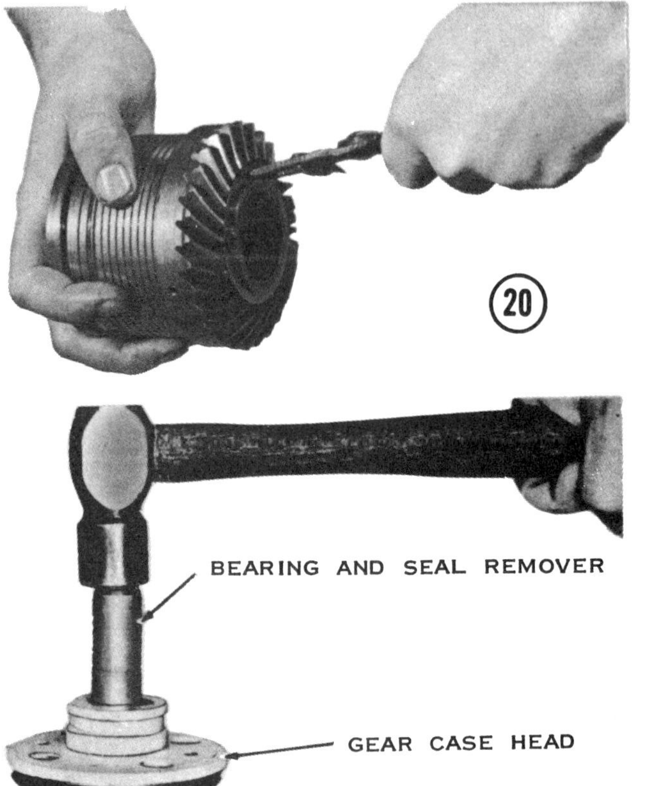

(20) To disassemble the forward or reverse gear assembly, remove the Truarc retainer. Slide the gear, spacer, and clutch spring off the hub. Remove the bearing. *NOTE: The forward gear assembly contains a bronze bearing, while the reverse gear assembly contains a needle bearing with 40 needles. In addition, the reverse gear assembly has a sleeve around the clutch spring.* Remove the setscrew in the gear and clutch assembly. Clean the setscrews, gears, spacers, and clutch springs with a degreasing solvent and allow the parts to dry.

(21) To disassemble the gear case head, place it on a suitable support, and then drive out the needle bearing assembly, using Tool No. 380659. Remove the two seals in the gear case head. Note the direction of the seal lips for assembly purposes. **CAUTION: The oil seals must not be reused.**

CLEANING AND INSPECTING

Clean all parts with solvent and dry with compressed air. Discard all oil seals, O-ring seals, and gaskets. Discard the upper pinion bearing, the upper driveshaft bearing, and the gear case head bearing, if these have been removed, because the thin steel case housing the needles will be damaged in removal.

(22) Check the parallelism on a plate with a surface gauge and a scriber. A drill press table will serve, using the spindle as a gauge. **CAUTION: Do not attempt to**

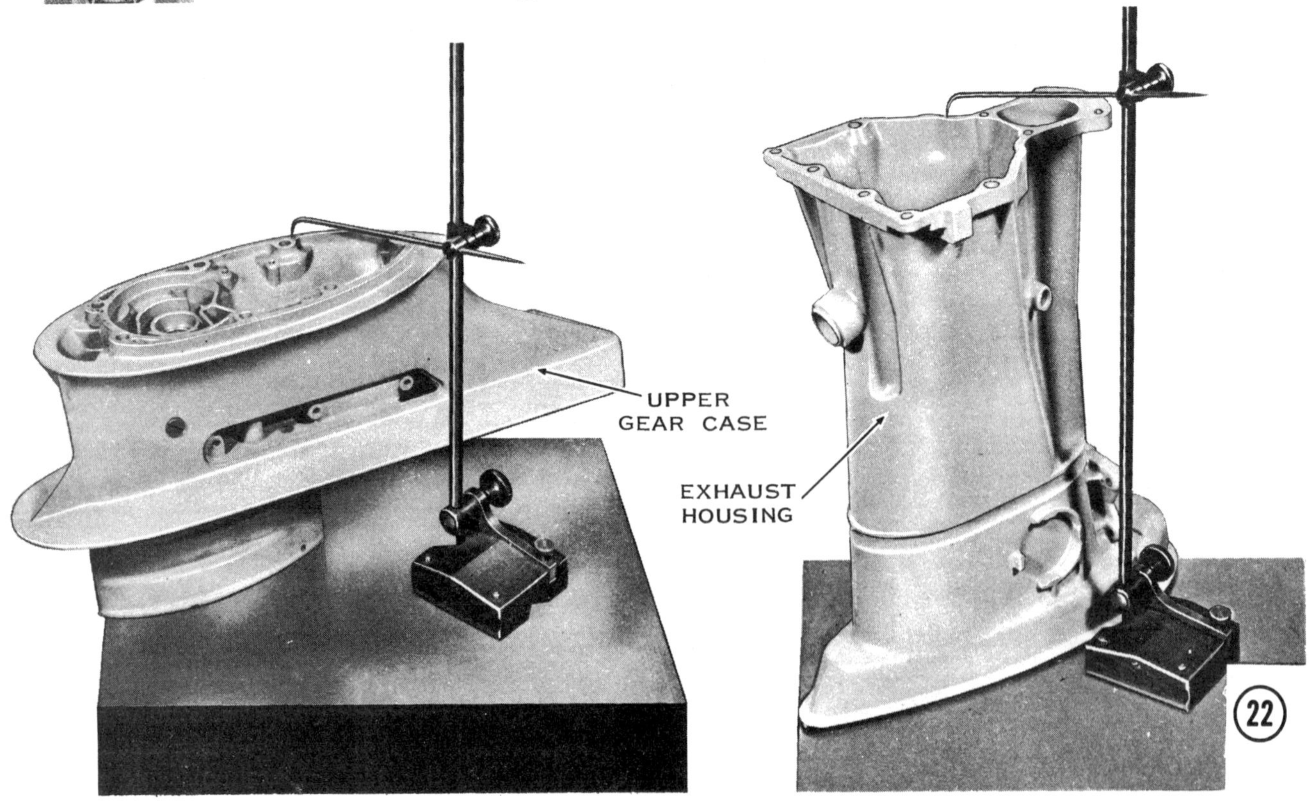

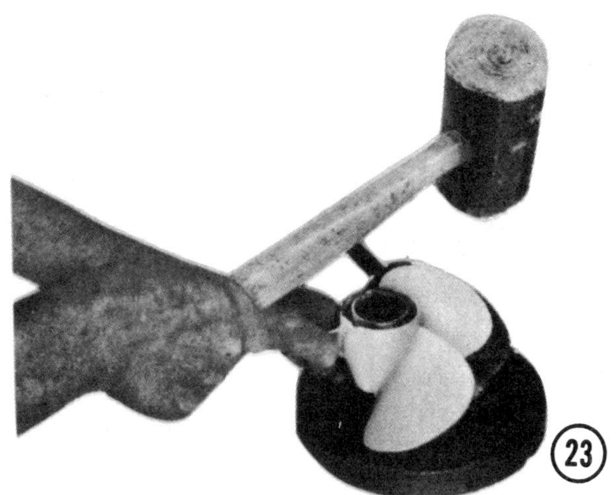
23

straighten a bent gear case; replace it. Inspect the gear case for nicks on the machined surfaces. Remove nicks and resurface the faces on a surface plate. Start with No. 120 grit emery cloth and finish with No. 180 grit. Inspect the driveshaft splines for wear. A lower unit bent from striking a submerged obstruction can cause extensive damage to the driveshaft. Replace the shaft if it is worn or bent.

Inspect the water tubes for obstructions or kinks, which may restrict the water flow. Check the opening of the 3/32" hole in the inlet water tube. This sprays a fine mist of cooling water on the shift cable. If it is clogged, serious damage can occur.

(23) Inspect the propeller for nicks, broken blades, and cracks. **CAUTION: Do not attempt to weld cracked or broken propellers.** Remove minor nicks with a file. *NOTE: The aft side of the propeller is flat while the other side is rounded.* File the blades accordingly to retain the shape. Check the pitch on a propeller pitch block. To straighten a bent blade, use a piece of leather strap or belting under the part of the blade that touches the fixture. Rap the high part of the blade smartly with a No. 3 rawhide mallet. The leather allows a slight overbend to correct for the blade's tendency to spring back. Check the rubber slip clutch, using the propeller torque fixture assembly, Tool No. 378448, with torque shaft, Tool No. 308114.

Inspect the water pump impeller and replace it if the vanes are damaged or worn. Inspect the pump housing for scoring and replace it if damaged. Inspect the impeller housing plate and replace it if scored or pitted.

Inspect the drive gears, pinion gear, and thrust washers for wear. Replace any that are worn.

Wash needle bearings in solvent, and oil immediately with clean, light spindle oil to prevent rusting. Inspect the bearings for wear. Replace if worn.

(24) Check the electromagnet coil windings on an ohmmeter or ammeter. The resistance should be approximately 6 ohms, or 2.0-2.4 amps if an ammeter is used. Check the shift cable leads for continuity. Check for shorts between the green and the blue (forward and reverse) leads which could cause both coils to operate at once. The green lead is for the FORWARD gear range and the blue lead is for the REVERSE.

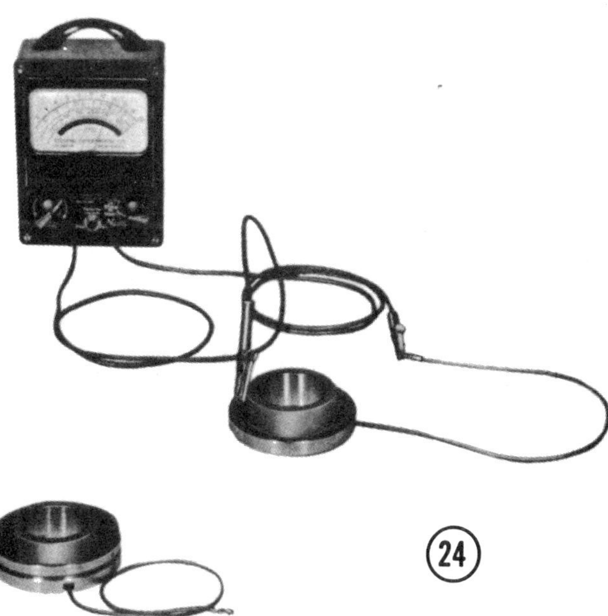
24

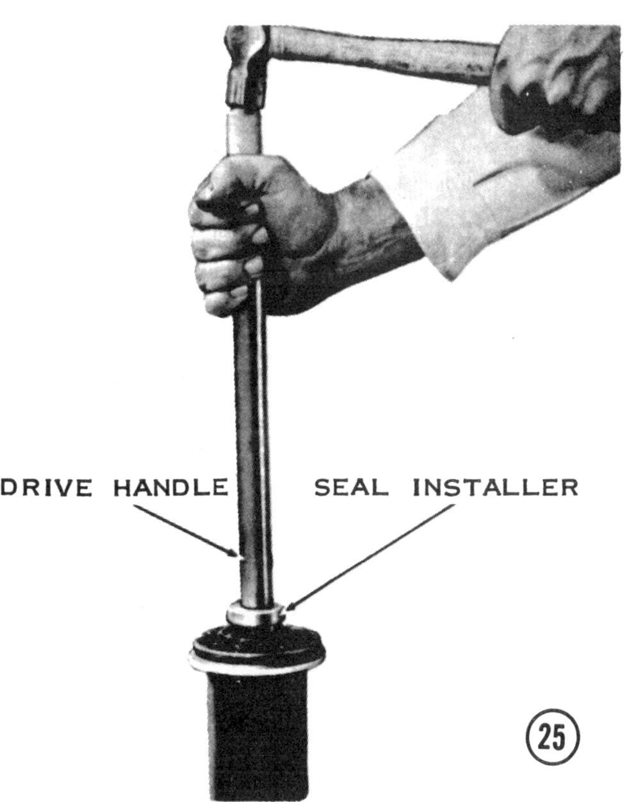

25

The magnets collect iron filings, and this prevents the particles from being circulated with the lubricating oil.

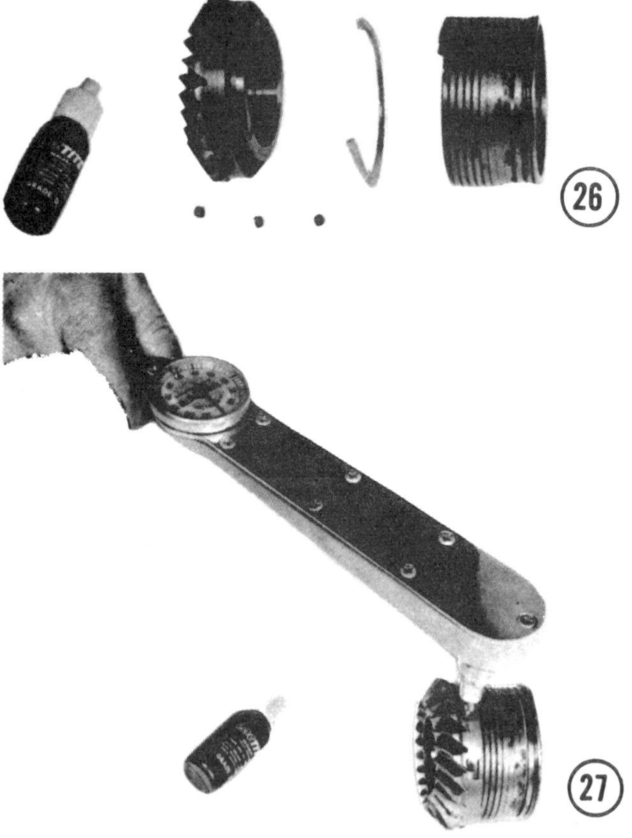

ASSEMBLING

(25) To assemble the gear case, install two new seals, using a seal installer, Tool No. 311877, attached to a drive handle, Tool No. 311880, as shown. The seals should be installed so that, when the assembly is completed, the lips of the seals will point away from each other. Install the gear case head needle bearing, using an installer, Tool No. 311869, attached to a drive handle, Tool No. 311880.

(26) Slip the spacer and clutch spring into the gear. Make sure that the spring engages the gear properly. Apply Loctite Sealant "D" sparingly to the threads of each screw. **CAUTION: Always use new screws. CAUTION: One drop of Loctite is the maximum to use. Don't allow the Loctite to enter any moving parts.**

(27) Torque the setscrews to 15-20 in-lbs. on gears with 8-32 × 5/32" setscrews or to 30-35 in-lbs. on gears with 10-32 × 3/16" setscrews. Bake the gear and clutch spring assembly at 300°F. for 20 minutes. Install the bronze bearing in the forward gear. Install the clutch hub on the gear and spring. Install the retaining ring, lettered side up. **CAUTION: In the event that the bronze bearing becomes cocked on the hub, do not force the assembly by wringing or tapping.** Apply needle bearing grease to the rear clutch hub bearing surface, and then place 40 needles around the hub. *NOTE: With the 40 needles in place, a slight gap between the first and last needle is normal.* Install the sleeve over the spring, with the flanged end facing the coil. Assemble the hub and gear, and then install the retaining ring. Install the gear case extension seals flush with the upper and lower casting surfaces, lips facing out. If removed, apply oil to the shift cable and pull the upper end up through the bottom of the extension until the lower end is seated in the casting. Install the retainer, and then slide the sleeve over the cable and down to the retainer.

(28) Install the bearing cup from the propeller shaft bearing assembly, using an installer, Tool No.

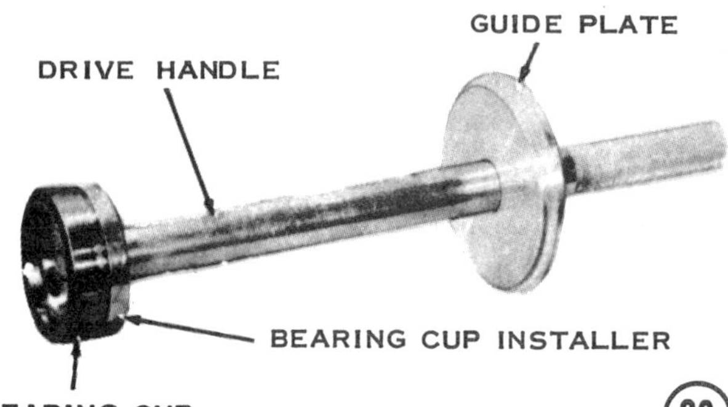

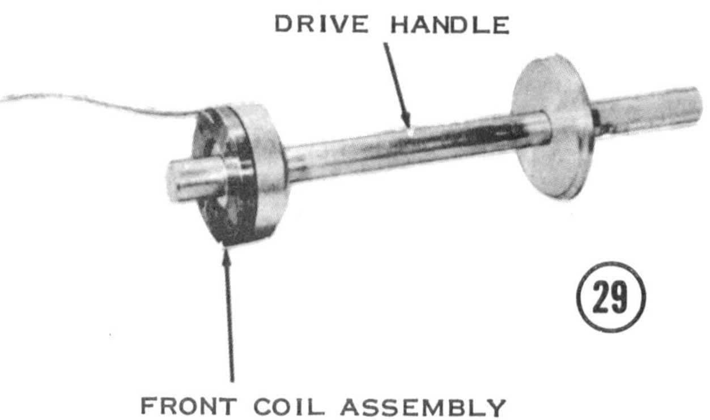

311872, attached to a drive handle, Tool No. 311880. The guide from the front coil installer, Tool No. 380691, should be placed on the drive handle to press in the bearing cup. Install the roller bearings. *NOTE: Assembly will be facilitated if a small amount of oil is used.*

(29) Assemble the front coil and lead assembly installer, Tool No. 380691 and No. 311880. Place the coil and lead assembly on the body of the installer, as shown. Attach an extra lead with a knife-disconnect to the front coil lead. Feed this wire into the gear case and up through the forward coil lead opening. Be careful not to damage the connection between the coil and lead. Insert the coil and installer into the gear case so that the coil lead is at the top of the coil. Carefully pull the attached lead while feeding the coil into the gear case. Drive the forward coil in until it seats. Remove the installer tool and the extra length of wire. With the coil installed, use an ohmmeter to check the resistance, which should be 6 ohms. An infinite resistance reading indicates an open circuit, such as a broken wire. Readings less than specifications indicate a short circuit to ground. Install the oil deflector, open side up, in its

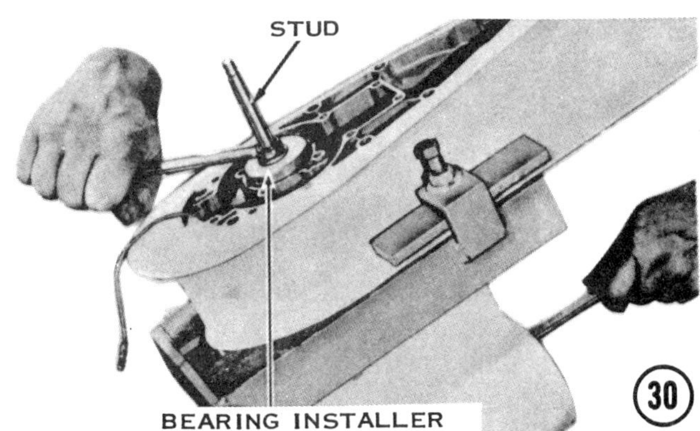

cavity, making sure that the notches in the side of the deflector line up with the drilled holes in the gear case.

(30) Place the upper needle bearing on the installer, Tool No. 311876, and the lower roller bearing on the pilot from Tool No. 380758. Place the stud No. 312019 from Tool No. 380759 through the driveshaft opening. The end of the stud with 1/2" of thread must be at the bottom. Place the lower roller bearing into the gear case and attach the installer to the stud. Place the

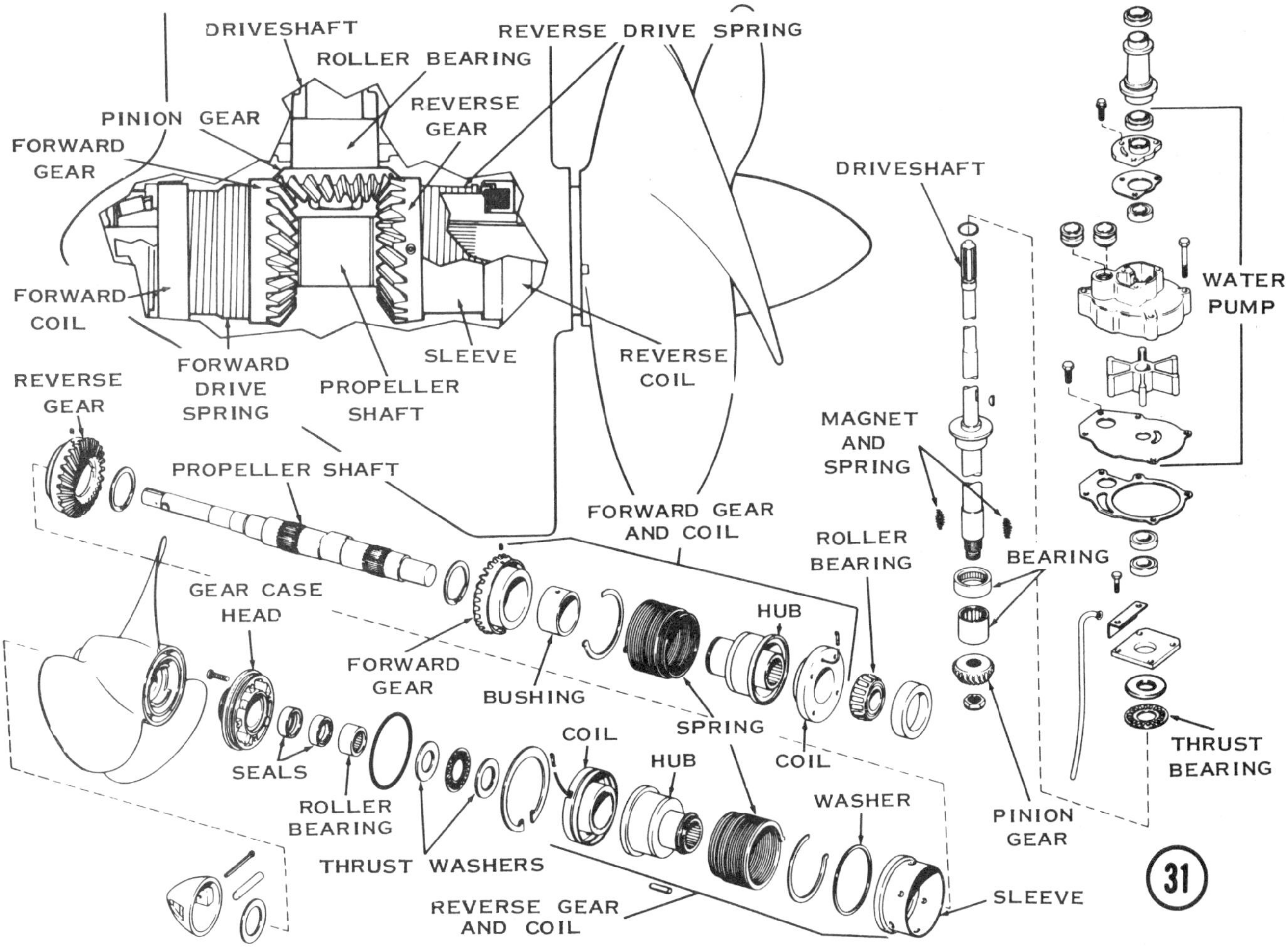

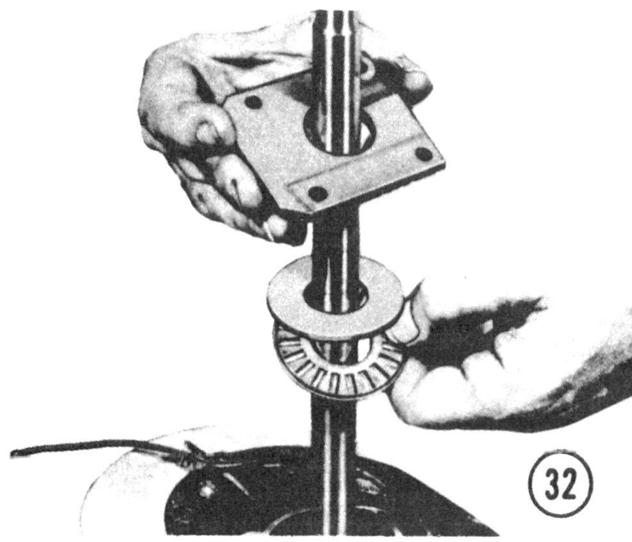

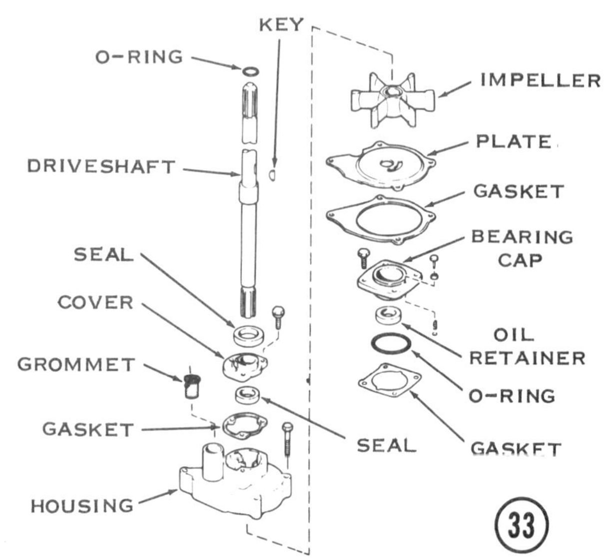

upper needle bearing (and the bearing installer) on the top of the stud. Next, place the 3/8" flat washer and the 3/8"-16 hex nut from the roller bearing installer, Tool No. 380758, on the stud. Draw up on the nut until both bearings are seated.

(31) Install the forward gear, clutch, and spring assembly. Install the driveshaft and the pinion gear. Torque the locknut to 70-80 ft-lbs. Install the oil pump and plunger, and then replace the propeller shaft. **CAUTION: Make sure that the pump cam faces away from the pump.** Turn the shaft slightly to engage the forward gear hub splines. Install the reverse gear, clutch, and spring assembly on the propeller shaft. **CAUTION: Align the splines with the propeller shaft. Don't force it. If the splines are aligned, the gear should slip into place easily.** Install the washer in the rear coil. *NOTE: Grease it to help in assembly.* Install the rear coil and lead assembly in the gear case. Before inserting the coil, make sure that the lead is at the top of the coil. After the coil is installed, feed the coil lead up through its passageway. With the coil installed, use an ohmmeter to check the resistance, which should be 6 ohms. Install the coil retaining ring (with the opening up) using pliers, Tool No. 311897. Install the thin thrust washer, the thrust bearing, and the second thrust washer on the propeller shaft. *NOTE: When installing the thrust washers, the one with the chamfer on the inner diameter goes nearest the coil. It should be noted also that this washer is the thinner of the two.* Install the gear case head. Align the countersunk holes in the gear case head with the tapped holes in the rear coil, and then seat the gear case head with a mallet. Install the four screws and tighten them securely.

(32) Clamp the blue reverse coil lead to the gear case, and then install the thrust bearing, plate, oil line bracket, and oil line.

INSTALLING THE GEAR CASE

40 Hp Engine

(33) Assemble the water pump by placing a new impeller housing gasket and impeller housing plate on the gear case, and then insert the impeller drive key. Install the impeller housing. Position the impeller for rotation in a counter-clockwise direction, when viewed from below. Attach the pump to the gear case with screws dipped in Perfect Seal #4. Tighten to 5-7 ft-lbs. of torque. Use a new gasket, seal, and seal rings, and then attach the pump cover with screws dipped in Perfect Seal #4. Torque the screws to 5-7 ft-lbs. Install a new grommet in the impeller housing to prevent exhaust gases from getting into the cooling system, which would cause overheating and pre-ignition. **CAUTION: It is especially important for the impeller housing seal ring to fit properly to prevent exhaust gases from feeding back into the intake manifold through the driveshaft housing.** Install a new O-ring seal on the driveshaft.

(34) Press new bearings and seals into the swivel bracket. Assemble the stern bracket and shock absorbers, and then attach them to the front exhaust cover. Install the upper and lower thrust washers as you tagged them. Place the exhaust housing in position in the front exhaust cover.

(35) Attach and tighten the four screws through the front exhaust cover-to-rubber mount on the outer exhaust housing. Attach the gear case extension. Place the adapter assembly, with the inner exhaust tube, water tubes, and new seals, gasket, and grommets in position. Tighten the two screws at each motor mount and the five screws to the outer exhaust housing. Make sure that the water tube grommets remain in position.

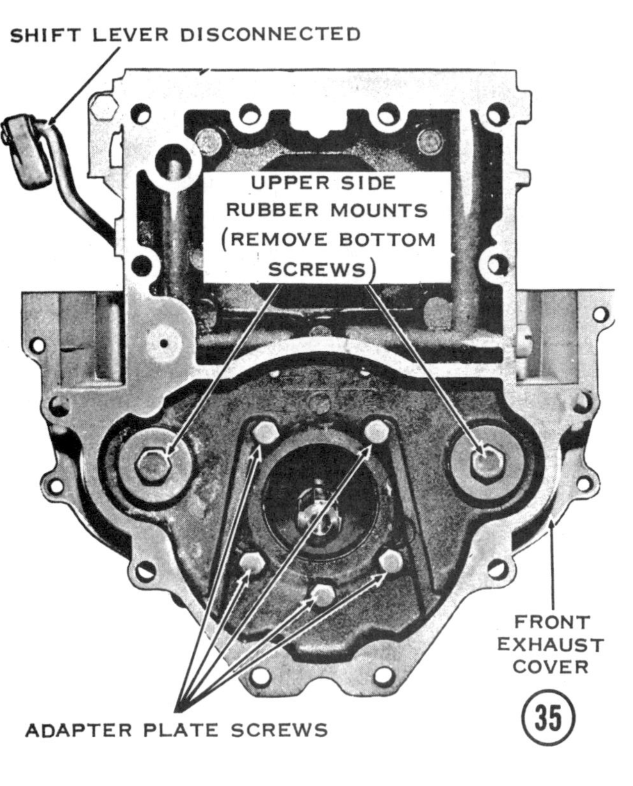

(35)

(36) Place a new O-ring on the driveshaft and then move the assembled gear case into position under the exhaust housing. Thread the shift cable through the exhaust housing opening and through the new gasket and exhaust housing plate and cable clamp. Carefully raise the gear case into position, making sure that the driveshaft is aligned with the crankshaft, water tubes with the grommets and connector. *NOTE: Oiling the ends of the water tubes will assist in assembly and avoid damaging the grommets and seals. NOTE: Although this illustration is of a four-cylinder engine, the process is the same for the 40 Hp motor.*

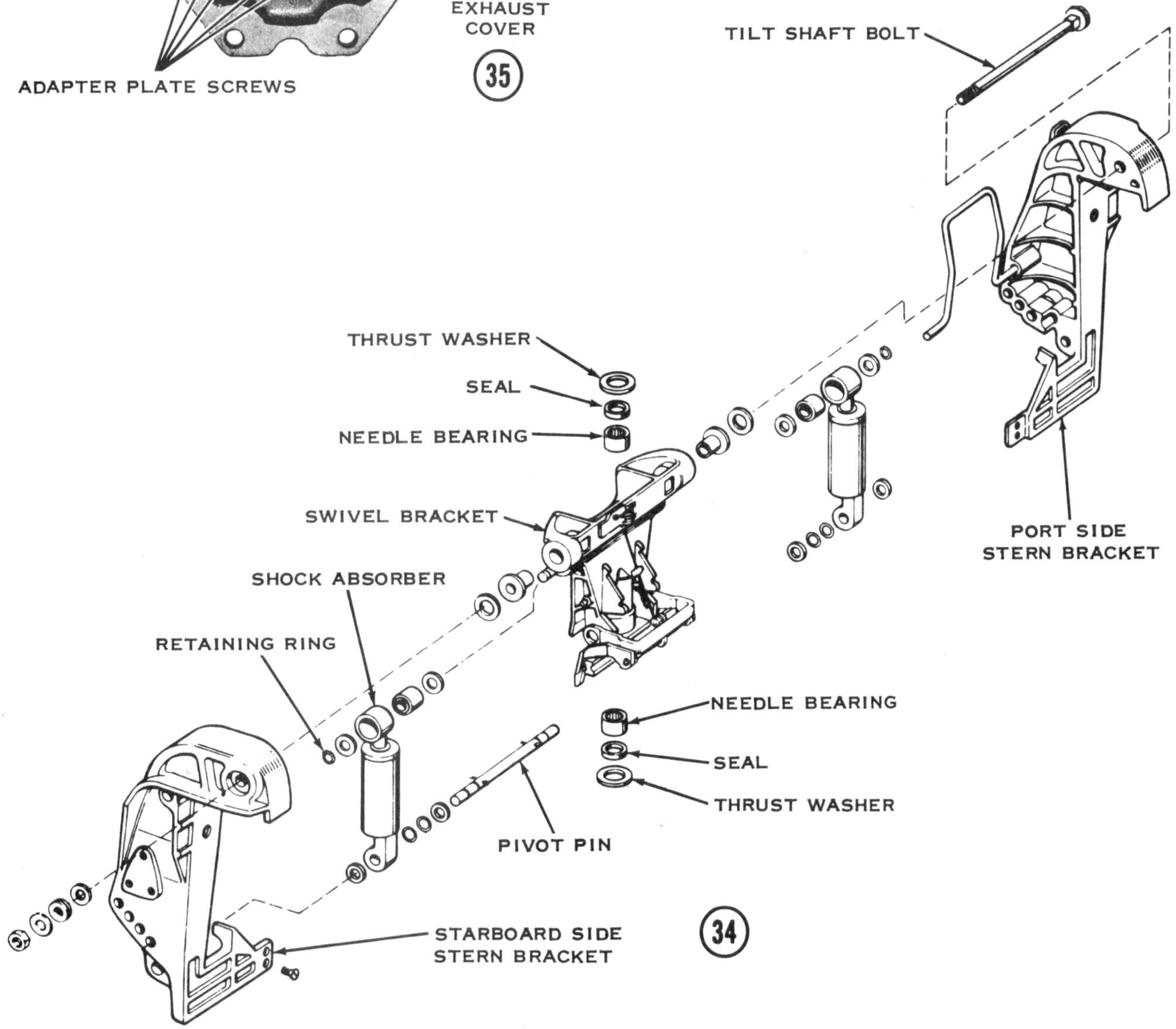

(34)

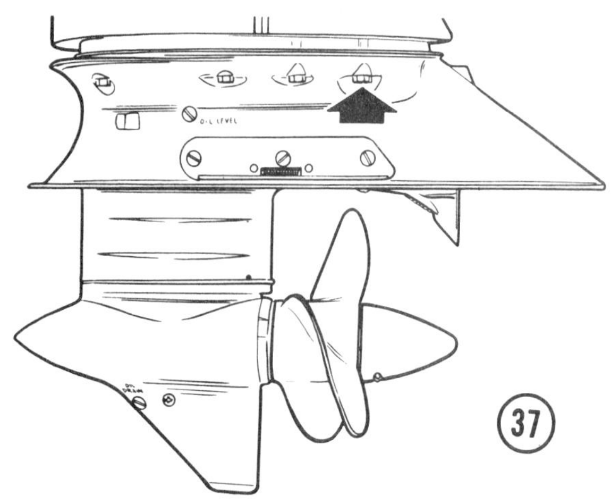

(37) Fasten the gear case to the exhaust housing, after dipping the screws in Perfect Seal #4. Torque the screws to 10-12 ft-lbs.

(38) Apply liquid soap to the electric shift cable, and then slide the exhaust housing plate gasket, plate, and cable clamp into position. Attach the inner and outer cover plates, using new gaskets. Coat the screws with Perfect Seal #4 and attach the exhaust relief boot. Check the shift cable leads with an ohmmeter to test for an open or short circuit between the leads. **CAUTION: A short circuit could cause the forward and reverse gears to engage at the same time.** Check the resistance of the coils by connecting the forward coil green lead to the ohmmeter and grounding the

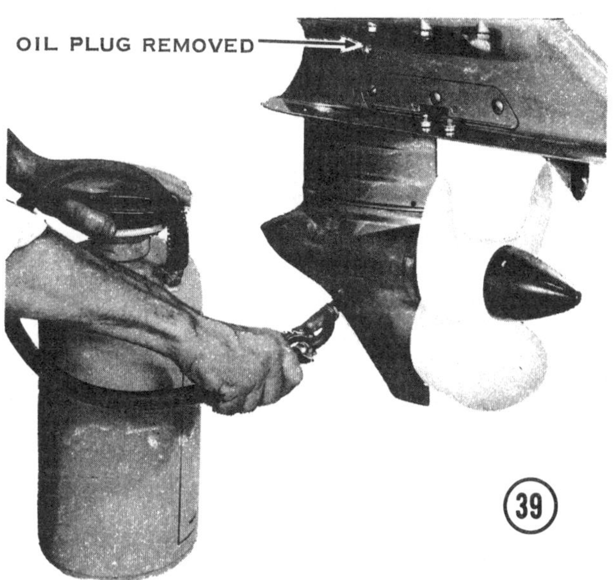

other ohmmeter lead; the meter should show 8 ohms. Test the reverse coil in the same manner by measuring between the blue lead and ground. Install the rear exhaust cover, using a new seal ring to prevent passing exhaust gases up into the motor cover, which would affect idle and high speed operation. Attach the rear lower cover.

(39) Fill the gear case with OMC Type "C" lubricant. Grease the propeller shaft with OMC Type "A" lubricant, and then install the propeller, thrust washer, new drive pin, and propeller nut, securing it with a new cotter pin. Connect the spark plug wires.

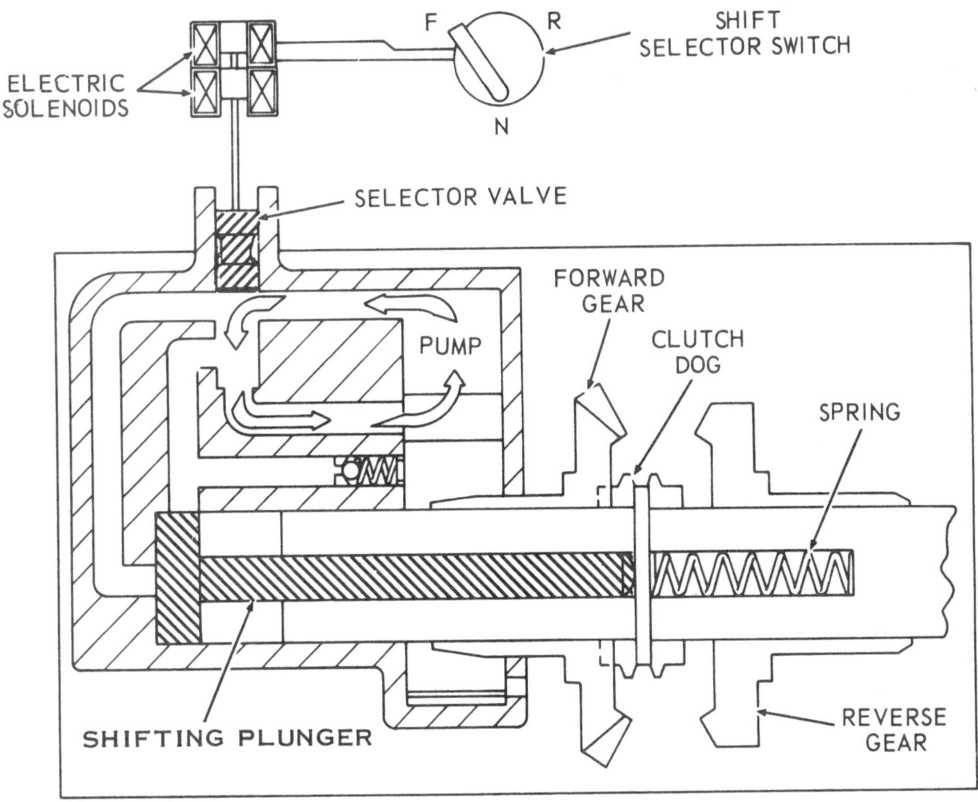

The shift mechanism of the hydro-electric gear shifting unit is in forward gear whenever there is an absence of oil pressure against the plunger. The engagement is made through spring pressure which forces the clutch dog to engage with the forward gear. Note how the selector valve is out of the hydraulic circuit, and the fluid circulates between the inlet and outlet ports of the pump itself.

SERVICING THE HYDRO-ELECTRIC SHIFT TYPE LOWER UNIT—1968-72

50 Hp Two-Cylinder Engine

This model contains an electric-hydraulic shift mechanism consisting of the usual gear case parts plus a vacuum switch, hydraulic pump, and selector valve. The hydraulic pump is mounted in the forward end of the gear case and is driven by the forward gear, using the gear case lubricating oil to supply the force needed for shifting. The solenoids operate the pump selector valve, which directs the hydraulic fluid to move the clutch dog to the selected position.

REMOVING

① The gear case can be removed from the exhaust housing and powerhead by disconnecting the spark plug wires. Drain the lubricant from the case. Slide back the insulating sleeve on the shift cable wires so that the terminals between the shift cable and the engine cable can be disconnected. *NOTE: The terminals are located on the port side, adjacent to the powerhead exhaust bypass cover.* Disconnect the terminals.

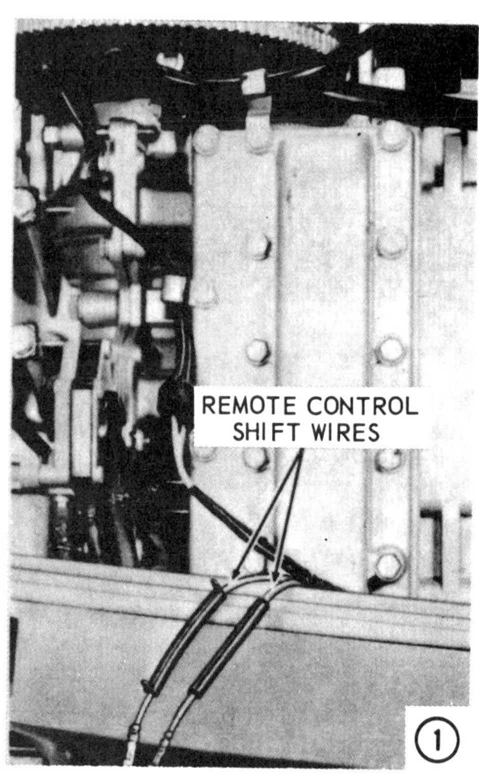

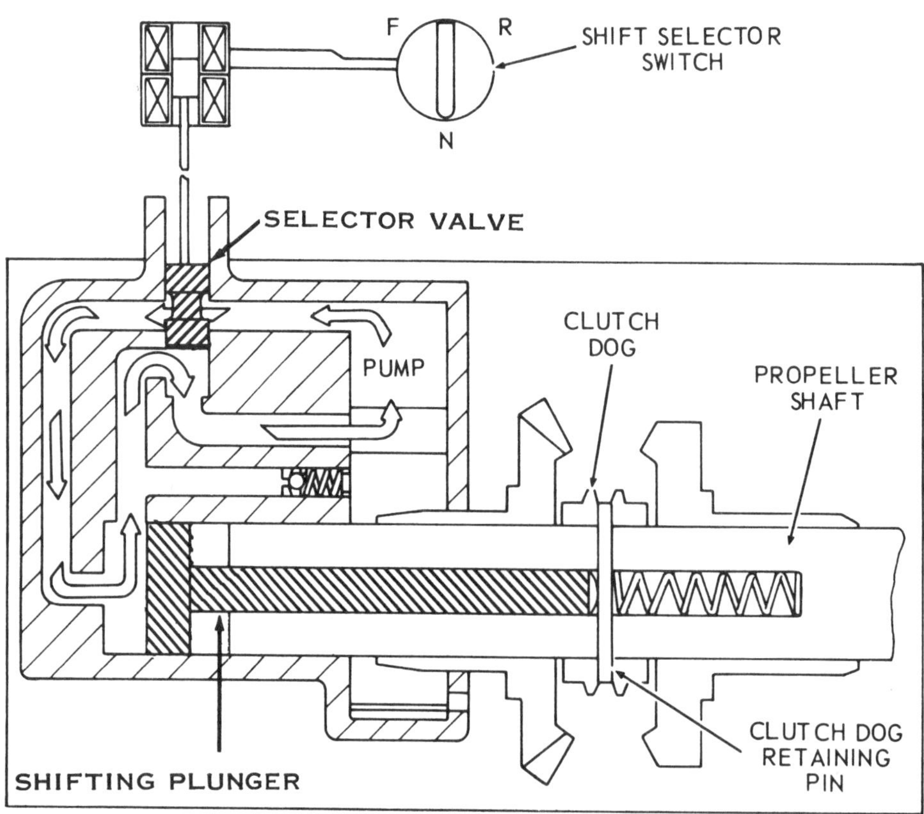

In neutral, the selector valve drops into the fluid circuit to direct the flow of fluid against the end of the plunger, which is just enough to balance the pressure of the shifting spring so that the plunger forces the clutch dog out of engagement with the forward gear. Note that the selector valve does not restrict the return flow of fluid to the pump intake.

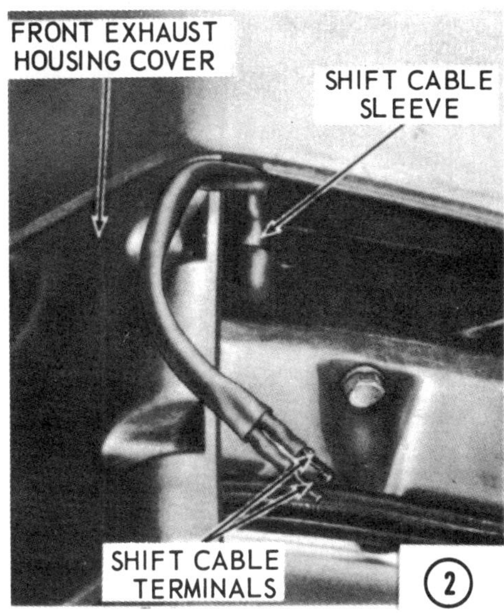

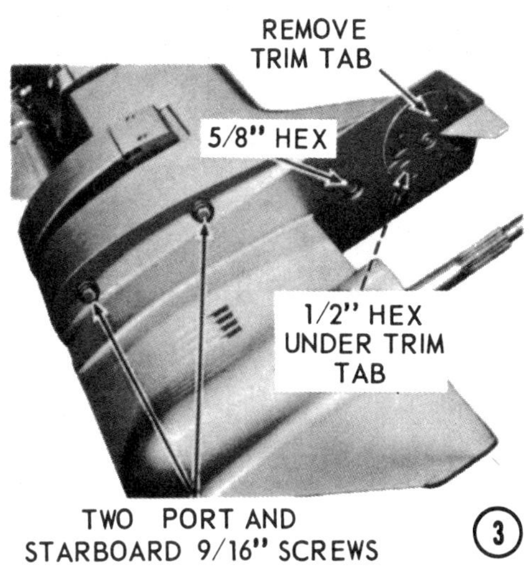

② Remove the four screws from the front exhaust cover and the two inside of the lower engine cover, and then take off the rear exhaust cover. Apply oil or liquid soap to the cable sleeve, pull down on the lower unit, and the cable will pull through the hole in the exhaust housing.

③ Scribe a mark on the gear case and adjustable trim tab so that it can be reinstalled in the same position. Remove the Allen-headed screw and the trim tab. Use a 1/2" socket and short extension to remove the screw from inside of the trim tab cavity. Use a 5/8" thin-wall socket to remove the countersunk

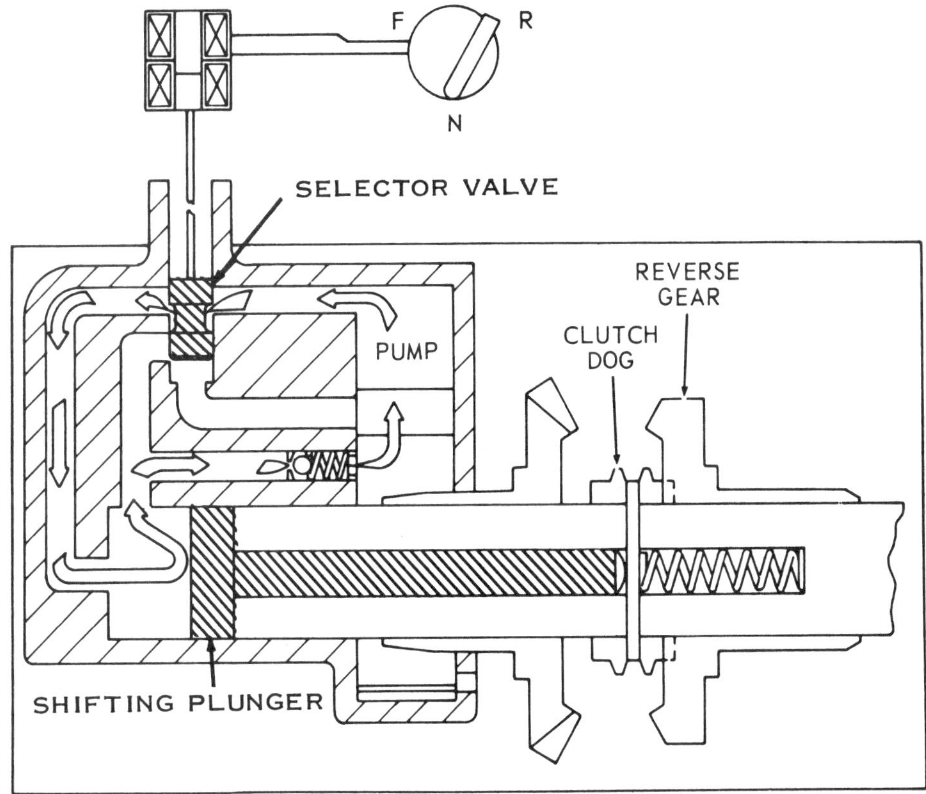

In reverse gear, the shifter valve is depressed enough to restrict the return flow of fluid so that all of the pump pressure is directed against the shifting plunger, overcoming all spring tension so that the clutch dog is forced into reverse gear.

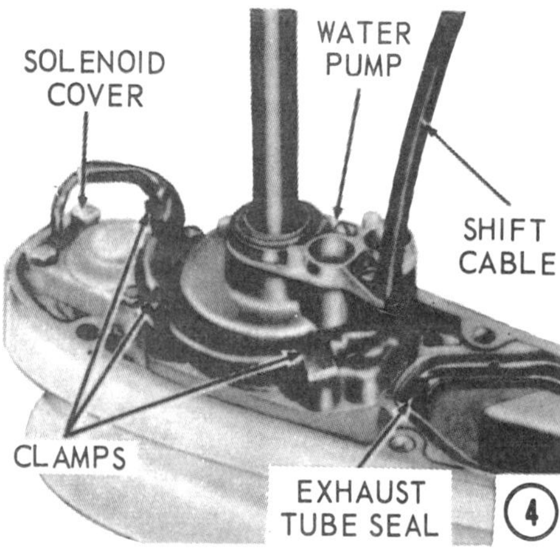

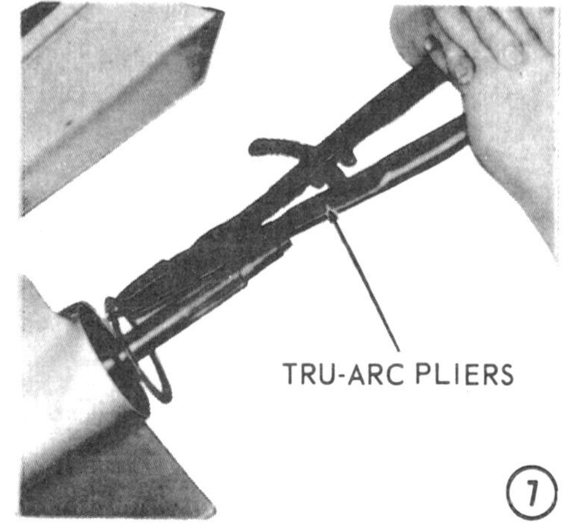

screw, take out the four 9/16" screws which hold the gear case to the exhaust housing, and then remove the gear case assembly. **CAUTION: Don't lose the plastic water tube guides, which are used to guide the water tube into the pump grommets during assembly.**

DISASSEMBLING

④ Remove the shift cable from the clamps around the pump housing. Take out the four screws holding the water pump housing to the case, and then slide off the housing and impeller. Remove the impeller drive key and the impeller plate. Remove the four upper driveshaft bearing housing screws.

⑤ Remove the four screws, solenoid cover, and wave washer. Disconnect the shift cable leads. Lift the solenoids and plunger assembly from the gear case.

⑥ Remove the propeller nut, washers, and propeller. Take out the four bearing housing screws, using a long 1/4" Allen wrench. Use a slide hammer with a hooked end to pull the bearing housing from the gear case.

⑦ Slide the thrust washer and the thrust bearing from the propeller shaft. Remove the two Truarc rings.

⑧ Withdraw the propeller shaft, retainer plate, reverse gear, thrust washer, and clutch dog as an assembly.

⑨ Remove the pinion locknut from the bottom of the driveshaft by using the special holder, Tool No. 312752. With the locknut removed, take out the pinion gear thrust bearing and washer. Pull the driveshaft out of the gear case. Lift out the forward gear. Remove the Truarc ring holding the pump housing, and then take out the screen. Remove the oil pump from the gear case. If necessary, remove the lower driveshaft bearing.

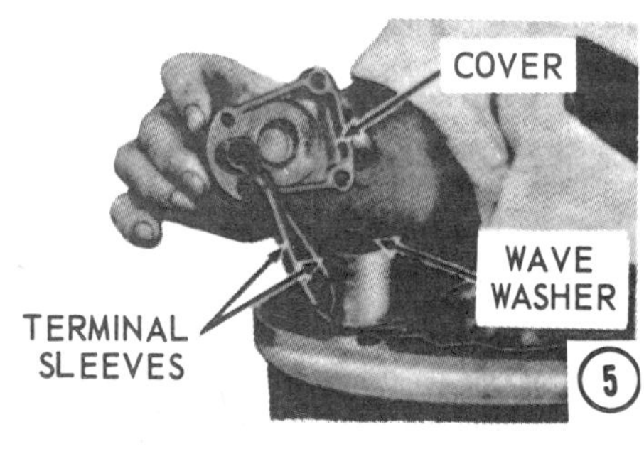

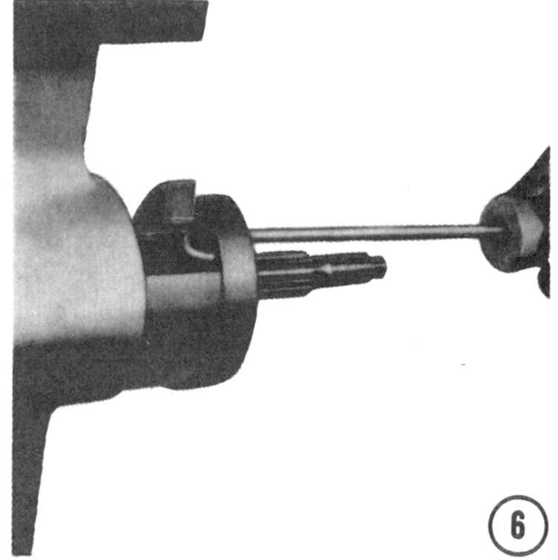

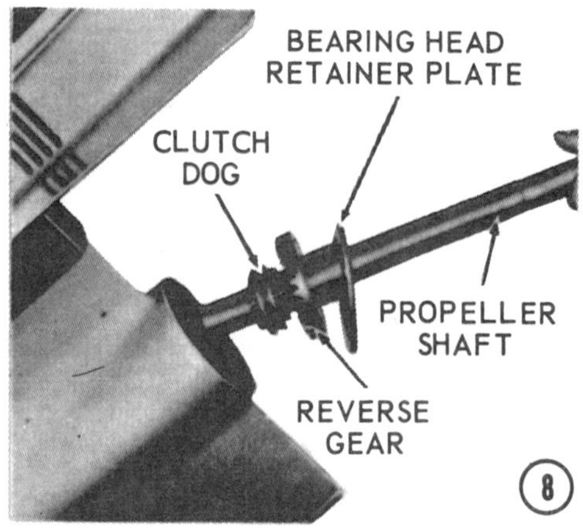

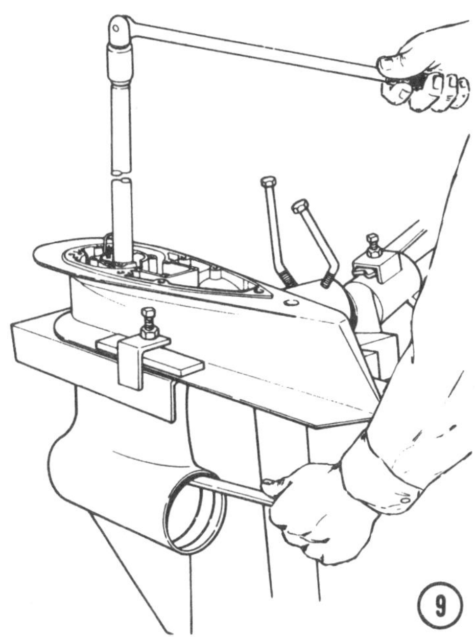

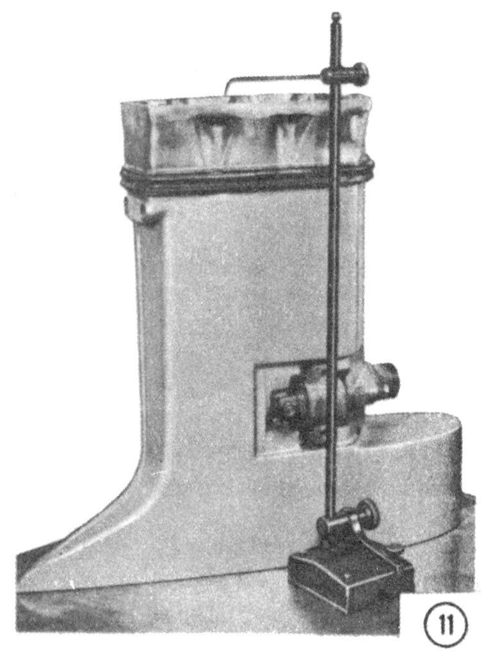

(10) Remove the piston from the oil pump, and then take out the cover screws and lockwashers. Lift off the pump cover. Remove the screw and screen from the cover. Remove the check valve and spring and the pump gears.

CLEANING AND INSPECTING

Clean all parts in solvent and dry with compressed air. Wash needle bearings in solvent. Oil the bearings immediately with light spindle oil to prevent rusting. Rotate the bearings a few times after draining the excess oil, and then place them in a covered container until assembly. Discard any bearing that has rusted rollers or races. Worn, galled, or abraded surfaces can be caused by too loose a fit or a bearing locked by dirt. A fractured bearing ring can be caused by forcing a cocked bearing off a shaft.

(11) Inspect the gear case for nicks on the machined surfaces. Remove the nicks and resurface the faces on a surface plate. Start with No. 120 emery cloth and finish with No. 180 cloth. Inspect and resurface the exhaust housing in a like manner. Replace the housing if it is bent. Check the parallelism on a surface plate, using a surface gauge. **CAUTION: Don't attempt to straighten a bent case; replace it.** Inspect the driveshaft splines for wear. A bent lower unit can cause extensive damage to the driveshaft splines. Also, a bent exhaust housing may cause the upper driveshaft splines to wear excessively and may also damage the crankshaft splines. Check the drive gears, pinion gear, and thrust washers and bearing for wear.

Replace all oil sals, O-ring seals, and gaskets. Always use a new upper pinion bearing and upper driveshaft bearing as well as new propeller shaft housing bearings, if they have been removed.

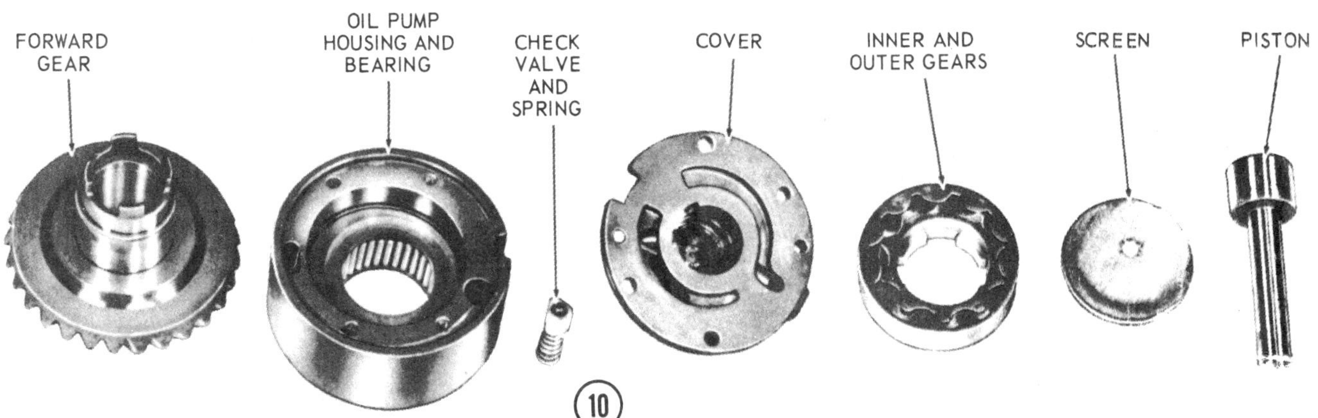

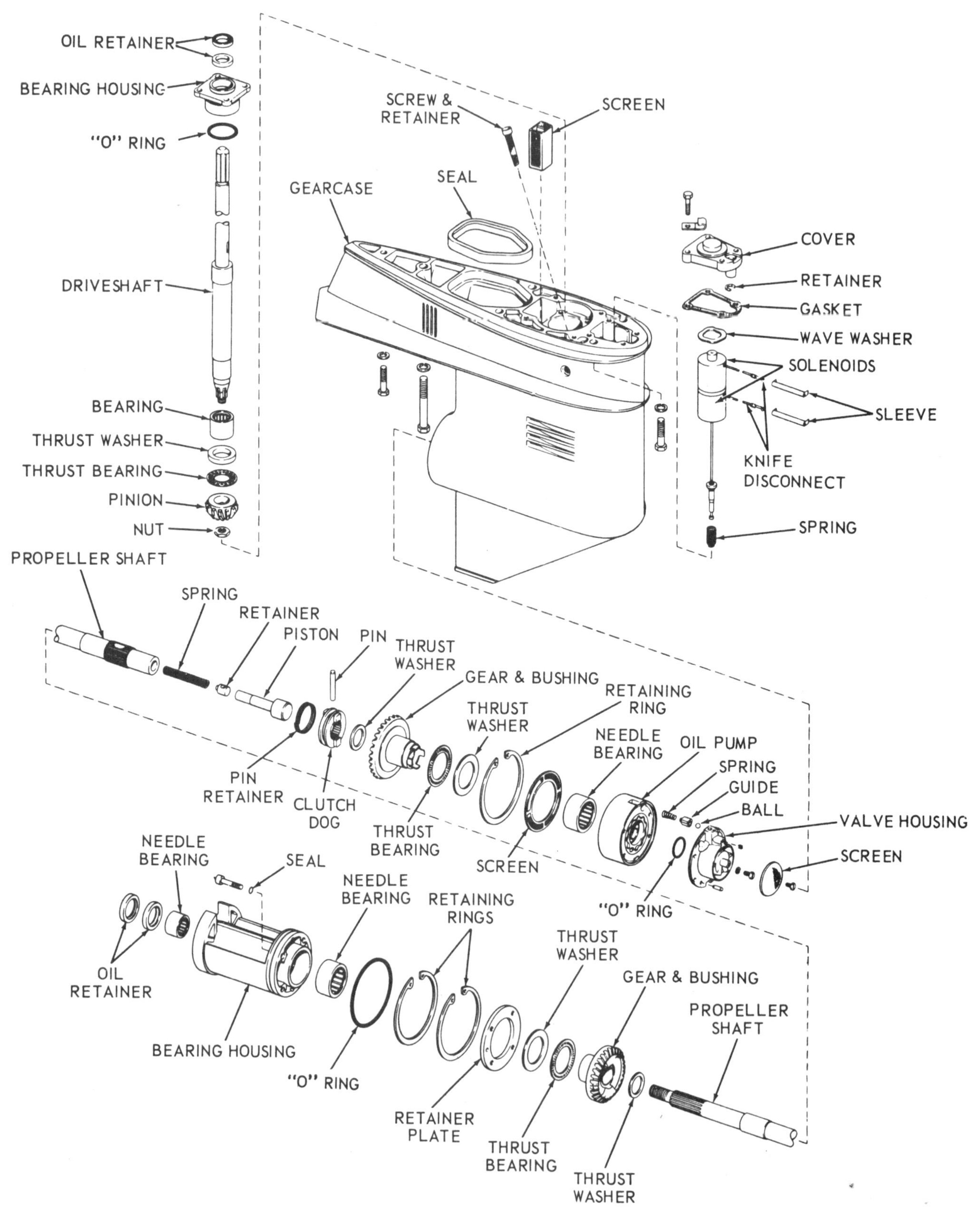

Exploded view of the hydro-electric shift type of lower unit.

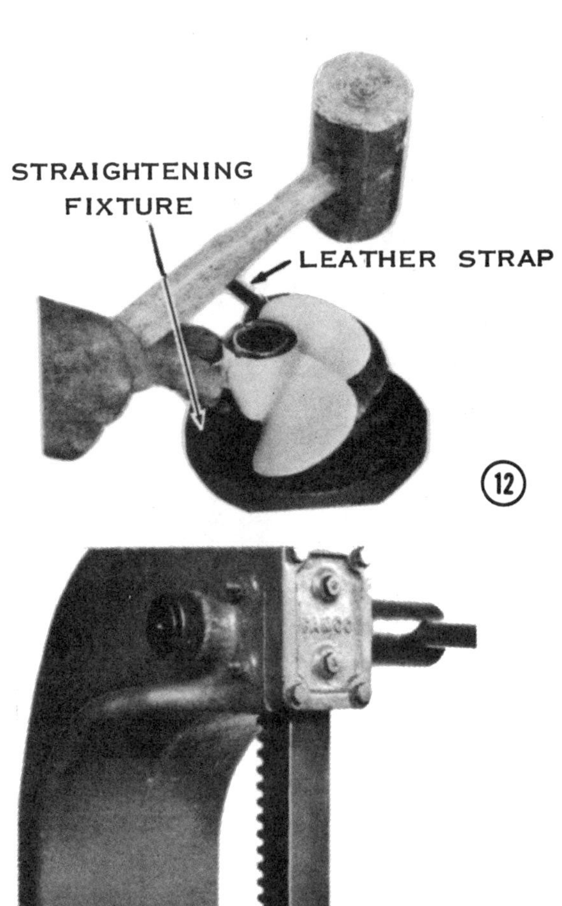

(12) Inspect the propeller for nicks, broken blades, and cracks. **CAUTION: Don't attempt to weld cracked or broken propeller blades.** Remove minor nicks with a file. Check the pitch on a propeller block. To straighten a bent blade, use a piece of leather strap or belting under the part of the blade that touches the fixture. Rap the high part of the blade smartly with a No. 3 rawhide mallet. The leather allows a slight over-bend to correct for the blade's natural tendency to spring back.

Inspect the water tubes for obstructions. Check the water pump impeller and replace it if the vanes are damaged. Inspect the water pump housing and the housing plate. Replace either if scored or pitted. Check the water intake screen.

Check the oil pump screen. Inspect the oil pump gears, housing, and cover for wear. Check the solenoid coil windings and shift cable leads for continuity. The solenoid windings should have 5-6 ohms resistance.

ASSEMBLING

(13) If removed, install a new roller bearing in the oil pump housing, using the special tool, No. 314641. Install the check valve in the smaller end of the spring, and then position the parts in the oil pump housing.

(14) Install the oil pump gears in the housing. **CAUTION: One side of each gear has a mark; both marks must be on the same side when installed in the housing.** The surface of the pump gears and housing must be parallel when the forward gear, thrust bearing, and washer are installed. Install the pump cover, gasket, and shaft. Tighten the cover screws securely. Install the screen on the cover.

(15) Slide the assembled pump into the gear case,

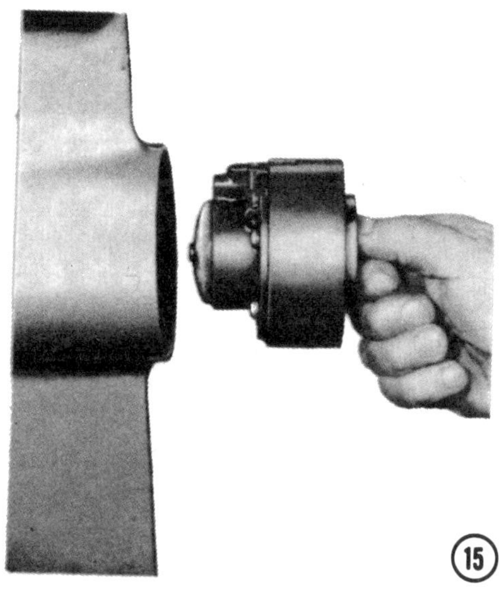

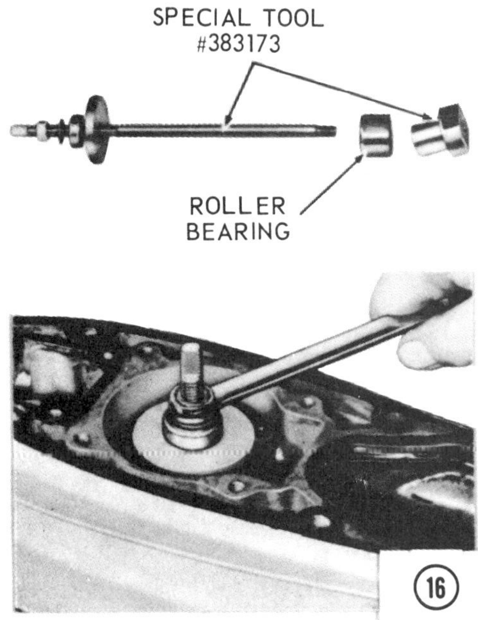

16

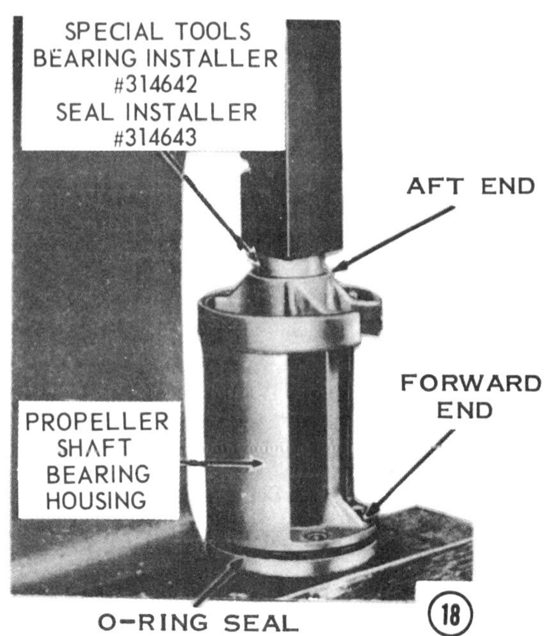

18

locating it on the pin and seating it as far forward as possible. **CAUTION: Unless properly seated, the solenoid plunger will not fit into the pump valve.** Install the large screen against the pump, with the loops facing out. Install the retaining ring, with the flat side toward the pump. Use Truarc pliers to install the retaining ring.

(16) Install the lower driveshaft bearing, using bearing installer, Tool No. 383173. Place the bearing on the driver, with the lettered side of the case toward the driver. Insert the tool (with the large washer, bearing, washer, and nut) through the top of the gear case. Thread the rod into the driver. Tighten the nut to draw the bearing into the case.

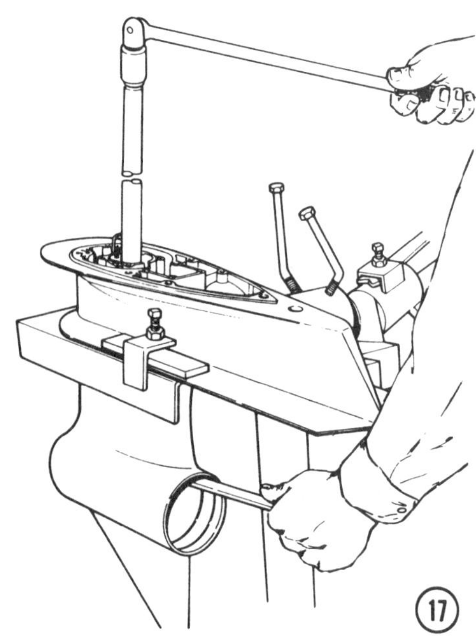
17

(17) Install the thrust washer, bearing, and forward gear as an assembly. Install the driveshaft, thrust washer, bearing, and pinion gear, using a special holding socket, Tool No. 312752, and then torque the nut to 40-45 ft-lbs.

(18) If removed, install new bearings in the propeller shaft bearing housing. For the large bearing, use Tool No. 314641. For the small bearing, Use Tool No. 314642. Install new seals back to back, with the lips of one seal facing out and those of the other facing in.

(19) To assemble the clutch dog, insert the spring and retainer in the propeller shaft. Install the clutch dog on the shaft. *NOTE: One face of the clutch dog has the mark PROP END on the side, and this face must be installed toward the propeller end of the shaft.* Depress the spring and retainer, and then insert the pin. Secure the pin with the retainer spring.

(20) Assemble the reverse gear and bearing housing retainer plate on the propeller shaft, and then insert the assembled shaft into the gear case.

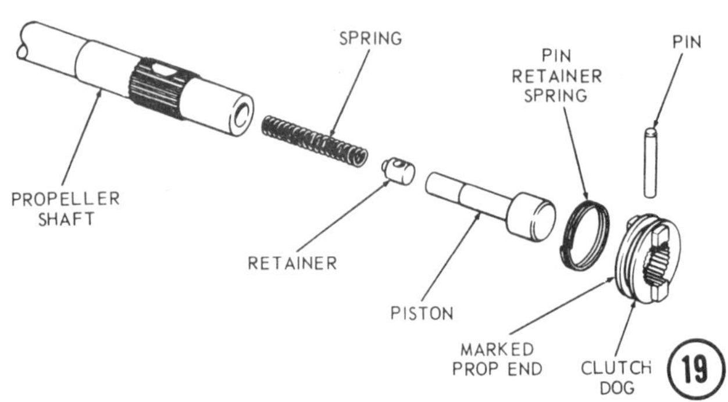

19

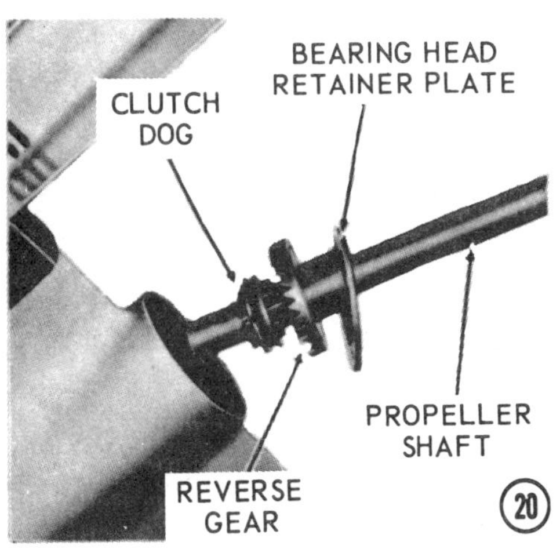

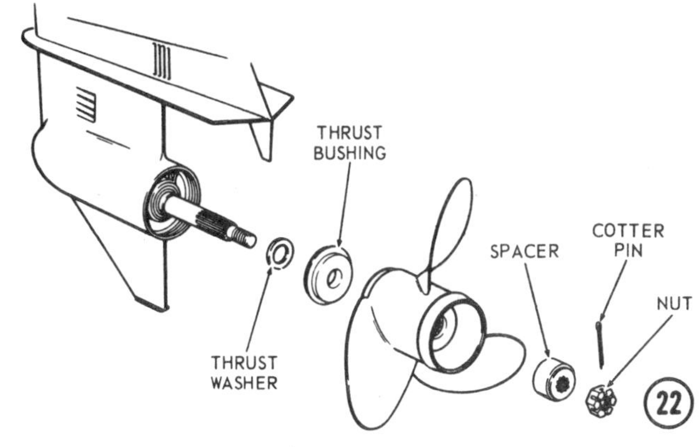

(21) Install two Truarc rings in the gear case. Position the thrust bearing and thrust washer on the reverse gear.

(22) Install a new seal in the driveshaft bearing housing, using a seal driver, Tool No. 314640. Position a new O-ring seal on the bearing housing, and then install the housing, with the bottom marking facing down. Secure it with the four Allen-headed screws dipped in Perfect Seal #4. Tighten the screws securely.

(23) Install the solenoid assembly, making sure that the plunger valve enters the oil pump body. **CAUTION: Don't force it.** Apply Perfect Seal #4 to both sides of the solenoid cover gasket, and then position the gasket on the gear case. Connect the shift cable leads, and then slide the sleeves over the terminals. Position the leads down in the gear case. Place the wave washer on top of the solenoid, and then install the solenoid cover.

(24) Apply Sealer 1000 to the bottom edge of the impeller plate, and then position the plate in the gear case. Insert the impeller drive key in the driveshaft. Install a new seal in the impeller housing cover. Insert the water tube extension in the pump and into the grommets. Attach the cover to the impeller housing. Slide the impeller over the driveshaft. If the impeller is new, either side can be facing up. Install the pump housing, using a seal protective sleeve. Oil the impeller blades and rotate the driveshaft clockwise while sliding the housing over the impeller. Secure the pump housing with screws dipped in Perfect Seal #4. Route the shift cable around the water pump and secure it in the clamps. Lubricate the propeller shaft, and then install the propeller.

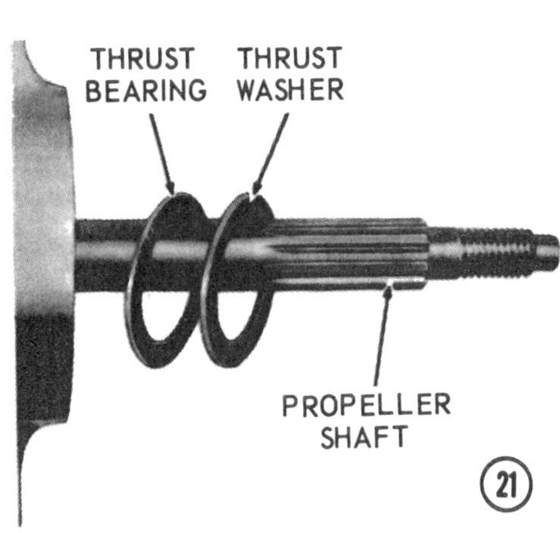

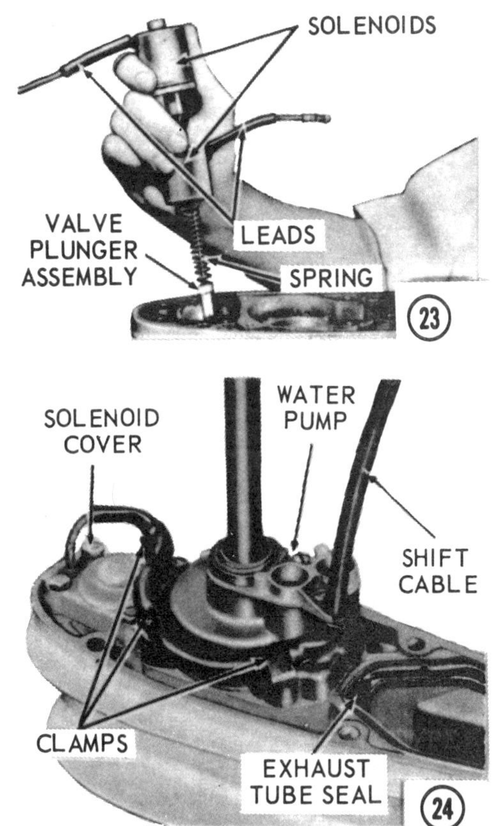

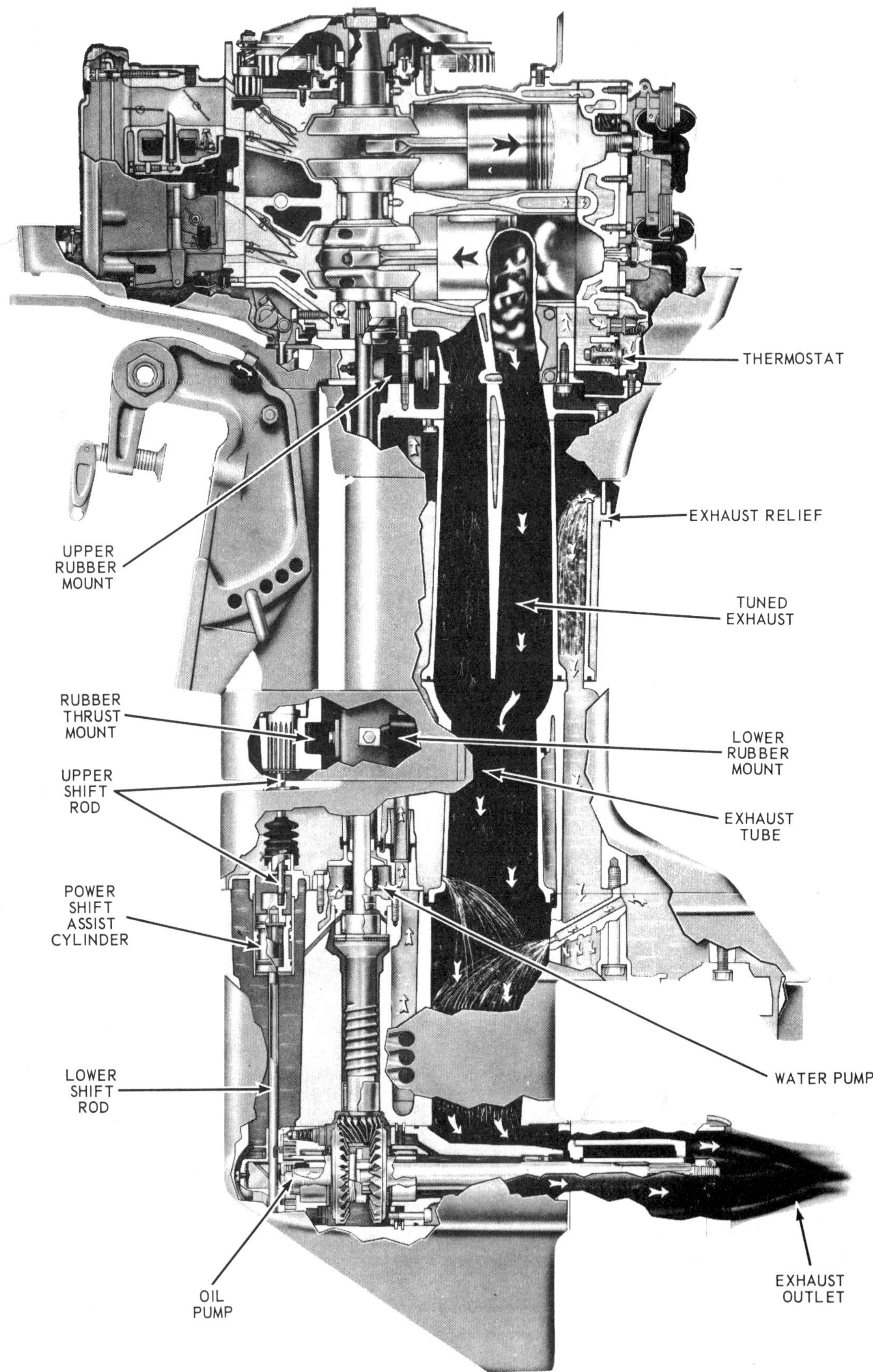

Sectioned view through the 50 Hp motor and lower unit, with the hydro-mechanical shift-type lower unit used since 1973.

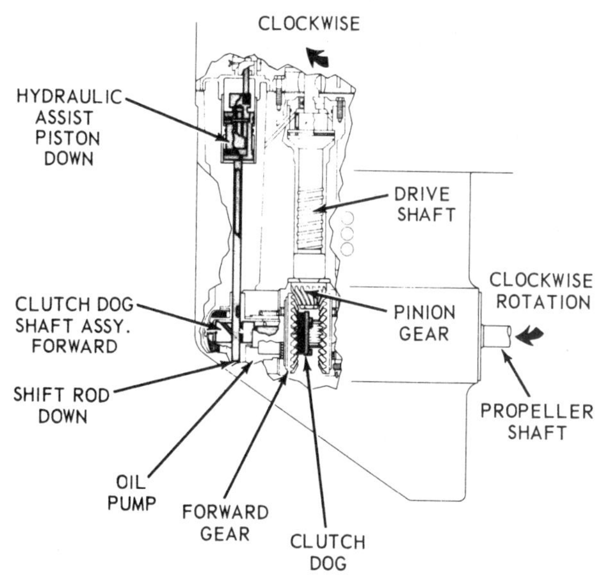

The hydro-mechanical shift lower unit in forward gear, with the clutch dog engaging the forward gear.

SERVICING THE HYDRO-MECHANICAL SHIFT TYPE LOWER UNIT—SINCE 1973

50 Hp Engines

This unit supersedes the hydraulic-shift type unit, which had a defect in that it would remain in FORWARD gear in the event of a defective solenoid, thus forcing the boat forward without control. This unit is a mechanically shifted device with the assistance of hydraulic power.

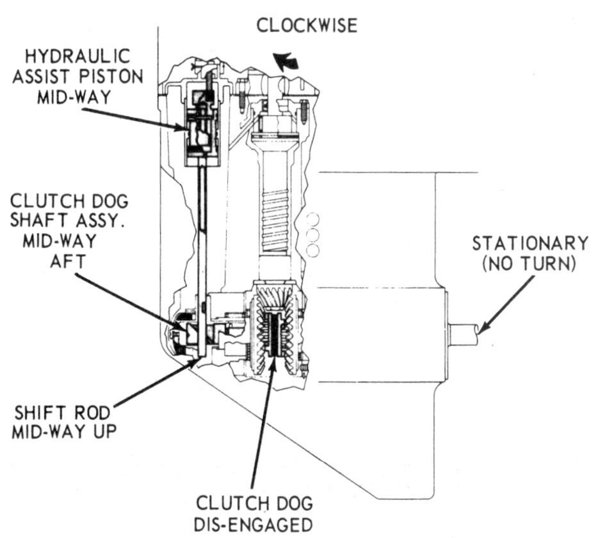

The hydro-mechanical shift lower unit in neutral.

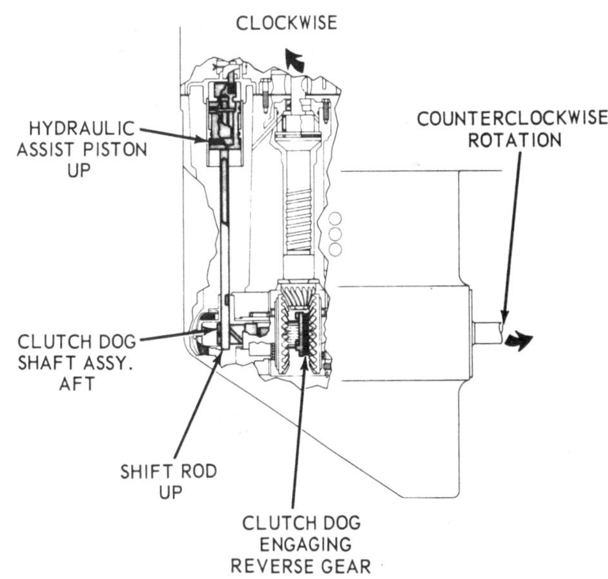

The hydro-mechanical shift lower unit in reverse gear. Note the clutch dog engaging the reverse gear.

REMOVING

① To remove the gear case, first disconnect the spark plug wires. Drain the lubricant from the gear case. Remove the three electric starting motor attaching screws and the cable nut.

② Remove the shift rod-to-lever screw.

③ Scribe a mark on the gear case and adjustable trim tab so that it can be installed in the same position. Remove the retaining screw and the trim tab. Use a 1/2″ socket and shaft extension to remove the screw from inside of the trim tab cavity. Use a 5/8″ thin-walled socket to remove the countersunk screw. Pull the gear case from the exhaust housing, taking care to avoid bending the shift rod.

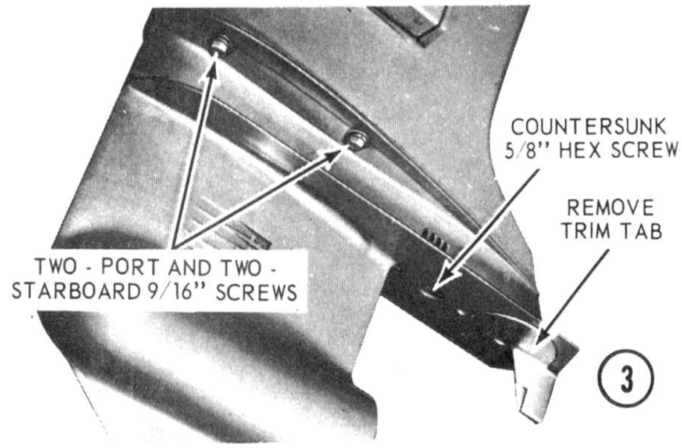

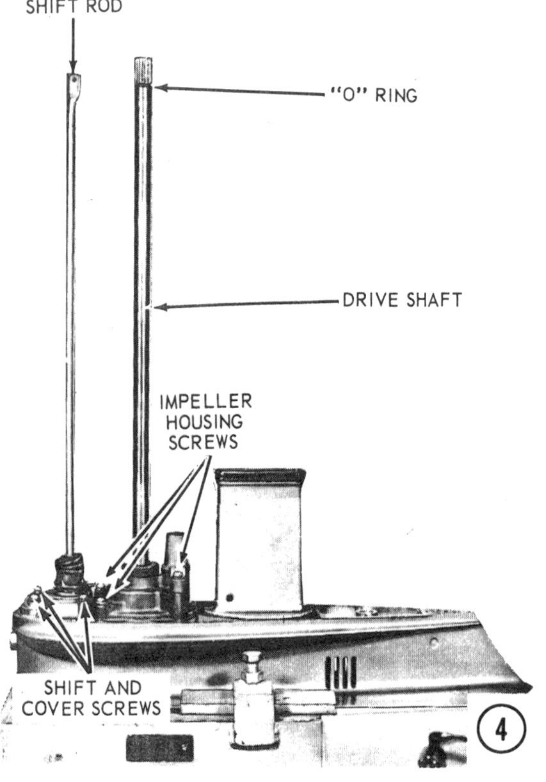

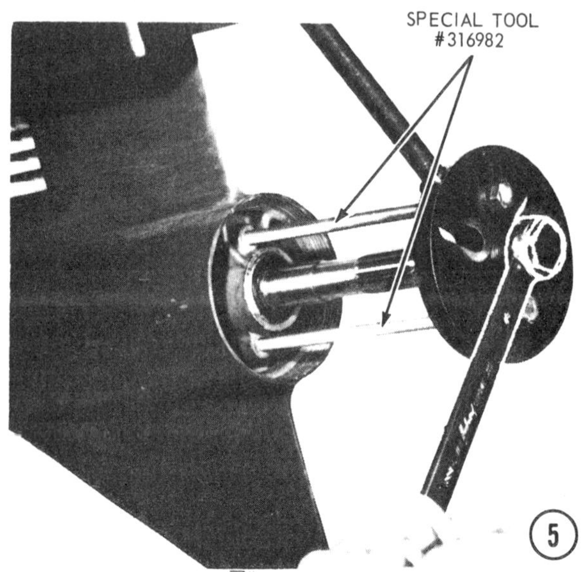

DISASSEMBLING THE GEAR CASE

(4) Remove the propeller nut, washers, and propeller. Take off the O-ring from the top of the driveshaft. Remove the four impeller housing screws, and then slide the impeller housing and the impeller off the driveshaft. Mark the impeller so it can be assembled in the same way it was removed. Remove the impeller drive key and the impeller plate.

(5) Remove the four propeller shaft bearing housing screws. Discard the O-rings on the screws. Using two 5/16" × 18 bolts, 8" long (Tool No. 316982) and flywheel puller (Tool No. 378103), pull the bearing housing from the gear case.

(6) Remove the thrust washer and thrust bearing.

(7) Remove the two Truarc rings using #7 Truarc pliers (Tool No. 311879). **CAUTION: The retaining rings are under extreme pressure. Wear safety goggles and proceed with care to prevent the pliers slipping off the rings.**

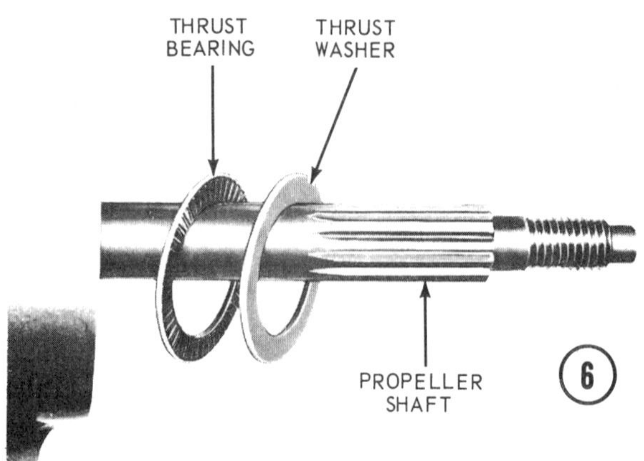

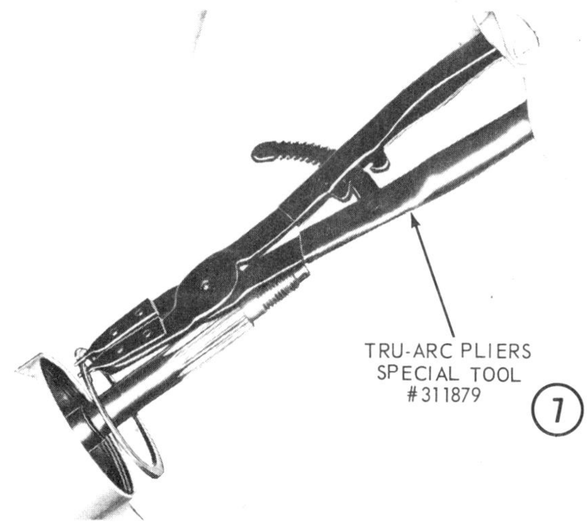

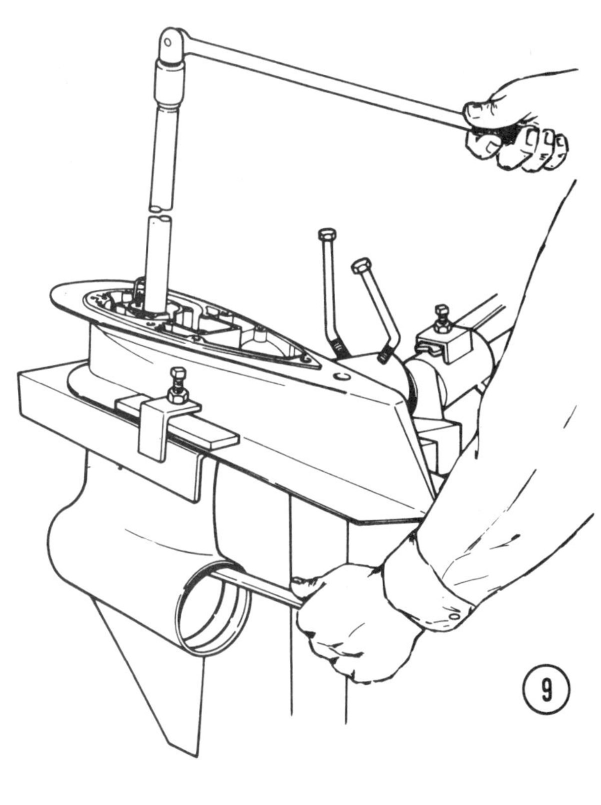

(8) Remove the shift rod cover retaining screws, and then pull out the power-assist cylinder, propeller shaft, reverse gear, retainer plate, and clutch dog from the gear case.

(9) Remove the pinion locknut from the bottom of the driveshaft with Tool No. 316612. Now, remove the pinion gear, take out the four upper driveshaft bearing housing screws, and then pull the driveshaft assembly out of the gear case.

(10) Remove the drain plug and magnet assembly, and then take out the forward gear. Remove the oil pump from the case with a slide hammer, Tool No. 311887, and two 1/4″ × 20 threaded rods, 16″ long.

(11) If the lower driveshaft bearing needs to be replaced, use Tool No. 385546 to pull it out. **CAUTION: The pinion bearing setscrew in the upper right of the illustration must be taken out first.** Position the washer, bearing, and plate on the screw as shown. **CAUTION: The shoulder of the tool must**

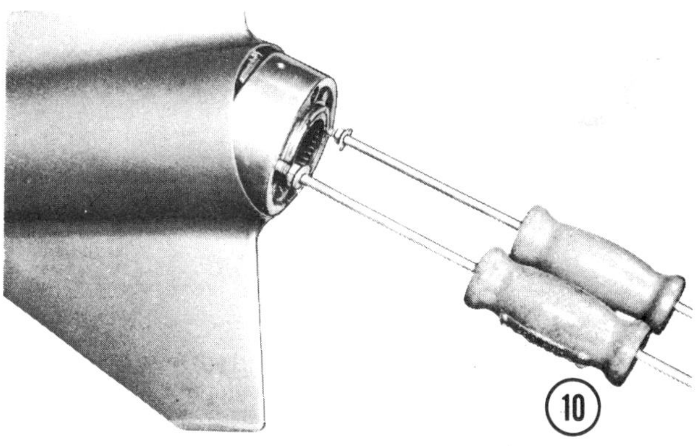

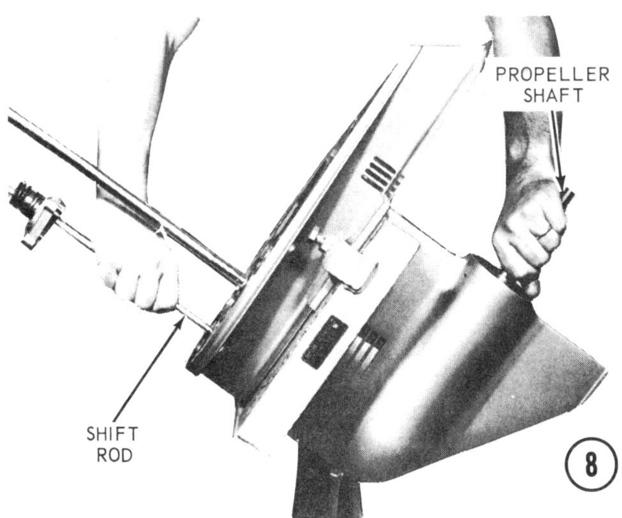

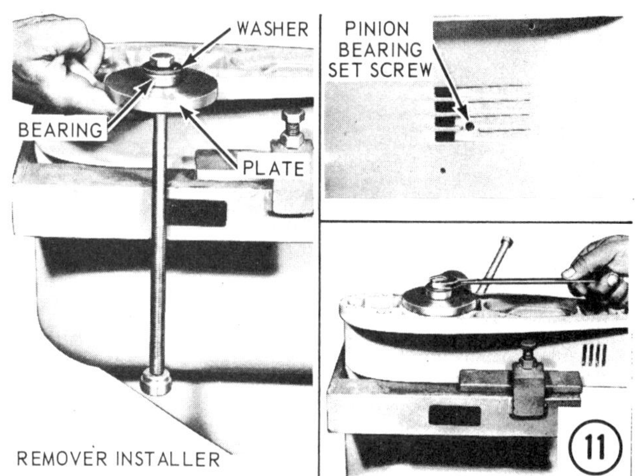

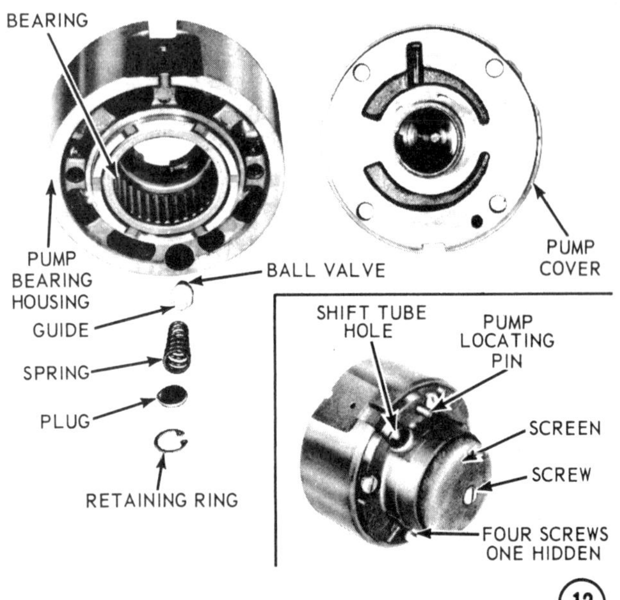

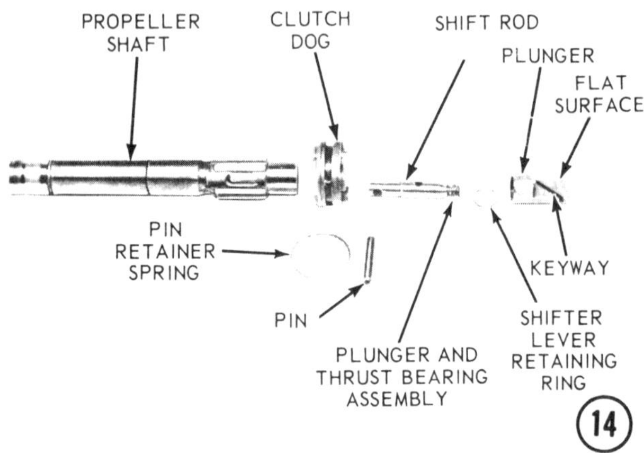

face the bearing. Tighten the screw to pull the bearing from the case. The propeller shaft bearing housing oil retainers and bearings can be pulled in the same manner.

⑫ To disassemble the oil pump, remove the four screws and lockwashers from the pump housing. Take out the screw and screen from the cover. Use #2 Truarc pliers to remove the retaining ring, plug, spring, guide, and ball valve from the oil pump.

⑬ To disassemble the power-assist piston, use one half of spanner wrench, Tool No. 386112, clamped in a soft-jawed vise, and then place the cylinder on the tool, as shown. Push the rod down to engage the pins of the tool with the holes provided in the bottom of the piston. **CAUTION: Use care to prevent bending the push rod.** Place the other half of the special tool on top of the cylinder engaging the pins in the holes of the piston cap. Use a socket wrench and turn it counterclockwise to disassemble the cylinder. Remove the pin to disassemble the push rod, piston, and valve.

⑭ To disassemble the propeller shaft and shifter assembly, remove the shifter clutch dog pin retainer, spring, and pin. The plunger can be removed from the shift rod and thrust bearing by taking out the retaining ring in the plunger.

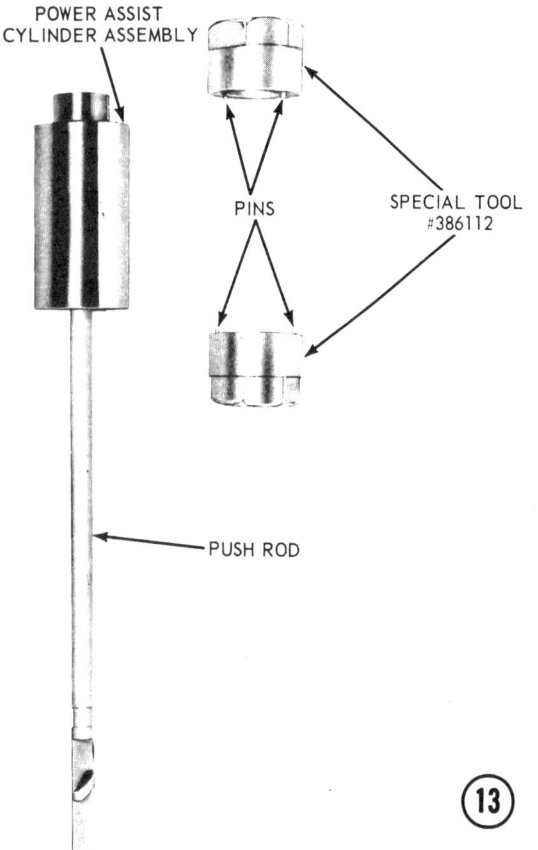

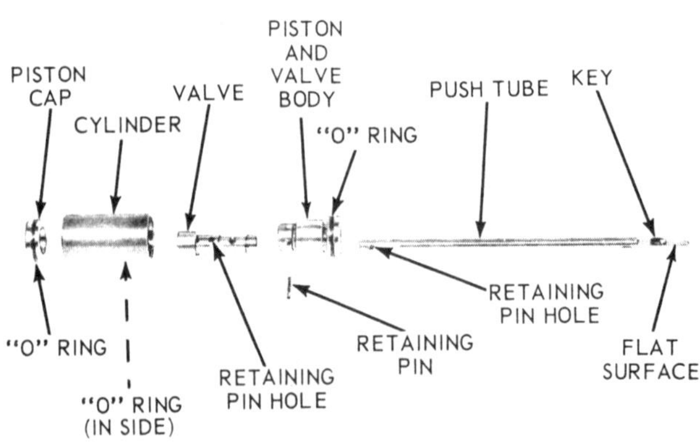

Details of the shift-assist parts.

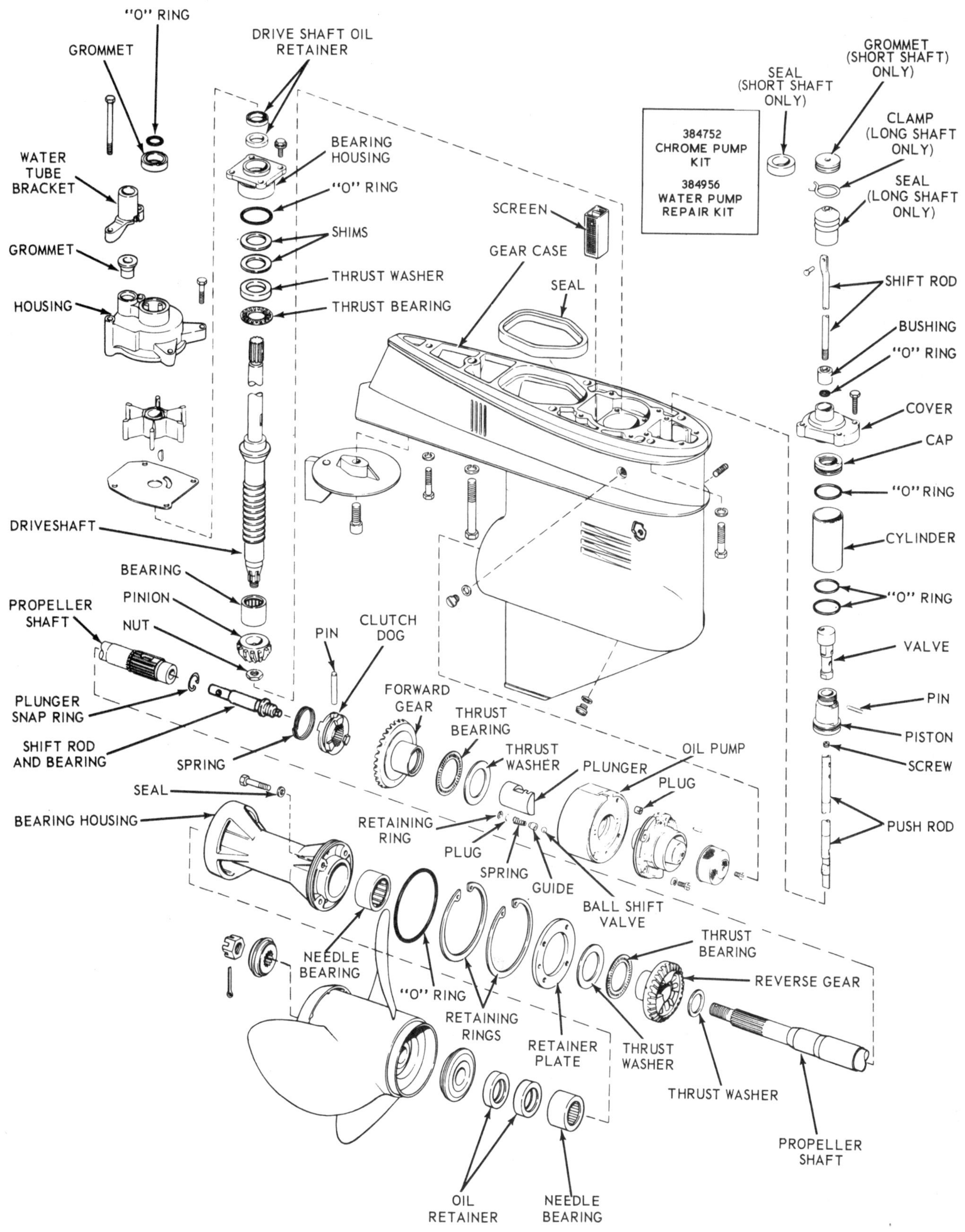

Exploded view of the hydro-mechanical shift-type lower unit used since 1973.

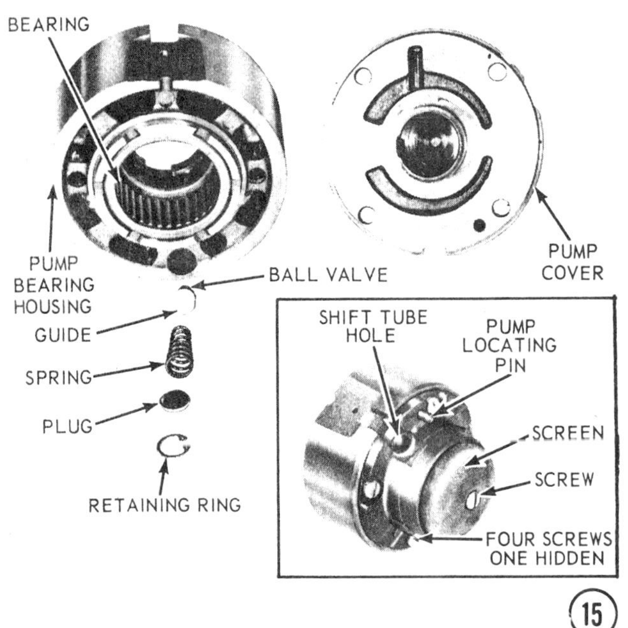

CLEANING AND INSPECTING

Clean all parts with solvent and dry with compressed air. All nuts and screw threads that were coated with Loctite must be thoroughly cleaned before assembly.

Discard all oil seals, O-rings, and gaskets.

Examine the rubber mounts and replace those that have deteriorated.

Inspect the driveshaft splines for wear. If the lower unit was bent by striking a submerged object, this can cause extensive damage to the driveshaft splines. Replace the shaft if it shows wear.

Inspect the propeller for nicks, broken blades, or cracks. Remove minor nicks with a file. **CAUTION: Don't attempt to weld cracked or broken blades.** Note that the aft side of the propeller is flat while the other side is rounded. Be careful to file the blades according to the original shape. Replace badly worn, bent, or broken propellers.

Inspect the gear case for nicks on the machined surfaces. Remove any nick and then resurface the machined surfaces on a flat plate. Start with 120 grit emery cloth and finish with 180 grit cloth. Inspect and resurface the exhaust housing in a similar manner. Check the parallelism and replace any unit that is bent. **CAUTION: A bent exhaust housing will cause the upper driveshaft splines to wear excessively and can also damage the crankshaft splines.**

Inspect the water tube for kinks or obstructions, which could restrict the flow of water. Inspect the water pump impeller and replace it if the vanes are damaged or worn. Inspect the pump housing for scoring and replace it if damaged. Inspect the impeller housing plate; replace it if worn or scored. Check the water intake screen; clean it or replace it as needed.

Check the oil pump screen. Clean it if it is clogged.

Inspect the drive gears, pinion gear, thrust washers, and bearings for wear. Replace all worn parts. Wash the needle bearings in clean solvent. Oil them immediately with clean spindle oil to prevent rusting. Replace all damaged or worn bearings.

Check the pump pressure relief valve, ball, and seat for grooves. Replace the ball if worn. Replace the pump if the bearing is damaged.

Inspect the shift components for wear. Check the clutch dog engagement surfaces, push rod key, plunger keyway, and shift rod thrust bearing. The shift rod and thrust bearing are serviced as an assembly.

Inspect the shift-assist components. All parts must be free of galling and burrs. Inspect the O-ring and bushing in the shift rod cover. Always replace the O-ring. Replace the bushing if worn.

ASSEMBLING

Always use OMC Sealing Compound, Part #317201, on all pressed-in seals. Use OMC Locquic Primer on the threads of nuts and screws on which Loctite will be used to reduce curing time.

(15) Assemble the oil pump by installing the pressure-relief valve, which consists of the ball, guide spring, and plug. **CAUTION: The flat side of the plug faces the spring and the flat side of the retaining ring must face out.**

(16) Install the oil pump gears into the housing, with the dots facing up. Use a straightedge to check that the surfaces of the pump gears and pump housing are even when the forward gear, thrust bearing, and washer are installed. If they are not, either the bearing

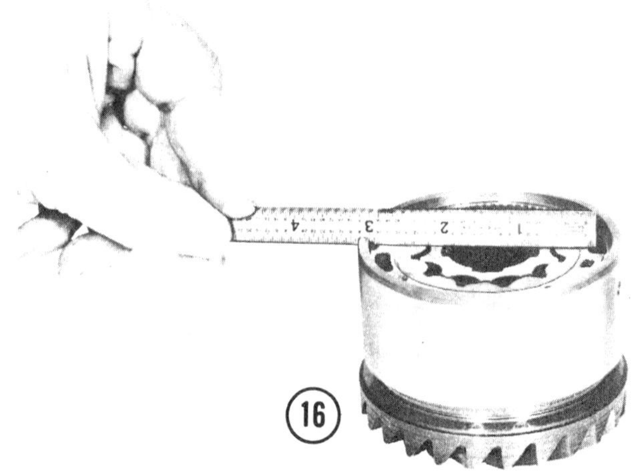

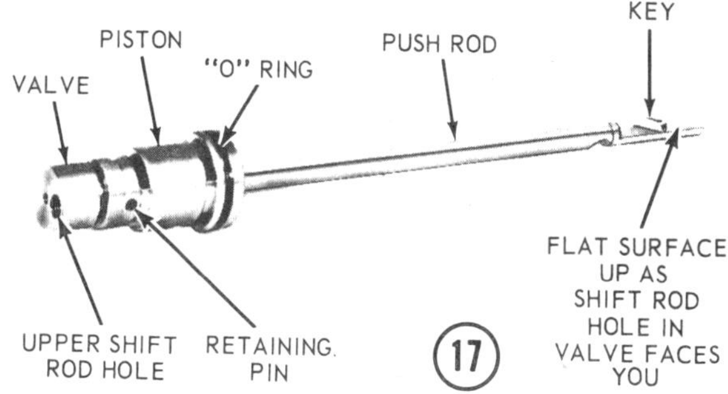

(17)

(19)

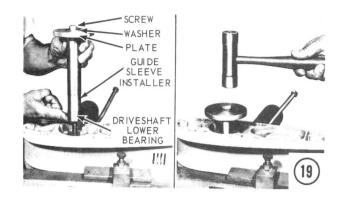

or gear bearing surfaces are worn, and these parts must be replaced. Install the oil pump cover, and tighten the screws securely. Install the screen on the valve housing. Install the pump assembly into the gear case. Note that the forward end of the pump has a locating pin in the cover, and this must locate in a pin hole in the gear case. Check the gear case through the propeller shaft end to note the hole in the lower starboard side, at the forward end of the case. **CAUTION: Unless the pump is seated in the gear case properly, you cannot complete the assembly.**

(17) To assemble the power-assist cylinder, oil all parts first, and then install three new O-rings: one on the piston, one in the cylinder, and one on the piston cap. Assemble the push rod and valve, and then secure them with the pin. A small amount of needle bearing grease on the pin will assist in assembly.

(18) Using Tool No. 386112, assemble the shift-assist cylinder and torque it to 12-15 ft-lbs. Check the piston for freedom of movement in the cylinder and the valve for freedom of movement in the piston.

(19) Install a new lower driveshaft bearing, using Tool No. 385546. Assemble the washer, guide sleeve, and part of the tool on the screw in the order shown. The shoulder of the tool must face down. Place the lower driveshaft bearing on the tool, with the lettered side of the bearing facing the shoulder on the tool. Drive the bearing into place. *NOTE: The bearing will be seated properly when the plate of the tool contacts the top surface of the gear case.* Apply Loctite to the setscrew and install it.

(20) The driveshaft pinion gear is precisely meshed with the forward and reverse gears by shims between the driveshaft thrust bearing, thrust washer, and bearing housing. To select the proper shims, assemble the pinion gear to the driveshaft, torquing the nut to 40-45 ft-lbs. Remove the thrust washer and bearing. Place the shims removed during disassembly on the driveshaft shoulder. Use gauge No. 315767 to measure the clearance between the bottom of the gauge and the pinion gear. If the shimming is correct, the bottom edge of the gauge should just touch the top of the pinion. The clearance must not exceed 0.002", or the shim pack thickness must be adjusted until it does. Install the properly shimmed driveshaft and pinion gear into the gear housing. Torque the nut to 40-45 ft-lbs.

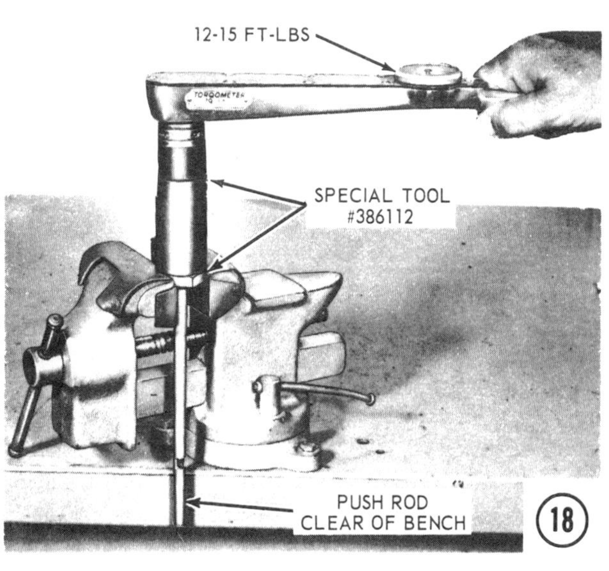

(18)

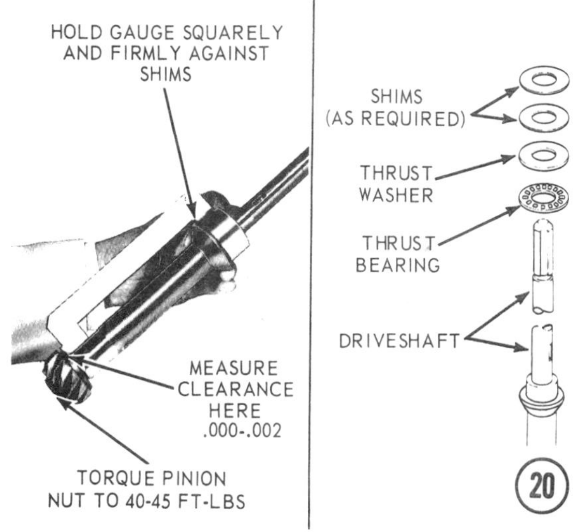

(20)

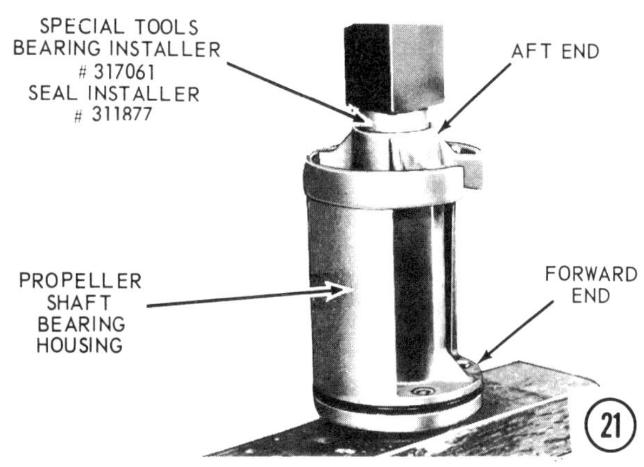

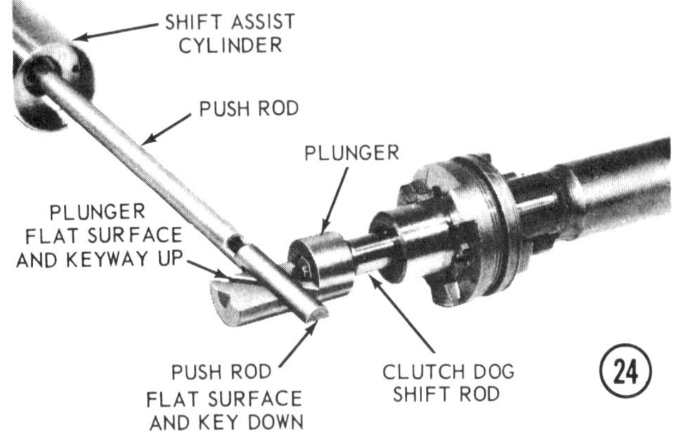

(21) If necessary, install new bearings in the propeller shaft bearing housing. Use Tool No. 314641 for the forward bearing or Tool No. 317061 for the aft bearing. Install new oil seals, back to back. One seal lip must be facing out and the other facing in. Use seal installer No. 311877 to assist in assembly.

(22) Attach the shift rod to the plunger with the retaining ring, flat side out. Install the clutch dog on the propeller shaft, with the grooved end on the dog facing the propeller end of the shaft. Align the holes in the clutch dog and the slot in the propeller shaft. Install the clutch dog pin and the retainer spring, making sure that no coils overlap.

(23) Place the gear case on the bench, with the port side facing up. Insert the propeller shaft into the gear case and oil pump, as far as it will go, with the flat side of the plunger and keyway facing up, as shown.

(24) Carefully insert the push rod and shift-assist assembly into the gear case, with the shift rod tapped hole in the shift-assist valve assembly facing the propeller end of the gear case, and the flat surface on the push rod and key facing down, as shown. Neither the valve or push rod should be able to be rotated when

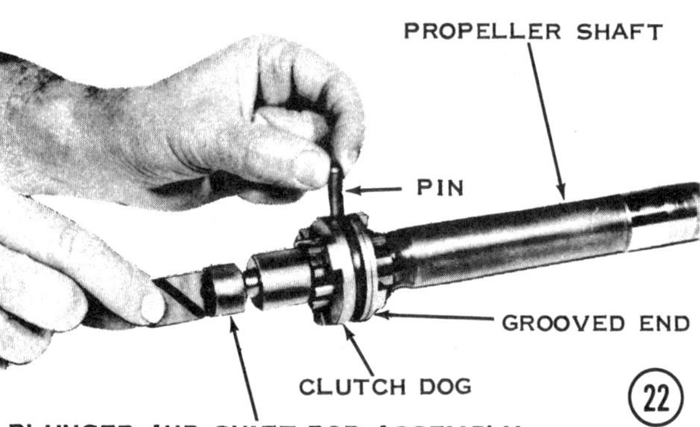

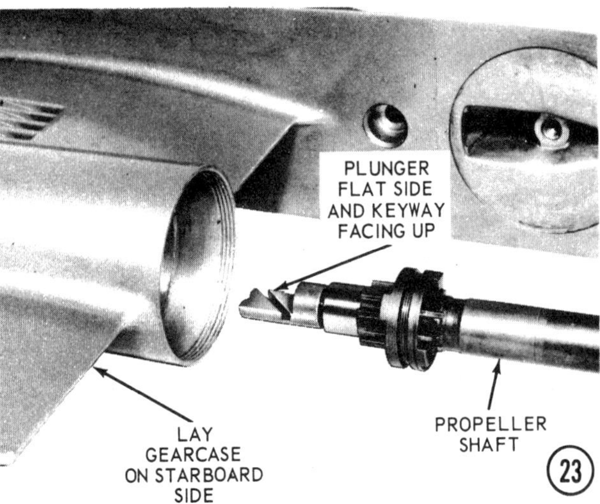

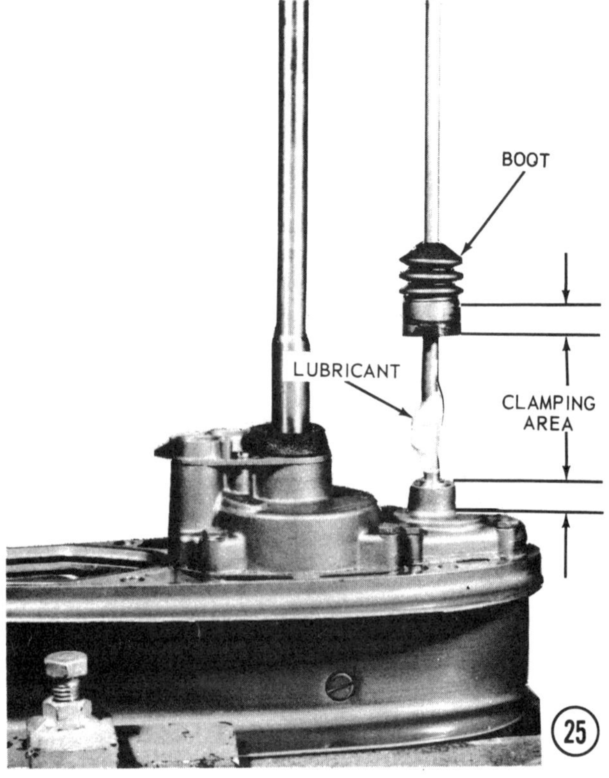

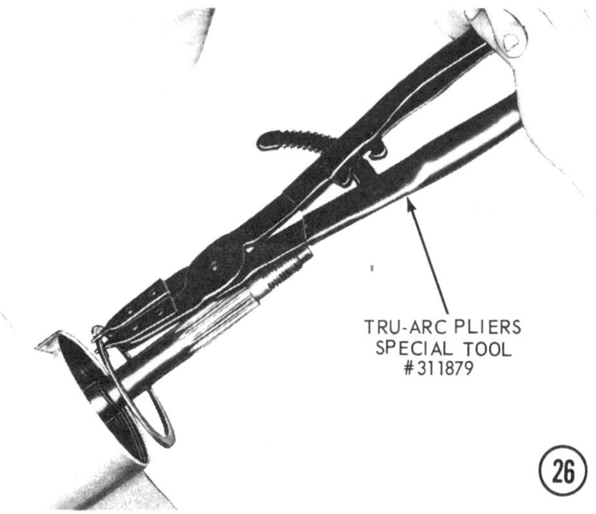

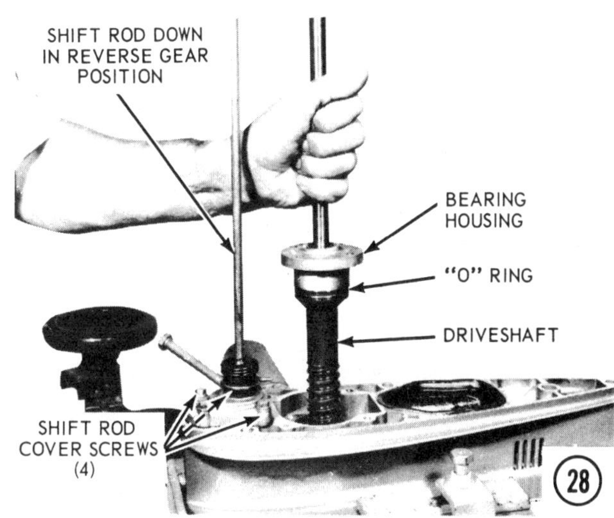

properly engaged, flat to flat, as shown. With gentle downward pressure on the assist cylinder and push rod assembly, carefully ease back on the propeller shaft to engage the push rod key and plunger keyway. Gentle downward pressure on the valve will help the push rod key slip into the keyway. When alignment is reached, push the propeller shaft and assist valve into complete engagement, as shown.

(25) Hold the gear case in a suitable fixture. Apply OMC Gasket Sealing Compound to both sides of the shift rod cover gasket, and then locate it on the gear case. With a new O-ring seal in the shift rod cover, install it, torquing the screws to 5-7 ft-lbs. Slip the shift rod through the bushing in the cover and thread it into the shift-assist cylinder valve. Apply OMC Sea-Lube Anti-Corrosion Lubricant to the shift rod for about 3", as shown. **CAUTION: Avoid getting lubricant on the clamping surface of the shift rod cover or inside of the boot, or the boot will slip off.** Slip the boot over the shift rod cover, and secure it with a clamp.

(26) Assemble the thrust washer, reverse gear, and retainer plate to the propeller shaft. Install two Truarc rings, flat side out, into the gear case, using #7 Truarc pliers. **CAUTION: The retaining rings are under extreme pressure during installation. Wear safety glasses and keep the pliers from slipping off the rings.** Install the thrust bearing and thrust washer on the reverse gear.

(27) Thread guide pins 10" long by 1/4"-28 into the retainer plate. Install the propeller shaft bearing housing with the UP mark facing the top, as shown, and then secure it with new O-rings and four screws dipped into OMC Gasket Sealing Compound. Torque the screws to 5-7 ft-lbs.

(28) Install new seals in the driveshaft bearing housing, using Tool No. 316615. Install a new O-ring on the housing. Insert the thrust bearing, thrust washer, and preselected shims on the driveshaft. Install the driveshaft housing, using seal protector #316614. Dip the screws in OMC Gasket Sealing Compound and tighten to 5-7 ft-lbs. of torque. Apply OMC Adhesive "M" to the bottom edge of the impeller plate, and then install the plate. Insert the impeller drive key into the driveshaft. Install the impeller over the key in the driveshaft. **CAUTION: If the old impeller is being reused, it must be installed the same way it came out. A new one can be installed either way.** Oil the impeller blades and rotate the driveshaft clockwise while sliding the pump housing over the impeller. Install a new water tube grommet into the pump housing. Secure the pump housing and water tube bracket with screws dipped in OMC Gasket Sealing Compound and torque them to 5-7 ft-lbs.

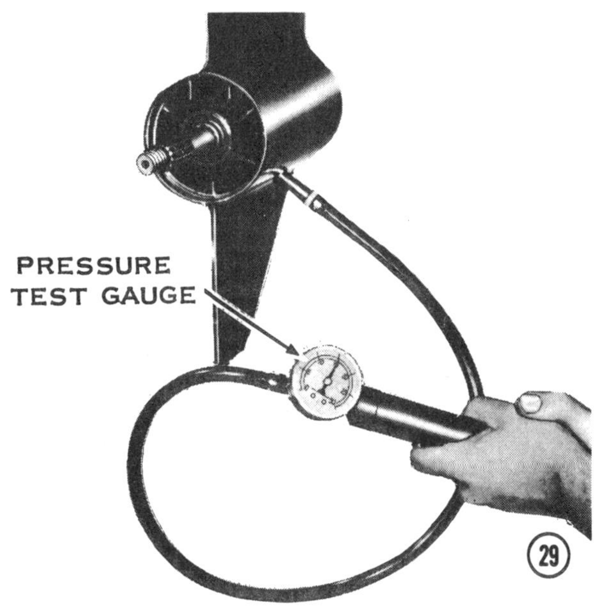

(29) To test the crankcase sealing, remove the drain plug and screw in a pressure test gauge. Pump up pressure to 16-18 psi and there should be no leak. If it does leak, submerge the case in water to see where the bubbles are coming from.

(30) Coat the propeller shaft with OMC Gasket Sealing Compound, and then install the thrust washer, propeller, spacer and nut. Tighten the nut to 130-150 ft-lbs. of torque, and then install the cotter pin to secure it.

INSTALLING THE GEAR CASE

(31) Check the dimensions of the shift shaft if parts have been replaced to determine that you have the correct ones installed. Do this by pulling up on the shift rod to engage reverse gear, while you rotate the propeller shaft. Measure from the surface of the gear case to the center of the shift rod hole. With the bend in the shift rod facing aft as shown, the dimension for short-shaft models should be 16-7/32". Long-shaft models should measure 21-7/32".

(32) Place an O-ring on the driveshaft. Apply OMC Adhesive "M" to the exhaust housing and the gear case surfaces, and then carefully install the gear case, making sure that the water tube enters the pump grommet, while the shift rod enters through the exhaust housing grommet (on short-shaft models only) and adaptor seal assembly. Rotate the flywheel clockwise to align the driveshaft and crankshaft splines. Dip the screws into OMC Gasket Sealing Compound and tighten them to 18-20 ft-lbs.

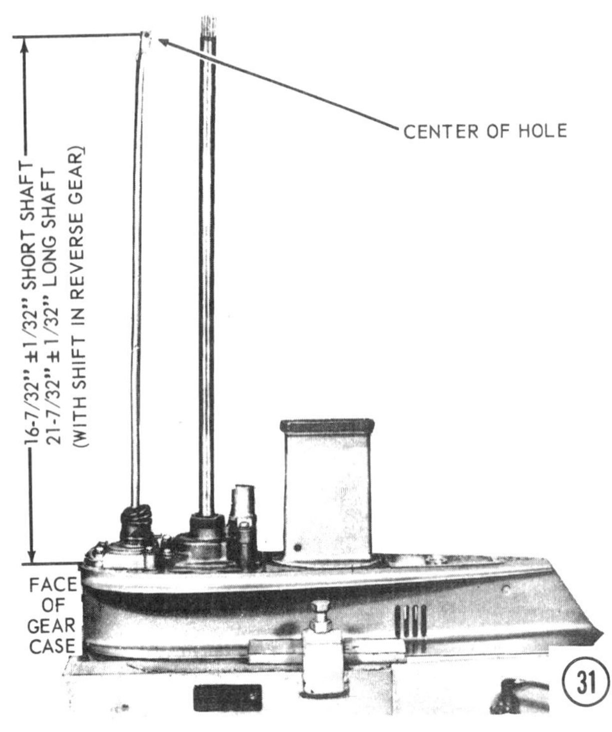

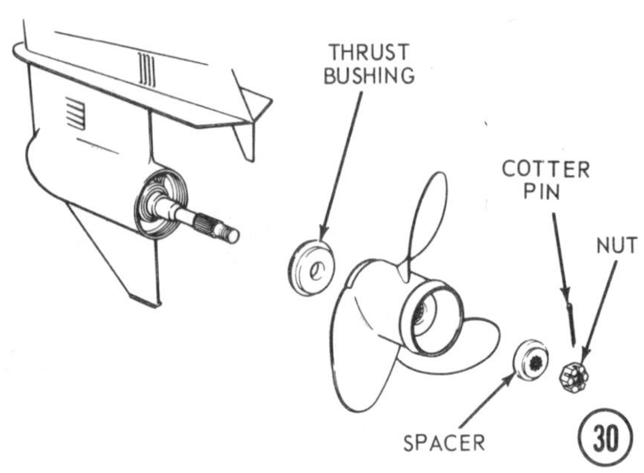

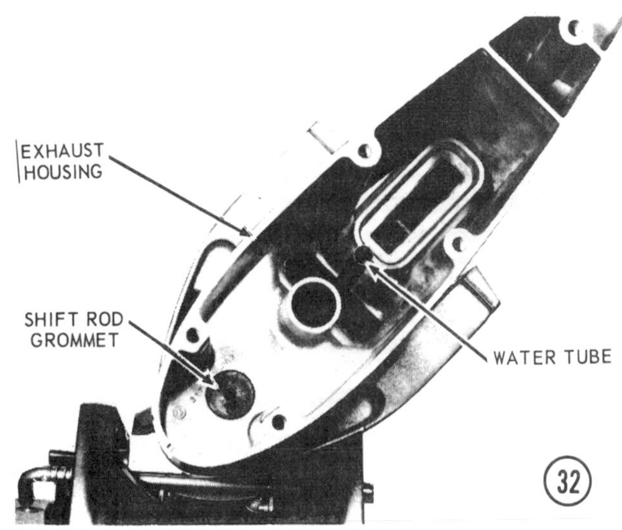

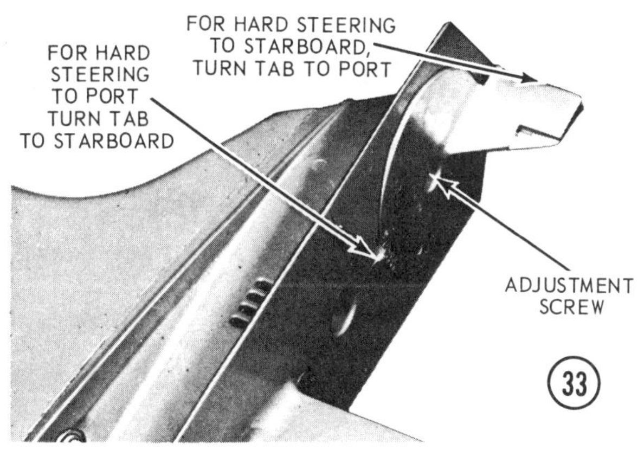

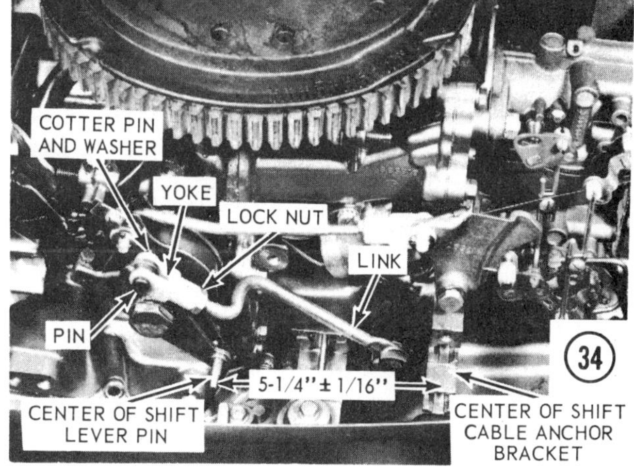

(33) Install the trim tab, aligning the scribed marks made during disassembly. If not marked, the factory setting is between 2 and 2-1/2.

(34) Connect the shift rod to the shift rod lever shaft. Move the shift lever into FORWARD gear while rotating the propeller to insure that the shifter clutch dog fully engages FORWARD gear. Check the distance between the center of the shift lever pin to the center of the shift cable anchor bracket, which should measure 5-1/4 ± 1/16" for all except the 65/75 Hp models, which should be 4-13/16 ± 1/16". No adjustment is needed on four-cylinder engines. If an adjustment is needed, remove the clevis pin, loosen the clevis nut, and then turn the yoke on the link as necessary. Fill the gear case with OMC Sea-Lube Gear Case Lubricant.

7

ELECTRICAL SYSTEM SERVICE

The first outboard motors were started by pulling on an attached rope, and even today most small engines still are started in that way. With the advent of the larger, higher-compression engines, though, it became necessary to replace the rope starter with an electric cranking system.

Since a starting motor requires a large amount of current, it is necessary to have a fully charged battery for the starting system. The battery can be externally charged or the engine optionally can be equipped with an alternator, which charges the battery while the engine is operating.

With the addition of the battery, the next logical improvement was to change the ignition system from a magneto type to a battery-ignition system. The latest improvement has been to replace the conventional ignition system with a capacitor-discharge type, using a solid-state amplifier.

THE ELECTRICAL SYSTEM

The electrical system consists of four circuits: the generating circuit, the starting circuit, the choke circuit, and the ignition circuit.

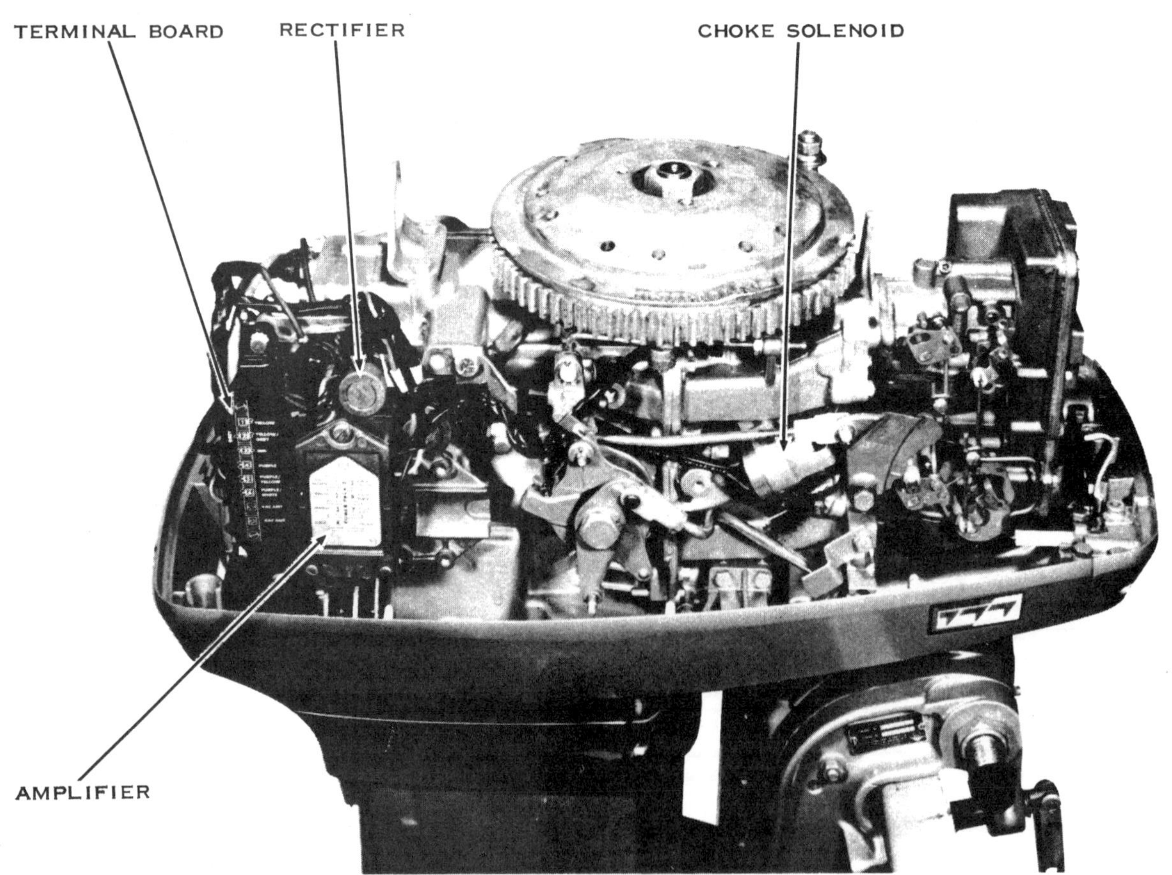

Starboard side of the 50 Hp engine.

GENERATING CIRCUIT

Permanent magnets and a stator are located within the flywheel. The alternating current, generated in the stator windings, passes to the rectifier which, in turn, changes the alternating current into direct current for charging the battery. The negative side of the rectifier is grounded. The positive side goes through the internal harness plug to the battery. The negative side of the battery is connected, through the connector, to the ground of the engine.

STARTING CIRCUIT

The starting circuit consists of the cranking motor and the starter-engaging mechanism. The solenoid is a heavy-duty switch used to carry the heavy current from the battery to the starting motor. The solenoid is actuated by turning the ignition key to the START position. A mechanically actuated safety switch prevents engaging the starting motor whenever the throttle is opened too wide.

CHOKE CIRCUIT

The choke is activated by a solenoid that attracts a plunger to close the choke valves. It is energized by turning the ignition key to the START position and holding the choke switch in the ON position until the engine starts.

IGNITION SYSTEM

The ignition system varies with engine type. Some engines have a magneto under the flywheel. Some of the larger engines used a belt-driven magneto. Most of the larger engines are now using a CD (Capacitor-Discharge) type ignition system. Some of these have contact points under the flywheel to actuate a solid-state amplifier for generating about 25,000 volts for

Port side of the 50 Hp engine.

firing the spark plugs. The latest versions have a sensor magnet under the flywheel which generates a small triggering voltage as it passes a sensor coil. This small voltage is stepped up in the charge coils to about 300 volts, rectified, and used to charge a capacitor for discharging into the ignition coil.

Tuning is covered in Chapter 3, and service procedures are covered in this chapter.

TROUBLESHOOTING

Trouble in the electrical system often is first evidenced by failure of the starter to operate, and may be caused by failure of any one or more of the electrical components. If the ammeter does not indicate charge with the engine running, or if the battery fails to retain enough charge to start the engine, the first things to check are the condition of the battery, polarity of the battery, and electrical connections throughout the circuit. A large percentage of electrical failures are caused by loose or dirty electrical wiring connections, especially in the starting circuit.

BATTERY

For best performance, use a 12-volt, 70-ampere hour battery, or better, with a minimum of two minutes cold starting capacity at 300 amperes discharge, zero degrees Fahrenheit, and a 10-second voltage reading of 7.5 volts. Frequently, poor starting is traceable to a battery with specifications not conforming to recommendations. **CAUTION: Correct battery polarity is extremely important. The battery must be connected so that its negative (−) post is connected to ground. If the positive (+) post is connected to ground, the rectifier diodes, voltage suppressor, and pulse pack may be damaged.**

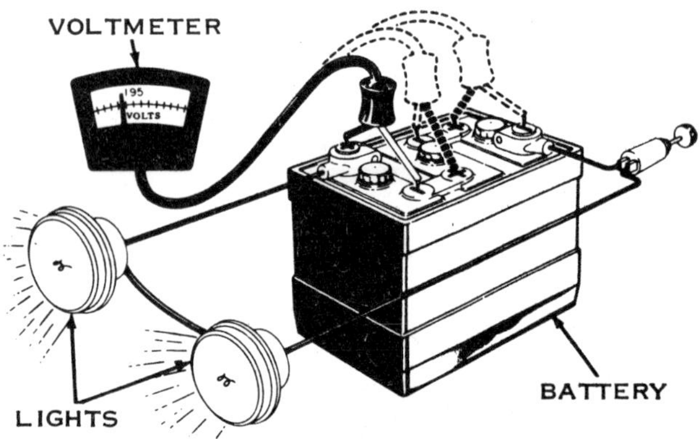

The battery can be tested by turning on the lights and accessories until there is an 8-10 ampere load and then measuring the individual cell voltages, as discussed in the text.

TESTING A BATTERY

The condition of the battery cells may be checked quickly and accurately by following the light-load test procedure. Before starting the test, add water as necessary to bring the electrolyte to the proper level. Place a load on the battery by holding the starter switch on for three seconds. It makes no difference whether the starter turns the engine or not. However, if the engine does start, turn off the ignition key to stop it immediately.

Establish an 8- to 10-ampere load by turning the ignition switch to the ON position. Turn on the lights or other accessories as necessary. After one minute, with an 8- to 10-ampere load still on, read the individual cell voltages with a voltmeter having a 0.01-volt scale division. *NOTE: After testing, close the openings in the sealing compound made by the probes of the voltmeter.*

If any cell reads 1.95 volts or more, and the difference between the highest and lowest cell reading is less than 0.05 volt, the battery is good and is sufficiently charged. If the cell readings are both above and below 1.95 volts, and the difference between the highest and lowest reading is less than 0.05 volt, the battery should be recharged. If any cell reads 1.95 volts or more but there is a difference of 0.05 volt or more between the highest and lowest cell, the battery should be replaced.

If the reading for each cell is less than 1.95 volts, the battery is too low to test properly; however, this does not necessarily indicate a defective battery. A battery in this condition should be boost-charged but not fully charged at this time, and the light-load test repeated. If the battery is found to be good after boost-charging, it should be fully recharged before being returned to service. If none of the cells comes up to 1.95 volts after the first boost charge, the battery should be given a second boost. Batteries which do not come up after the second boost-charge should be replaced.

BATTERY CHARGING

Boost-charge 12-volt batteries at 50 amperes for 20 minutes. **CAUTION: Do not boost-charge the battery more than this amount for the light-load test.** If batteries are to be fully charged by means of a "quick charger," the charging rate must be "tapered" (reduced to a safe limit) when the electrolyte temperature reaches 125°F., or when gassing becomes excessive. **CAUTION: Failure to do so may harm the battery.**

If the battery is to be slow-charged, adjust the electrolyte to the proper level by adding water, and then charge the battery at five amperes until it is fully charged. A full charge of the battery is indicated when all cell gravity readings do not increase when checked at three intervals of one hour, and when all cells are gassing freely. Plenty of time must be allowed for slow-charging. Charging period of 24 hours or more are often required.

BATTERY CARE

The battery should be kept charged at all times. The state of charge should be checked by taking specific gravity readings with a hydrometer. It is suggested that specific gravity readings and checking for replacement of water be made every two weeks. If the battery has been standing for 30 days, it should be recharged before being placed in service.

The specific gravity of the battery electrolyte should be checked with a battery hydrometer which has a built-in thermometer and correction chart. No other method is accurate in determining the condition of a battery. Note, also, that a hydrometer reading is not accurate if water has been added recently, due to the fact that the water has not had a chance to mix thoroughly with the electrolyte.

The proper water level should be maintained at all times. If water is added in freezing weather, the battery should be charged to a full charge at once or the water may freeze and crack the battery case. Only pure distilled water should be added to the battery to replace water lost through evaporation. **CAUTION: Never add acid except when acid has been lost by spilling.**

Install the battery near the engine. For mounting the battery, use a frame securely fastened to the boat. A loose battery may shift in the boat, damaging itself or other equipment. Tighten the hold-down nuts evenly until the battery is secure. If the hold-down nuts are tightened too much, distortion and damage to the battery case will result.

STARTING MOTOR

The electric starting system consists of the starting motor, starter and choke switches, starter and choke solenoids, safety switch, and the necessary cables and wires with their connectors. The starting motor supplies cranking power to the engine by converting electrical energy into mechanical power, which is transmitted through the drive pinion gear and the flywheel ring gear to crank the engine. The starter switch controls the operation by activating the starter solenoid, which makes the circuit between the battery and starting motor.

The starter solenoid completes the circuit through a movable contact disc which strikes two terminal contacts that are connected to the starting motor circuit. The solenoid contains many turns of wire which, when energized by the starter switch, exert a magnetic pull on the solenoid plunger, causing it to move the contact disc against the terminal contacts.

The starting motor drive pinion is disengaged when at rest and is made to mesh with the flywheel ring gear by the rotation of the starting motor armature. After the engine has started, the starter pinion is driven faster than the starting motor shaft and moves down the screw shaft and out of mesh with the flywheel.

The safety switch opens the starting motor circuit, preventing accidental engaging of the starting motor whenever the throttle lever is set beyond the START position. The switch is operated by a plunger which rides on a cam on the lower distributor housing.

Due to the construction of the starting motor, maintenance operations are generally limited to periodic checking for loose mounting bolts. Unless it is certain that the starting motor requires attention, do not remove it. A thorough check should be made of the battery, cables, starter solenoid, and switch. Check the starting motor by using the no-load test. With 12.0 volts applied to the starting motor, the maximum current should be 60 amperes, and the minimum speed should be 8,000 rpm.

OVERHAULING THE STARTING MOTOR

REMOVING

Disconnect the battery lead at the starting motor. Remove the three cap screws holding the starting motor bracket and the mounting bracket to the crankcase, and then lift off the starting motor-and-bracket assembly from the studs. On some later engines with an air silencer, it is necessary to remove the silencer because one of the mounting screws is behind it.

DISASSEMBLING

Use the accompanying exploded view to disassemble the type of starting motor you have.

CLEANING AND INSPECTING

① Clean all parts with a solvent-soaked rag. **CAUTION: Don't dip electrical parts in solvent, or you will damage the insulation.** Clean the commutator with grade 00 sandpaper. If the surface is worn or deeply pitted, it should be turned in a lathe. Check the armature on a growler for shorted turns by holding a hacksaw blade over the laminations while slowly turning the armature. If the hacksaw blade vibrates, the armature coils are shorted. Check the insulating segments between the commutator bars for a short, which will give the same indication. This type of short circuit can often be corrected by digging out the metallic piece causing the trouble.

② Check the commutator for ground by touching one test prod to the commutator and the other to the shaft. If the test lamp lights, the armature is defective.

③ Check the field windings with a test light for continuity and ground. Check for continuity by touching the test prods to both brushes; the test lamp should light. To test for ground, place one of the test prods on the metal part of the housing and the other on one of the brushes. If the test lamp lights, the field windings are grounded.

④ The starter solenoid is a sealed unit. To test it, apply 12 volts to the small terminals, and the solenoid plunger should click as it operates.

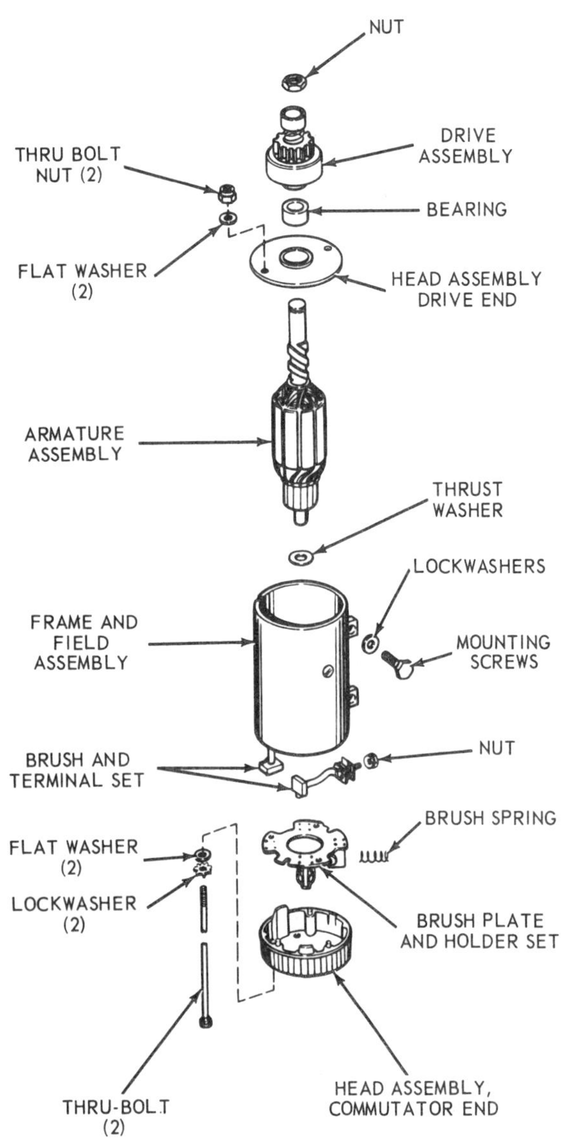

Exploded view of the cranking motor used on the 50 Hp two-cylinder engine.

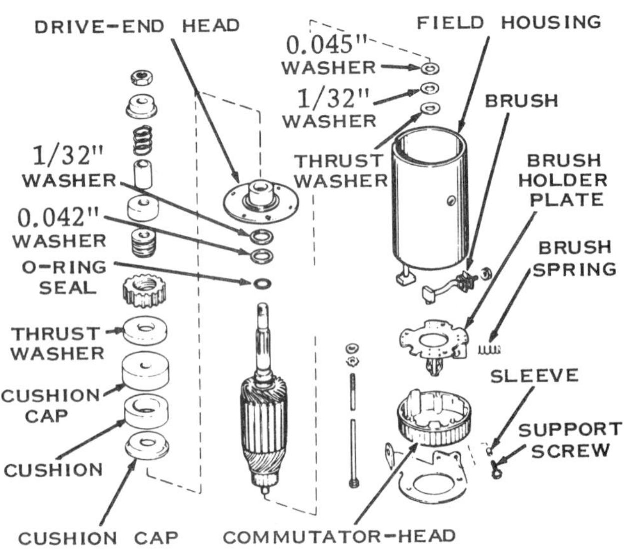

Exploded view of the starting motor used on the 18 through 40 Hp engines.

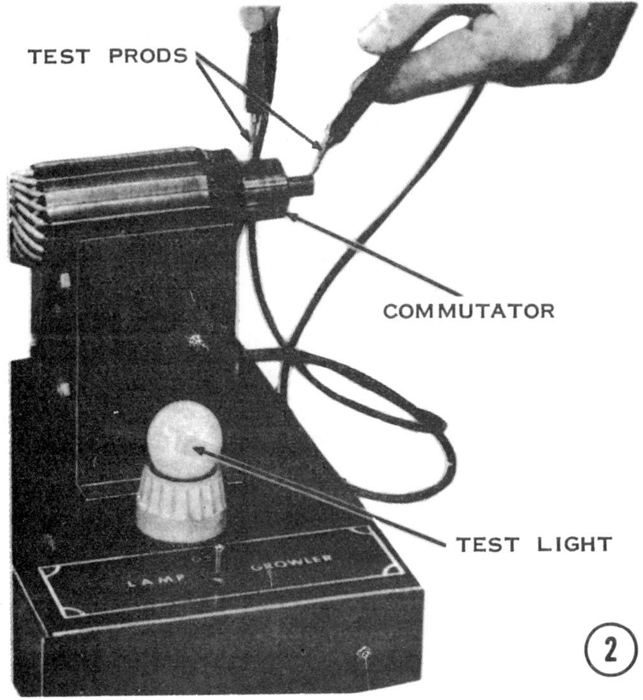

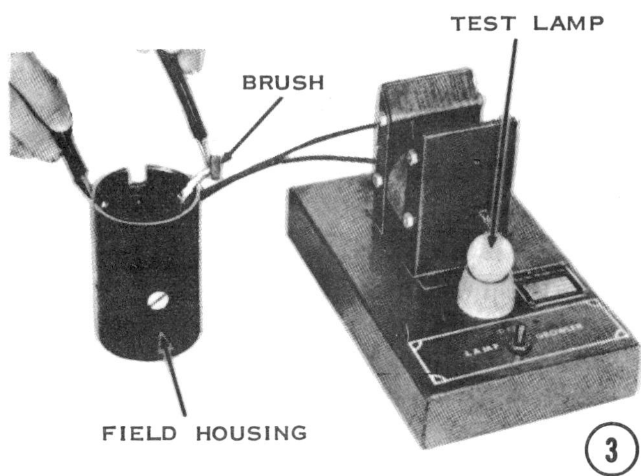

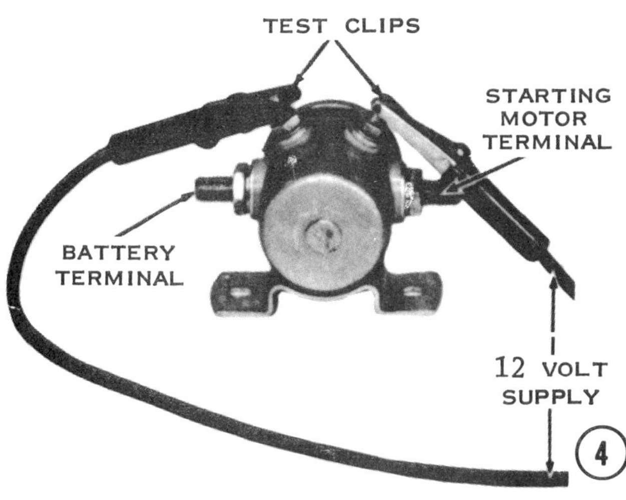

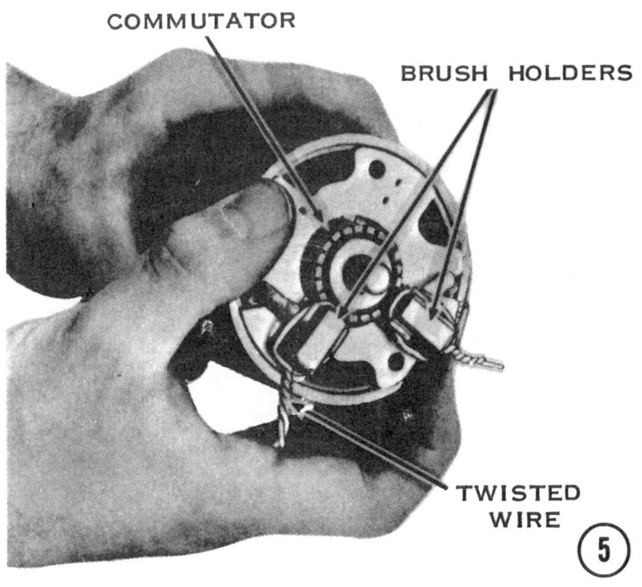

ASSEMBLING

⑤ To facilitate assembly of the starting motor, insert the brushes and brush springs in the holders. Tie them in place with a piece of fine wire. Assemble the brush holder and armature to the field housing, and then remove the wires. Replace the commutator- and drive-end heads to complete the assembly. Use the exploded views for assembling the parts of the drives.

DC CHARGING CIRCUIT

The charging system consists of a DC generator, voltage regulator, and battery. The three functions of the regulator are: (1) to prevent the battery from discharging through the generator when the engine is idling or stopped (cut-out relay), (2) to limit the charging current to a safe value (current regulator), and (3) to limit the voltage to a safe value (voltage regulator).

OUTPUT TESTS

Connect a voltmeter across the battery terminals, using the 15-volt scale. The voltmeter should indicate a voltage of 12.6 for a fully charged battery. Start the engine and run it about 3,500 rpm with the propeller in water; the voltage should rise to the regulated setting, which should be 14.0-15.0 volts.

If the voltage does not rise, then the generator or regulator is at fault. The trouble can be isolated by grounding the field terminal with a jumper wire while the engine is operating at 3,500 rpm. If the regulator is defective, the generator output will now rise to about 10 amperes and the voltage should rise above 16 volts. This is because the regulator has been removed from

Troubleshooting the DC generator can be accomplished by grounding the generator field terminal with a jumper wire, as shown. If the generator now charges, the trouble is in the regulator, as discussed in the text.

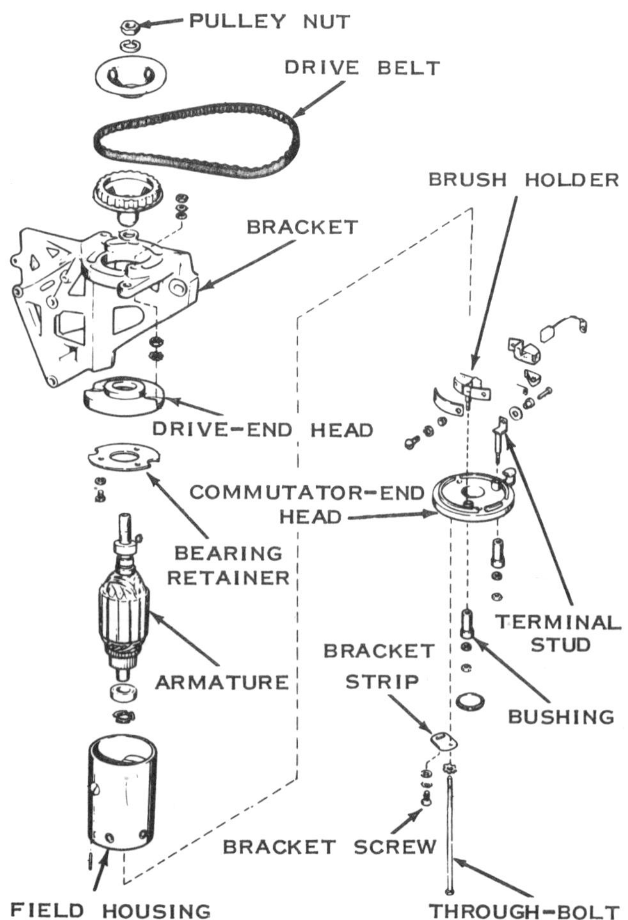

Exploded view of the DC generator.

the circuit by the jumper wire, and the generator is now operating without any regulation. **CAUTION: Don't run the engine with the jumper wire in place, or you will burn up the generator.**

REMOVING THE GENERATOR

Remove the generator pulley flange by taking off the attaching nut and lockwasher. Loosen the through-bolt nuts to release the belt tension. Lift the drive belt off the pulley. Disconnect the generator armature and field leads. Remove the nuts from the generator bracket studs. Remove the attaching bolt holding the ring gear guard to the generator bracket, and then lift the bracket and generator from the powerhead as an assembly.

DISASSEMBLING THE GENERATOR

Remove the pulley. Take off the bracket strap from the mounting bracket by taking out the attaching bolt. Remove the nuts, lockwashers, and through-bolts from the generator. Hold the generator with the shaft end facing down, and then drop it lightly on a soft wooden block until the heads separate. Remove the drive-end head and armature. Remove the terminal stud nuts, and then take off the commutator-end head.

CLEANING AND INSPECTING

Check the bearings for roughness or play. Replace any bearing that shows signs of excessive looseness. **CAUTION: Don't wash or lubricate the ball bearings because they are factory-packed with a special lubricant.**

Check the brushes for wear; replace them if they are worn to half of their original length.

Check the fields and armature with a growler and test lamp for a short, a ground, or an open circuit as shown in the preceding starting motor section.

ASSEMBLING

Assemble the armature, bearing, and bearing retainer to the drive-end head. Install the brushes in their holders. Place the armature and drive-end head in position in the field housing. **CAUTION: The dowel pin in the head must be aligned with the notch in the case.**

Install the terminal stud bushings and nuts. Attach the generator to the mounting bracket, leaving the nuts on the through-bolts loose enough to allow for adjusting the drive belt tension. Install the bracket strap attaching screw. Place the key and pulley on the generator shaft.

INSTALLING

Attach the armature and field leads to the studs on the bottom of the generator. *NOTE: The holes in the lead terminals and the terminal studs are different sizes to prevent incorrect assembly.* Position the generator and bracket assembly on the powerhead studs. Install the stud nuts, but don't tighten them. Push the generator bracket toward the rear of the engine until the stops on back of the generator bracket make contact with the two machined pads on the cylinder. Tighten the mounting bracket nuts.

Place the belt on the generator pulley. Install the pulley flange, lockwasher, and nut. Adjust the drive belt tension by pivoting the generator until the belt deflects 1/4"-3/8" under finger pressure. *NOTE: The strap and one bolt hole in the bracket are slotted for this adjustment.* Tighten the nuts and capscrews securely. **CAUTION: The generator bearings will wear excessively if the belt tension is too tight.**

Before starting the motor, it is necessary to polarize the generator to be sure that it will charge with the correct polarity. Do this by shorting across the voltage

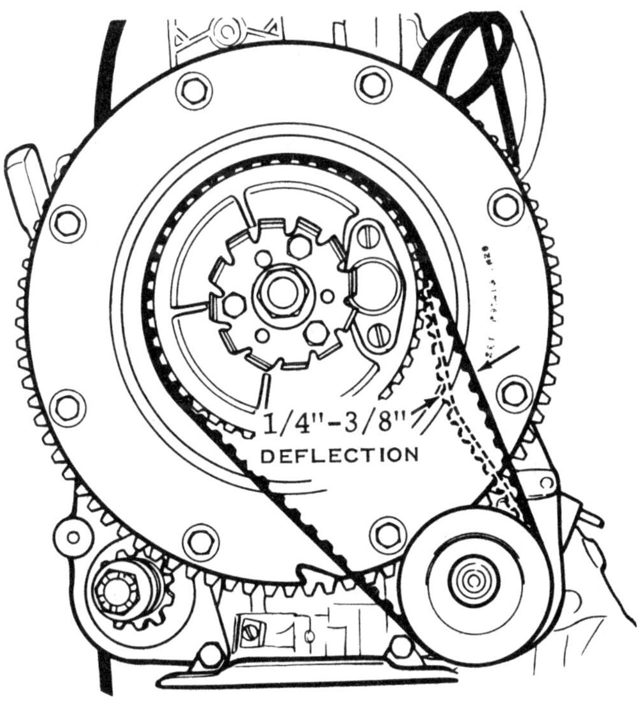

The generator drive belt should deflect 1/4"-3/8" under moderate finger pressure.

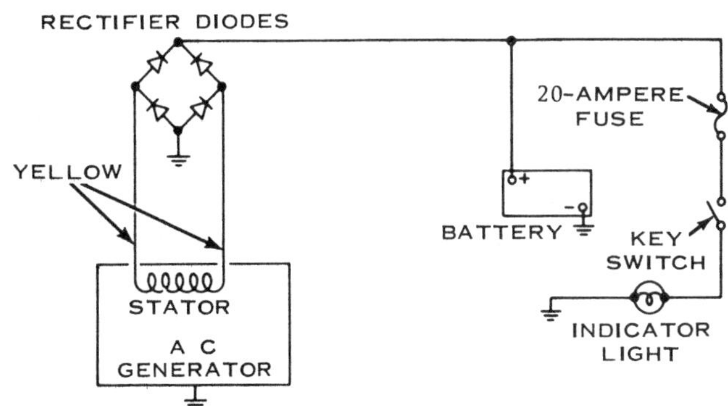

Wiring diagram for the 9-ampere alternator charging circuit.

regulator terminals FIELD and BATTERY for a few moments with a jumper wire.

AC CHARGING CIRCUIT

The charging circuit consists of an alternator, a rectifier, and a battery. The alternator is made up of two parts, the flywheel, with cast-in magnets, and the stator assembly, which is bolted to the crankcase. The stator is made up of a circular field winding with 12 coils wound over laminated iron cores. The flywheel, with cast-in magnets, turns around this assembly, inducing alternating current in the coils. A rectifier converts the alternating current into direct current.

Three types of charging circuits are used; 6-ampere, 9-ampere, and 15-ampere systems. All contain bridge-type rectifiers and have similar charging circuits. The 15-ampere charging circuit has, in addition, a transistorized voltage regulator and a charge indicator light.

SERVICING THE 6/9 AMPERE CHARGING CIRCUIT

CHECKING THE RECTIFIER DIODES

① Turn the test meter control knob to the HIGH OHMS position. Disconnect the diode leads at the connector. Connect the ohmmeter red test lead to the rectifier case (ground). Note the meter reading and then reverse the test leads. A normal diode will show a reading with the test leads connected in one direction and no reading in the other direction. An infinite (very high) reading in both checks indicates that the diode is open circuited (defective). A zero reading in both tests indicates that the diode is shorted (defective). Repeat the tests for the other diodes by connecting the test leads between the other diode leads and the rectifier case.

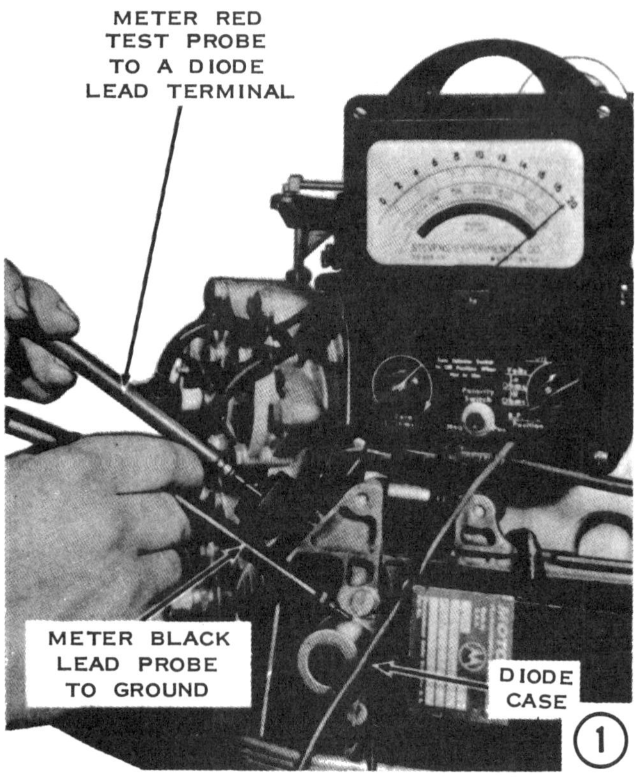

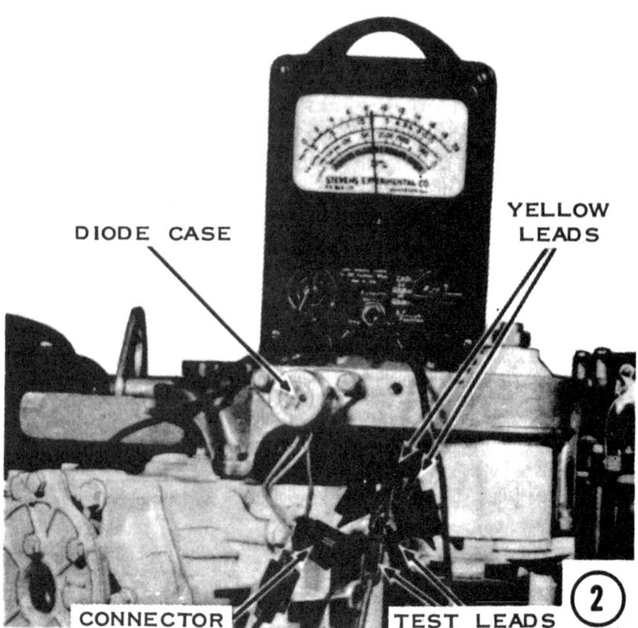

CHECKING THE STATOR WINDINGS

② To check the stator windings for ground, disconnect the leads at the powerhead. Connect the red meter lead between either lead and the black meter test lead to ground. Any reading indicates that the windings are grounded (defective). To test the stator windings for continuity, turn the ohmmeter control knob to the LOW OHMS position and connect the meter test leads between the two stator leads; the meter should read 0.75-1.0 ohm if the windings are good. An infinite reading means that the windings are open circuited (defective).

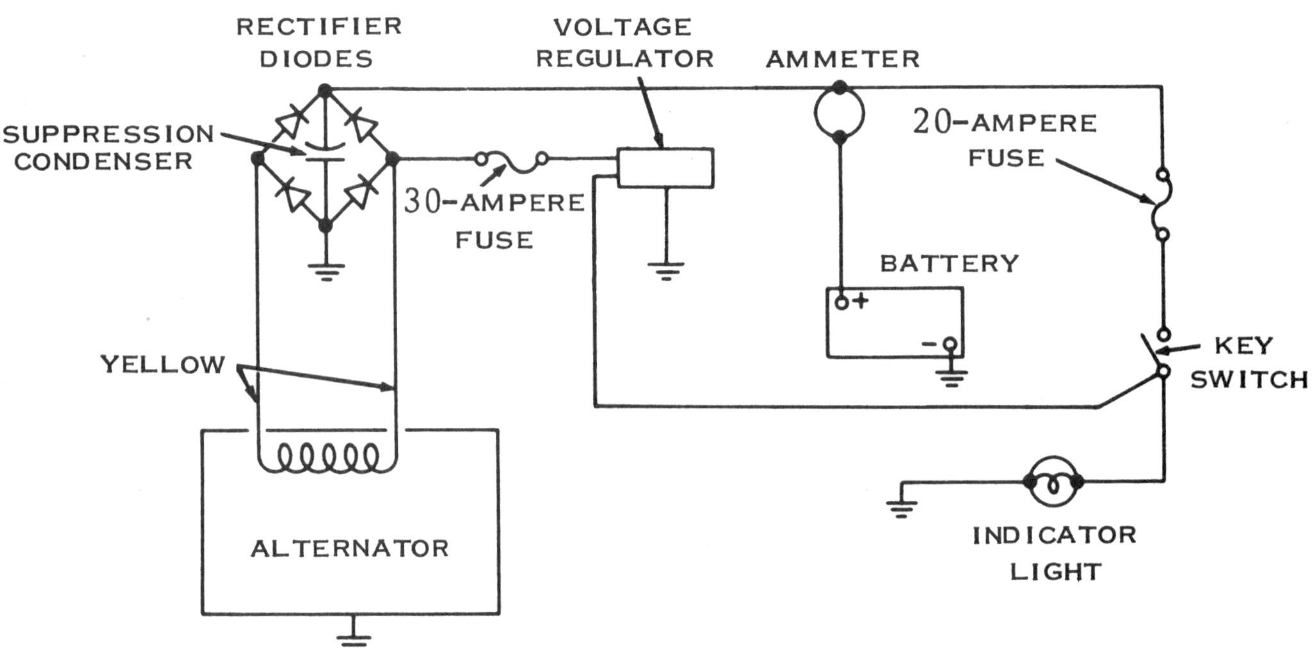

Wiring diagram for the 15-ampere alternator charging circuit.

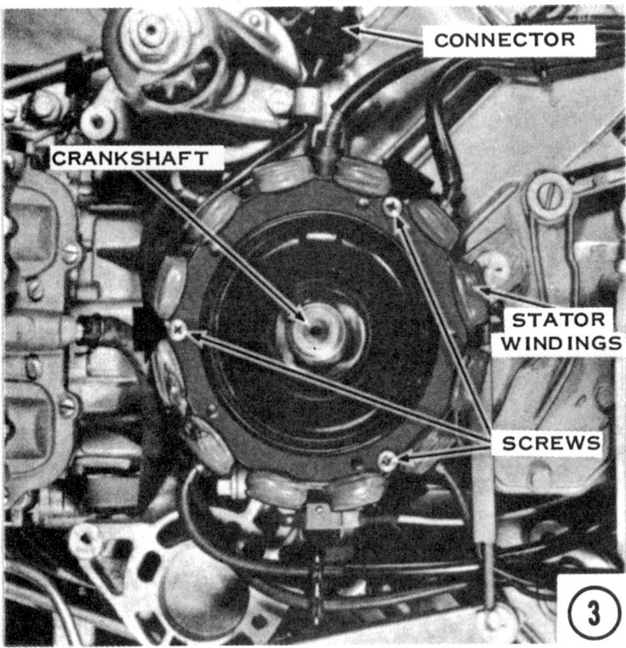

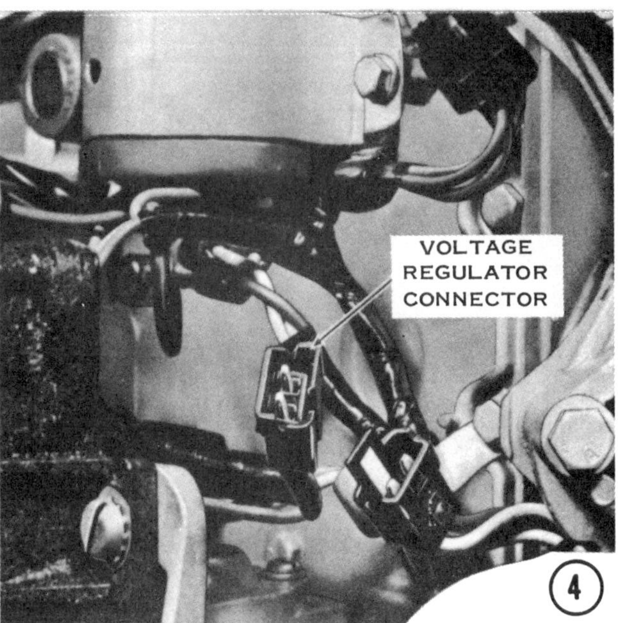

REPLACING THE STATOR WINDINGS

③ If the windings are defective, the stator can be replaced by removing the flywheel with a puller. Disconnect the stator lead connector, remove the three retaining screws, and then lift the stator from the powerhead. Place a new stator in position, and attach it with the three screws dipped in Loctite. Torque the screws to 48-60 in-lbs. Reconnect the stator lead connector.

SERVICING THE FIFTEEN-AMPERE CHARGING CIRCUIT

CHECKING THE VOLTAGE REGULATOR

④ With the solid-state voltage regulator used, there can be only two types of failures: (1) no output, resulting in an undercharged battery, or (2) too much output, resulting in an overcharged battery. The following tests must be performed with a fully charged battery and with the engine running at 3,000-3,600 rpm with the propeller in water. If the battery is undercharged and the ammeter does not indicate a charge, stop the engine and disconnect the regulator leads at the connector in the regulator circuit. **CAUTION: Make sure that all accessories are turned off because the uncontrolled voltage during the test could damage the accessories.** Restart the engine and run it at 3,000-3,600 rpm. If the ammeter now shows a full charge, the stator windings are good but the regulator must be replaced. If there is no ammeter reading, check the stator windings.

If the battery is overcharged, check the 30-ampere fuse in the voltage regulator line. If the battery is consistently being overcharged (ammeter indicates continuous maximum charge or the battery uses excessive amounts of water), then check the battery

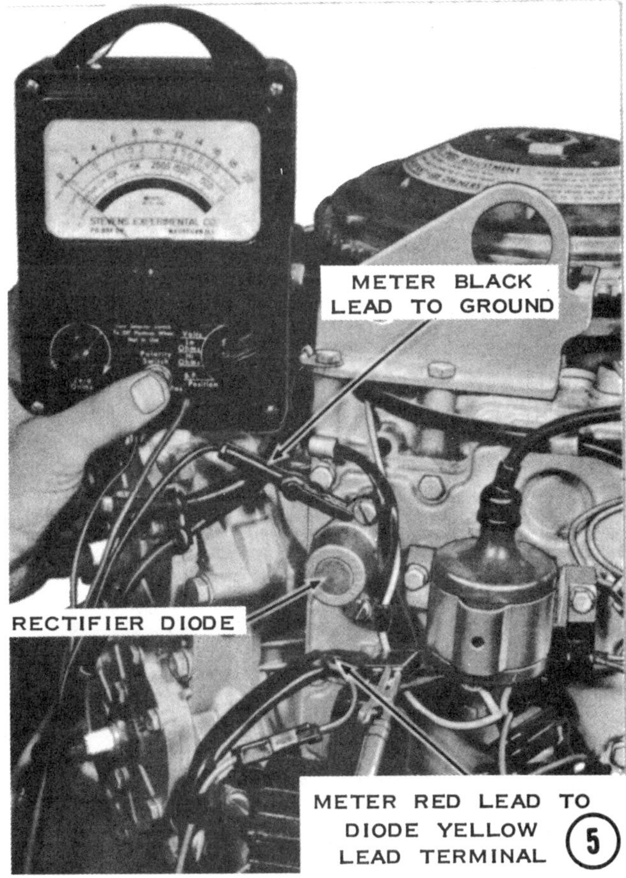

voltage by running the engine at 3,000-3,600 rpm with all accessories turned off. Check the battery voltage and, if it is in excess of 15 volts, replace the regulator.

CHECKING THE RECTIFIER DIODES

⑤ To check the rectifier diodes, turn the test meter knob to the HIGH OHMS position. Disconnect the three wire plugs. Connect one meter test lead to one of the yellow wire diode terminals and the other meter test lead to the diode case. Note the meter reading, and then reverse the test leads. A normal diode will show a reading with the test leads connected in one direction and no reading in the other direction. An infinite (very high) reading in both tests indicates that the diode is open circuited (defective). A zero reading in both tests indicates that the diode is shorted (defected). Repeat the test procedure for the other diodes by connecting the test leads between the other yellow wire spade terminal and the diode case. Then connect the test leads between one yellow terminal and the brown terminal. The meter must read in only one direction.

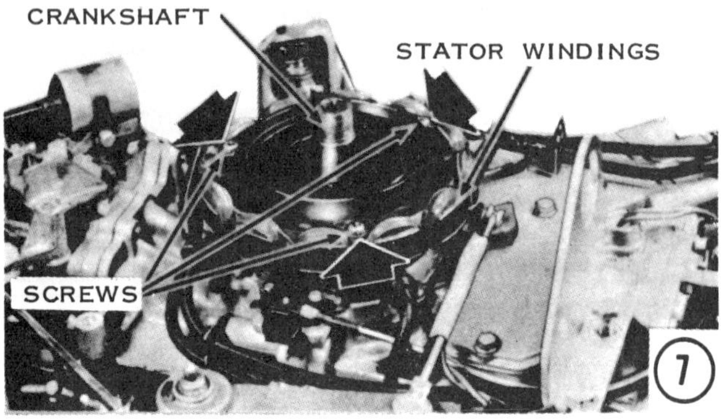

CHECKING THE STATOR WINDINGS

⑥ To check the stator windings on the engine, disconnect the leads at the powerhead. With the test meter on HIGH OHMS, connect the test lead to either yellow stator lead and the other test lead to a good ground. An infinite reading indicates that the windings are not grounded (good). To check the stator windings for continuity, turn the test meter control knob to the LOW OHMS position. Connect the two test leads to the two stator yellow leads and the meter should read 0.5 ± 0.2 ohm if the windings are good. An infinite reading indicates that the windings are open circuited (defective).

REPLACING THE STATOR WINDINGS

⑦ If the stator windings have to be replaced, remove the flywheel. Disconnect the stator lead connectors. Remove the three screws, and then lift the stator from the powerhead. Place a new stator winding in position and attach it with three screws dipped in Loctite. Tighten the screws to 48-60 in-lbs. of torque. Replace the flywheel, and then reconnect the stator lead connectors.

IGNITION SYSTEM SERVICE

General ignition system service procedures are covered in the first part of Chapter 3, Tuning for Performance. This section will cover the service procedures for checking and replacing components of the CD ignition systems used on late-model engines.

SERVICE PRECAUTIONS

Because of the higher voltages, it is extremely important to observe special precautions for troubleshooting a CD ignition system. Some of them are: (1) Conduct all tests with the spark plug high-tension leads connected to the spark plugs or to a good ground, unless otherwise specified. (2) When running the engine, be sure the battery is connected or damage to the ignition system will result. (3) Always hold the spark plug wire with insulated pliers when making a spark test. The high voltages in the system could result in a severe shock if you held the high-tension wire with your hand. (4) The coil lead is sealed in the ignition coil; therefore, don't attempt to remove it. **CAUTION: Whenever hooking up a battery to an engine with a CD ignition system, it is essential that you connect it properly. If the terminals are reversed, even for an instant, you will burn out the power pack.**

A malfunction in the ignition system will result in (1) engine misfiring, (2) engine surge, or (3) failure of the engine to run. It should be noted, too, that a malfunctioning vacuum switch may also prevent the engine from starting or cause erratic operation. Engine misfiring or surging can also be caused by a carburetor condition, and this should be checked as a possible cause of trouble before checking the ignition system. Any ignition system malfunction should be checked in a logical order, as discussed below:

CHECKING FOR A SPARK

Use a neon tester to check for high-tension voltage at the spark plug leads, or hold the high-tension wire with a pair of insulated pliers to see if the spark jumps a small gap to the spark plug terminal when the engine is being cranked. **CAUTION: Don't hold the spark plug wire in your hand while making this check because of the high voltages in the system, and keep the wire away from the vicinity of the carburetor to avoid fire.**

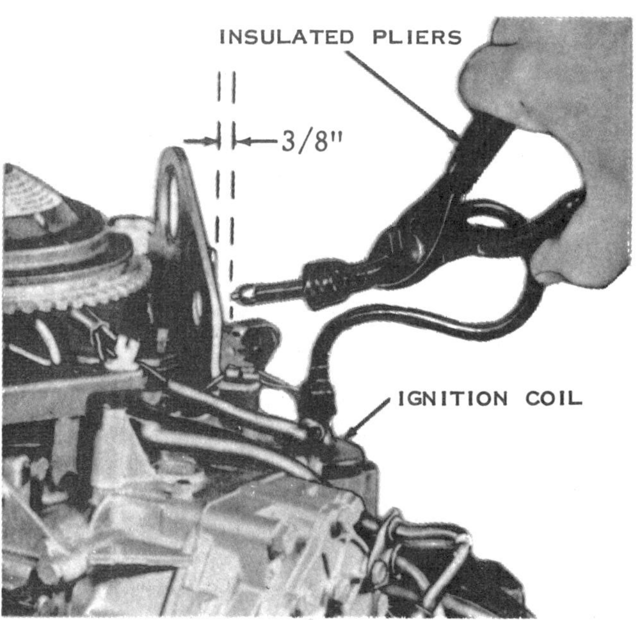

Always use a pair of insulated pliers to hold the high-tension wire when checking for a spark. CAUTION: Don't hold the wire in your hand, or you can get a severe shock.

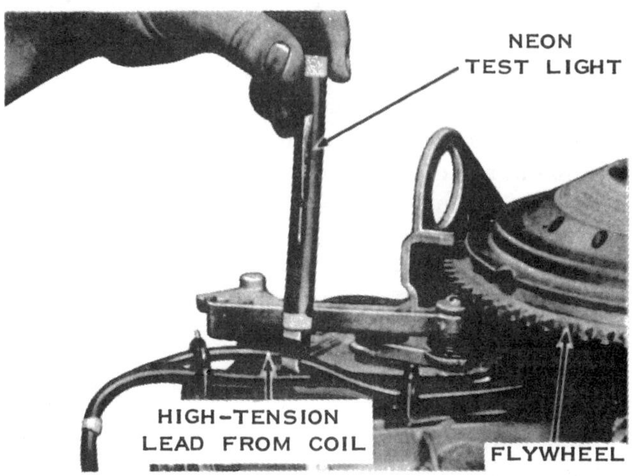

A neon tester can be used to check for high-tension voltage by holding the tester alongside of the main coil wire.

CHECKING THE WIRING

Insert a probe, from a continuity tester using a #57 bulb, into the socket of the hot lead which runs to the amplifier. Touch the other test lead to a good ground. Turn on the ignition switch and the bulb should light brightly. *NOTE: A voltmeter also can be used for this test.* No voltage to this point means that the circuit to the amplifier is open.

Check all wires associated with the system for loose or corroded connections, especially plug-in connections. Make sure that there is a clean, tight connection from the negative terminal of the ignition coil to ground. Also check for a good battery ground cable connection. Check all high-tension leads for cracks or oil-soaked insulation. The high-tension leads should also be checked with an ohmmeter for excessive resistance or an open circuit.

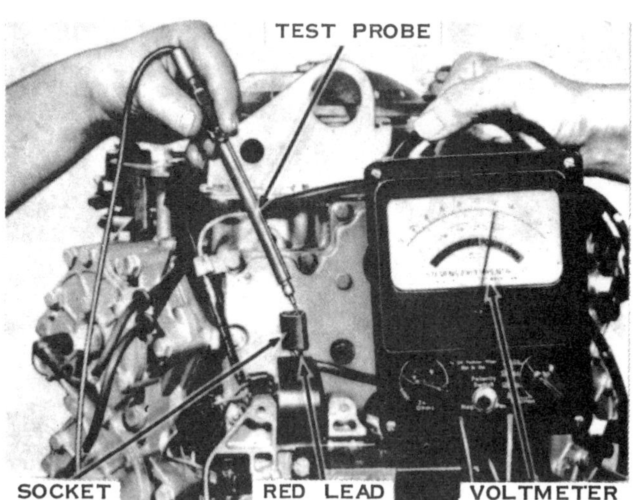

To check the wiring, use a #57 bulb or a voltmeter, as discussed in the text.

TROUBLESHOOTING A MAG-FLASH IGNITION SYSTEM—50 HP ENGINE—SINCE 1971

Since 1971, a "Mag-Flash" CD ignition system has been used on the 50 Hp engine, with charge coils mounted on the alternator stator under the flywheel. The flywheel magnets, which induce current in the alternator coils, also induce current in the charge coils so that no external voltage is needed. A sensor magnet in the flywheel hub triggers the circuit.

PRELIMINARY STEPS

Make sure that all connections are clean and tight, especially ground connections. Check to see that the plug-in connections are fully engaged and that all terminals are free of corrosion. Make sure that all wiring is located so that it cannot rub against metal edges, where vibration will wear through the insulation. Hold the spark plug wire with insulated pliers to avoid shocks, which can be very severe with this system.

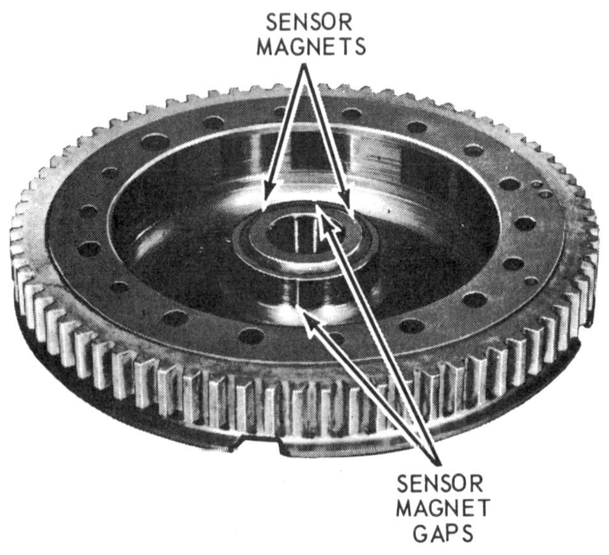

The sensor magnets are located in the flywheel hub.

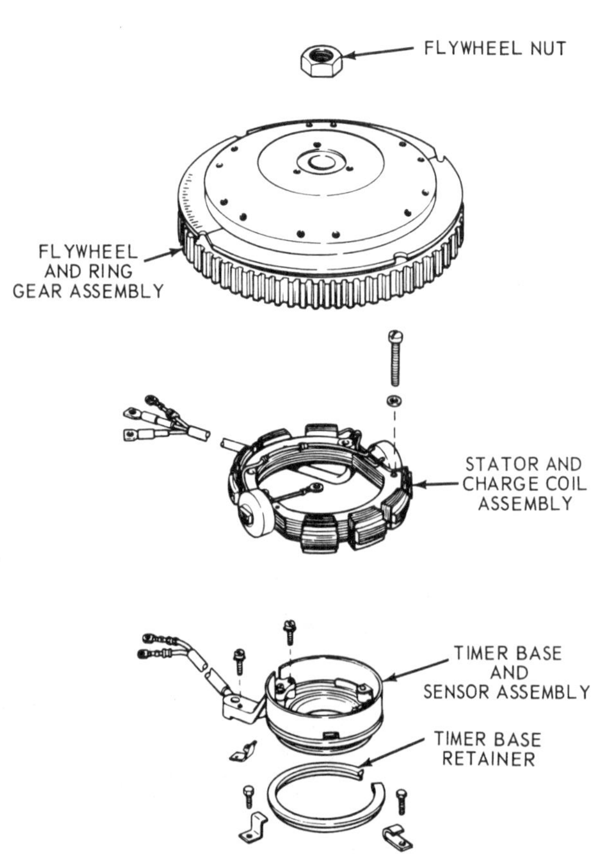

Exploded view of the Mag-Flash CD ignition system used on the 50 Hp engine.

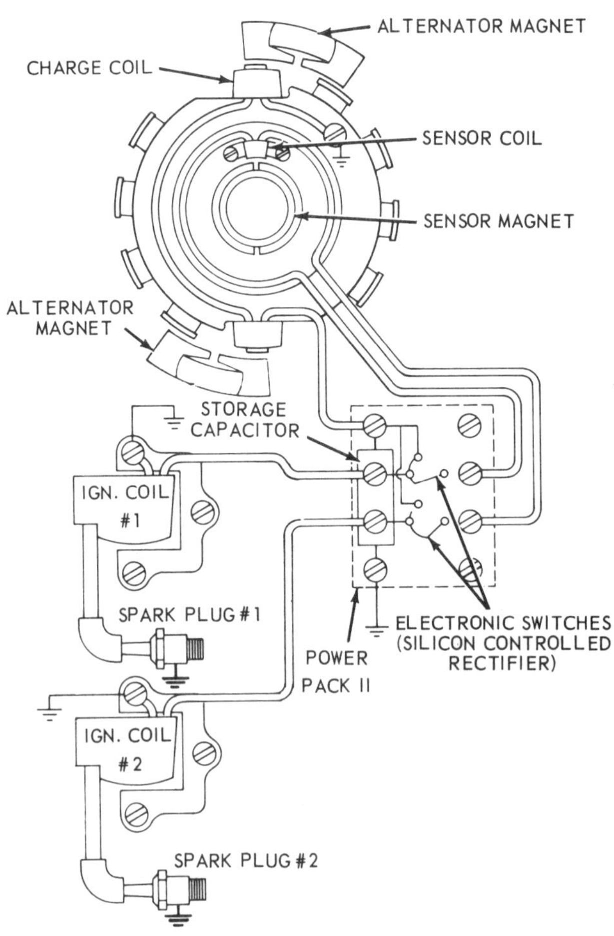

Wiring diagram of the Mag-Flash CD ignition system used on the 50 Hp engine.

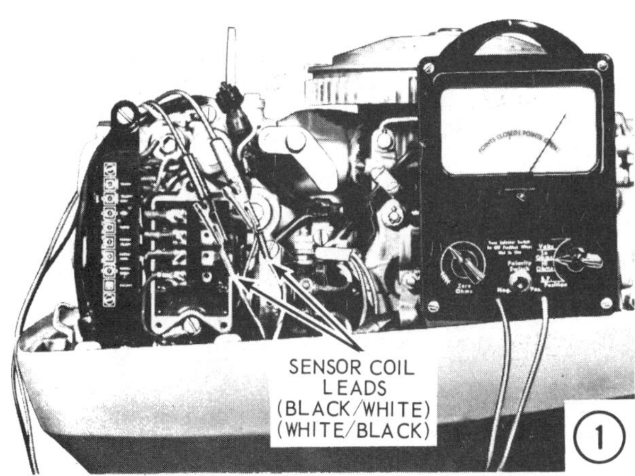

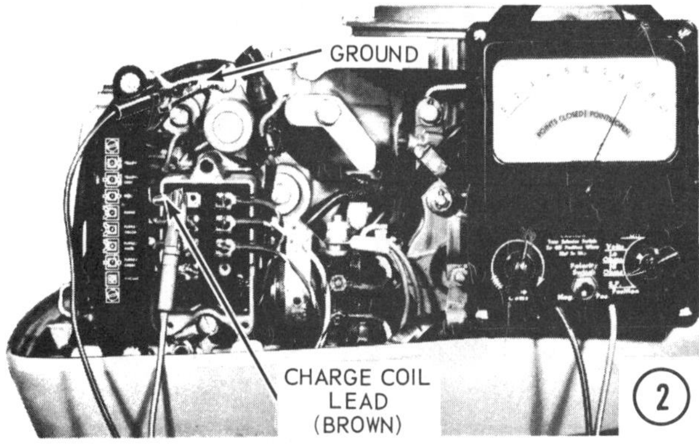

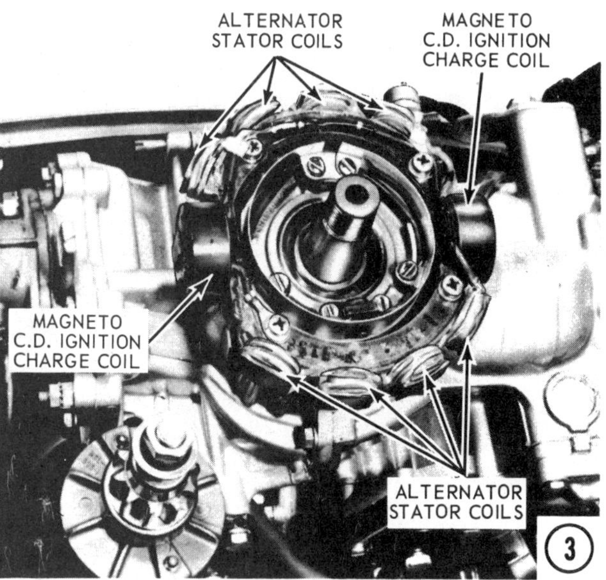

Don't open the Power Pack; it is serviced as an assembly. Don't pull on high-tension wires at the ignition coils. Don't open any plug-in connector with the engine running. Don't connect a tachometer which has not been approved for use with this system. Don't connect this system to any voltage source other than specified.

① *To check the sensor coil,* disconnect the sensor leads from the power pack terminals Nos. 6 and 7 and then connect an ohmmeter to the sensor coil leads (white and black stripe and black with white stripe). The meter should read 15 ± 5 ohms. With the sensor leads still disconnected, use the ohmmeter on the high-ohm scale to check either lead to ground. A reading indicates that the sensor coil or one of the leads is grounded, and the coil must be replaced. Because the sensor coil and timer base are serviced as an assembly, it is necessary to remove the flywheel to take off the timer base.

② *To check the charge coils,* disconnect the charge coil lead, and then connect one test lead of an ohmmeter to the charge coil lead (brown) from power pack terminal No. 1. Connect the other ohmmeter test lead to ground. The meter must read 875 ± 75 ohms. *NOTE: The charge coils are part of the stator and cannot be serviced separately.*

③ *To replace the charge coils,* pull off the flywheel. Disconnect the stator leads (yellow and yellow/grey) at the terminal board of the amplifier. Take out the four stator retaining screws, and then lift off the stator. Remove the four timer screws and clips which engage a Delrin ring of T-shaped cross-section that fits around the timer base, and then lift off the timer assembly. **CAUTION: Be careful not to cut the Delrin ring.**

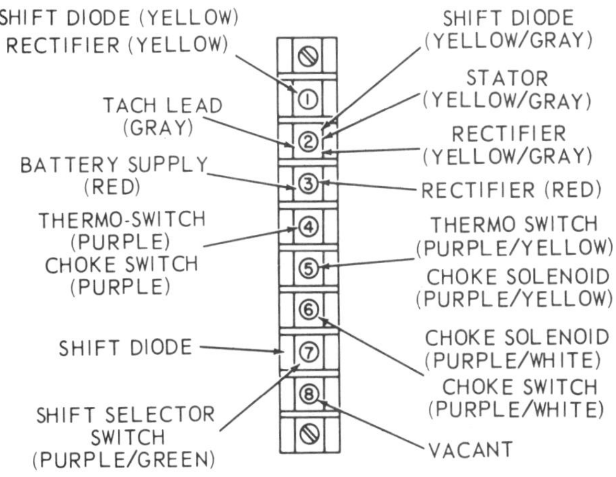

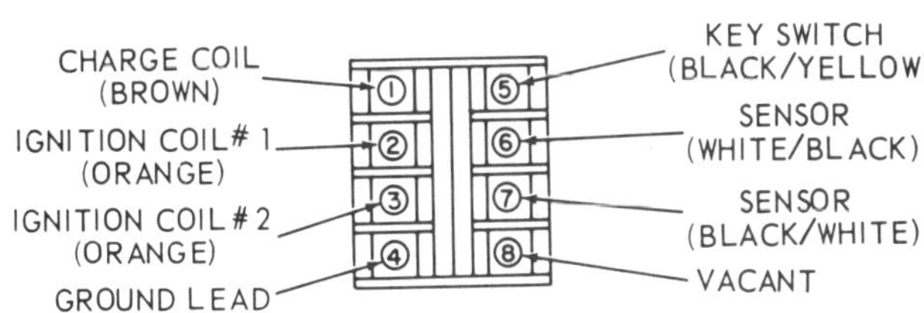

Terminal board used on the 50 Hp engine.

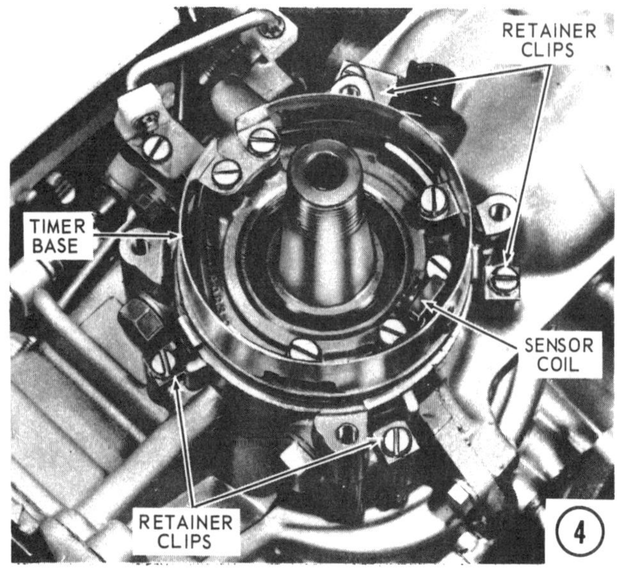

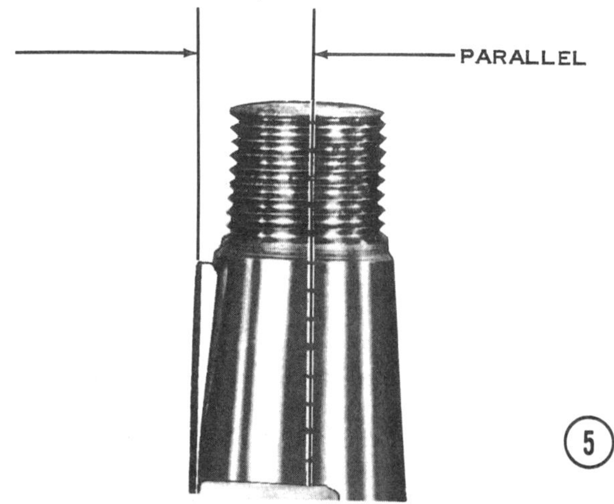

④ *To replace the timer base,* first remove all dirt and chips from the upper bearing on which the timer base rotates. **CAUTION: Because of the close clearance, any grit will cause difficulty in rotating the timer base.** Oil and assemble the Delrin ring and retainers to the timer base, and then attach the assembly to the crankcase with the four retaining clips and screws. Replace the stator and charge coils, tightening the four retaining screws to 48-60 in-lbs. of torque. Connect the stator leads to the terminal board of the amplifier.

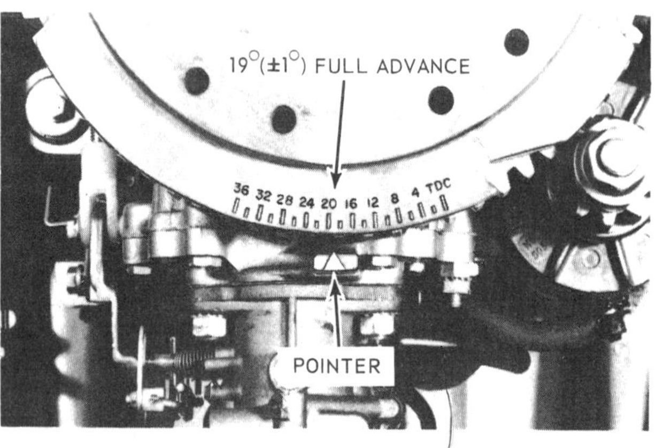

The full advance timing on the 50 Hp engine should be 19 ± 1°.

The full-spark advance stop screw is used to adjust the timing on the 50 Hp engine.

⑤ *To replace the flywheel,* first check the flywheel key to be sure that it is parallel to the centerline of the crankshaft, and then install the flywheel. **CAUTION: The inside of the flywheel and crankshaft tapers must be perfectly dry.** Swab the tapered surfaces with solvent, and then blow them dry before assembling. Tighten the flywheel nut to 100-105 ft-lbs. of torque.

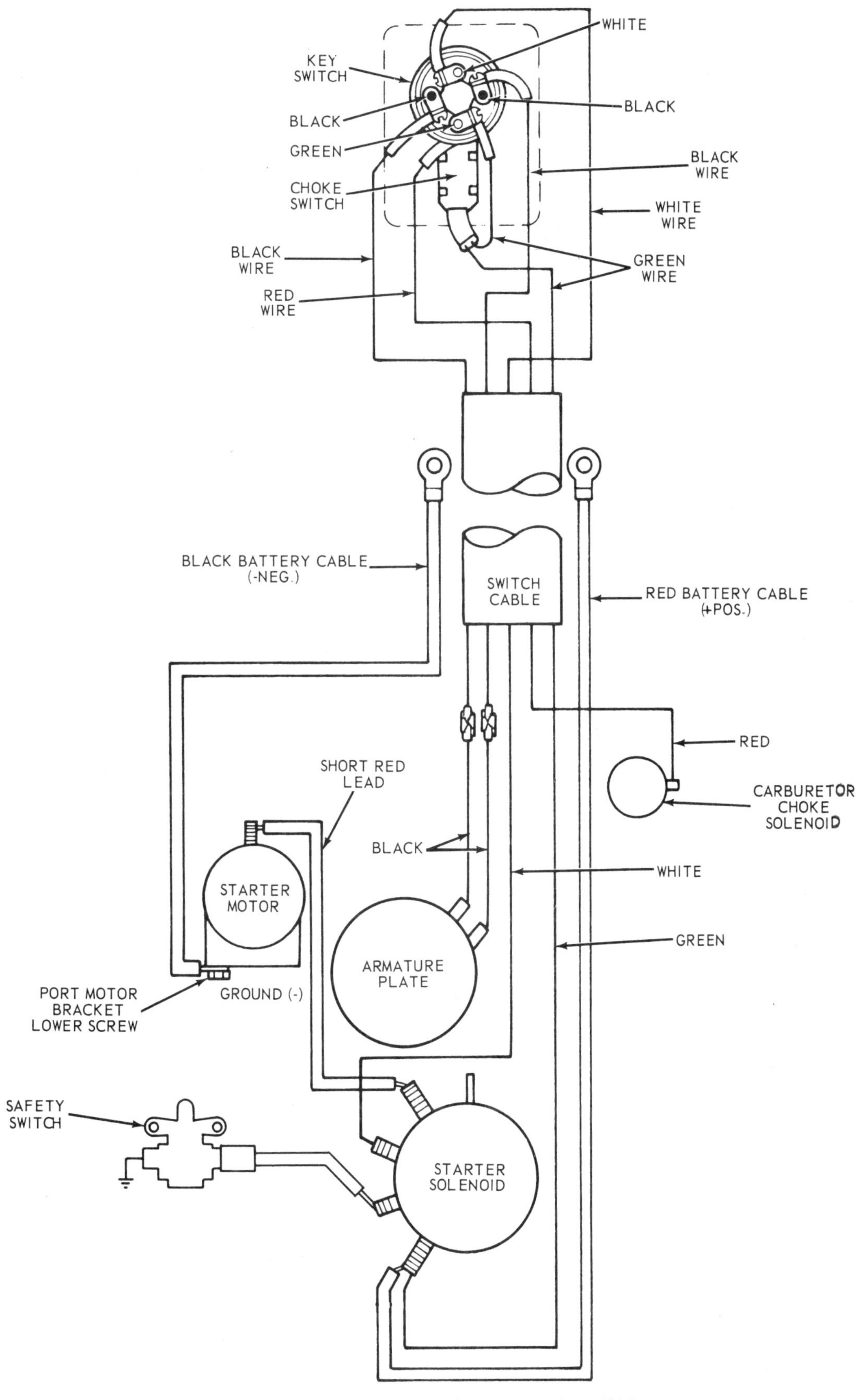

Wiring diagram of the 25 Hp motor, since 1969.

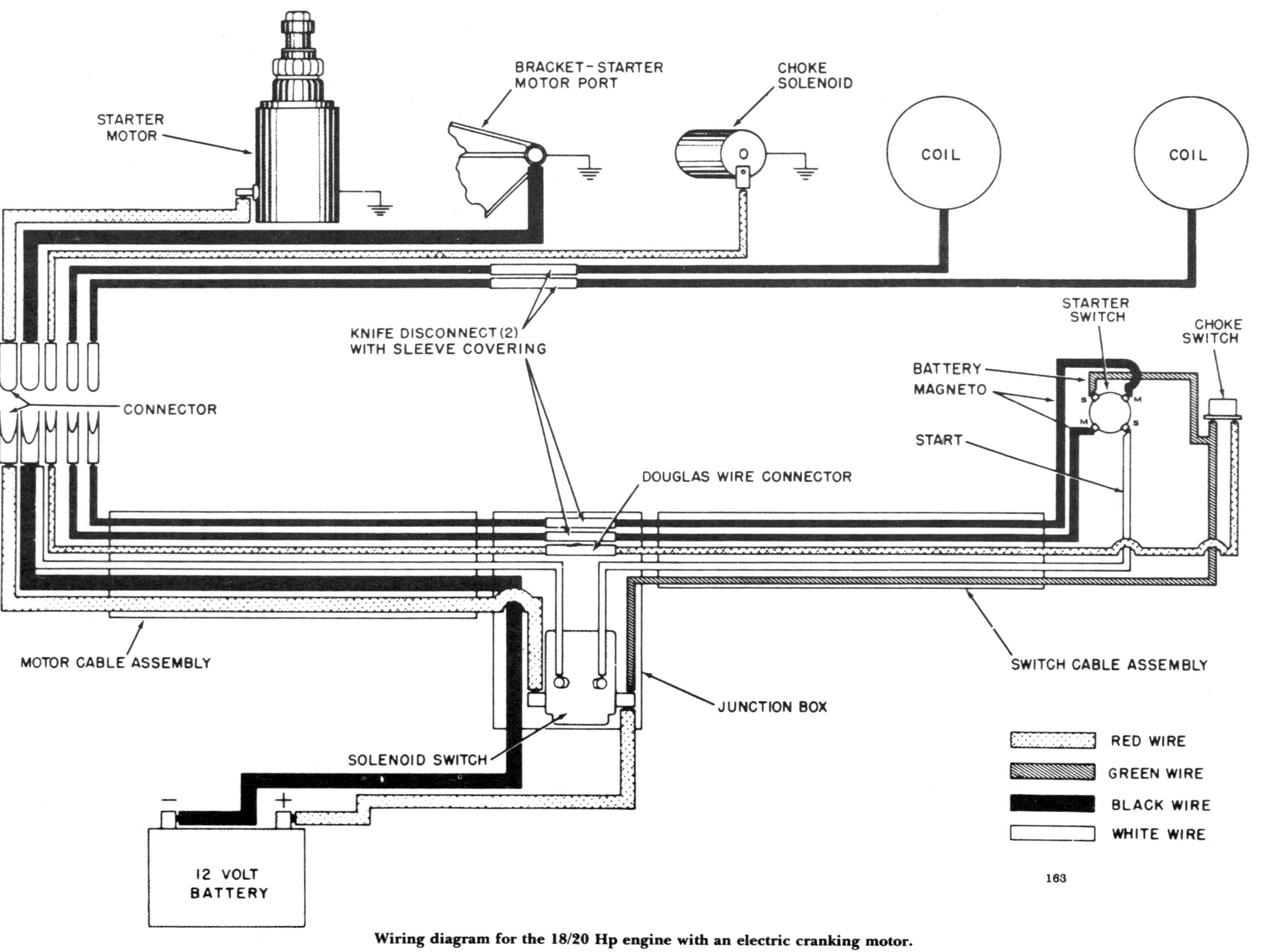

Wiring diagram for the 18/20 Hp engine with an electric cranking motor.

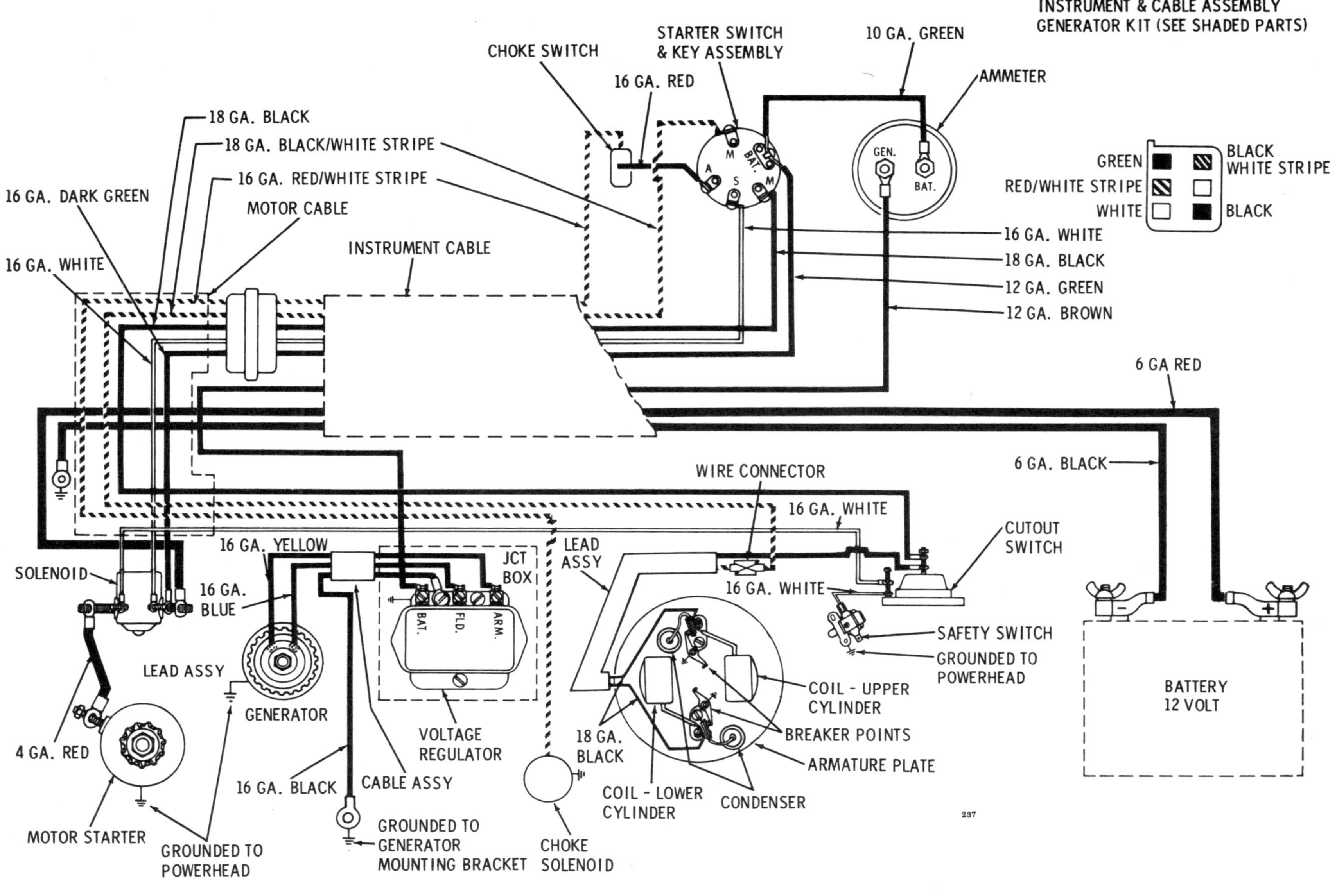

Wiring diagram for the 33 Hp engine with a DC generator.

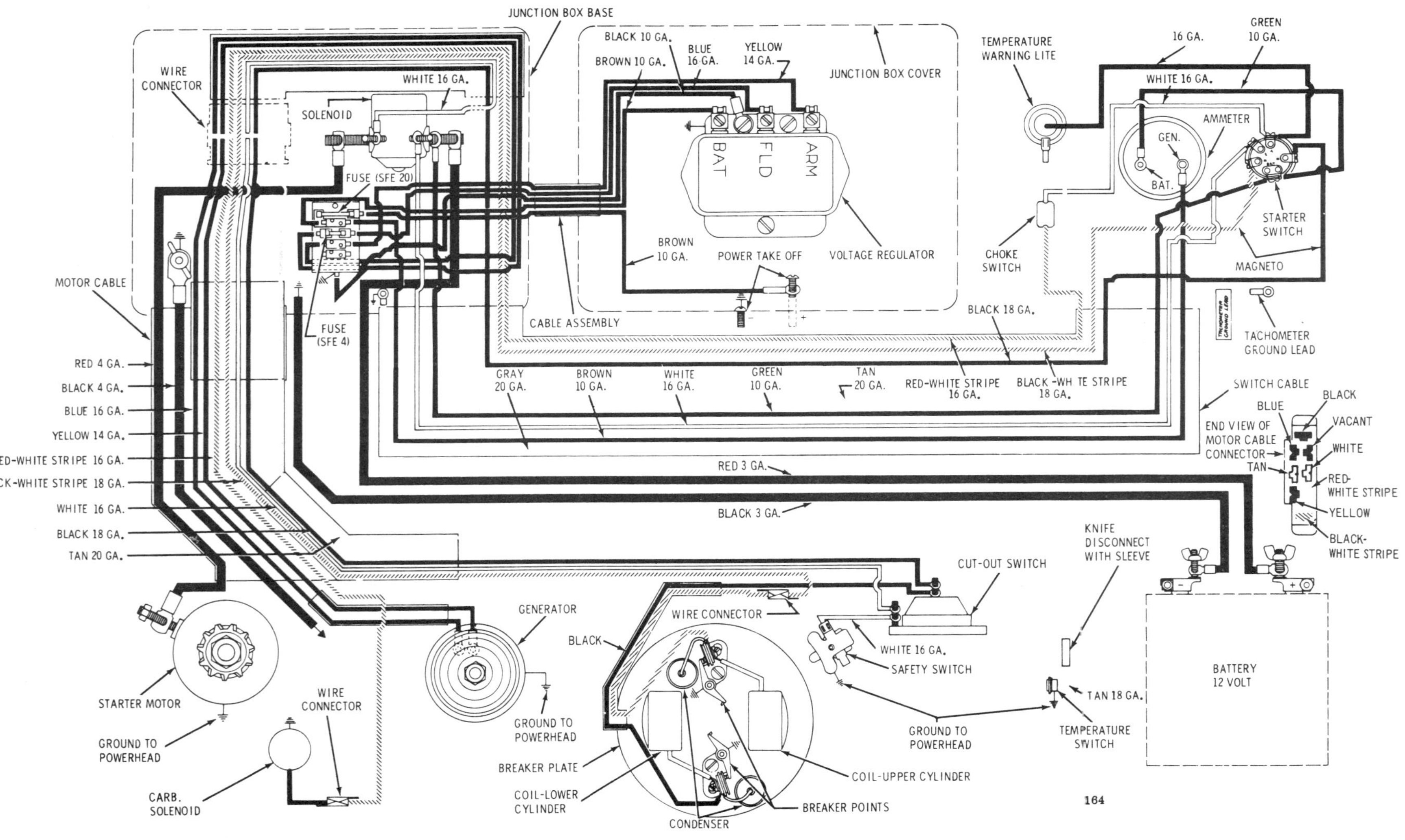

Wiring diagram for the 40 Hp engine with a DC generator.

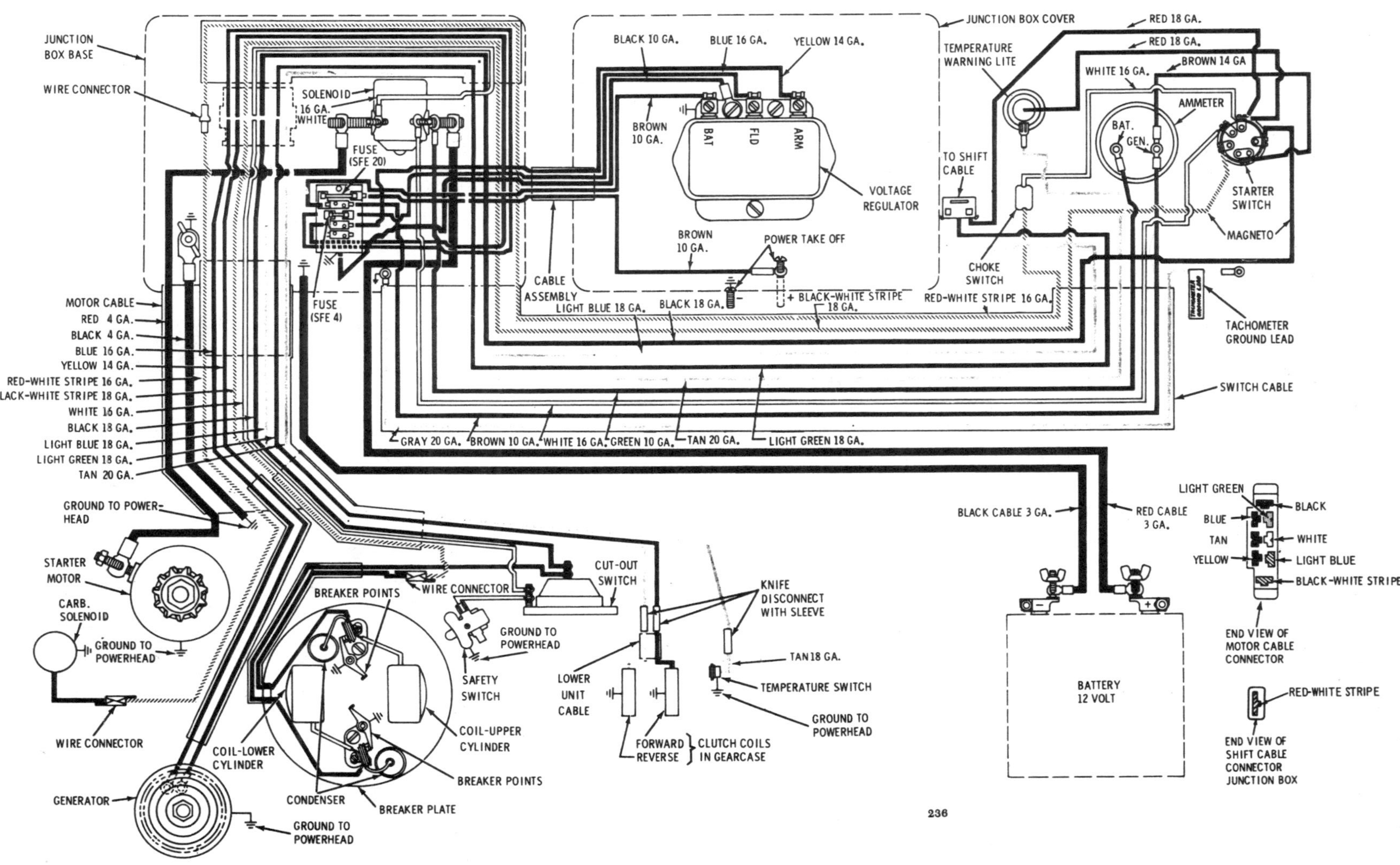

Wiring diagram for the 40 Hp engine with an electric shift.

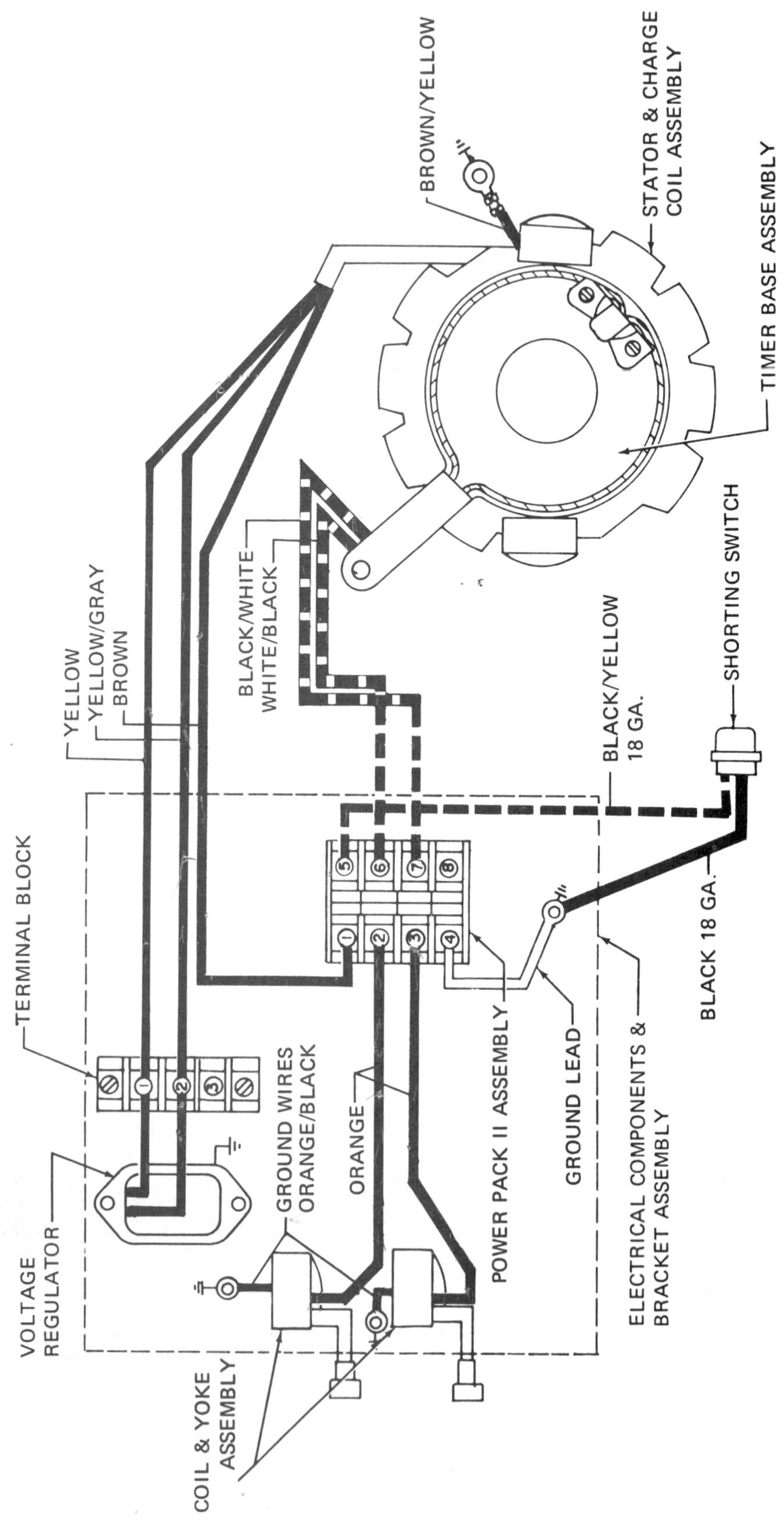

Wiring diagram of the 50 Hp engine with manual start, since 1971.

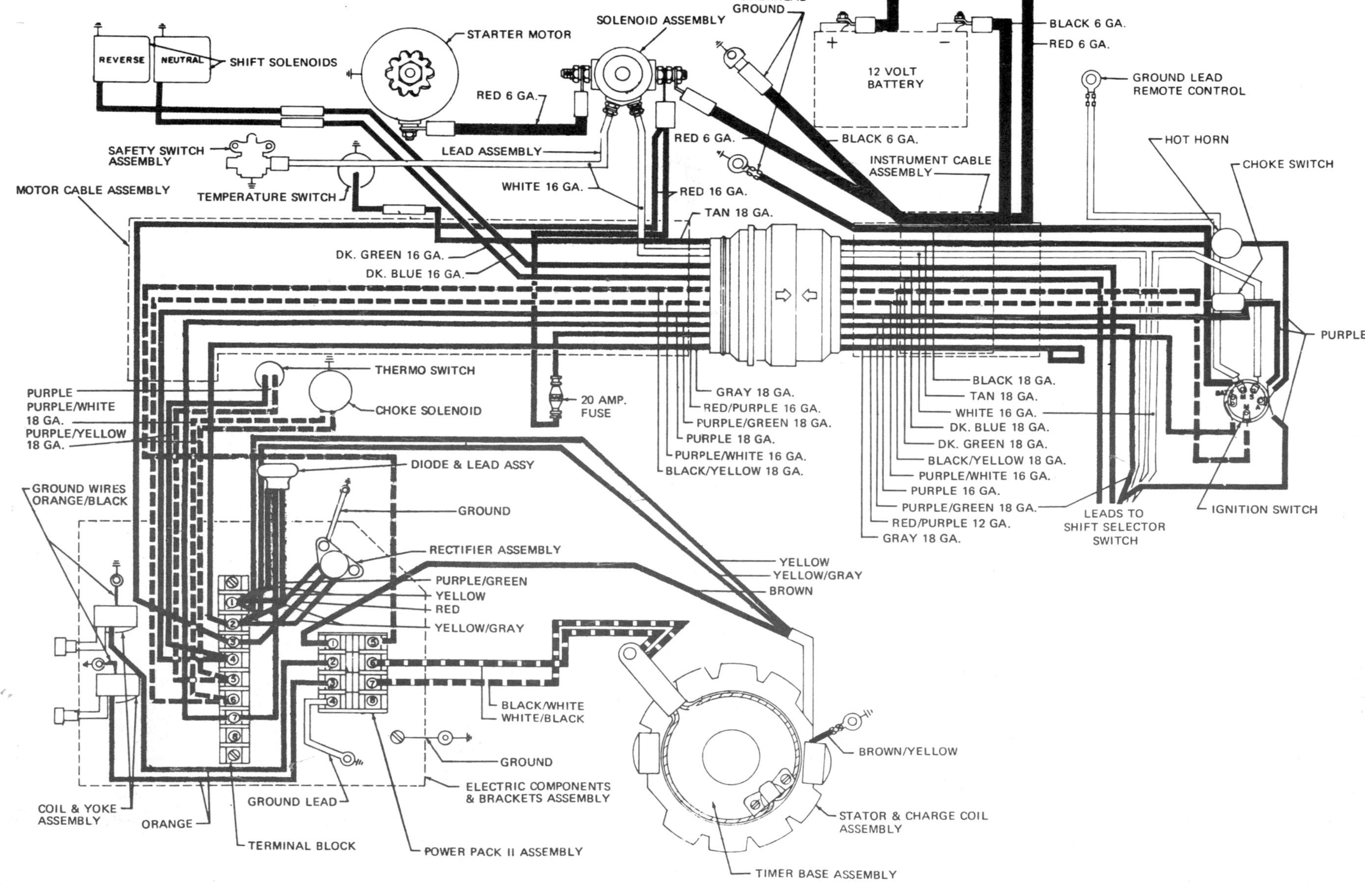

Wiring diagram of the 50 Hp engine with electric start, since 1971.

APPENDIX

TUNE-UP SPECIFICATIONS

Models (Hp)	Cyl.	Year	Spark Plugs Type (Champion)	Spark Plugs Gap (Inches)	Ignition System Type	Ignition System Breaker Point Gap (Inches)	Ignition System Condenser Capacity (Mfd.)	Idle Speed (In gear)	Full-Throttle Rpm
1.5	1	1968-70	J4J	.030	①	.020	.18-.22	550	3500-4500
2.0	1	1971-75	J6J	.030	①	.020	.18-.22	550	4200-4800
3.0	2	1952-68	J4J	.030	①	.020	.18-.22	550	3500-4500
4.0	2	1969-75	J4J	.030	①	.020	.18-.22	550	4000-5000
5.0	2	1965-68	J4J	.030	①	.020	.18-.22	550	3500-4500
5.5	2	1956-64	J4J	.030	①	.020	.18-.22	550	3500-4500
6.0	2	1965-75	J4J	.030	①	.020	.18-.22	550	3500-4500
9.5	2	1964-73	J4J	.030	①	.020	.18-.22	550	4000-5000
9.9	2	1974-75	UL4J	.030	①	.020	.25-.29	600	4500-5500
15	2	1974-75	UL4J	.030	①	.020	.25-.29	600	5500-6500
18/20	2	1957-73	J4J	.030	①	.020	.25-.29	550	4000-5000
25	2	1969-75	J4J	.030	①	.020	.25-.29	550	5000-6000
28	2	1962-64	J4J	.030	①	.020	.25-.29	600-650	4000-5000
33	2	1965-70	J4J	.030	①	.020	.25-.29	550	4000-5000
40	2	1960-75	J4J	.030	①	.020	.25-.29	650	4000-5000
50	2	1971-75	UL77V	—	②	—	—	650	5000-6000

① Breaker points under the flywheel.
② Mag-Flash ignition system.

MECHANICAL ENGINE SPECIFICATIONS

Models (Hp)	Cyl.	Year	Bore (Inches)	Stroke (Inches)	Displacement (Cu. In.)	Crankshaft Sizes Crankpin	Crankshaft Sizes Top Main	Crankshaft Sizes Center Main	Crankshaft Sizes Bottom Main
1.5	1	1968-70	1-9/16	1-3/8	2.64	.6685-.6690	.7497-.7502	—	.7497-.7502
2.0	1	1971-75	1-9/16	1-3/8	2.64	.6685-.6690	.7497-.7502	—	.7497-.7502
3.0	2	1952-68	1-9/16	1-3/8	5.28	.6250-.6255	.6849-.6854	.6849-.6854	.6849-.6854
4.0	2	1969-75	1-9/16	1-3/8	5.28	.6250-.6255	.7515-.7520	.6849-.6854	.6849-.6854
5.0	2	1965-68	1-15/16	1-1/2	8.84	.6685-.6690	.8075-.8080	.8075-.8080	.8075-.8080
5.5	2	1956-64	1-15/16	1-1/2	8.84	.6685-.6690	.8075-.8080	.8075-.8080	.8075-.8080
6.0	2	1965-75	1-15/16	1-1/2	8.84	.6685-.6690	.8075-.8080	.8075-.8080	.8075-.8080
9.5	2	1964-73	2-5/16	1-13/16	15.2	.8127-.8132	.8120-.8125	.8127-.8132	.8120-.8125
9.9	2	1974-75	2-3/16	1.760	13.20	1.0630-1.0635	.8120-.8125	.8120-.8125	.8120-.8125
15	2	1974-75	2.188	1.760	13.20	1.0630-1.0635	.8120-.8125	.8120-.8125	.8120-.8125
18/20	2	1957-73	2-1/2	2-1/4	22.0	1.0000-1.0005	.9995-1.0000	.9995-1.0000	.9995-1.0000
25	2	1969-75	2-1/2	2-1/4	22.0	1.0000-1.0005	.9995-1.0000	.9995-1.0000	.9995-1.0000
28	2	1962-64	2-7/8	2-3/4	35.7	1.1823-1.1828	1.2495-1.2500	.9995-1.0000	.9995-1.0000
33	2	1965-70	3-1/16	2-3/4	40.5	1.1823-1.1828	1.2495-1.2500	.9995-1.0000	.9995-1.0000
40	2	1960-75	3-3/16	2-3/4	43.9	1.1823-1.1828	1.2495-1.2500	.9995-1.0000	.9995-1.0000
50	2	1971-75	3-1/16	2-13/16	41.5	1.1823-1.1828	1.4974-1.4979	1.3748-1.3752	1.1810-1.1815

ENGINE CLEARANCE CHART (INCHES)

Models (Hp-Cyl)	Piston: Ring End Gap	Piston: Ring Side Clearance	Piston: Bore Clearance	Crankshaft: Upper Main	Crankshaft: Center Main	Crankshaft: Lower Main	Crankshaft: End Play	Connecting Rod: Piston End	Connecting Rod: Crankshaft End
1.5-1	.005-.015	.0010-.0035	.0043-.0055	②	—	②	.001-.024	.0004-.0011	②
2.0-1	.005-.015	.0010-.0035	.0043-.0055	②	—	②	.001-.024	.0004-.0011	②
3.0-2	.005-.015	.0010-.0035	.0013-.0025	.0013-.0023	.0013-.0023	.0013-.0023	.002-.010	.0004-.0011	.0007-.0017
4.0-2	.005-.015	.0010-.0035	.0008-.0020	②	.0013-.0023	.0013-.0023	.002-.007	.0004-.0011	.0007-.0017
5.0-2	.005-.015	.0010-.0035	.0018-.0030	.0015-.0025	.0015-.0025	.0015-.0025	.002-.010	.0003-.0010	②
5.5-2	.005-.015	.0010-.0035	.0018-.0030	.0015-.0025	.0015-.0025	.0015-.0025	.002-.010	.0003-.0010	②
6.0-2	.005-.015	.0010-.0035	.0018-.0030	.0015-.0025	.0015-.0025	.0015-.0025	.002-.010	.0003-.0010	②
9.5-2	.007-.017	.0010-.0035	.0035-.0050	①	②	①	.002-.012	②	②
9.9-2	.005-.015	.0025-.0035	.0040-.0053	②	②	③	—	②	②
15-2	.005-.015	.0025-.0035	.0040-.0053	②	②	③	—	②	②
18/20-2	.007-.017	.0020-.0040	.0032-.0047	①	①	①	.004-.023	①	①
25-2	.007-.017	.0020-.0040	.0033-.0048	①	①	①	.004-.023	①	①
28-2	.007-.017	.0045-.0070	.0030-.0045	①	①	①	.003-.011	①	①
33-2	.007-.017	.0045-.0070	.0030-.0045	①	①	①	.003-.011	①	①
40-2	.007-.017	.0020-.0045	.0030-.0045	①	①	①	.003-.011	①	①
50-2	.007-.017	.0015-.0040	.0045-.0065	①	①	③	.006-.0165	①	①

① Roller bearing.
② Needle bearing.
③ Ball bearing.

ENGINE TORQUE CHART

Models (Hp-Cyl)	Spark Plugs (Ft-lbs.)	Flywheel Nut (Ft-lbs.)	Connecting Rod Screws (In-lbs.)	Cylinder Head Screws (In-lbs.)	Crankcase-to-Cylinder Screws (In-lbs.)			Crankcase Head (Bearing Housing) Screws (In-lbs.)	
					Upper	Center	Lower	Upper	Lower
1.5	17.5-20.5	22-25	60-66	60-80	—	—	—	—	60-80
2.0	17.5-20.5	22-25	60-66	60-80	—	—	—	—	60-80
3.0	17.5-20.5	30-40	60-66	60-80	60-80	60-80	60-80	—	—
4.0	17.5-20.5	30-40	60-66	60-80	60-80	60-80	60-80	—	—
5.0	17.5-20.5	40-45	60-66	60-80	60-80	60-80	60-80	—	—
5.5	17.5-20.5	40-45	60-66	60-80	60-80	60-80	60-80	—	—
6.0	17.5-20.5	40-45	60-66	60-80	60-80	60-80	60-80	—	—
9.5	17.5-20.5	40-45	90-100	96-120	120-145	120-145	120-145	—	—
9.9	17.5-20.5	45-50	48-60	145-170	145-170	—	145-170	—	—
15	17.5-20.5	45-50	48-60	145-170	145-170	—	145-170	—	—
18/20	17.5-20.5	40-45	180-186	96-120	110-130	120-130	110-130	—	—
25	17.5-20.5	40-45	180-186	96-120	110-130	120-130	110-130	—	—
28	17.5-20.5	100-105	348-372	168-192	150-170	162-168	150-170	—	—
33	17.5-20.5	100-105	348-372	168-192	150-170	162-168	150-170	—	—
40	17.5-20.5	100-105	348-372	168-192	150-170	162-168	150-170	—	—
50	17.5-20.5	100-105	348-372	168-192	144-168	144-168	144-168	—	—

STANDARD SCREWS:

	Inch-Pounds	Foot-Pounds
No. 6	7-10	
No. 8	15-22	
No. 10	25-35	2-3
No. 12	35-40	3-4
1/4″	60-80	5-7
5/16″	120-140	10-12
3/8″	220-240	18-20

① Retorque the cylinder head screws to 192-216 in-lbs. after the engine has been tested and tuned.
② Retorque the cylinder head screws to 216-240 in-lbs. after the engine has been tested and tuned.

GEAR CASE CAPACITIES

H.P.	Year	Capacity (ounces)
1-1/2	1968-70	.75
2	1971-75	1.28
3	1952-68	2.9
5	1965-68	2.9
5-1/2	1954-64	8.5
6	1968-75	8.5
7-1/2	1956-58	8.5
9-1/2	1964-73	9.7
9.9	1974-75	9.7
10	1949-57	10.0
10	1958-63	9.7
15	1956	8.3
15	1974-75	8.3
18	1957-65	8.3
20	1966-73	8.3
25	1969-75	8.3
25	1951-55	11.0
28	1962-65	13.9
30	1956	11.0
33	1965-70	13.9
35	1957-58	13.9
35	1958	13.9
35	1959	13.9
40	1960-75	13.9
50	1958-59	34.8
50	1971-75	25.3
55-60-65-70	1968-73	25.3
60	1964-67	19.5
65	1968	19.5
65	1968	34.8
75	1960-65	19.5
80	1966-67	17.4
85	1968	17.4
85	1969-75	27.9
90	1964-65	17.4
100	1966	27.6*
100	1967-68	37.2
100	1971-72	26.9
115	1969-75	27.9
125	1971-72	26.9
135	1973-75	27.9

*Gear cases with fill plug above cavitation plate, 32.2 ounces.